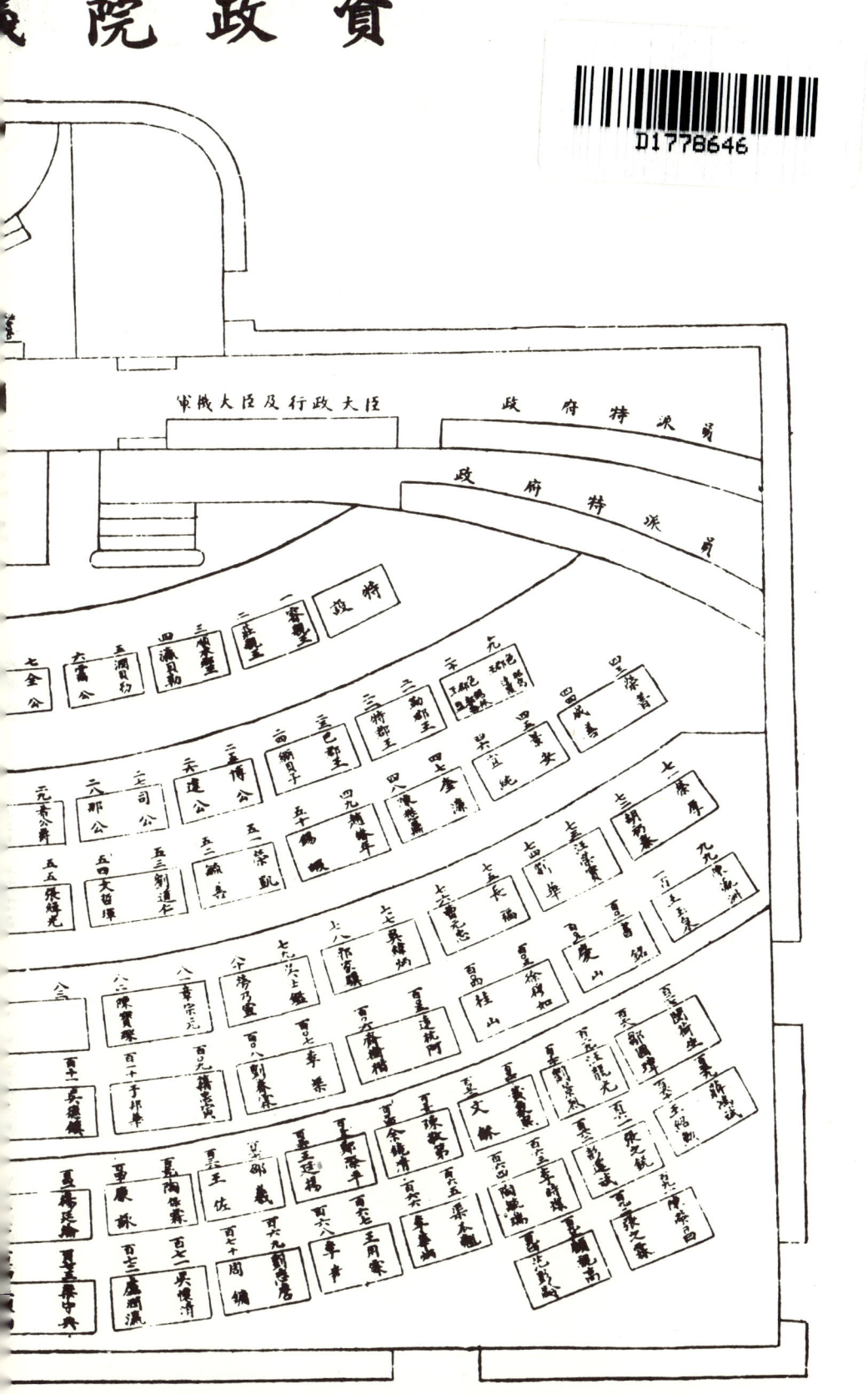

National Polity
and Local Power

Harvard-Yenching Institute Monograph Series 27

by
MIN TU-KI
edited by
PHILIP A. KUHN
and TIMOTHY BROOK

Published by
THE COUNCIL ON EAST ASIAN STUDIES / HARVARD UNIVERSITY
and
THE HARVARD-YENCHING INSTITUTE
Distributed by the Harvard University Press
Cambridge (Massachusetts) and London   1989

National Polity and Local Power

The Transformation of Late Imperial China

© *Copyright 1989 by the President and Fellows of Harvard College*
Printed in the United States of America

The Harvard-Yenching Institute, founded in 1928 and headquartered at Harvard University, is a foundation dedicated to the advancement of higher education in the humanities and social sciences in East and Southeast Asia. The Institute supports advanced research at Harvard by faculty members of certain Asian universities, and doctoral studies at Harvard and other universities by junior faculty of the same universities. It also supports East Asian studies at Harvard through contributions to the Harvard-Yenching Library and publication of the Harvard Journal of Asiatic Studies *and books on premodern East Asian history and literature.*

Library of Congress Cataloging in Publication Data

Min, Tu-ki.
    National polity and local power : the transformation of late imperial China / by Min Tu-ki ; edited by Philip A. Kuhn and Timothy Brook.
    p. cm. – (Harvard-Yenching Institute monograph series ; 27)
Bibliography: p.
Includes index.
ISBN 0-674-60225-0
    1. China–Politics and government–1644–1912. 2. Local government–China.   I. Kuhn, Philip A.   II. Brook, Timothy.
III. Title.   IV. Series.
JQ1508.M56 1988
320.8'0951–dc19   87-36474
                                                                                                                  CIP

FOREWORD

Getting to know Professor Min Tu-ki and his work is like meeting a fellow voyager in a far country: one who has traveled the same route, but who has certain special insights and talents which have enabled him to see things you have not seen, and to understand more deeply those things you have both seen. It is therefore with considerable excitement that one reads the work of this eminent Korean Sinologist and realizes, if one did not before, how much Korean scholars can tell us about China.* Since it is the nearly universal shortcoming of American China scholars not to be trained in Korean, for the present we can but rely on the kindness of our Korean colleagues to go through the trouble of having their work translated. Although some Korean China scholarship has been available in Japanese, I believe this

---

*A partial bibliography of Professor Min's work, in its context of Korean China scholarship, can be found in Min Tu-ki and Oh Keum-sung, "Korean Studies of Ch'ing China: A Bibliographical Note," *Ch'ing-shih wen-t'i* 4.3:95–105 (1980). In 1986, Min wrote two papers to introduce Korean studies of Chinese history to Japanese readers: "Kankoku ni okeru Chugoku gendaishi kenkyū ni tsuite," and "Kankoku ni okeru Chugokushi kenkyū no tenkai."

is one of the few extended works to have been translated into English. Is it too much to hope that Americans will someday consider learning Korean to be an indispensable part of their training as students of China?

Min Tu-ki was born in 1932 in Haenam, South Chŏlla province, to the family of Min Byong-ha, a small landlord. Until his first year of middle school, his education was conducted in Japanese, the language of Korea's colonial rulers. Professor Min's complete fluency in Japanese (his was the last academic generation to have had that kind of exposure) clearly established a breadth in him as an East Asia scholar that American scholars envy, yet must have been the occasion for some very ambivalent feelings. His vibrant sense of his own national identity was nourished by his mother's insistence, in defiance of official prohibition, that he learn the Korean written alphabet at home. During the Korean War, he attended university under conditions of bleak privation at Pusan, where Seoul National University had taken refuge in drafty, dirt-floored, makeshift barracks. Although the relative intellectual freedom of the period immediately following World War II had given way to a strict orthodoxy which shunned projects on the history of popular movements, he gained access to some rare original sources on the Tonghak Rebellion of 1894, which fired his interest in social history. Searching for a wider perspective on popular movements in East Asia, Min became interested in the Boxer Rebellion in China on which he wrote his bachelor's thesis. For this thesis he drew upon the Ch'ing *Veritable Records,* which had been part of the Japanese reference library on Chinese affairs at SNU. Since then his scholarly work has focused on Chinese history.

His mentor was the classical scholar and bibliophile Kim Sang-ki, who taught at SNU from 1945 until his death in 1972. Kim, from a Confucian *yangban* family, had received a rich classical training and had also attended Waseda University. The effect of this warm-hearted and deeply cultivated scholar on Min Tu-ki's development probably began with a fervent devotion to learning for its own sake, and admonitions to "stick to one thing" and avoid dilettantism. It did not, however, include forcing him into a particular channel of study, for Professor Kim believed in letting his students find their own way. Under Kim's guidance, Min went into Han studies initially, but later became fascinated with the voluminous sources of the Ch'ing period and the transition to modern times.

An early project revealed the hallmarks of his emerging style: to blend the classical Sinologue's sense of China's cultural integrity, with the historian's sense of context and change. At SNU library he came across an edition of the *Ta-i chueh-mi-lu,* a polemic by the Yung-cheng Emperor defending himself and his throne against his alleged defamers. In the process, Yung-cheng lambasted the theory of "political feudalism" (*feng-chien*) as a dangerous anachronism in the China of his day. Min was intrigued by the long history of the "political feudalism" concept and pursued it through its historical permutations. Not only did he expose fundamental shifts in political thought during the late empires; he also discovered that in recent history "political feudalism" had a peculiar role to play: as a transitional idea in the constitutionalism of the late Ch'ing, which bound imperial and modern history together in a single structure of political philosophy. Sharp distinctions between "tradition" and "modernity" blur; the interaction of logical structure with changing historical context takes the place of simple "periodization."

Min's earliest acquaintance with American scholarship on China had the effect of strengthening his dissatisfaction with over-simple distinctions between "traditional" and "modern" civilizations. The work of Joseph Levenson, for all its brilliance and sophistication, left him even more inclined to pursue a historiography that would show interpenetration of the modern age by the longstanding agenda of the past. As a young part-time instructor in colleges in Seoul in the 1960s, during which he was responsible for, among other things, teaching the history of world civilization, Min read widely in Western history and anthropology. The work of Boas and Linton, in particular, gave him a sense of the comparability of cultures and strengthened his interest in topics that spanned national boundaries. His work on the "principle/utility" concept in Japan and China (Chapter 3 of this book) reaches beyond the differences in context between Meiji and late Ch'ing by its sensitivity to the similarities with which these cultures handled the agonizing problem of preserving native values in the face of Western penetration.

In 1969, Min joined the SNU faculty full time, was awarded a Doctorate of Literature in 1974, and became Chairman of the Department of Asian History in 1977. Under his leadership the department has added positions in Japanese and Central Asian history, with the aim of a more comprehensive curriculum than any available before in

Korean education. As we become better acquainted with the work of this group of scholars we may be pleasantly startled by the new insights into Asian affairs that Korean historiography offers us. Pondering the distinctive perspectives of Min Tu-ki's work, for example, one is reminded of the experiences of that sophisticated traveler Pak Chi-wŏn two centuries ago (Chapter 1 of this book). An accomplished Confucian scholar himself, Pak was able to penetrate the Ch'ing scene with that unique capacity generated by the union of intimacy and detachment. Pak, like Min, was in some sense a participant in the human experiences he described, yet his independent cultural stand (that part of him which is distinctly Korean) enables him to see it with an objectivity not available to the Chinese themselves. Min, like the Chinese he writes about, is himself close to the experience of a premodern civilization passing through the agonizing reevaluation of its own culture under the pressures of the modern world. The view is both sympathetic and objective in a way that neither we nor the Chinese can attain. It emphasizes, with an authority we cannot match, the degree to which modern East Asian civilization, for all its Western infusions, drew its main character from the issues of the late traditional world and evolved at the prompting of its own internal agenda.

> Philip A. Kuhn
> Professor of History
> Harvard University
>
> Timothy Brook
> Assistant Professor of History
> University of Toronto

Editors' note:
In this English version of Professor Min's work, the text has been altered somewhat in the interest of making it more accessible to Western readers. Its production would not have been possible without the expert and dedicated effort of Olive Holmes. Her immense labors in transcending the difficulties posed by a multi-language, multi-translator draft are deeply appreciated. We are also grateful to Florence Trefethen for her skill and patience in seeing the manuscript through to publication.

CONTENTS

Foreword v

Author's Preface xi

1 *The* Jehol Diary *and the Character of Ch'ing Rule* 1
    Social and Political Changes 3
    Ethnic Differences 6
    Sinocentrism and the Acceptance of the Status Quo 9
    Editorial Projects and the Chinese Literati 14
    Chu Hsi Studies under the Ch'ing 15

2 *The* Sheng-yuan–Chien-sheng *Stratum (*Sheng-Chien*) in Ch'ing Society* 21
    The Shen-shih *and the* Sheng-chien: *Basic Characteristics of the* Shen-shih 25
    Debates on the Structure of the Gentry and the Problem of the Sheng-chien *Stratum* 28
    Political Aspects of the Sheng-chien 32
    Social Aspects of the Sheng-chien 43

3 Chinese "Principle" and Western "Utility," a Reassessment 51

    Ethics/Technology (Tōyō dōtoku seiyō geijutsu ron) in Japan 58
    Principle/Utility in China 64

4 The Theory of Political Feudalism in the Ch'ing Period 89

    Introduction 89
    Feng-chien as a Theory of Institutional Reform 92
    Debates over Feudalism from the K'ang-hsi through the Chia-ch'ing Era 100
    Debates over Feudalism in the Late Nineteenth Century 105
    Late-Ch'ing Debates on Local Self-Government 112
    The 1898 Reform Movement and Debates on Local Self-Government 122

5 The Late-Ch'ing Provincial Assembly 137

    Debates on the Establishment of the Provincial Assembly (1900–1907) 138
    The Establishment of the Provincial Assemblies (tzu-i-chü) 147
    Characteristics of the Newly Established Provincial Assemblies 159
    The Authority of the Provincial Assembly 168

6 The Soochow-Hangchow-Ningpo Railway Dispute 181

    The Background of the Dispute 182
    The Movement to Annul the Sino-British Loan Agreement 191
    The Movement to Abrogate the Loan Deposit Agreement and Oppose the Dismissal of T'ang Shou-ch'ien 199
    The Changing Attitude of the Gentry Class 207
    Conclusions 217

Notes 221

Bibliography 275

Glossary/Index 293

AUTHOR'S PREFACE

There is no common theme binding together the six articles[1] collected here. Three of them, however,—"The Theory of Political Feudalism in the Ch'ing Period," "The Late Ch'ing Provincial Assembly," and "The Soochow-Hangchow-Ningpo Railway Dispute"—are focused on the same questions. How did the traditional political ideas of *feng-chien* and *chün-hsien* change in the Ch'ing period, and how does this change provide a transitional device in our modern study of Chinese history?

In an article entitled "Traditional Political Ideas of China: The Debates around *feng-chien* and *chün-hsien*," written in 1966, I analyzed the debates from the Ch'in to the Sung dynasties that centered on whether feudalistic administration or centralized administration was the ideal political institution.[2] One of my main concerns in that article was how the concepts of "public" (*kung*) and "private" (*ssu*) were changed during the period. The purpose of "The Theory of Political Feudalism in the Ch'ing Period" (Chapter 4 of the present volume) is to analyze the evolution of those concepts of "public" and "private" during the Ch'ing period. The concept of "public" in the

Ch'ing period contained the centrifugal idea of local self-government, which the gentry demanded, and which was one of the most important goals of the late Ch'ing constitutional movement.

The idea of constitutionalism, originating in Western political tradition, gave birth to the Chinese-style constitutional movement only after it was linked with traditional Chinese political ideas. In Chapter 4, I try to show one of the reasons why the Ch'ing government's attempt to use constitutionalism for the purpose of centralization faced strong opposition from the gentry and failed to achieve its goal. I suggest that there still remains a question that I have not touched upon: how the traditional ideas of *feng-chien* and *chün-hsien* (which I discuss mainly on the provincial level) were developed in the late Ch'ing period on the sub-provincial level after the introduction of the modern (or Western) theory of local self-government.

As a result of the constitutional movement launched by the gentry, the provincial assembly was established. Through analyzing the process of establishing the provincial assembly, I show in Chapter 5 ("The Late Ch'ing Provincial Assembly") how the assembly, through which the Ch'ing Court tried to bolster its centralized bureaucratic rule, became the main stage for the anti-government activities of the gentry, who utilized the idea of *feng-chien* as a transitional device. In Chapter 5, I also point out that, in the creation and in the operation of the provincial assembly, neither the upper nor the lower gentry played a leading role; but the enlightened gentry did, and this group should be understood from a new perspective.[3]

I describe in Chapter 6 ("The Soochow-Hangchow-Ningpo Railway Dispute") how these enlightened gentry concerned with local interests became disillusioned with the Ch'ing government during the turmoil of the Chekiang-Kiangsu railway dispute (1905–1911). The provincial assembly in which these enlightened gentry were active turned into a podium for their localistic nationalism, and their anti-government activities in the railway disputes were closely related to the Republican Revolution in Chekiang and Kiangsu provinces.

Let me now comment on the three essays that are the first three chapters of this book. Chapter 1 ("The *Jehol Diary* and the Character of Ch'ing Rule") presents several features of Manchu rule in China through the eyes of Pak Chi-wŏn, one of the most sensitive intellectuals in eighteenth-century Korea. I have added some analytic comments of my own to this valuable report. Pak's diary is a unique historical source not only because it contains his penetrating observations but because it was written beyond the reach of the Ch'ing literary inquisition.

Chapter 2 ("The *Sheng-yuan–Chien-sheng* Stratum (*Sheng-Chien*) in Ch'ing Society"), dealing with the question of the gentry class, was stimulated by the studies of Chung-li Chang, Ping-ti Ho, and T'ung-tsu Ch'ü. In this chapter I emphasize the significance of the independent and static features of that lower gentry class.

Chapter 3 ("Chinese 'Principle' and Western 'Utility'"), the most recent of the articles in this book, published in 1978, pursues the role of the much disputed political-cultural theory used in China to accommodate modern (Western) culture. In it I have questioned whether it is really useful to understand any *specific stage* of introduction or accommodation of Western ideas in China in terms of the traditional Chinese cultural theory of *Chung-t'i hsi-yung* (Chinese principles, Western utility) or not. I have had this question in mind since the 1960s when I began my study of the Reform Movement of 1898.[4] Was there any argument similar to *Chung-t'i hsi-yung* in Japanese modernization which was regarded as a model by those who led the Reform Movement in China? If there was such an argument, how was it understood by modern Japanese? On the basis of these questions I analyze the *Chung-t'i hsi-yung* theory and show that the theory is not an adequate tool for explaining the specific stage of ideological transformation in the late Ch'ing. The idea should be considered as a rather "universalistic pattern" which took shape especially in countries that underwent severe cultural conflict in modern times.

The articles collected here, except the last one, were written before 1970. Articles by other scholars have since appeared, dealing with similar topics, with differing viewpoints and explanations centering on specific trends, using more recent materials than mine. Those studies may make my work outdated in part. Still the difference in viewpoint should be noticed, and that in itself would justify publication.[5]

This project began almost six years ago. The perseverance and enthusiasm that my respected friend Professor Philip A. Kuhn at Harvard University showed, in spite of all the difficulties during those years, defies description. Without his effort and the assistance of Timothy Brook this book would not exist. Professor Kim Yong-deok in Seoul, also, has given continuing support to the project. I would like particularly to thank those who undertook the tasks of translation and editing despite a variety of difficulties—Peter Perdue (Chapters 1 and 2), Choe Hei-je (Chapters 3, 4, and part of 6), Kim Hong-myong (Chapter 5) and Kim Ho-dong (part of Chapter 6). I sincerely hope that all their endeavors will be partly rewarded by a favorable response from readers of English. Finally, Olive Holmes, my editor, has toiled enduringly and cheerfully to bring this book to fruition.

CHAPTER ONE

The Jehol Diary and the Character of Ch'ing Rule

The Manchus, calling themselves the Latter Chin, invaded Korea between 1629 and 1636. In 1637, T'ai-tsung (Abahai) sent Ingguldai to Korea to open normal diplomatic relations, and Korean missions, called the "dispatch of envoys of submission" (*shih-ta shih-hsing*), were sent to China under various names every year.[1] These missions not only created a diplomatic exchange between the two countries but opened an officially recognized pathway for contact with Chinese culture. Although Koreans despised the Manchus as a barbarian tribe, they now had to treat the Ch'ing dynasty (at least superficially) with the deference due from "a smaller country serving a large one" (*shih-ta chih-li*), just as they had done with the Ming dynasty. The *Yŏnhaeng-nok* (Records of visits to Yen [Peking]), covering these missions from their beginnings, have been collected and studied.[2] This chapter is concerned with one of these records, the *Yŏlha ilgi* (Jehol diary), an account of travels in southern Manchuria, Peking, and Jehol written by a Korean of the Yŏngjo reign (mid-eighteenth century), Pak Chi-wŏn. Pak's visit to Peking occurred in 1780, the 45th year of the Ch'ien-lung Emperor's reign.

The *Records of Visits to Yen* have several characteristics in common. First, they are all critical of the Ch'ing dynasty, although there are qualitative differences and differences of degree among the individual diaries. The Korean attitude toward the Ch'ing dynasty differed from their attitude toward the Ming. The records of the missions to the Ming dynasty had been called *Choch'ŏn-nok* (Records of tributary visits to the imperial capital). The Koreans were grateful to the Ming dynasty because the Ming had defended Korea against the invasion of Toyotomi Hideyoshi and had restored the Chosŏn (Yi) dynasty in Korea (*chaejo chiŭn*). When the Manchus, whom the Koreans had for a long time despised as a "barbarian tribe" (*hojok*), destroyed the Ming dynasty, Koreans were humiliated at being forced to submit to them. In using the ancient term Yen (Yŏn in Korean) for the Peking area, instead of the customary "heavenly capital," in the overall title of the *Yŏnhaeng-nok,* the Koreans showed that they did not recognize the Ch'ing as a true Chinese dynasty. Although they submitted formally to the dynasty, they were contemptuous of it.

Second, in addition to their critical tone, these records contain a wide range of experience and observation. China was the only foreign country that Koreans of the time were familiar with. Although they had reservations about the Ch'ing dynasty, they were intensely curious about Chinese culture, and even the landscape. The instant Pak Chi-wŏn crossed the Yalu River and set foot on Chinese territory he told his servant, "From now on, as soon as you see anything, even if I am sleeping, wake me up and tell me about it."[3]

Third, the *Yŏnhaeng-nok* form an annual record of observations of China during the Ch'ing. Each year, three seasonal tributary missions visited Peking. Various temporary missions were also sent, passing through southern Manchuria to Peking. Over a long period of time, into the later years of the Ch'ing, not one year was missed. It would be difficult to find anywhere a similar continuous record of contemporary observations.

Fourth, the *Yŏnhaeng-nok* contain uninhibited descriptions of the society and policies of the Ch'ing dynasty. Because the Manchus were foreign conquerors who kept tight control over thought and expression, native Chinese writers were unable to record conditions as they saw them. The Koreans, however, lived beyond the direct control of the dynasty and could risk recording facts that might offend the Ch'ing rulers.

How does the *Yŏlha ilgi* (Jehol diary) of Pak Chi-wŏn fit into the *Yŏnhaeng-nok* as a whole? Pak left Korea at the age of forty-four in 1780, traveling first to Peking, and from there to Jehol. In Korean intellectual history, he was a thinker and writer of the Pukhak, or "Learn from Ch'ing" school. He was free of the narrowness of some of his contemporaries and was able to develop a flexible style of thought. His acute observations, his original style, broad knowledge, and liberal ideas, as expressed in the *Jehol Diary*, shocked the Korean literati of his time. King Chŏngjo personally initiated a campaign to "restore the orthodoxy of literary style" (*munch'e panjŏng*) in response to the great impact of the *Jehol Diary*.[4]

During his travels, Pak met and conversed with a *chü-jen* named Wang Min-hao, as well as literati such as Yin Chia-ch'üan, the former director of the Court of Judicature and Revision (the highest-ranking Chinese Pak met); Ch'i Feng-o, the Kweichow provincial judicial commissioner (a Manchu of Korean origin); First Captain Hao-ch'eng of Shantung, and others.[5] On his route across southern Manchuria he also met ordinary Chinese, including several *sheng-yuan*, merchants, and peasants. Because of his contacts with many social strata, he was able to observe a cross section of Ch'ing society.

SOCIAL AND POLITICAL CHANGES

It is commonly thought that the Ch'ien-lung period of 1736–1795 marks a dividing line in the periodization of Ch'ing society.[6] Hwang Chae visited Peking in 1734 and 1750. He summarized the changes in China between these two visits as follows:

No one, whether Manchu or Chinese, dared to speak of affairs concerning the Emperor. If you asked about them, no one answered. This is what I noticed in 1734. Now, on this [second] journey, those who call themselves Confucian scholars speak openly of the Emperor's faults and fear nothing. This is the difference between what I saw before and what I have seen now. People say that there are also differences between earlier times and now in the desolation of the villages and the difficulties of making a living. But, as I hurried along my route [to

Peking], there was no way to find out the real situation. Generally speaking, even though the K'ang-hsi Emperor repeatedly visited Kiangnan and went far out into the deserts, he never heard a word of resentment anywhere. Now, with Ch'ien-lung's travels, it is not so. Slander fills the streets. Can this be due only to the difference in the ostentation of the Emperor's baggage train? We cannot tell.[7]

The biggest change that Hwang noticed over this period was that the social order had begun to decline, and general dissatisfaction was increasing. Kim Ch'ang-ŏp, who visited Peking in 1713, saw the K'ang-hsi Emperor this way:

Because K'ang-hsi ruled with thrift, leniency, and simplicity, curbed the merchants in order to promote agriculture, and economized in order to spare the people [by reducing their taxes], we naturally enjoyed fifty years of peace. Since he also esteemed the arts of scholarship, honored Confucius and Chu Hsi, personally practiced filial piety and served his mother well, he need not be ashamed of being compared to [Emperor] Hsiao-wen of the Northern Wei [467–499] or Emperor Yung [Shih-tsung] of Chin [1161–1189].[8]

Like his predecessor, Pak Chi-wŏn gave his own evaluation of the Ch'ien-lung Emperor:

The Emperor is old and has ruled for a long time. His authority remains strong and his understanding has not weakened; his health remains vigorous. But, although there is peace within the four seas, the ruler's conduct becomes daily more violent; he is suspicious, brutal, and overly strict; he has unpredictable fits of glee and rage. His ministers at court all find it the best policy to patch things up for the present, and feel that anticipating the Emperor's desires and pleasing him are the only realistic things to do.[9]

The descriptions of the two emperors differ, but the two accounts agree that public order in the Ch'ien-lung period had weakened. Pak Chi-wŏn tells us that the Ch'ien-lung Emperor had become "suspicious, brutal, and overly strict." In the quotation below he writes of "the cruel severity of imperial regulations." These two statements tell of an autocratic ruler attempting to shore up a government that had been weak and lax by a merciless use of his personal power.

Pak criticized the strictness of the new ruler as follows:

In whatever the Chinese write, even in the most ordinary letters of a few lines, they must extol the achievements of successive reigns and express deep gratitude for the beneficence of the present age. The Chinese still consider themselves loyal to the Ming, constantly harbor feelings of pain and despair, and they need to be on guard against hatred and suspicion. Therefore, when they open their mouths, it is to sing praises and write flattering words, which makes them feel even more out of place in the present age. The Chinese take great pains to be circumspect. When they talk to others, even about the most commonplace affairs, they burn the records of their conversations without leaving a scrap of paper. The Chinese are not alone in this; the Manchus are even worse. The Manchus all live and work close to the palace, so they know even better the cruel severity of imperial regulations. Thus, not only are the Chinese pained, but those who execute the laws of the Emperor also suffer.[10]

Both Han and Manchus, although in different circumstances, were under severe constraints. Pak wrote: "All respect the laws and thus act cautiously toward officials. Because everyone acts cautiously toward officials, the polity works uniformly."[11]

This "cruel severity of imperial regulations" forced the Chinese literati to be careful with written words. The repeated literary inquisitions under Ch'ing rule made them extremely wary of written evidence; they were forced, as the *Jehol Diary* says, to "shred paper" and "black out characters." For example, it was important to avoid any possible misuse of the words *ming* (bright, the Ming dynasty) or *ch'ing* (clear, the Ch'ing dynasty). The *Jehol Diary* refers to the avoidance of these terms many times, as for example in the following description of a "written conversation" (*pi-t'an*) with the *chü-jen* Wang Hu-ting:

On the occasion, it was already dusk and, as it had grown dark in the inner room, he had lit a candle. I wrote: "There is no need in the human world to waste wax by lighting a candle / The sun and moon together are suspended in the sky and illuminate Heaven and Earth." Hu-ting waved his hand and blacked out *shuang-hsuan jih-yueh* ("the sun and the moon together are suspended in the sky"), for writing *jih* (sun) and *yueh* (moon) together forms the character *ming* [for Ming dynasty].[12]

We can find similar examples of such taboos in the account written by Yu Tŏk-kong (a Korean scholar who went to Peking) ten years later in 1790. "Imperial strictness" appears to have increased, and many more terms were thought dangerous:

Wu Chao asked the monk Liang-feng to paint a picture of "The Fisherman and His Son Living in Seclusion at Stone Lake" and asked [the Korean scholar] Pak

Chae-ga to write the title. When Weng Fang-kang saw this, he was greatly alarmed and sent a letter, saying: "You scholars do not understand practical politics. How can anyone live secluded when the Sacred Emperor rules?" Wu Chao hastily altered the title to read: "Plowing the Fields at Stone Lake." Chinese scholars must always take care with their words this way.[13]

ETHNIC DIFFERENCES

Any treatment of Ch'ing society must include a discussion of the distinction between Chinese and Manchu culture. Kim Ch'ang-ŏp noticed the differences between Manchus and Chinese in the late K'ang-hsi period, and commented on the Sinicization of the Manchus:

The Manchus have splendid physiques, but they have little refinement. Because they lack refinement, many of them are pure and sincere. The Chinese are the opposite. The southerners are particularly insincere and crafty, although not all of them are like this. The Manchus have now been in China a long time, and the Emperor also respects the refinements of culture, so their simple character is disappearing.

There follows an example of the increasing refinement of the Manchus:

The Manchus can all speak Chinese, but the Chinese cannot speak Manchu. It is not that they are unable to; they do not want to. Not speaking Manchu, however, hinders them in official life. In general, the Court and the yamen all use Manchu, because memorials and documents are all translated into Manchu. In the streets, Chinese and Manchus both speak Chinese. For this reason, many of the children of Manchus cannot speak Manchu. The Emperor was concerned and selected intelligent young people and sent them to Ningguta to learn Manchu.[14]

In addition, Kim Ch'ang-ŏp reported that "after the Manchus had lived in China for seventy years . . . their customs of food and drink gradually became extravagant, and they lost their original simplicity." The emperors found it necessary to practice such traditional Manchu skills as horseback-riding and archery, and to encourage thrift.[15] Hong Tae-yong, who recorded his observations after those of Kim, also noted that the Manchus were a simpler people than the Chinese: "In general, the Chinese have highly developed talents, while the Manchus are, for the most part, plain and sincere. When it comes to character, the Manchus are superior to the Chinese."[16]

Pak Chi-wŏn confirmed this view of the relative merits of Manchu and Chinese character in the following anecdote about a peddlar who cheated people when he sold melons: "My servant said: 'This man must be a Chinese. He used deceptive practices when selling melons. Such a wicked man cannot be found among the Manchus.'"[17] Kim noted that these differences were gradually disappearing as the Manchus became Sinicized, and Pak again agreed.[18] Their descriptions indicate that the Sinicization of the Manchu rulers was at a peak during the Ch'ien-lung reign.

Pak was also interested in the Mongols, who appeared to be a simple people much like the Manchus. He wanted to learn what position the Mongols, so different from the frivolous Chinese, might occupy in the Manchu empire.[19] Pak was aware of the battles between the Manchus and the Mongolian Dzungars in the K'ang-hsi period, and was interested in the relations between Mongols and Manchus. He wrote:

There are many nationalities in the empire. When I went to Jehol, I met many who had gathered there for a council of princes. Those Mongols who had grown up in China possessed learning and culture equal to the Manchus and Chinese, but in their sturdy physiques they are quite different. This is even more true of the chieftains of the forty-eight tribes. The chiefs claim princely titles like "Left Hsien Prince" or "Ku-li Prince" [ancient Hsiung-nu titles] and refuse to submit to each other. They match each other in strength, so no one dares to make the first move [against the other]. For this reason the Chinese can sit idly by and face no trouble from them . . . Now, although the Manchus have a large population, it is less than half that of the whole empire. The Manchus have been in China for over a hundred years, so under the influence of the natural environment they have absorbed the local character and become no different from the Chinese. Decadent and refined, they have weakened to the point of being fit only for literary work. Looking at all the forces in the empire, the only ones to fear are still the Mongols, and no other barbarians. Why is this? In strength and audacity the Mongols are not equal to the Tibetans or Moslems, but the Tibetans and Moslems do not have the social constitution or cultural achievement needed to rival the Chinese. Mongolia, however, is geographically close—only a hundred *li* from China. From the ancient Hsiung-nu to the Turks and on down to the Khitans, there are remnants of great empires in this region. Since the days of Wei Lü and Chung-hang Yueh [who fled the Han dynasty to serve the Hsiung-nu], it has been a refuge for runaways. And, as for social constitution and cultural achievement, do not the customs of the former Yuan dynasty still persist there? Add to this the strength of their soldiers and horses and their native acceptance of life in the steppe, then as soon as the order of the empire weakens a little, there will suddenly be a crisis. When that happens, will the kings of these forty-eight tribes be content to just keep on hunting foxes and rabbits outside the Great Wall?[20]

Pak's prediction that the Mongols were potentially dangerous to the Ch'ing was not fulfilled because of the later cultural and military threat of the Western barbarians, but the extreme care that the Ch'ing took toward the Mongols testifies to Pak's good judgment.

After pointing out the hidden menace of the Mongols, Pak went on to discuss Ch'ing policies in response to this threat. Among Pak's predecessors, there were those who had perceived that successive Ch'ing emperors summered in Jehol not simply to escape the heat but for military purposes as well.[21] Pak, however, had a more penetrating view:

I find now that geographically Jehol is the brain of the empire. The Emperor goes to the north for no other reason than to master this vital point. Simply by sitting there, he can control the throat of Mongolia. Otherwise, the Mongols would long ago have been breaking out daily and disturbing Liaotung. Once Liaotung is disturbed, the left arm of the empire is cut off. When the left arm is cut off, the right arm at Ninghsia cannot function alone. Then the various western tribes that I have seen will begin to come out and aim at Kansu and Shensi.[22]

Yu Tŏk-kong, a contemporary, confirmed that the summer residence in Jehol was a means of controlling the Mongols: "In name it is to avoid the heat, but in fact the Emperor is personally overseeing readiness along the border."[23] Contemporary Chinese records show no appreciation of the military importance of the Emperor's Jehol residence.[24]

The Koreans inaccurately regarded the Tibetans as another group of Mongols. As it says in the *Jehol Diary:*

The forty-eight tribes of the Mongols are certainly strong, but the Tibetans are the fiercest of all. The Tibetans are barbarians of the northwest, one of the tribes of the Mongols, and the object of the Emperor's extreme concern.[25]

Pak was perceptive in noting the extreme concern the Ch'ing emperors felt toward Tibet, and he interpreted the Ch'ing support of Lamaism as a conciliatory gesture toward Tibet:

The Tibetans are strong and bold, but they stand in great awe of the Yellow Sect. Thus, the emperors follow their customs and personally worship the Yellow Sect, welcome their Lama [Panchen] to China and give him splendid residences to please him. They enfeoff several princes in order to divide up their strength. These are the arts by which the Manchus control the tribes in all directions.[26]

Pak described here the policy of placating the Panchen Lama as a means of undermining the Dalai Lama. This viewpoint is commonly accepted today, but was unusual among foreign observers of the time.

SINOCENTRISM AND THE ACCEPTANCE OF THE STATUS QUO

Korean intellectuals under the Chosŏn (Yi) dynasty were primarily interested in two aspects of Ch'ing thought: the Sinocentrism of the Chinese literati, and the nature of the Chu Hsi school of Neo-Confucianism. Korean scholars were interested in the latter because, unlike Korea where it held absolute authority, the Chu Hsi school under the Ch'ing was in decline in spite of its official standing. Pak's inquiry into the nature of the Chinese literati accordingly focused on these issues.

Regarding the attitude of Ch'ing literati toward foreigners he wrote:

Before K'ang-hsi, the Chinese were leftover subjects of the Ming. With the reign of K'ang-hsi, however, they saw themselves as subjects of the Ch'ing house. It is therefore natural that they maintained their loyalty to the Ch'ing and respected its laws. If in conversation they were to reveal dissident feelings to a foreigner [like me], they would be considered rebels and traitors to the present dynasty. When one meets Chinese scholars and hears them boast about this dynasty's beneficence, one sighs that there is no one in China who has read the *Spring and Autumn Annals* [and who understands the distinction between Chinese and barbarians in it].[27]

Pak did not accept the Chinese as willing servants of the Ch'ing "barbarians." Instead, he claimed to see underneath the boasting about the beneficence of the Ch'ing a feeling for the identity of the Chinese race, or a "longing for a Chinese ruler" (*ssu-Han*). He distinguished between different generations in their attitudes toward the new dynasty, saying that, by the time of K'ang-hsi, the Chinese recognized the Ch'ing as the ruling dynasty. The Yung-cheng Emperor in his *Ta-i chüeh-mi lu* also made this distinction and demanded that his subjects be loyal to his rule.[28]

In the *Tamhŏn yŏn'gi* (Description of a journey to Peking), Hong Tae-yong wrote:

I told Yen-ch'eng [a Chinese scholar and friend] that ten years ago a district magistrate of an eastern province met a Korean emissary and invited him into his inner chambers. [The Korean was wearing clothing resembling the official clothing of the Ming dynasty.] He borrowed the Korean's hat and belt, faced his wife, and began crying. Up to this day the Koreans transmit this story and pity the district magistrate. Yen-ch'eng hung his head and was silent. P'an T'ing-yun sighed and said, "What a good district magistrate he was!" I said, "If he felt that way, why didn't he quit his official post?" P'an said, "That would not have been an easy thing to do. We wouldn't be able to do it. How can we blame him for not resigning?" Everybody blushed with shame.[29]

Pak, too, appreciated the complex psychology of the scholar class. "It is not easy to resign one's official post" corresponds to Pak's observation that it was natural for Chinese not to want to become "disloyal ministers and rebels." The scholars may have "longed for a Chinese ruler," but they had to adapt to existing conditions so they blocked out tabooed characters, tore up their writings, and feared the laws.[30] These Chinese scholars kept the longing for a Chinese ruler hidden in their hearts.

How could an outsider discover whether or not the scholars felt this longing? Pak used the following method:

Some Korean scholars boast about wearing clothes that remind the Chinese of the Ming dynasty, in order to shame the Chinese. Some ask the Chinese directly if they long for a Chinese ruler, embarrassing them greatly. These are not only subjects that the Chinese abhor, but [bringing them up this way] causes them to think that we have no consideration. Therefore, if you want them to open up to you, you must first deliberately praise their country's culture and teachings, making them feel at ease. Show them that there is no gap between Chinese and foreigners and try to get them to let down their guard. You may show great interest in Chinese rituals and music and show that you are well bred, or you may discuss historical events, instead of discussing current affairs. By showing a humble willingness to learn and, while discussing this and that, pretending that you do not understand something, you will make them anxious [to explain things to you], and in an instant you can see whether or not they are sincere. By smiling and chatting in this way, you can probe their real feelings. This is how I learned something of their inner thoughts, which they do not entrust to pen and paper.[31]

Pak developed this style during his conversations with Wang Hu-ting. He wrote about their discussion:

Hu-ting, when discussing past and present personalities, scholarship, and classical philosophical principles, often gave radical and liberal evaluations of praise and blame, but he was only testing me. At first I did not realize it, and feared only that everyone would laugh at me. When he questioned me I modestly adhered to orthodox responses. Then every time Hu-ting finished writing a few lines, he mumbled something, as if he wanted to say more. It took me quite a while to understand him. I sought his opinion on a phrase from Mencius, and only then did I realize that Hu-ting's views were pure and orthodox.[32]

Most Korean scholars of the time thought that opposition to Chu Hsi's learning meant impurity and heterodoxy. Was Pak correct in equating opposition to Chu Hsi's thought with opposition to the Ch'ing dynasty? If we agree with Pak that "longing for a Chinese ruler" was to be found in Chinese hearts, to what extent can we say that it regulated their behavior as a logical consequence of their thinking? Let us examine Wang Hu-ting's views further. In a discussion of the historical evaluation of the Ch'in dynasty, Wang said:

In general, in ruling the empire, "the people can be made to follow the Way, but they cannot be made to understand it." This was the intention of Yao and Shun. Confucius transmitted it, the Ch'in enacted it . . . When Confucius returned from the state of Wei to the state of Lu, he edited the *Book of Poetry*, the *Book of History*, and corrected the *Book of Rites* and the *Book of Music*. This was something he had to do for the world of his time. On the other hand, [Ch'in Shih Huang-ti's acts of] eliminating the system of enfeoffments, destroying the well-field system, burning the Classics and burying the Confucian scholars alive were of great effectiveness in unifying the empire. From ancient times, emperors have been pleased to have their virtue compared to Yao and Shun. When their virtue is compared to Ch'in Shih Huang-ti they get angry. But I have never heard of one of them who really models himself on Yao and Shun. In fact, they all transmit Ch'in Shih Huang-ti's teachings and put them into law. And I have never heard of a single emperor who, in giving commands to the empire, said, "This is something in the style of Yao and Shun: let it be carried out," or "This is something that brought the downfall of the Ch'in: let it be stopped." You cannot find this kind of emperor anywhere in the thirteen classics or the twenty-one dynastic histories. When a minister is compared to Hsiao Ho [who aided Han Kao-tsu in conquering the empire] or Ts'ao Shen [who succeeded Hsiao Ho as prime minister], he says hesitantly: "I do not dare compare myself." But, when he is compared to [the famous Legalists] Shang Yang and Li Ssu, he becomes extremely angry. But the so-called good ministers who distinguished themselves through history, such as Hsiao Ho, Ts'ao Shen, Fang Hsuan-ling [famous minister of the T'ang who aided T'ai-tsung], and Tu Ju-hui [also a minister to T'ang T'ai-tsung], cannot be compared to Shang Yang and Li Ssu, who are held up to blame. Yet Shang Yang and Li Ssu were able to strengthen the public welfare and repress private interest, and promote good faith between superior and inferior. Those who would achieve what they did would be mistaken to take Hsiao Ho and Ts'ao Shen as models. They would not be mistaken, however, if they were to learn how to protect themselves while carrying out their policies.[33]

This kind of thinking must have been considered (not only by the Chu Hsi school, but by scholars in general) impermissible heresy. Praising the abolition of feudalism, the elimination of the well-field system, the burning of the books, and the burial of the scholars practiced by the Ch'in ruler in front of a foreigner is not at all the same as praising the beneficence of the present dynasty. However, both views derived from a practical acceptance of reality.

The most extreme example of Wang Hu-ting's pragmatism occurred when Pak prompted Wang with the following comments: "Of all the objects and events in the empire, any that have not been investigated by Chu Hsi must be considered false." Wang replied, "Do you mean to say that everyone who was born after Chu Hsi is only a wood and earthen shape [without a thinking mind]?"[34] Wang's philosophy, whether derived from a kind of resignation to barbarian rule, or from pure theory, is, in the end, no different from a legitimation of barbarian rule. Ch'in Shih Huang-ti's abolition of the well-field system, burning of the books, and burial of the scholars is put in the same category as the reality of the foreign conquest and the domination of China.

Wang was ashamed of wearing the queue and Manchu clothing, but admitted that he would not go so far as to ignore the actual state of affairs.[35] He did not lack a feeling of *ssu-Han* or "longing for a Chinese ruler" but, faced with reality, he pushed it to the back of his mind. Wang's theory of "the principle of righteousness" (*i*) expressed this feeling best. He said:

From ancient times, the principle of righteousness has been like melting metal and pouring it into a mold. The metal has no form of its own. It is formed by the mold into a utensil. Or it is like looking at a shell. The shell has its own color, but the color differs when looked at directly or obliquely. Whether water flows east or flows west, the water itself is the same.[36]

Wang went so far as to say:

We Confucians, when we talk about the Mandate of Heaven, never go beyond the two ideas of material force (*ch'i*) and fate (*shu*), though these two ideas of *ch'i* and *shu* are simply the labels we put on success and failure. Everyone talking about Heaven constantly says that "Heaven grants [the position of Son of Heaven] to man," and "the minds of all men unite with the [new] Emperor." This is a lot of stupid talk. When rebels over the ages seize power and then successfully protect their position, are they not favored by the Heavenly Mandate? As long as agriculture flourishes and the Way of the ministers is upheld, do they not bring pleasure to the gods and peace to the people? I have often heard the Chinese people praise the virtues of Wang Mang, and I have never seen the spirit of Yü reject an incense offering from Chin [conqueror of Yü].[37]

Wang's statement that in times of peace the Chinese people would praise even the usurper Wang Mang, regarded by later generations as a symbol of immorality, was not mere cynicism.[38] Rather, it reflected the situation in which he himself was placed. Wang's views should be taken as an affirmation of actuality, a kind of resignation which accepts that orthodox principle may be powerless before the force of reality.

Pak and Wang discussed the famous debate between Shih K'o-fa and Dorgon over the principle of righteousness described in the *Spring and Autumn Annals*.[39] Wang was asked which of them had truly discerned the meaning of "righteousness" (*i*). He replied with a smile, "They each cite the *Spring and Autumn Annals*, but [since Wang An-shih] it has long been no more than a fragmentary work. They both talk about the Mandate of Heaven, but [as Mencius said], "Who will listen when Heaven speaks?" After he wrote this, he blotted it all out.[40] Here, too, even if he thought that Shih K'o-fa's theory was correct, he could not say so. He was suffering as a Chinese under Manchu rule, but he was expressing not only the inability to resist the forces of his time but also his doubts about the absoluteness of *i*. Can this not be called "the affirmation of present reality"? Wang's evaluation of the discussion of the Ming-Ch'ing transition in *Yü-p'i li-tai t'ung-chien chi-lan* (Comprehensive mirror of successive dynasties imperially annotated), compiled under the Ch'ien-lung Emperor, as "public-minded and orthodox," and his praise of the Ch'ien-lung Emperor's "Edict Praising Loyalty" also reflected his practical attitude.[41]

Wang Hu-ting's views are of particular interest because he was not a famous scholar or a high official but an ordinary *chü-jen*. If it had not been for the chance occurrence of the "written conversation" with Pak Chi-wŏn, Wang's views would never have been recorded. They are the ordinary, deeply buried thoughts of one member of the gentry class under barbarian rule. For this reason, Wang can serve as a spokesman for the gentry class in general.

In discussing Wang's theories, Pak was striving to find a psychological "longing for a Chinese ruler" hidden behind the shadow of

Wang's affirmation of the Ch'ing dynasty. It is worth noting that Pak himself expounded almost exactly the same views on Shang Yang and Li Ssu in another part of his *Jehol Diary*.⁴² Pak's inability to adopt a consistent attitude was due to an unrealistic disregard of Manchu rule, but may also have stemmed from deference to powerful readers in Korea.

EDITORIAL PROJECTS AND THE CHINESE LITERATI

In discussing the intellectual situation of the Chinese literati, we must take note of the *Ssu-k'u ch'üan-shu* editorial project, a massive bibliographical project, which was completed in 1784, four years after Pak entered China. Just as he had viewed the Emperor's residence in Jehol and his worship of the Tibetan Yellow Sect as deliberate policies, Pak discussed the *Ssu-k'u ch'üan-shu* from a broad perspective. He saw this project as a means of controlling the Chinese literati, in a passage which has been quoted often by some modern scholars:⁴³

> Because there was no suitable way for the Ch'ing rulers to pacify the scholars of the empire, they have deliberately honored Chu Hsi's teachings in order to please the less serious scholars. The courageous scholars dare to be angry but they do not dare to say anything, while the shallow sycophants follow the tide and seek personal profit. [By following this policy, the Ch'ing] has been able to weaken any resistance from the Chinese literati on the one hand, and take credit for promoting culture on the other. Instead of burying the scholars alive as the Ch'in did, the Court buries them in labors of collation; instead of burning the books as the Ch'in did, it scatters them in the Bureau of Assembled Pearls.⁴⁴ Alas! These techniques for fooling the empire are crafty and deep! The saying "The calamity caused by buying up all the books is worse than that of burning" refers precisely to this policy.⁴⁵

Pak had a similar idea in mind when he asked Wang Hu-ting if the *Ku-chin t'u-shu chi-ch'eng* (Synthesis of books and illustrations of ancient and modern times) was not analogous to the *Yung-lo ta-tien*, which the Yung-lo Emperor had ordered compiled in order to keep scholars critical of his usurpation of the throne so busy that they would have no time to formulate their criticisms. Wang Hu-ting replied that the books proscribed and destroyed in connection with the *Ssu-k'u ch'üan-shu* project were all unimportant, that the present dynasty's policy on the development of culture was quite outstanding, and that Ku Yen-wu's collected works "were of no use because they were not included in the *Ssu-k'u ch'üan-shu*."⁴⁶ This statement seems excessive even for a servant of the Ch'ing, but the frank recognition of the great scholarly significance of the *Ssu-k'u ch'üan-shu* should also be noted. The Japanese scholar Yano Jin'ichi said that one must not ignore the possibility that Pak thought that the rulers were revitalizing culture.⁴⁷ It is unclear to what extent Pak understood the real significance of the *Ssu-k'u ch'üan-shu* project or its connection with the rise of the anti-philosophical Han Learning, but the accuracy of his overall judgment is astonishing.⁴⁸

CHU HSI STUDIES UNDER THE CH'ING

Korean scholars followed only the Chu Hsi school, and were extremely sensitive to Chu Hsi studies in China. Pak was no exception. As the foregoing discussion shows, Pak saw the dynasty's respect for Chu Hsi learning as a means of controlling the scholar class. He expressed his views on Chu Hsi studies under the Ch'ing in these words:

When the Manchus entered China, they secretly investigated which were the dominant trends in scholarship and which had many followers and which had few. They chose the trend with the most followers and actively supported it. They raised Chu Hsi up to be one of the ten greatest philosophers in history and proclaimed to the empire that "the way of Chu Hsi is the school of our Imperial House." Consequently, there were those in the empire who were pleased with this and submitted to it. There were also those who followed it in order to make a name for themselves in the world. The school of Lu Hsiang-shan disappeared almost entirely.

Alas! How could those Manchus possibly understand Chu Hsi's teachings sufficiently well to recognize his orthodoxy? They honored him only superficially with their imperial authority. Their real intention was to spy out the opinions of the Chinese people and, preempting their position, place a gag on the people of the empire so that no one would dare to call them barbarians. How do I know this? Chu Hsi honored the Chinese and rejected the barbarians. Yet the Emperor himself [knowing this] once wrote a treatise criticizing Emperor Kao-tsung of the Sung dynasty for failing to understand the meaning of "righteousness" in the *Spring and Autumn Annals* and attacked Ch'in Kuei [Sung prime minister who counseled peace with the Jurchens] for counseling peace. Chu Hsi had written commentaries on many books, so the Emperor gathered together the scholars of the empire and collected the books of the empire to compile the *T'u-shu chi-ch'eng* and *Ssu-k'u ch'üan-shu* collections, and led the empire in praising them, saying: "These are Chu Hsi's ideas and hidden thoughts." This is the only reason that the Ch'ing emperors revere Chu Hsi. They ride on the necks of the literati, grasp their throats, and pat them on the back. The scholars of the empire are all duped and cowed by them. They only stick to the study of regulations about formal rituals and and are unable to understand their own position.⁴⁹

Pak felt that some courageous Chinese literati discerned the motives for the Ch'ing support of Chu Hsi and moved to the opposite pole. Thus, criticism of Chu Hsi gained momentum as scholars sought to find errors in Chu Hsi's commentaries in retaliation against the Emperor's policies. Pak believed that Ch'ing critics of Chu Hsi differed greatly from Lu Hsiang-shan, who opposed Chu Hsi from a philosophical standpoint. Pak said that Ch'ing scholars opposed Chu Hsi, not because they disagreed with the content of Chu Hsi's thought, but because they were critical of the barbarian dynasty that supported it.[50] He reflected the views of the Korean scholars of that time, who were convinced that the Chu Hsi school held the only key to knowledge.

Pak's point of view can be vindicated by an examination of the way the Yung-cheng Emperor chose to handle the Chinese-barbarian distinction contained in Chu Hsi. Yung-cheng wrote in the *Ta-i chüeh-mi lu* that, while he recognized the distinction between Chinese and barbarian in Chu Hsi, it could be explained by saying that the criterion for this distinction was the refinement or crudity of the culture, not race or residence.[51]

Is it possible to explain the stagnation of Chu Hsi studies in the Ch'ing by this anti-Ch'ing temper alone? Shortly after the *Jehol Diary* was written, Chao-lien wrote in his *Hsiao-t'ing tsa-lu:*

After Yü Min-chung [1773–1780] and Ho-shen [1777–1799] became grand councillors, the scholars at court competed to establish contact with them. The crafty scholars flattered the councillors and denounced the upright scholars, saying that their own scholarship was superior to theirs. Those who were unwilling to do this stuck stubbornly to the collation of texts and picked flaws in the works of Sung scholars. No one dared to read works of Sung Neo-Confucians. I once tried to buy the *Tu-shu chi* of Hsueh Hsuan [1389–1464] and the *Chü-yeh lu* of Hu Chü-jen [1434–1484], but the bookstore owner said: "In the last twenty years or more I have not kept that kind of book in my store. I am afraid that there is no market for them and that I would only lose my investment [if I stocked them]." I was unhappy to hear this.[52]

In 1801, the Korean scholar Yu Tŏk-kong went to Peking again, and Chi Yun (editor-in-chief of the *Ssu-k'u ch'üan-shu* project) remarked to him: "The main stream of scholarship is found in the *Erh ya* or *Shuo wen* [ancient dictionaries]. If you go to the south, you might possibly be able to buy some books of the Chu Hsi school."[53] Yu lamented, "It has apparently been a long time since the books of the Ch'eng brothers and Chu Hsi were discussed. That the scholarship of China should have reached this point is deeply regrettable." The Han Learning had its roots in the school of practical statecraft which formed in response to the social reality of the late Ming and early Ch'ing periods. The inability of Chu Hsi (or Wang Yang-ming) studies to respond to reality was a major cause of the rise of the statecraft school. When the statecraft school itself, however, failed to respond to the reality of the firm Ch'ing rule (and thought control), the faction within the statecraft movement that studied mainly the classics and histories remained alive and became identified with the "labor of collation" for the Ch'ing Court, and Han Learning flourished.[54] As a result, the development of Han Learning brought about the decline of the Chu Hsi school. One of Pak's important contributions is that he pointed out that anti-Ch'ing feeling was one cause of this decline. The lack of an energetic response to reality by the Chu Hsi school itself, however, must be considered another important factor.

The study of philosophical principles in the Chu Hsi school (which included a discussion of the distinction between Chinese and barbarian and rigid adherence to orthodoxy in its historical view) under the rigid barbarian rule was bound to fail to provide impetus for a response to the present reality of barbarian rule.[55]

As the distance between Chinese scholars and barbarian rulers disappeared, however, the Chu Hsi school moved in the direction of "statecraft" (responding to reality). The proof of this change is that, in the late Ch'ing period, Tseng Kuo-fan tried to establish the foundations of a theory of statecraft from a Chu Hsi school standpoint, calling it a "compromise between the Han and Sung schools" (*Han-Sung che-chung*). The internal distance between Han and Manchu shrank greatly before the new threat of the Western barbarians. Only by locating the barbarians outside China was the Chu Hsi school able to find a base from which to respond to reality in a confrontation with Western barbarian values.[56]

We have commented on various features of the Ch'ing policy of control in the late eighteenth century as seen in Pak Chi-wŏn's *Jehol Diary*. Since he had to some degree the objectivity of a foreigner, his critical views are extremely interesting, not so much for his detailed descriptions, but rather for his perceptions of the great currents that flowed beneath the Ch'ing rulers' policies. As we have noted, Pak's dealings were mainly with lower gentry, which made possible a closer approach to the views of the ordinary Chinese of that time.

Pak differed greatly from nearly all the other Korean scholars of the time in stressing that, even though barbarians were in power, China was still China. He believed there were many things to be learned from China under the Ch'ing, and he tried to be realistic and flexible in his understanding of the Chinese literati under Ch'ing rule. Pak was still a Korean scholar, however, in his view of the Ch'ing dynasty as thoroughly barbarian and in his devotion to the Chu Hsi school. Furthermore, inasmuch as he shared the views of his readers, he was, of course, biased to some degree. Most of his colleagues believed that the Chinese literati, in superficially accepting the Ch'ing dynasty, had ceased to recognize the difference between Chinese and barbarian. Pak, however, took the outward expression of the literati as a façade behind which he recognized a psychological awareness of the Chinese-Manchu distinction. In this respect he was certainly in advance of his contemporaries, but he was not able to see that the Chinese literati had no choice but to accept reality. The weakness of anti-barbarian thought reflected the social character of the gentry class, which was dependent on the current dynasty for its very survival.

The theoretical basis for this lack of strong anti-Manchu sentiment is found in doubts Pak had about the traditional historical view of legitimacy. Although these doubts turned into an affirmation of the real historical role of Shang Yang and Ch'in Shih Huang-ti, Pak did not accept them at face value. Two hundred years later we can analyze his discussion with a wider perspective and a freer point of view, and can see in Pak's description the subtleties of Ch'ing literati thought which he had overlooked. Pak himself was not bound solely to the classical viewpoint but tried to look at China historically. His inability to take a more comprehensive view of Ch'ing governing policies, however, was an inescapable result of contemporary cultural restrictions.

Pak's views on the situation of the Chu Hsi school in the Ch'ing dynasty were extremely perceptive. However, although he was particularly aware of the significance of the *Ssu-k'u ch'üan-shu* project, his views were narrowly focused. He is open to the charge of being too distant from the general trend of Chinese scholarship, thus perceiving only one side of the situation and failing to explain the whole. We, however, can use Pak's description to discuss Ch'ing cultural policies and thought control from a wider perspective. Pak's comments on Ch'ing policy toward the Inner Asian peoples were also remarkable. His sharp insight that the "severity of imperial regulations" of the Ch'ien-lung period concealed a contradictory relaxation of control is also useful to us in establishing a view of the Ch'ien-lung reign.

We cannot draw any general conclusions about Ch'ing rule and intellectual trends based solely upon Pak's comments. He interviewed only a handful of gentry and his experiences were limited. It may, however, be stimulating to make use of Pak's acute observations in our broader study of the whole Ch'ing period.

CHAPTER TWO

The Sheng-yuan–Chien-sheng Stratum (Sheng-Chien) in Ch'ing Society

For a broad understanding of Ch'ing history it is essential to study the social structure and local government of the period. On this assumption, much research has been conducted on Ch'ing local government and the "gentry."[1] Until recently, however, there have not been many studies of the mechanics of local government and of the relationship of the *shen-shih* (that is, gentry) to the central government. This relationship demands clarification because it is the ultimate penetration of state power into the lives of the people.

The term *gentry* can be more broadly defined, but we use it here to refer to those people who received degrees from the state authorities either through the examination system, the school system, or the purchase system, and who were directly or indirectly tied to official positions. It includes both those directly connected to official posts (officials in office, retired officials, and officials relieved of their posts) and aspirants to official posts (those who held the degrees of *chü-jen, kung-sheng, chien-sheng, sheng-yuan,* and so forth). These people were granted special privileges by the government and engaged in social interaction with officials. They sometimes supported the ideals of the Confucian state and cooperated in the maintenance of order (while protecting their own positions), but at times part of this stratum engaged in anti-state or anti-official activities to protect their own interests. They promoted public works which the state could not participate in directly, but they could also disrupt local administrative order by disturbing "proper administration"; when that happened, the state stepped in to control them. Because the social activities of the gentry were so complex, and because their significance was so great, it is impossible to treat their institutional roles in isolation if we are to understand their place in Chinese society.

The gentry had much in common in character and ideals with the ancient *shih-ta-fu* (upper elite) but, unlike the *shih-ta-fu,* their status was guaranteed by the state through degrees, and existed as such only from the Ming period (1368–1644) on. Officials in office were included in the term *gentry* because of their links with their home areas. My present concern, however, is not with the ruling stratum but with the ruled and their response to rule. Officials in office are therefore not included in the term *gentry* for purposes of this discussion.

Most of the recent work on the institutional aspects of the gentry is written in English, and the word *gentry* is borrowed from English history to translate the Chinese term *shen-shih.* The meaning of the English term is approximately the same as the Chinese *shen-shih,* but *shen-shih* can be divided into the two concepts of *shen* (official gentry) and *shih* (scholar gentry). If we use the term *gentry,* we cannot distinguish these two components.[2] The association of *gentry* with a ruling class or a sense of domination also comes from the implications of the English word, because the original term indicates that the gentry lived in their home district, had a social status distinct from commoners, and a preeminent position in local government. The term *local elite*[3] and the Japanese term *kyōshin* also emphasize local residence and preeminence in the local scene.[4] The term *shen-shih* encompasses a variety of social groups, and often lumps together the distinct social activities of these groups. Thus, after investigating the activities of the groups composing the gentry, it may be better not to use the traditional term *shen-shih* if it appears inappropriate to include such a variety of behavior. Here I use *shen-shih* only in its official and institutional meaning and do not wish to imply that the gentry in all cases formed a unified group.

Nor do I aim to study the gentry as a whole, but to clarify the character of the *sheng-yuan* and *chien-sheng* strata (called *sheng-chien*), which composed the overwhelming majority of the gentry and had an important influence on society. The *sheng-chien* are called *shih* (or *chin*, another term for scholar gentry), and are usually treated together with the *shen* (official gentry), as in the term *shen-shih*. I doubt, however, whether the *sheng-chien* can be unreservedly included with the *shen*, and I will try to describe the actual character of the *sheng-chien* and their effects on traditional Chinese society. Starting from an examination of earlier studies concerning the common character of *shen* and *shih*, we shall emphasize the extent to which *shen* and *shih* cannot be treated together (that is, the independent character of the *shih*), and we shall also investigate the connection between the *shih* and the common people. We shall evaluate this independence and judge its importance for gaining an understanding of the traditional Chinese social order.[5]

The major works on the character of the *sheng-chien* are the studies of Chung-li Chang, Ping-ti Ho, and T'ung-tsu Ch'ü. Chang divided the gentry into "upper gentry" and "lower gentry," the former including officials, *chin-shih*, *chü-jen*, and *kung-sheng*, the latter including *li-kung-sheng*, *sheng-yuan*, and *chien-sheng*. Chang based his discussion of the differences between the upper and lower strata on the concept of *gentry* as an encompassing term. Ho's distinction between upper and lower gentry is in general the same as Chang's, but he defined the composition of the upper and lower gentry somewhat differently. He separated *sheng-yuan* and *chien-sheng* from the gentry and did not see them as part of the elite. He stressed that they were a leading group among the commoners. Ch'ü, following the traditional distinction between *shen* and *shih*, saw the lower stratum of scholar gentry as a middle stratum distinct from both the upper, official gentry, and the commoners, but he included both strata under the term *gentry*.

Three criteria may be used to define the character of the *sheng-chien*. We can first look at the institutional structure, that is, the degree of distance from state power. Second, we can examine the relationship of the *sheng-chien* to local government, that is, the county magistrates who served concurrently as tools for the execution of imperial policies and were masters of an independent unit of local administration. Third, we can investigate the behavioral patterns of the *sheng-chien* themselves.

County magistrates in the administative system were no more than cogs in the administrative machine, manipulated by their superiors, who were often arbitrary and who, themselves, represented state or dynastic authority. Seen from the perspective of the common Confucian order of successive dynasties, however, county magistrates might be regarded as supervisors of an independent order; their real function was no different from that of the emperor. Their duties were as broad as his, ranging from education (the strengthening of the Confucian order) to tax collection, the settlement of lawsuits, and even the capture of locusts. Like the emperor, they were free to select their assistants (*mu-yu*). Their fiscal prerogatives, as seen in the setting of customary fees (*lou-kuei*) and so on, also resembled the emperor's.[6] At least this would appear to be the case from the people's point of view.

The ideal Confucian political order was expressed in the vocabulary of family relationships. The use of such terminology denotes the moral responsibility of the ruler for his subjects. The emperor was called the father and mother of the people. Similarly, the county magistrate was the father and mother of the people in his jursidction, and he referred to the people as his children (*ch'ih-tzu*).[7] In the Ch'ien-lung period (1736–1795), Hsieh Chin-luan said: "The reason Heaven established emperors was to benefit the people. Emperors could not reach the entire empire with their own eyes, ears, hands, and feet, so that they had to subdivide it into administrative units to rule it. The county magistrate actually administers and rules these units. *As emperors are masters of the empire, county magistrates are the masters of their counties.*"[8]

Hsieh accurately expressed the dual character of the county magistrate as both the representative of the emperor and the master of a designated region. There were two kinds of popular resistance, therefore, often addressed to one aspect of the dual character. Opposition to a particular local official, however, could easily be translated into anti-state rebellion because of this dual character. When we consider the anti-official movements of the *sheng-chien*, we must keep this duality in mind.

THE *SHEN-SHIH* AND THE *SHENG-CHIEN*: BASIC CHARACTERISTICS OF THE *SHEN-SHIH*

There is general agreement that the *shen-shih* were composed of *shen* (official gentry) and *shih* (scholar gentry), but there is a difference between the meaning of the concept in principle and its real content. The word *shen* means "those holding office," but in an expanded sense it includes retired officials, who remained closely connected with officialdom.[9] Those holding official status but not serving in office because of mourning, as well as degree-holders waiting for official assignment, were also included in the *shen*.[10] When the local residence of the *shen* is emphasized, the term *hsiang-shen* is usually used. In *Fu-hui ch'üan-shu* (A complete book concerning happiness and benevolence), a handbook for local officials written in 1699, Huang Liu-hung describes the *shen-shih* of a locality as the *hsiang-shen, chü-jen, kung-sheng, chien-sheng*, military and civil *sheng-yuan*, and so on.[11] He thus distinguishes the *hsiang-shen*, who hold official posts, from the lower strata. He also writes in a sub-chapter entitled "Treatment of *shen-shih*": "Among the local gentry (*hsiang-shen*) there are those who have served as local officials; others who have returned to their native place on leave of absence; and still others who have retired from official positions and now live at home. In social intercourse they should be treated with proper courtesy."[12] Here the term *shen-shih* actually refers to *hsiang-shen*, which was supposed to include officials presently in office in places other than their native districts. *Hsiang-shen* is sometimes used as a general term describing a variety of groups and sometimes designates one of the component groups.[13]

If in principle the *shen* were directly connected to officialdom, what was the nature of the *shih*? They were not directly tied to officialdom, but through the examination and school systems they could attain an official post. Yet there was a certain legally recognized and guaranteed distance between the *shih* and the attainment of official posts.[14]

Beneath the highest-ranking group (*chin-shih*) among the *shen* were the *chü-jen. Chü-jen*, however, as a product of the examination system, which was a level higher than the school system, differed from the *kung-sheng* and *sheng-yuan* below them. They enjoyed great social prestige because they had a good chance of getting official posts by virtue of their degrees, and because there were fewer of them than the degree-holders below them.[15] They were highly respected in their own localities and exerted a considerable influence.[16] The legal guarantees of their status were a direct expression of this social esteem. Like the *chin-shih*, they could only be stripped of their status with imperial approval. In contrast, the *kung-sheng* and *chien-sheng* could lose their status by order of the provincial governor, and the *sheng-yuan* by order of the provincial directors of schools.[17]

All the groups below *chü-jen* (*kung-sheng*, *li-kung-sheng*, *chien-sheng*, *li-chien-sheng*, and *sheng-yuan*) were statuses within the school system, not the examination system. *Kung-sheng* were selected from among the *sheng-yuan* registered at county and prefectural schools (*fu-sheng*, *tseng-sheng*, *lin-sheng*). *Kung-sheng* and *chien-sheng*, whether they obtained their degrees by the orthodox route or by purchase, had the special privilege of participating directly in the provincial examinations, without having to take the *k'o-shih* qualifying examinations. The best among the *kung-sheng* could obtain posts as education officials at the county or prefectural level, or even as county magistrates, so the privileges of *kung-sheng* were quite different from those of the other degrees. *Li-kung-sheng* (who bought the *kung-sheng* degree by contribution) could not obtain an official post by virtue of the degree itself.

Regular *chien-sheng* were students at the Imperial Academy, itself a link in the school system. There were not many *chien-sheng* (only a few hundred), and they did not follow a regular course of study,[18] so they are of little significance. *Li-chien-sheng* bought *chien-sheng* degrees. (Most of those recorded as *chien-sheng* were in fact *li-chien-sheng*.) They were the most numerous group next to *sheng-yuan* and thus extremely important. (According to Chung-li Chang's calculations, they numbered about 355,000 in the early nineteenth century.)[19]

Sheng-yuan were at the lowest end of the school system, and were the most numerous of the gentry. In order to enter the examination system, they had to pass through a number of intermediate exams, including the yearly exam and the *k'o-shih* qualifying exam. Except in unusual circumstances, they could not obtain any official post with their degrees alone. Although they were the degree-holders who were furthest away from officialdom, they still differed greatly from commoners, who had absolutely no connection with officialdom.

The common characteristic of all the groups from *chü-jen* down to *sheng-yuan* was that, although they were a middle stratum, which had to get higher degrees in order to obtain official posts, they were all in a position to hope for an official post. As intellectuals connected with officialdom, they composed the traditional *shih-ta-fu* class and formed a source of future officials, which was their main distinction from commoners. Although there were differences between these groups, they received special treatment from the state because they were connected with officialdom, and they held publicly recognized rights to privileged treatment in the judicial and tax systems.[20]

The groups from *chü-jen* to *sheng-yuan* were not directly tied to officialdom; they were generally called *shih* or *chin*. The clearest explanation of their status appears in two essays by Feng Kuei-fen: "Chün-fu shuo-ch'üan chin" (Persuading the *chin* to equalize taxes), and "Chün-fu shuo-ch'üan shen" (Persuading the *shen* to equalize taxes). These are essays explaining a proposal for the reform of the grain-tribute taxes in the Su-Sung area. Feng wrote separate proclamations to the *shen* and *chin*. In the *chin* he clearly included *chü-jen, kung-sheng, chien-sheng,* and *sheng-yuan*.[21] Even when these four groups are not so clearly described as *shih* or *chin*, they are included in a separate category from the *shen*, as in the *Fu-hui ch'üan-shu* cited above.

There are, however, many cases in which the largest group, the *sheng-yuan*, is distinguished from the other groups and described as *chin*. When the functions of *sheng-yuan* and *chien-sheng* became alienated from local government, expressions like "wicked *sheng*" (*sheng-yuan*) and "vicious *chien*" (*chien-sheng*) were frequently used. These terms appear innumerable times in collections of regulations controlling the activities of *sheng-yuan*, such as the *Ta-Ch'ing hui-tien shih-li* and other administrative handbooks like *Ching-shih wen-pien* and *Mu-ling shu*. In addition, the term *chin-chien* is sometimes used instead of *sheng-chien* (as, for example, in *Fu-hui ch'üan-shu*).[22] This term describes all the *sheng-yuan* as *chin*, while the *chin* in Feng Kuei-fen's "Persuading the *chin*" above has the same meaning as *shih* and denotes broadly all the strata of *chü-jen* and lower. In most cases, however, uses of the words *shih* or *chin* refer to *sheng-yuan*. This is an outgrowth of the special status of *sheng-yuan* within the *shen-shih*.

To summarize the above discussion, there are three ways to divide up the *shen-shih:* (1) officials vs. non-officials, that is, in the strict meaning of *shen* and *shih,* dividing present and retired officials from *chü-jen* and below; (2) examination system vs. school system, putting officials, *chin-shih,* and *chü-jen* in the upper category, and *kung-sheng* and below in the lower category; (3) having or lacking the qualification to obtain an official post, dividing orthodox *kung-sheng, chü-jen,* and *chin-shih* (who can obtain an official post by virtue of their degrees alone and are grouped together with officials) from *li-kung-sheng, chien-sheng,* and *sheng-yuan. Sheng-yuan,* in particular, are in a special category. If we look at the way the government actually worked, we must go beyond our analysis and see how the *shen-shih* functioned in the real world of the time.

DEBATES ON THE STRUCTURE OF THE GENTRY AND THE PROBLEM OF THE *SHENG-CHIEN* STRATUM

T'ung-tsu Ch'ü made a basic distinction between official and scholar gentry, since all gentry were part of the political order. "Official gentry" (the traditional *shen*) included presently serving officials, retired officials, dismissed officials, and official posts by contribution; "scholar gentry" (*shih*) included *chü-jen, kung-sheng, chien-sheng,* and *sheng-yuan.* The *shih* were therefore part of the gentry; the commoners formed a separate group.[23]

Some contemporary examples suggest an interpretation that differs from Ch'ü's, stressing instead the gap between the official and scholar gentry. For instance, Yueh Yuan-sheng of the late Ming wrote, "*Shih* are the most eminent of the four categories of people, and the local *shen* are the most eminent of the *shih*," and his contemporary Yen Mao-yu wrote, "The local *shen* are the most eminent people in the country, . . . and their merit is a hundred times greater than that of the *shih.*"[24] Yuan Mei of the mid-Ch'ing, writing from the point of view of a county magistrate, said: "Respecting the gentry (*shen*) is the way to respect the Court; the other *sheng-yuan* and *t'ung-sheng* [students] are all my sons and younger brothers." Here the *shen* are seen as having the same character as the Court, or central authority. Yuan Mei clearly treated the *t'ung-sheng* the same as the *sheng-yuan* and differentiated them from the official gentry, or *shen.*[25]

People of the time were clearly aware of the great distinction between *shen* and the *sheng-yuan;* they considered the *sheng-yuan* close to the level of commoners. Feng Kuei-fen, for example, in "Chün-fu shuo-ch'üan chin" described how the attitude of county magistrates toward the *chin* (mainly *sheng-chien*) differed from their attitude toward the *shen:*

Presently, in handling grain-tribute taxes, the subprefectural and county officials hate the *shen*, but they hate the *chin* even more. Why is this? The *shen* are few and are easily kept under surveillance. The *chin* are many . . . and all are damaged by them. Therefore the officials resent the *shen* slightly, but they resent the *chin* deeply . . . In the division of proceeds from the grain-tribute system, runners, clerks, and corvée laborers share a hundred parts, officials ten parts, the *shen* two or three parts. But the *chin* get only one part, sometimes not even that. Because of the authority of a department or county magistrate is such that it is difficult to punish the *shen*, but easy to punish the *chin* . . . To strip a *sheng-yuan* or *chien-sheng* of his rank, one need only draw up an official letter in the morning and inform him in the evening.[26]

The departmental and county officials thus discriminated against the *sheng-chien* as compared with the *shen*.

Ch'ü put the "scholar gentry" in an intermediate group between the ruling and the ruled.[27] There is some basis for Ch'ü's distinction, and we shall soon propose the concept of an "intermediate group" as appropriate. Ch'ü, however, was in the end faithful to the literal concept of the traditional vocabulary of *shen-shih*[28] and ignored the differences of various groups within the traditional category of *shih* (*chü-jen* vs. *sheng-chien*, and so forth). He called them an "intermediate group" but still included them in the gentry. In this respect, his explanation of the connections between the different strata is inadequate.

If we introduce a new viewpoint, the analysis of social strata based on the degree of unity between the social stratum and state power or the ruling authority, then it is not necessary to cling to the traditional vocabulary. It is, of course, important to know the traditional use of words and the concepts of people of the time, but contemporaries clearly were not completely aware of the real functioning, attitudes, and effects that we are studying today. It is possible that within the *shih* class there were various groups that differed in their relationship to state power.

Chung-li Chang, unlike Ch'ü, tried to draw distinctions based on the real functions of the groups, rather than on traditional categories.[29] Upper gentry were distinguished from lower gentry by their qualification for assignment to official posts, their leadership of the lower gentry in social activities ("gentry functions"), and by a much greater number of officially granted special privileges. Differences in marriage and funeral ceremonies were also mentioned. As we have seen, in Chang's view, "upper gentry" included officials, *chin-shih*, *chü-jen*, and *kung-sheng;* the "lower gentry" included *li-kung-sheng, sheng-yuan,* and *li-chien-sheng.*

The problem with Chang's interpretation, however, is that, in discussing upper and lower gentry and in distinguishing them from commoners, he exaggerated the distance between lower gentry and commoners. Chang was correct in stressing the predominance of upper gentry in gaining tax privileges and in controlling militia organization. The upper gentry were the overall organizers; the lower gentry led only small units. Chang, however, focused on the unity of the lower gentry with the government and seldom discussed their alienation from it. Even though he spoke briefly of alienation, he mentioned only that of the gentry in general, without touching on the question of which group, upper or lower, was the most active. As will be shown below, Chang's lower gentry, unlike the upper gentry, often united with the commoners in activities that diverged from state interests. This phenomenon hints at the need for analysis in terms of the concept of an "intermediate group" in a different sense from that of Ch'ü.

According to Chang, there were two kinds of distinctions in the marriage and funeral ceremonies: one was that of ranked officials (*p'in-kuan*) and the other was that of lower literati (*shu-shih*), which included officials of the 8th rank. Privileges granted to ranked officials were applicable to *chin-shih, chü-jen,* and *kung-sheng;* those of lower literati were applicable to *sheng-yuan, chien-sheng,* and *li-kung-sheng.*[30]

Ping-ti Ho included *sheng-yuan* and *chien-sheng* in the commoner class, but as "a privileged class among commoners and an important social transitional group." For Ho, the "official class" included retired officials, present officials, expectant officials, *chin-shih, chü-jen, kung-sheng,* and *li-kung-sheng.*[31] Ho's view is a long way from the general concept of *shen-shih. Shen-shih,* for Ho, connoted officialism and ruling authority and thus often did not include *shih* (with the meaning of *sheng-chien*). Ho tried to prove this theory by citing lists of donors in establishing schools and school land, which included, under *shen-shih,* only *kung-sheng* and *li-kung-sheng,* but not *sheng-yuan* and *chien-sheng.* This argument is weak, because Ho did not say whether *sheng-chien* never gave aid to schools or if there is simply no record of it. Other reasons given by Ho for regarding *sheng-chien* as commoners are: (1)They could not obtain official posts. (2) They were not important enough to be included in the "class lists" (*teng-k'o lu,* and so forth). (3) Most local gazetteers did not record their names, or, if they did, they did not record their ancestors. (4) Their households were not wealthy and engaged in low-status occupations. Ho also differed from Chang in including *li-kung-sheng* along with *kung-sheng* in the gentry (official class), as potential officials.[32]

Ho emphasized the strikingly low social and institutional position of *sheng-chien* compared with the other groups. This aspect of the *sheng-chien* class is not addressed by the the traditional concept, and Ho's approach has merit in allowing the opportunity for reconsideration of their status. Ho, however, failed to give an adequate explanation of the extent to which his separation of *sheng-chien* from his "official class" differs from the views that include *sheng-chien* as lower gentry or scholar gentry. A more diversified analysis is necessary.

Ho and Ch'ü differed in their conception of the official ruling class.[33] Both excluded *sheng-chien* from the ruling stratum, but for Ch'ü this exclusion was for both political and institutional reasons; Ho, on the other hand, discussed social isolation. There is still room to consider the exact scope of the Ch'ing ruling stratum. Chang saw the entire gentry group as part of the ruling class, while Kung-ch'üan Hsiao stressed the difference of interests between the state and the gentry or potential gentry (*t'ung-sheng*) who provided leadership in their home communities and who rendered services to local government. Hsiao maintained:

Leadership in their home communities and services in the administration, however, did not make the gentry a part of the ruling class, nor cause their interests to become identical. In fact as well as in theory, scholar-officials remained subjects of the emperor and, together with commoners, were subject to imperial control. Those who, in their capacity as government officials, functioned as mediums through which imperial authority was brought to bear on the masses, were at the same time a part of "the people" over whom and ostensibly for whose benefit the emperors ruled.[34]

When the gentry are excluded completely from the ruling class in this way, the definition of "ruling class" becomes even more confused.

The ruling class must be defined as the group that identifies the interests of state power with its own interests and always, in promoting the penetration of political authority, automatically pursues its own interests. If we accept this definition, then the relations of this class with state power can be investigated in detail. Here, rather than focusing on a component designated clearly as the "ruling class" by some researchers, we shall analyze only the *sheng-chien* stratum, who have sometimes been called part of the ruling class, part of the subject class, and also a middle stratum, in an attempt to define the lower bounds of the ruling class.

We shall consider the following four points: (1) the distance between state power and the *sheng-chien* class, (2) the degree of social mobility of the *sheng-chien*, (3) the behavioral pattern and thought of the *sheng-chien*, (4) the relations between *sheng-chien* and commoners.[35]

POLITICAL ASPECTS OF THE *SHENG-CHIEN*

State Power and the Sheng-chien

Ku Yen-wu, in his essay "Sheng-yuan lun,"[36] said of the late Ming (and he was probably thinking of early Ch'ing *sheng-yuan* as well), "There are three groups in the realm who injure the people: (1) the *hsiang-huan* (upper local gentry), (2) the *sheng-yuan*, and (3) the clerks." He thus recognized the difference between *sheng-yuan* and *hsiang-huan* or *hsiang-shen*. Ku here spoke only of *sheng-yuan* and not *chien-sheng*, since in the Ming *chien-sheng* were not numerous. The situation changed in the Ch'ing, when the ranks of the *chien-sheng* were swollen by the ever-increasing *li-chien-sheng*, and both were seen as being in the same stratum and enjoying equal social treatment as *sheng-yuan*.[37]

Ku Yen-wu wrote:

Why did the state establish *sheng-yuan*? Generally speaking, it was in order to gather together the talented young men of the empire and to cultivate them in local schools such that they might be made to make them perfect their virtue and develop their talent, understand the Way of the former kings, and grasp the affairs of their age, and thus serve as officials and share the rule of the empire with the emperor.

He saw the *sheng-yuan* as guardians of Confucian ideals and as a source of able officials. From the Ming on, the school system and the examination system were united and the significance of the *sheng-yuan* became even more debatable. In addition to preserving Confucian ideals and serving as a source of officials, they became tools of state control. These literate intellectuals had great influence on the mass of commoners, and were granted various legal privileges. They were thus easily controlled and aided state control or at least were less likely to interfere with it.

A man named Wu Le-kuang wrote as follows on the subject of

local administration (*yang-min*, or "nourishing the people") is quoted in the *Mu-ling shu* (The magistrates' handbook):

> There are many ways of promoting an administration that nourishes the people. There is the registration of the population to settle them in their residences, and the organization of the *pao-chia* and village defense against thieves to control the depredations of brigands. There is the promotion of agriculture, the clearance of new land, and the repair of dikes to encourage production, and there are restrictions on the use of land and grain to eliminate waste. There is the control of locusts and flies to eliminate their damage, the construction of bridges and ferries to benefit transportation and of granaries to prepare against famine, famine relief to provide assistance after a disaster strikes, charitable institutions to aid the impoverished, and the recording of the benevolent and the aged. These are all important aspects of government recorded in the *Hui-tien* (Regulations of government). As for building reservoirs for irrigation, preparing equipment to save people from floods, distributing clothes in cold weather, establishing soup kitchens for the starving, and providing tea for the thirsty, drugs for the ill, coffins and shrouds to bury the dead, and graveyards for burial—these are all activities of government vital for the livelihood of the people. But much of this important work is done by public-spirited gentry (*hao-i shen-chin*) and is not recorded in the *Hui-tien*. Local officials should urgently exhort the gentry to transform the people with their efforts.[38]

Wu Le-kuang divided government activities into two types: those that were recorded in the *Hui-tien*, and those that were not. He emphasized the latter, which were to be carried out only by public-spirited gentry. Of course all these activities were directly connected to local interests (particularly irrigation, famine relief, and the organization of local militia against rebellion and thieves) and were sources of economic gain for the gentry who participated in them, so the interests of the two coincided.[39] The participation of the *sheng-yuan* in these public works and their aid to local government is significant.

The activities not recorded in the *Hui-tien* were called "gentry functions" by Chung-li Chang, and the particular interests of the *sheng-yuan* themselves lie behind these social activities. When this self-interest came in conflict with government control, there was a potential for damage to local government by illegal schemes of the gentry.[40] Not only *sheng-yuan*, but the gentry class as a whole, standing between the officials and the commoners, were apt to pursue illegal profit, but the *sheng-yuan* were particularly prone to corruption and may even have participated in anti-official and anti-government activity. The *sheng-yuan* often collaborated for mutual economic benefit, and exerted various kinds of pressure on the local officials. This is why the phrase "manipulating officials" (*ch'ih-li ch'ang-tuan*), used since the Han dynasty, appeared frequently in the Ch'ing administrative handbooks. Sometimes their pressure appears to be a collective one.

Many of the administrative handbooks instructed local officials to "treat the gentry (*shih*) according to ritual," not only because of the tradition of favorable treatment for the literati, but also because of their propensity for illegal activities. As we mentioned earlier, the *sheng-yuan*, because of their low status, differed from the *shen* in that they were put under the supervision of the local magistrates. The primary responsibility for supervision of the *sheng-yuan* fell on the county school director. *Sheng-yuan* could not deal arbitrarily with subprefecture and county magistrates, who were empowered to strip *sheng-yuan* of their degrees.[41] *Li-chien-sheng*, unlike the *sheng-yuan*, could not be deprived of their rank without the approval of the governor or governor general.[42] Actually, however, both *sheng-yuan* and *chien-sheng* were under the direct supervision of the magistrates as well.

Both Ch'ü and Chang wrote from the viewpoint of the emperor or the officials in their discussions of the distinction of *sheng-yuan* from commoners. In the *Yŏlha ilgi* (Jehol diary) of the Korean traveler Pak Chi-wŏn, there is an interesting passage that describes the *sheng-chien* from the commoner's perspective. Pak reported this conversation with a merchant surnamed Li in Manchuria in 1780:

I said, "Once someone becomes a student, is he considered part of the gentry (*shih*)?" Li answered, "Yes. The students have various classes, such as *lin-sheng*, *chien-sheng*, and *kung-sheng*, who are promoted from the *sheng-yuan*. Once someone becomes a *sheng-yuan*, he brings glory to his relatives and harm to his neighbors. He manipulates officials and tyrannizes the countryside. These are the special tricks of the *sheng-yuan*."[43]

The *sheng-yuan* did take advantage of the commoners. The question remains, however, to what extent did their interests coincide with those of the officials, *chü-jen*, and other superior strata? Ku Yen-wu and the Manchurian merchant both saw the need for the repression of the *sheng-chien* and thus distinguished them from other groups. We shall examine below the extent to which this distinction outweighed the unity between the *sheng-chien* and other strata.

Beating the Sheng-chien

The *Kuo-ch'ao ch'i-hsien lei-cheng, Pei-chuan chi,* and *Hsu pei-chuan chi,* which are collections of biographies of Ch'ing local officials, include "loving the *shih*" and "treating the *shih* according to ritual" as requirements for the ideal local official,[44] implying that the general practice was the opposite. Here is an example from a biography of an exemplary county magistrate contained in the *Pei-chuan chi:* "He was in office for twelve years and never once humiliated a member of the gentry. If someone acted in an evil way, he simply gave him sincere moral instruction, allowing him to correct his own mistakes. Thus, wherever he went, the people were all at ease." Humiliating the lower gentry (usually called "beating the *shih*") was thus so common that those who did not practice it were singled out as particularly virtuous.[45] Many administrative manuals, of course, also urged "treating the gentry according to ritual," "respecting the gentry," and "receiving the gentry with humility."[46] Fang Ta-shih's *P'ing-p'ing yen* (1887) stated that most county magistrates in fact treated the *sheng-yuan* cruelly.[47]

Some examples of local officials "beating the *shih*" are the following: Kao T'ing-yao, a local official in the Ch'ien-lung period, stated that one *chien-sheng* was struck on the jaw for trying to bribe an official in connection with a lawsuit; another *sheng-yuan* was beaten on the hands for having himself recorded, ignoring custom, under a courtesy name (*pieh-hao*) in the registry of civil and military *sheng-yuan*; and another *chien-sheng* was struck on the jaw for attempting to interfere with a coronor's inquest.[48] The *Mu-ling shu* also described the beating of a *sheng-yuan* who refused to pay his taxes, and a student who defied the law to obtain a post as *li-cheng* (a captain in the *li-chia* system).[49] The *Pei-chuan chi* also described the beating of *sheng-yuan* involved in lawsuits, the "frequent beating of *sheng-yuan* to collect tax payments," and the forced kneeling of *sheng-yuan* in the county court.[50]

These beatings were administered arbitrarily by local officials, all for violations of the regulations, but it is worth noting that these sources mention almost no beatings of groups higher than *sheng-yuan*. A decree of 1653 stated:

If *sheng-yuan* commit misdemeanors, they shall be punished by prefectural, departmental, or county education officials; if they commit major crimes, they shall be reported to the provincial director of education to be deprived of rank and have their punishment determined. If local officials arbitrarily punish *sheng-yuan*, the provincial director of education shall impeach them.

This rule provided some protection for *sheng-yuan* against willful local officials. A 1759 decree stated:

Henceforth it is the responsibility of the prefectural or county magistrates to investigate and control those who hold *kung-sheng* and *chien-sheng* degrees by purchase. They no longer have to list the holders of these degrees and send them to education officials. If these *li-kung-sheng* and *li-chien-sheng* commit misdemeanors, the local officials together with the local education officials shall personally beat and punish them. Education officials may not interfere in other incidents. Prefectural, departmental, and county magistrates shall still, according to precedent, report the details of the crimes [of *li-kung-sheng* and *li-chien-sheng*] to the provincial governor and provincial director of education for investigation.[51]

The primary responsibility for those who purchased *kung-sheng* and *chien-sheng* degrees was thus returned to local officials and, like the *sheng-yuan*, these groups were still protected from the arbitrary punishment of local officials.[52]

Why did the beating of *sheng-yuan* occur so frequently, despite the apparent legal protection based on traditional conceptions of literati status? The distance between *sheng-yuan* and officials was so great that officials felt no great sympathy with them, that is, the officials considered them to be an independent group far removed from the official class. This suggests that upward mobility was difficult for the *sheng-chien* and that the traditional ideal of "treating the *shih* according to ritual" had its limitations.

There are other examples of low regard for the *sheng-yuan* that may have been almost as humiliating as the beatings. In dealing with the grain-tribute officials, lower gentry were the only degree-holders required to appear at the official yamen in person. County magistrates could intimidate both *sheng-chien* and commoners who were subject to the grain tribute under the protection of the grain circuit attendant.[53] *Sheng-chien* were punished much more severely for illegalities in tax collection than were upper gentry.[54] *Sheng-yuan* were treated differently from higher status groups in the *pao-chia* system,[55] and prohibitions against proxy tax collection or engrossment (*pao-lan*) were directed particularly at *kung-sheng*, *chien-sheng*, and *sheng-yuan*.[56] In the management of local granaries, *kung-sheng*, *sheng-yuan*, and *chien-sheng* were distinguished from superior groups.⁵⁷ Local officials lecturing on the Sacred Edict stressed particularly the duty of *shih* (those below *chü-jen*) to present themselves for duty.⁵⁸

The Anti-Official Character of Sheng-chien Engrossments and Tax Resistance

The most important duties of local officials were the collection of taxes and the settlement of lawsuits. The gentry clearly used their special privileges to become closely involved in both. In tax collection, gentry were able to reduce the surtax charged them for "waste,"⁵⁹ to obtain a beneficial commutation rate into silver for the grain-tribute tax, and to extort customary fees for grain tribute from the county magistrate. The gentry not only benefited personally but could also use their position to take over the tax payments of their lineage or others close to them. Many official sources reveal that among the gentry the overwhelming majority of those practicing engrossment *pao-lan* were *sheng-chien*.⁶⁰

Shen were also implicated in engrossment. A decree of 1690 stated: "Furthermore, *shen* and *chin* engross tax payments, paying land and poll taxes on behalf of others and putting all the surtaxes in their own pockets."⁶¹ Tai Chao-ch'en in *Hsueh-shih lu* (1867) and the memorials of Kiangsu Governor Li Hsing-yuan in the Tao-kuang era also referred to both the *shen* and *chin*, but they cannot compare in scale to the engrossment committed by *sheng-chien*, as shown in detail by Kung-ch'üan Hsiao and T'ung-tsu Ch'ü.⁶² Feng Kuei-fen in his "Chün-fu i" (Discussion of equalization of taxes) blamed the *shen* and *chin* for deliberately delaying tax payments and accumulating arrears, and he said that "circumstances are such that people must find an agent to entrust their taxes to; they begin with yamen runners and then proceed to use the *chin* and *chien* [that is, *sheng-yuan* and *chien-sheng*]."⁶³

The *sheng-chien* took the lead in engrossment, and this tax-collection procedure was largely a result of their greed. A memorial of Chekiang Governor T'ao Shu in the Tao-kuang reign stated: "There are those who do not even have one *mu* of land but pay taxes of several hundred *tan* on behalf of others. They are not assessed for even a *sheng* or *ho* of grain but collect customary fees of several ten to several hundred taels. In the most populated areas, the *sheng-chien* may pay 300 to 400 *tan* in tax and collect fees of 10 to 20 thousand taels."⁶⁴

T'ung-tsu Ch'ü said:

Both propertied and propertyless persons belonged to the same status group. While it is true that most gentry members did possess property, particularly landed property, the fact is often overlooked that many of them, as portrayed in the satirical novel *Ju-lin wai-shih* (The scholars), acquired landed property after they had acquired gentry membership. In their case land ownership was the effect rather than the cause of status.[65]

Ch'ü referred to the gentry as a whole, including officials who used their special privileges as officials to get rich. The *sheng-yuan* therefore reflected a general tendency in the society when they used their special status (as compared to commoners) to gain wealth by illegal means. Tax engrossment by the *sheng-chien* was forced on them by officials in some cases, or was done out of good will,[66] but in general it was considered to be disruptive of the tax-collection administration and was dealt with severely.

In addition to the use of the privilege of low customary surcharges and the delaying of complete payment of taxes for profit, the gentry could also substitute poor quality silver, or poor quality rice, to enhance profits. These activities further confused the tax administration. Despite all the state's efforts to correct it,[67] engrossment by *sheng-chien* was a constant problem, indicating that, at least objectively, the *sheng-chien* tended to work in opposition to the state.

Tax resistance was regarded as even more serious than engrossment and was forbidden many times,[68] as, for example, in this edict of 1825:

Chu Shih-yen memorialized to prohibit tax resistance by "lawsuit households" (*sung-hu*) in order to rectify the practices of the *shih*. The *shih* are the leaders among the four categories of people; they should strictly follow the inscribed regulations of restraint for students in the Confucian temple and discipline themselves. Moreover, the land tax is the most fundamental resource of the state. According to precedent, poor scholars are allowed to delay tax payments until the 2nd or 4th month of the following year, several months later than the commoners. Now, if the *shih* are already treated so generously, how can they be allowed to resist taxation for years? As the provincial director of schools has memorialized, in the three prefectures of Hang-chou, Chia-hsing, and Hu-chou of Chekiang, recently arrears have been great and all of them are caused by *sheng-chien*. There are cases of suits brought to higher authorities—concerning engrossment, the disruption of grain tribute, tax resistance, and incomplete payment—and local officials cannot collect all the taxes. In addition, even if they are called "lawsuit households," which is no different from professional pettifoggers, these *sheng-chien* are not at all concerned. These practices greatly endanger the habits of the *shih* and must be severely punished . . . If there are still worthless *sheng-chien* who use their privileges to resist payment of arrears and extend the deadlines without paying, strip them all of their ranks and show no leniency in punishment.[69]

The major motives for tax resistance were the heavy burden of excess collection and dissatisfaction with the oppressive engrossment system. Tax resistance for these motives often developed into violent demonstrations. This violence was especially prominent when state power weakened, as at the time of the Opium War and the Taiping Rebellion. The leaders were *sheng-yuan* or *ti-pao* (local constables) and the targets were officials of "city gentry" (absentee landlords; *ch'eng-shen*).[70]

In some cases the outbreaks of rent and tax resistance came together in the conflict between the landlords in rural areas with smaller holdings and city-dwelling gentry who held large areas of land. The rural landlords might sometimes have included some *chü-jen*, but they were mainly in the *sheng-chien* group.[71] The Kiangnan tax-protest case in the early Ch'ing involved the punishment of 13,000 gentry in an attempt by the central government to discourage any future anti-Ch'ing protests.[72]

After the Opium War in the first half of the nineteenth century, the tax-resistance movements expanded and joined with the Taiping Rebellion, as the *sheng-yuan* and *chien-sheng*, village elders, and constables[73] (all of whom were supposed to support central authority) incited large-scale outbreaks of violence, killing officials and destroying county government offices. Local militia and village strong men sometimes became the key organizers of tax resistance. Thus an edict of 1862 stated: "Wicked gentry are refusing to obey the leadership of local officials and are arbitrarily forming local militia, and even the officially organized militia incite the masses to resist the payment of taxes. They must be investigated and suppressed."[74] Most of the anti-tax movements, of course, were not major rebellions aimed at destroying the existing political order; they were only "anti-official" movements.[75] Given the proper opportunity, however, they could easily expand and merge into anti-state rebellions. For example, the Taiping Army[76] and the Ch'in-lien Revolt of the T'ung-meng hui in 1907 both absorbed many anti-tax activists.[77]

Kung-ch'üan Hsiao has discussed the concept of "good government," which was the basis of the gentry's political philosophy, in relation to the imperial ideology. The ideology of the rulers was based on a rationalization of paternalistic autocracy in terms of the idea of "good government"; the gentry found in it a convenient theoretical defense for their own economic interests against what they perceived as cruel and violent officials. When the preservation of their status was guaranteed, the gentry accepted government control. But, if this condition changed, their relations with the dynasty became antagonistic. The non-official components of the gentry obtained their gentry status for the purpose of furthering their individual family interests, not for the purpose of cooperation with the government. These non-official gentry were mainly the *sheng-chien*. Ku Yen-wu described their self-interested attitude: "Nowadays, those who want to become *sheng-yuan* do not necessarily aim at the renown of an academic degree. Seven-tenths of them are only trying to protect the interests of themselves and their families; they number about 350,000 people [out of a total of 500,000]. This is a perverse rejection of the original intention of the examination system and runs counter to the interests of the state."[78] In other words, they saw in the examination system, not a channel for bureaucratic recruitment and social mobility, but a shield for their local status.

The efforts of the majority of *sheng-yuan* to protect the interests of their families, therefore abandoning (or being forced to abandon) the prospects for upward mobility from the outset, reinforced the static quality of the *sheng-chien* class. But, if they could not protect their family interests by the attainment of a *sheng-chien* degree, that is, if the state was not able to protect their families sufficiently, they tended to use selfishly (or in opposition to officials) the very political order by which they had obtained their status as *sheng-chien*. If they failed completely to protect their family interests by opposing the officials, they might reject the ruling order itself.[79]

Commoners, of course, were the main participants in these movements. A large number of *sheng-chien* were economically impoverished, and they were closer to the peasants than to the *shen* in their standard of living, but they could not have mobilized the peasants to resist rent or taxes without a pre-existing peasant dissatisfaction. Although we cannot necessarily assume that the proximity of *sheng-chien* and commoners itself served as a positive basis for unity, it may be helpful in explaining the vast gap between the *sheng-chien* and the upper gentry. The officials themselves and the *shen*, who usually had great hopes of official positions and received special treatment from the state, saw their interests as closely tied to the existing political order, but the *sheng-chien* were liable to conduct anti-official or anti-government actions when threatened economically. Both the upper gentry and the *sheng-chien* used the power conferred by their degrees to further their particular interests. The social immobility of the *sheng-chien* forced them to use their degrees in anti-government activities. When they became involved in anti-tax and anti-rent movements, the unity of the *sheng-chien* with the upper gentry was disrupted and they could no longer be seen as part of the ruling class. They are therefore better characterized as a fixed and alienated stratum.

Involvement in Proxy Lawsuits

We can see a trend toward alienation between the state and the *sheng-chien* in lawsuits as well. A decree of 1651 enforced severe restrictions on the entrance of *sheng-yuan* into official yamens. It ordered the registration of names and intentions of all who entered the yamens and punished by deprivation of rank all those who "entered the yamen on affairs unconnected with them personally."[80] It ordered the erection of a "stele of restraint" (*wo-pei*) with eight instructions in the Confucian hall of each school. The placement of such stern limitations on the activities of the *sheng-yuan* was a reaction to their active political involvement during the late Ming. The direct purpose of the regulations was to prevent *sheng-yuan* from involving themselves in other people's lawsuits, thus disturbing local administration. As the stele clearly stated: "*Sheng-yuan* must practice forbearance. They may not lightly enter official yamens. If someone has an urgent case, only family members are allowed to represent him. *Sheng-yuan* may not become involved in other people's lawsuits, and others similarly may not drag in *sheng-yuan* to be their witnesses."[81] Because the relative freedom of *sheng-yuan* to enter the yamen was due to their equality with 9th-rank officials, a 1730 edict applied the same restrictions on entering the yamen to the similarly placed *kung-sheng* and *chien-sheng*.[82]

The essence of the lawsuit in question was the possibility that the *sheng-chien* might use their literacy and their leadership roles in the villages, in addition to their privileges, to involve themselves as proxies in commoners' lawsuits and by so doing make improper profits. Like tax engrossment, these proxy lawsuits (*pao-lan tz'u-sung*) disturbed local administration; there are innumerable prohibitions against them in the *Hui-tien shih-li.* Ch'en Hung-mou's admonition to county magistrates instructed them to ascertain as soon as they arrived at their post "the practices of the gentry in your area and how many *sheng-chien* enjoy bringing lawsuits." Ch'eng Han-cheng also asked local officials, "If there are wicked *sheng-yuan* and *chien-sheng* who manipulate public affairs, engage in proxy lawsuits, and tyrannize the countryside, how will you punish them?"[83]

Sheng-chien were thus the main proponents of proxy lawsuits. A decree of 1876 stated, "The *sung-kun* (pettifoggers) are mostly *kung-sheng, chien-sheng,* and military and civil *sheng-yuan.*"[84] *Sung-kun* were those who made a specialty of proxy lawsuits; they were referred to as "lawsuit households" in some other sources. There were actually pettifoggers who were commoners, but those who were lower gentry were the most powerful and most troublesome because of their special privileges.[85]

Pettifoggers, who helped corrupt magistrates to collect unreasonable tax contributions, could also organize movements to unseat a magistrate who made such profiteering by proxy lawsuits difficult, by slandering the magistrate to superior authorities.[86] These activities by pettifoggers not only endangered local order but threatened the security of the local official himself. One source tells of a pettifogger who forced the magistrate to pay him a regular fee from the grain tribute,[86] in order to have an excuse to blackmail him into dividing the profits from an illegal verdict. The government used local officials to take every opportunity to repress the pettifoggers.

In some respects, however, officials did not reject, but rather encouraged, the participation of gentry in the settlement of disputes, just as they did in tax collection. The real capability of the county magistrate to carry out his official duties was limited, and a deeply rooted tradition of community among the people resisted official intervention in their lives. Officials urged the literati to take charge of the settlement of most disputes because they recognized their moral superiority. One governor proclaimed, "Fair and just gentry should be particularly respected, so that they may establish good customs in their home areas. Let them settle petty conflicts by persuasion and mediation, so that officials need not be involved."[88] In this way, lower gentry familiar with the community could settle disputes.

SOCIAL ASPECTS OF THE *SHENG-CHIEN*

Poverty

Tax engrossment, tax resistance, and proxy lawsuits were usually inspired by the poverty of the *sheng-chien*. If enough income from the land had been guaranteed to all of the gentry, lawsuits and uprisings would have been unnecessary.

It is impossible, of course, to prove that all *sheng-chien* were poor, but it is certainly possible to show from source materials that not all of them were well-off. The *Pei-chuan chi* and *Hsu pei-chuan chi*, biographies of local officials, frequently stressed as one of their virtues that they were closer to "poor gentry" (*p'in-shih*) than to rich merchants. One late-Ch'ing reader in the Hanlin Academy memorialized that *sheng-yuan* in schools were "impoverished scholars who make a living with their pen and work sincerely at their studies. Nine-tenths of them have no landed property for their family."[89] Chung-li Chang maintained that, although some high-level bureaucrats and upper gentry were large landlords, most of the gentry owned no land at all, or at most only a small amount. Because of the custom of partible inheritance, nearly all the great landlords enjoyed wealth in one generation, and most of them became wealthy through officeholding.[90]

The majority of the lower gentry who did not hold landed property must have been *sheng-chien*. Some of them engaged in occupations forbidden to them, such as village henchmen and military posts, pandering and gambling, or the management of pawnshops. Some of them even traded in farm animals or engaged in peddling.[91] Many *sheng-yuan* also worked as teachers or private secretaries. The Taiping leader Hung Hsiu-ch'üan, who aspired to become a *sheng-yuan*, was a farmer who owned one ox to share in plowing with his brother; he is an example of how some of the would-be *sheng-yuan* resorted to menial occupations.[92] The famous protagonist of the literary inquisition in the Yung-cheng period, Tseng Ching (a *sheng-yuan* who was stripped of his rank at the year school examination), owned only a few *mu* of land, and his father and brothers were farmers.[93] A recent study of those who purchased degrees indicates that the economic status of the poorest aspirants to the civil examinations was that of small farmer. The study told of a Shansi county magistrate in the Chia-ch'ing period "who was poor and fed himself by his own labor and, even after becoming *sheng-yuan*, trod the water wheel with hired laborers."⁹⁴ Some *sheng-yuan* received a small income from the *hsiang-yueh* village lectures. According to Kung-ch'üan Hsiao, most of the *hsiang-yueh* posts were filled by *sheng-yuan* because higher-level groups had no need of the small salary.⁹⁵

As part of the "good government" of local officials, charitable land was established to provide money to pay the expenses of poor *sheng-yuan* at village exams. They were exempted from payment of exam-book fees at yearly exams, or their expenses were subsidized from charitable land (*chuan-chin-t'ien*).⁹⁶ The existence of such financial aid suggests the poverty of the *sheng-yuan*. Their lack of landed property and pursuit of low-status occupations make it difficult to classify them as part of the ruling class, because a ruling class is generally thought to have economic privileges in addition to an institutional and political role. There were poor people among the *shen* (as in the case of Liang Chang-chü, discussed by Chung-li Chang), and there were some wealthy *sheng-chien*, but large landlords appeared more often in the ranks of *shen*, who had many opportunities to profit from their official positions.

Chung-li Chang has estimated that 2 to 4 percent of the gentry in the nineteenth century were large landlords, a total of 30,000 to 60,000.⁹⁷ These were the most powerful upper elite of a total of 200,000 upper gentry.⁹⁸ Since it is still commonly believed that all gentry were landlords, it is worth stressing the fact that most lower gentry held little or no land. The economic status of the *sheng-chien* is another factor that distinguished them from the upper gentry.

Social Mobility

The total number of "immobile" *sheng-chien* (both military and civil) who never rose to a higher degree is estimated at 965,000 of a total of 1.1 million before the Taiping Rebellion, and 1.23 million of a total 1.45 million after the Taipings.⁹⁹

This inability of the *sheng-chien* to rise within the status system only increased their lack of rapport with members of the upper gentry and encouraged them to use the few privileges they had already won to preserve their own interests, to "protect the interests of their homes and families," in Ku Yen-wu's phrase, and to clash with officials. Ping-ti Ho's statistics on social mobility demonstrate that 62.8 percent of the Ch'ing *chin-shih* had an ancestor within three generations who had held a degree higher than *sheng-yuan*, thus reinforcing our conclusion about the immobility of the *sheng-chien*.[100]

Common Consciousness and Collective Action

The immobility of the *sheng-yuan* aroused in them a strong sense of solidarity with their fellow degree-holders, causing them to act together to protect their mutual interests. Yuan Shou-ting in his *T'u-min lu* (1839) stated: "If one *shih* is pleased, all the *shih* are pleased; if one *shih* is humiliated, all the *shih* are angered." T'ung-tsu Ch'ü cited this passage in demonstrating that the gentry as a whole shared a consciousness, interests, and Confucian values, and that they acted and thought differently from commoners.[101] It is true that all the gentry had a good deal in common, but the differences within the gentry probably prevented the realization of this rather abstract consciousness. In particular, since collective action based on this common consciousness usually resulted from the conflict of interests between the gentry and officials, anti-official actions by the superior gentry groups (who had few conflicts of interest with officials) were rare. The people who were humiliated and whose interests were easily infringed upon by officials were the *sheng-chien*. As a result, their own particular common consciousness was strong, and they frequently organized collective actions.

The most representative collective actions of the *sheng-yuan* were examination strikes, held by both *t'ung-sheng* (aspirants to the *sheng-yuan* degree) and *sheng-yuan*. When the *t'ung-sheng* as a group refused to attend the *t'ung-shih* exam, they put district magistrates in extreme difficulty.[102] The examination strikes by the *sheng-yuan* caused even greater problems because of their special status. An edict of 1734 strictly forbade these examination strikes and specified penalties, following the example of the punishment of the "bullies of Shansi and Shensi." The ringleaders were to be stripped of their degrees if *sheng-yuan*, and *t'ung-sheng* were to be prevented from taking further exams. If an entire country or an entire school participated in an examination strike, all the participants would be punished by deprivation of rank and the termination of exams.[103]

A typical *sheng-yuan* examination strike took place in Feng-ch'iu county, Honan, in the Yung-cheng period, and was touched off by the refusal of the provincial treasurer, T'ien Wen-ching, to observe the customary exemption of gentry from corvée labor levies. (He levied duties for work on the Yellow River on the gentry as well as on the common people.)[104] T'ien Wen-ching's levies were assessed on the entire gentry class, but the leaders of the opposition were Wang Sun and other military and civil *sheng-yuan*. They first presented petitions to the county magistrate, and, when the petitions had no effect, they boycotted the examination. We know that *chin-shih* and *chü-jen* did not participate in the boycott, because Wang and the others forged the names of *chin-shih* and *chü-jen* on the petition.

Another example of an examination strike is the one in 1851 in the county schools of Nan-hai and Tung-kuan counties, Kwangtung.[105] This stike was aroused by the "suicide under duress" of a *sheng-yuan* who had resisted payment of taxes and was allegedly forced to commit suicide by the county magistrate. There are many examples of such actions, motivated not only by economic interests, but also by the common consciousness of the *sheng-yuan* class. The *Pei-chuan chi* recorded that a secretary in charge of canal repairs "mistakenly beat several *sheng-yuan*," and that the *sheng-yuan* organized a collective demonstration of force against him.[106] Other sources recorded examples of revolts by *sheng-yuan* against oppression by yamen clerks, leading to attacks on jails and the freeing of prisoners.[107]

These *sheng-yuan* revolts sometimes led to the killing of county magistrates and required the despatch of troops to put down the rebellion. Kung-ch'üan Hsiao has given two examples of the humiliation of county magistrates by *sheng-yuan*: a market strike led by *sheng-yuan* dissatisfied with relief after a flood, and the destruction of prisons and official buildings by village people led by *sheng-yuan* protesting the corvée for river works. He also recorded an example of a mass revolt led by *sheng-yuan*, which culminated in the killing of a county magistrate who was too zealous in his investigation of the illegal activities of *sheng-yuan*.[108]

Kao T'ing-yao in his *Huan-yu chi-lueh* noted that, when he arrived to take up his post as magistrate of Ta-an in the Ch'ien-lung era, he investigated the prisoners and released those sentenced to minor punishments. The *sheng-yuan*, however, gathered in a crowd, saying that one prisoner had stolen a *sheng-yuan*'s clothes, another had stolen a *chien-sheng*'s ring, and that to release them would "let loose bandits to injure the people."[109] This is a good example of an action taken not for concrete interests but only as an expression of the solidarity of the *sheng-yuan*. It is also an example of the collective action of the *sheng-yuan* aimed not at officials, but at commoners (in this case, the prisoners).

In stressing the collective influence of the *sheng-yuan*, T'ung-tsu Ch'ü has stated:

> As the *sheng-yuan* were outside the power hierarchy, they were the least influential among the gentry. Any power or strength they had derived mainly from group solidarity and collective action—as, for example, in joint petitions, or mass refusals to participate in an examination. At times, acting as a group, they even defied and insulted the local magistrate, who often found it difficult to control or punish them. But as individuals, the *sheng-yuan* had little influence with a magistrate. Nevertheless, the strength and influence of the *sheng-yuan* should by no means be underestimated.[110]

It must be emphasized that the collective actions of the *sheng-yuan*, weak individually but strong in their collective consciousness, distinguished them sharply from upper-level groups. This collective action based on collective consciousness is a result of the peculiar immobility of the *sheng-chien* as a stratum.

We have investigated the negative aspects of the relationship between the *sheng-chien* and state power: their social immobility and the collective actions based on their common consciousness. We have concluded that, in general, the *sheng-chien* must be regarded neither as simply one stratum among the gentry nor as a part of the ruling class. We have emphasized mainly the negative aspects of the relations between the *sheng-chien* and state power on the one hand and the *shen* stratum on the other, because, until now, the institutional and social proximity between them (the positive side) has been stressed, and the opposite pole ignored. *Sheng-chien* were regarded as direct threats to local government (although there was some cooperation) because of the poverty of their lives and their social immobility. Their exclusivist consciousness and their collective actions are expressions of their isolation as a stratum.

Although we can agree that there is a certain degree of unity between *sheng-chien*, *shen*, and state authority, there is a greater degree of separateness. They must be seen as a stratum clearly distinct from the *shen*. It is possible to deal only with the institutional aspects of their relations, including them with the *shen* in a single-gentry class, and taking into consideration the large gap between *sheng-chien* and commoners. In discussing the social reality of their position, however, there is a danger of reaching a misleading evaluation of their highly influential activities if their clear distinction from the *shen* class is ignored. Seen in terms of domination and subjection, they are in no way members of a ruling class. If the terms *shen-shih* and "gentry" presuppose a real concept of social and political domination, then these terms cannot be applied to the *sheng-chien*. *Shen-shih* or "gentry" can be applied to *sheng-chien* only in discussing their institutional position.

What, then, is the relation of *sheng-chien* to commoners? Should they be included in the commoner class, as Ping-ti Ho has insisted? Even though *sheng-chien* are distinguished from the upper gentry, their consciousness and activities are not at all the same as those of commoners. *Sheng-chien* are sometimes included in literature with the "people" and sometimes with the *shen,* but these explanations of the meanings of terms are of no use in solving the real problem. Sources like the *Ta-Ch'ing hui-tien shih-li,* edicts of 1726, 1825, and 1813,[111] as well as various administrative handbooks,[112] referred to the *shih* as "leaders of the people" (*ch'i-min chih shou*). An edict of 1651 spoke of stripping the *sheng-chien* of their rank, "reducing them to commoners" (*ch'u wei min*), and an edict of 1825 described "treating them differently from commoners by extending their deadline for tax payments several additional months."[113]

We must, after all, look at their real situation. Previous studies stressed the unity between the *sheng-chien* and the upper strata because of the special institutional privileges differentiating them from the commoners. These cannot be ignored, for they are an important basis for the distinction between *sheng-chien* and commoners. There is a formal and institutional unity between *sheng-chien* and *shen* which excludes commoners. Also, from the viewpoint of Confucian ideals, the state authorities recognized intellectuals as superior, so that at least ideally they were all included in the gentry as "virtuous" Confucian rulers.

In collective action, too, the *sheng-chien* stood apart from commoners. Even in anti-tax and anti-rent movements, although they may have united with the people and used their forces of mobilization, in the end they acted to preserve their own interests, and did not take the people's point of view. Their common consciousness was exclusivist regarding both their inferiors and their superiors. Their aim was to rise into a higher stratum, but, when this hope was frustrated because of their weak position, they did not direct their frustration downward. On the contrary, by reinforcing the feeling of distinction between them and commoners, they could neutralize their frustration. Rebellions, sometimes leading as far as resistance to state authority, arose from increasing frustration and were aimed ultimately at domination over the commoners and the establishment of a new dynasty. The view of the common people, as Pak Chi-wŏn's diary shows, was that *sheng-chien* were oppressors of the people. I have not investigated this separation from the commoners in this essay, but it needs to be emphasized in assessing the character of the *sheng-yuan*.

We may call the *sheng-chien* a middle stratum which strove to join the upper stratum and to cooperate with it, but which in the end found its aspirations frustrated, although they were supported ideologically and institutionally. This concept reveals the unity of the upper stratum and shows that in reality the strata were fixed.

The term *sheng-chien* differs, both in its meaning and in its composition, from T'ung-tsu Ch'ü's "middle stratum," which he used in discussing the relationship between ruler and ruled. The *sheng-chien* were distinct from *chü-jen* and higher degree-holders. On the institutional side alone, the *sheng-chien* lay within the limits of the school system. *Chü-jen* and higher-degree holders, however, were products of the examination system. Therefore, the treatment of the *chü-jen* was not modeled on that of *sheng-chien* but on that of *chin-shih*.[114] *Sheng-chien* also differed from higher groups in their ability to obtain official posts; it was not possible for *sheng-chien* to obtain official posts until they had attained a higher degree.

My conclusion agrees with previous studies that have demonstrated the real social status of the *sheng-chien* as a middle stratum, but it differs in connecting this fact with the alienation of the *sheng-chien* from officials and with their exclusivist, independent character. Although I have followed Chang, Ch'ü, and Ho on many points, I have, with I think more accuracy, placed the politically isolated and socially immobile *sheng-chien* stratum in a place of its own.

CHAPTER THREE

Chinese "Principle" and Western "Utility" A Reassessment

The Chinese reformers of the late nineteenth century have usually been considered conservative in their approach to the adoption of Western technology. They believed that the West had much to offer China in the realm of machinery (particularly military) and the manner of its use, but the basis of China's value system would always have to come from within. According to the formula: "Chinese learning for basic principle and Western learning for practical utility" (*Chung-hsueh wei t'i, hsi-hsueh wei yung*),[1] it would be possible to graft Western methods onto Chinese values, each functioning in its proper sphere. The formula was regarded by many historians of China's modernization as the principal component of the idea of *yang-wu* ("Western affairs"), which connoted all Chinese activities in the foreign sector (but principally military and technological innovation), which was favored by the proponents of the *yang-wu* movement.[2] This movement marked the initial stage of China's modernization drive, but was rejected in favor of *pien-fa* ("institutional reform"), the subsequent movement which sought a reorganization of the governmental system. I questioned in an earlier article of mine[3] whether the formula could really be taken as a separate one representing the initial stages of the modernization drive only. I should like therefore to examine the relationship between the principle/utility idea and the ideas of two successive stages of the modernization effort in the final phase of the Ch'ing period.

In the process I shall offer a critical review of the literature on these subjects in both China and Japan. The Japanese case will be of particular interest here, because the analogous concept in that country is usually credited with a progressive rather than a conservative effect on modernization.

Recent Chinese historians have been careful to differentiate among schools of reformist thought in the late Ch'ing period and, in particular, to find the dividing line between conservative modernizers with a "feudal" orientation and the more progressive "bourgeois" innovators. For example, Huang I-feng and Chiang Feng, writing in 1963, contrasted the Chinese *yang-wu* movement with the modernizers of Japan's Meiji Restoration. They asserted that the dominant faction of the *yang-wu* group attempted to preserve the feudal system by advancing the concept of principle/utility and did not call for institutional reforms. Another faction among the *yang-wu* group, however, including Cheng Kuan-ying, the comprador-reformer, and the pioneer journalist Wang T'ao argued for institutional reform, in effect a kind of bourgeois reformism, which recognized that technological modernization could not succeed without institutional change. This group, the authors have asserted, was ignored by the *yang-wu* group in power.[4] The logical grounds upon which these authors made the distinction between the two *yang-wu* factions are far from clear, however, and I am not persuaded by their argument that the subordinate faction argued for institutional reform and still held to the principle/utility concept. If we link principle/utility to the *yang-wu* group alone, we cannot logically include reformers such as Cheng Kuan-ying and Wang T'ao within that group.

Criticizing this kind of logical discrepancy, the historian Hsia Tung-yuan doubted that we can use principle/utility as a hallmark of the *yang-wu* group: "Although some portion of the bourgeois reformists' thought goes beyond this concept, a greater part of their thought is based on it." He argued that, although principle/utility is basic to the *yang-wu* group as a whole, a more effective way of distinguishing groups is by their "political programs and actions." He concluded: "The differences between the landlord reformists, such as Wei Yuan, bourgeois reformists (the *pien-fa* group), and the *yang-wu* group should not be considered inflexible; they shared both class characteristics and modes of thinking, among which was principle/utility."[5]

Hsia's behavior-oriented view avoids an oversimplified link between principle/utility and the *yang-wu* group, and contributes to our understanding of the rapid transformations of thought during this very short span of time. Yet it is unclear what parts of the principle/utility concept were shared by the *yang-wu* group and the bourgeois reformists, since Hsia has not given us a precise definition of principle/utility. Though he has succeeded in transcending the confusing connection between principle/utility and the *yang-wu* group, it is doubtful whether principle/utility can serve as an effective analytic principle to help us sort out these groups.

Discussing the difference between the constitutionalist Liang Ch'i-ch'ao and the conservative modernizer Chang Chih-tung, the philosopher Feng Yu-lan pointed out that Liang considered that Western learning included political systems (*cheng*), while Chang restricted it to technology (*chi-i*).[6] They agreed, however, that Confucianism was the best of all teachings. Later I shall consider whether Chang, who has been called one of the most important proponents of the principle/utility concept, understood Western learning to include only technology. But, for now, it seems correct to say that Liang and Chang both revered the teachings of Confucius as principle (*t'i*), at least if we take the words *t'i* and *yung* in the flexible sense to imply something principal and something subordinate.[7] If that which is Chinese is considered "principle," then "utility" (whether it is technology or political systems) must be considered Western. If this view of mine can be affirmed, then it would be meaningless to take principle/utility as a yardstick by which to measure the divisions of late Ch'ing thought. For both the *yang-wu* technological modernizers and the *pien-fa* constitutionalists will turn out to be believers in the principle/utility distinction.

Some scholars have stressed the fundamental difference between the two groups by saying that the *yang-wu* group did not advocate popular political rights (*min-ch'üan*) in their political programs. For example, Kondo Kuniyasu has pointed out that Chang Chih-tung's principle/utility concept was aimed against arguments for institutional reform and popular political rights. Principle/utility was, in Kondo's view, not so much a logical formula but rather an attempt to preserve the primacy of Chinese culture (*pen*, root) over Western (*mo*, branch).[8] Though Chang's thought was indeed conservative in this sense, I wonder whether it necessarily follows that the institutional reformers were less committed to the long-term maintenance of the ruling system, whatever their short-term goals may have been. Both sides seem to me convinced that Chinese culture should remain the root, and Western culture the branch, in whatever future system China developed. Furthermore, Kondo failed to clarify whether the principle of principle/utility itself was instrumental in bringing about attitudes opposed to popular political rights.

Another analytic approach has been to distinguish earlier reformers from later ones, in respect to whether they separated "principle" from "utility" in their views of China and the West. The noted historian Li Tse-hou, for example, has argued that early reformers, such as Cheng Kuan-ying, Ch'en Ch'ih, and Hsueh Fu-ch'eng, rejected the social and political doctrines of the West while calling for the importation of scientific thought to save the nation. Assuming the permanence of traditional social doctrine (*kang-ch'ang ming-chiao*), they were close to the *yang-wu* group in their insistence on the primacy of Chinese culture. Although they advocated the establishment of a national assembly and a constitution, their ignorance of Western capitalism prevented them from seeing the connection between such institutional changes and the concepts of freedom and equality, which are the theoretical foundations of the Western parliamentary system, and the principle of *min-ch'üan*.[9] Li saw a basic difference between Chang Chih-tung's famous *Ch'üan-hsueh p'ien* (Exhortation to study), the most institutionally reformist document of the *yang-wu* group, and the thought of later reformists such as K'ang Yu-wei and Liang Ch'i-ch'ao. This latter group, Li maintained, linked institutional reform to the bourgeois principles of popular political rights and equality. In this sense, the later reformists did not distinguish between "principle" and "utility," which sets them off from Chang Chih-tung and his followers, who rejected popular political rights and equality in favor of steamships and railroads.

Here again we face the problem of whether principle/utility is a logical structure based on the total divisibility of the two elements (*t'i* and *yung*), or whether it simply indicates a preference for keeping Chinese culture as the foundation of programs for modernization. Li Tse-hou was absolutely correct in his assertion that Cheng Kuan-ying and other early reformers failed to see the connection between liberalism (the advocacy of popular political rights and equality) and the Western representative system because they knew too little about Western society. Yet it is doubtful that this group's understanding of the West was much inferior to that of K'ang Yu-wei and Liang Ch'i-ch'ao. I find it hard to agree completely with Li's argument that the K'ang-Liang reformers believed "principle" and "utility" to be inseparable, if we acknowledge that even this later reformist group believed in preserving that which was Chinese, specifically Confucianism in the broad sense (*K'ung-chiao*) or "the Way of the Sages" (*sheng-jen chih tao*), while advocating the Western parliamentary system. This view led to some reservations in their advocacy of the parliamentary system.

A confrontation between *t'i* and *yung* lay at the base of the principle/utility concept, according to the Japanese intellectual historian Onogawa Hidemi, but the development of late nineteenth-century thought eventually harmonized them.[10] Yet, if one believes as I do that principle/utility, in a larger sense of recognizing the fundamental difference between Chinese and Western culture, also lay behind the thought of institutional reformers such as K'ang Yu-wei and Liang Chi-ch'ao, then Onogawa's argument may not be supportable. Whether there is a basic confrontation built into the principle/utility concept remains to be determined.

Principle/utility as a formula for modernization has generally been denigrated in both the late Ch'ing and the Republican contexts. Opposing Chiang Kai-shek's New Life Movement in the 1930s, Wang Ching-wei blamed principle/utility for China's inability to progress for the preceding fifty years.[11] The "Declaration for Chinese-Centered Culture," issued by ten professors in support of the Kuomintang's neo-traditionalist cultural movement in the 1930s, said that the *yang-wu* movement of Li Hung-chang and Tseng Kuo-fan had emphasized only strong armed forces, electricity, and other technical innovations, and thus their principle/utility was only a superficial imitation of Western technology.[12] In reply, Hu Shih scoffed that the declaration itself was an up-to-date disguise for principle/utility. Chinese-centered culture could be interpreted as "principle," while the declaration's call for "critical acceptance of Western technology" was identical to "utility." Both these cases illustrate the universal disapprobation of the principle/utility concept among modern writers. This negative assessment offers no real analysis of its contents, which leads me to believe that something is wrong with our current understanding of principle/utility.[13]

Part of the trouble has been that the *yang-wu* movement, of which principle/utility was a major intellectual component, failed to achieve its aim of strengthening China. Principle/utility has therefore been blamed for the whole effort to bring in technology and reject the other essential components of modernization. By contrast, the Japanese analog, known as "East Asian ethics and Western technology" (*tōyō dōtoku seiyō geijutsu ron*), has not been evaluated as reactionary. I suggest that this view is attributable to the success of the Meiji Restoration for which the idea served as a rationale.

Because of the success of the Meiji modernization program, comparisons of this Japanese doctrine with its Chinese counterpart have not been objective.[14] For example, Nomura Kōichi compared the Japanese ethics/technology concept as used by Sakuma Shōzan with its Chinese counterpart, the principle/utility concept.[15] A significant difference, Nomura thinks, is that Sakuma believed in a "self-evident truth of heaven and earth" (*tenchi kōri*) as something that penetrated both West and East. Thus, human relations and the practices of daily life were all subordinate to the law of "things" (*wu*), in whatever country they might be found. Nomura went on to point out that the concept of "reason" (*jōri*) found in the Neo-Confucian Yokoi Shōnan (1809–1860) was similar to this "self-evident truth" of Sakuma's. Both, he thought, are different from the spirit of Chang Chih-tung's *Exhortation to Study*, which defended traditional Confucian concepts of "filial piety, obedience of younger to older brothers, loyalty, and sincerity," rather than seeking a universal cross-cultural basis for truth. Nomura concluded that in Japan the idea of heavenly principle (*tenri*) was transformed into the idea of a self-evident truth applicable to all nations, which served as a basis for advocating an open door to the West. In China, on the other hand, heavenly principle remained inherent in, and inseparable from, the existing social system. Thus, he compared the freshness and receptivity of the Japanese ethics/technology concept with the conservatism of the Chinese principle/utility concept,[16] which was only a desperate attempt to reinforce the traditional order.

Nomura did not, however, adduce logical grounds for his analysis, in that he failed to explain the relationship between "Eastern ethics" and "Western technology," or that between "Chinese principle" and "Western utility."[17] Furthermore, it may be doubted that the mental structure he perceived behind ethics/technology is restricted to Japan alone. For example, Hsueh Fu-ch'eng, who remarked that the Chinese should safeguard the Way of the Sages by adopting Western technology, also said that the scientific basis of steam, electricity, and chemistry could not be owned or monopolized by Westerners, because they are public instruments for all the world to use.[18] Hsueh added that "both China and the Western countries are benefiting the people by using the spirit of nature (*tsao-hua chih ling*) ... Why can only Westerners monopolize it? And why should China not surpass the Western countries in a hundred years or so? ... Now, by adopting Western technological learning (*hsi-jen ch'i-shu chih hsueh*), we could preserve the Way of the Sages, not allowing Westerners to despise China, and in the future the Way would spread all across the world."[19]

How is Hsueh's concept of ubiquitous "public principles" (*kung-kung chih li*) different from Sakuma's "self-evident truth of heaven and earth" (*tenchi kōri*)? Is there nothing new in Hsueh's resolve to surpass the West in the future by learning Western scientific knowledge and spreading the Chinese Way all over the world? Can we say that the Japanese ethics/technology idea intended to negate the existing social system, while the Chinese principle/utility sought to reinforce it? Did not the Japanese regard their feudal system as a natural order? To be sure, ethics/technology thought in Japan developed into a doctrine of modernization without much difficulty, while principle/utility in China did not. Considering only the structure of the concepts themselves, however, as distinct from their historical environment, I do not agree that one should necessarily be positively evaluated and the other negatively.[20] Here we have, I am afraid, a projection of the eventual success story of the Meiji Restoration upon the analysis of the original concepts. To confirm this conclusion, however, we shall have to compare the structures of these concepts in greater detail.

ETHICS/TECHNOLOGY (*TŌYŌ DŌTOKU SEIYŌ GEIJUTSU RON*) IN JAPAN

What was the essential structure of the ethics/technology concept? Seriously concerned about the Western military threat, Sakuma Shōzan (1811–1864) advocated the opening of the country and searched for Western learning. He is well known for his influence on modern Japanese thought as the teacher of Yoshida Shōin, who was credited with inspiring the leaders of the Meiji Restoration, as well as of Tsuda Masamichi, Nishimura Shigeki, and Katō Hiroyuki, all of whom led the intellectual world during the early Meiji Restoration.[21] Sakuma argued that useful aspects of Western culture could reinforce Confucianism, the Great Learning of Japan, with the slogan: "Ethics of East Asia combined with the technology of the West" (*tōyō dōtoku seiyō geijutsu*). According to Minamoto Ryōen:

> Although it goes without saying again that the metaphysical and speculative principle (*li*) of Chu Hsi is not identical with rationality in the modern natural sciences, it was not unimportant to Sakuma to dig into the relationship of the two. To him it was possible to embrace the natural sciences of the West without losing confidence in Japanese culture and thought based on the speculative character of Neo-Confucianism. Once this position had been taken by Sakuma, samurai of later generations who were weak in Neo-Confucianism could begin to study Western learning without concern for the ideological relationship of Confucianism and natural sciences. For studying Western learning no longer meant yielding to the barbarians but rather perfecting the teachings (*tao*) of the sages. Sakuma thus opened for outstanding samurai across the country the doors leading to Western learning.[22]

According to Uete Michiari, Hashimoto Sanai and Yokoi Shōnan held opinions similar to Sakuma's. As Hashimoto argued: "We should adopt Western mechanical arts, but we have humanity, justice, loyalty, and filial piety." Yokoi advocated studying Western machine technology while promoting the *tao* of Yao, Shun, and Confucius. Their Confucian ideas mediated the formation of modern thought in Japan. But, if this was so, Confucianism did not function in the traditional manner. Modern thought, generated within the womb of a transforming Confucianism, came eventually to negate its origin.[23]

Then how can we account for the emergence of Sakuma's ethics/technology, which furthered his contemporaries' acceptance of Western learning and transformed Confucianism, thus giving birth to modern thought?[24] The academic foundation of the later Mito school, the basis of *sonnō jōi ron* (Honor the emperor, Expel the barbarians), was the restoration of ancient forms and principles of statecraft as the original aim of the early Confucian school. Thus, the later interpretations of classics by Chu Hsi came to be rejected. The argument for restoring "correct human relationships" (*ta-i ming-fen*), however, was enhanced, focusing on the "five relations" (*wu-lun*) as the great Way of all the world and nature, including the relationship between lord and subjects. Here we encounter the idea: "Honor the emperor, Expel the barbarians." Meanwhile, at the start of the Tempō period, with both domestic and foreign crises intensifying, demands arose for the vigorous adoption of Western ideas, primarily in military, scientific, and technological areas. These were seen as concrete means to meet the foreign threat, or to materialize the idea "Expel the barbarians." Sakuma overcame the Mito school's argument for closing the door and rejecting the barbarians (*sakoku jōi*) and began to champion the opening of the country.

Sakuma himself believed in the doctrines of Chu Hsi as the "true learning" before taking up "Dutch Learning" (*Rangaku*). He exhibited a deep interest in statecraft (*keisei saimin*) and the pursuit of the Neo-Confucian empiricism of *ko-wu chih-chih* (investigating things and extending one's knowledge). After studying the principle of "things" (*wu-li*), he included within "things" the human relations and principles of daily life. Considering himself the advocate of the "pure learning of Ch'eng-Chu," Sakuma conceived his task as rejecting heretical teachings (*i-hsueh*) and rebuilding orthodox learning (*cheng-hsueh*). Later, however, he began to study Dutch Learning, recognizing the threat from abroad and worrying about maritime defense after the Opium War in China. Stimulated by the sense of crisis from abroad, he began to learn and practice military techniques. Sakuma thus partook of the traditional doctrine of controlling the barbarians with the techniques of the barbarians. In Sakuma's reasoning, power was a common element in all cultures. Thus, the West, now taken as an object of comparison, was no longer contemptible as barbarian, and Japanese ethnocentrism was something to be shattered. He approached "expelling the barbarians" from the military point of view, asking whether the Japanese could possibly win a military victory. Then he became an advocate of the opening of the country.

Sakuma is significant in the history of thought because he accepted the Western impact as an intellectual challenge to Confucianism. He therefore tried to cope with the challenge by reinterpreting Confucianism. He argued that the intellectual difference between the West and the East (Japan) was attributable to the Chinese and Japanese emphasis on empirical textual criticism. This preoccupation resulted in the failure to explore the *li* of the natural world. Sakuma understood Western intellectual power as a knowledge of natural sciences, the foundation of military strength. He found the basis for the new encouragement of the natural sciences, however, in Neo-Confucianism itself, or the doctrines of Chu Hsi. Sakuma understood that physical quality goes beyond metaphysical quality (the two qualities that compose the *li* of Neo-Confucianism). In their original form they were undivided, and on that understanding he approached the scientific knowledge of the West. He tried to rationalize his position by saying that, since the natural sciences of the West correspond to the essence of Ch'eng-Chu Neo-Confucianism, "Western learning is only part of ours [the doctrines of Chu Hsi] and no more than that." The argument that the principles of Chinese Neo-Confucianism and the natural sciences of the West are the same must be based on the belief in the oneness and universality of the principle (*li*) of the cosmos. As expected, Sakuma said: "A lot of Western learning in recent times has been for practical use, and thus is sufficient to reinforce our sagely learning," and "those who had learned the principles of nature in *The Great Learning* [*Ta-hsueh*, a Confucian classic] would know Western learning at the same time."

Sakuma thus expanded the sphere of *li* (the *li* of the West was essentially identical to the *li* of the East). But, by stressing the physical character of *li*, he could rely on Confucianism only for the metaphysical realm as a supporting structure for the physical. For the world of value, he could not be satisfied with natural sciences alone. When he spoke of "Eastern ethics and Western technology" and "taking the teachings of sages in Chinese culture as longitude, and the various disciplines of Western arts [technology] as latitude," Sakuma indicated that he was still relying on "ethics" and "the teachings of sages" for the world of value,[25] thus giving the natural sciences of the West an adequate home to settle in.

Sakuma had a narrow view of the world of politics; the sharpness of his sense of the world was primarily restricted to technology and did not penetrate into the dimension of social systems. In his works he rarely mentioned the social systems of Western civilization. In Confucianism, politics should not only govern the people but should also lead to a realization of the *tao*. But Sakuma was not concerned about political and social systems because he lacked a deep observation of the world of ultimate value and morality.[26] For political doctrines, Sakuma followed the traditional thought of Neo-Confucianism and responded to crises in foreign relations with no greater call for institutional changes than the selection of fit persons for higher positions and the opening up of channels of communication with the ruler (*yen-lu*). He held to the basic Neo-Confucian idea that class relationships within the *bakufu-han* system constituted the order of nature.

He admitted, however, the changes in Confucianism, which had begun to be absorbed into the fields of social and political thought. As his knowledge of the West increased, he said: "The political system of the United States, however good it may be, cannot be applied to (or practiced in) our country. For Westerners do not install monarchs, but select a person who is equipped with the highest virtue, wisdom, and scholarship to be the head of their country, regardless of where in the country he may come from, and replace him with another every four years in order to transfer the governing power. This is as different from Japan's imperial system, in which one king and his descendants rule the country for a long time, as ice is from coal."[27] I think we can see here how the observation of facts led Sakuma to relativism, as he argued that Japan and the West have their appropriate ways.[28]

Summing up Sakuma's thought, Uete wrote:

After Sakuma, Confucianism began to be dissolved and its ideas on nature and society to be disrupted. Trying to reinterpret the Neo-Confucian doctrine of considering the principles of nature compatible with modern scientific method obviously deviates, I think, from trying to preserve traditional political thought by accepting relativism. In that his thoughts involved this deviant tendency, Sakuma could be said to have opened the door for modernization in the name of *tōyō dōtoku seiyō geijutsu ron* ... Sakuma himself, however, did not necessarily recognize this deviation. He related natural sciences to the *ko-wu ch'iung-li* formula. He did not even care, in his later years, to take *ko-wu ch'iung-li* in the traditional moralistic sense. He saw *li* as one and Confucianism as the universal teaching penetrating nature and society. In other words, he was immersed in adopting Western natural sciences without recognizing that they were gradually destroying the foundation of his own thought. As long as he thought that social orders were part of the order of nature (whether the nature of heaven and earth or historical nature), he could not overcome Confucian metaphysics... To the end, he identified the natural laws modern science is seeking to discover with the *li* mentioned in *I-ching* (Book of changes) or in Neo-Confucianism... The criticism of Confucian cosmology whose sprout is first spotted in Sakuma could be developed to its ultimate form, making scientific rationalism bloom, only when there had to be a consciousness that social orders are the product of artificial efforts and could be transformed with human opinions and actions, consequently liberating society from nature.[29]

In sum, we can say that the significance of Sakuma in the history of thought lies in his having opened the door for the acceptance of natural sciences by putting together Confucian *li* and Western natural sciences, whose connection was described in the formula of ethics/technology. Sakuma had little concern for Western political systems and understood the existing class order as part of the overall order in the Confucian sense (the order of heaven and earth), thus worthy of being safeguarded. Sakuma's influence was positive in the sense that his pursuit of Western sciences planted the seeds of criticism against the Confucian order.

Yokoi Shōnan was a contemporary of Sakuma's who went a step beyond him by opening the door to social and political systems of the modern West, breaking away from the traditional view of Western civilization as a purely material culture.[30] Although he believed in Confucianism (the Way of Yao, Shun, Confucius, and Mencius) no less than Sakuma, Yokoi took the initial step to total acceptance of Western civilization by reinterpreting Confucianism from a different direction. He transformed Japanese ethnocentrism from the ground up. His ideas have been called "practical learning," since they were aimed at restoring the original practical learning of Confucianism, which had degenerated into formulaic literary exercises.[31] Yokoi was a sincere Neo-Confucianist who believed that the Neo-Confucian idea of *ko-wu chih-chih* (understood as "studying the principles of nature") was connected with the goal of Confucian self-cultivation, a "sincere and purified mind" (*ch'eng-i cheng-hsin*). He also related the governing of the nation to mental discipline (*hsin-shu*).

Although at first he strongly advocated "expelling the barbarians," Yokoi later became an advocate of opening the country, for he knew that strategic realities made it impossible to expel the barbarians, and that the Japanese political system had reached a blind alley. Judging that the crisis in foreign relations could be overcome only by reforms, he insisted that the reforms should be attained by returning to the ancient Three Dynasties (San-tai). He felt that at the core of the Three Dynasties lay the purity of mind of the rulers as well as the spirit of public good (*kung*), rather than private advantage (*ssu*). "The world should be for the public" (*t'ien-hsia wei-kung*), or the idea of Confucian democracy, came to the fore and was directed at overthrowing the existing system.[32]

Yokoi was deeply interested in enriching the nation and stabilizing the lives of the people. He understood the values of Western technology. At the same time, he stressed the practicality of Confucianism, believing that enriching the nation, strengthening the armed forces (*fukoku kyōhei*), and improving the lot of the people was the work of sages. In politics, he advocated valuing public opinion (*kyōgi yōron*). Thus, he insisted on opening the channels of communication with the ruler and recruiting talented persons for public office. The Confucian idea of valuing the opinions of the broad mass of literati was here reinterpreted as the modern idea of respecting public opinion.[33]

In Yokoi's advocacy of a return to the Three Dynasties, he was responding to the impact of the West, which he learned about through Wei Yuan's *Hai-kuo t'u-chih* (Illustrated gazetteer of the maritime nations). Apparently he no longer believed that the existing system embodied *tao* or the laws of nature. By emphasizing the universality of *tao* (or heavenly principle) he could now proceed to acknowledge that even barbarians may have *tao*. Thus, he repudiated Sinocentrism, which viewed both China and Japan as Chinese in the broader sense of the word and the West as barbarian. Once Japan and the West became equal in the face of the *tao* of the Three Dynasties, the strong points of the West could be accepted. The social and political systems of the two cultures could also be compared. Yokoi came to believe that the American system of "transferring power not to one's son but to the wise" (the democratic election system), the English political system based on the will of the people, and Western amenities, such as hospitals, kindergartens, and institutions for the deaf and dumb, were all in accord with the teachings and governing system of the Three Dynasties.[34]

Sakuma intended primarily to adopt the natural sciences of the West; Yokoi expanded his concern to social and political systems, paving the way for the vigorous adoption of Western social and political thought and institutions. Yokoi's own contribution, however, was no more than just the beginning of the opening of the door, for he maintained to the end that Western civilization as such is excellent only in science and technology and that the West thus "has the branch but not the root." In assessing Western civilization, he focused on its correspondence to the achievement in the Three Dynasties, without understanding that the political systems of the modern West were based on principles fundamentally different from the political teachings of the Three Dynasties.

He did not rule out, however, the dangerous possibility of drowning in Western civilization, adding that one would drown if one did not adhere to the fundamental idea of the governing system of the Three Dynasties. Reflecting his attachment to the politics of the Three Dynasties and to humanity and justice, Yokoi said: "The teachings of Yao, Shun, and Confucius should be elucidated and every sort of Western machine and technology should be sought. And how can we be satisfied with a wealthy nation? How can we be satisfied with strong military power? These are merely ways of expanding the great cause (of the sages) to the four seas." Yokoi started as a Neo-Confucianist, but he became critical of the doctrines of Chu Hsi. He emphasized the difference between the doctrines of Chu Hsi, which stressed principle (*li*) and mind (*hsin*), and the teachings of the Three Dynasties, which stressed study (*kung-fu*). Thus *li* was understood as a principle that changed in accordance with circumstances (*shih*) – not an ultimate principle of all things in the universe.

In their search for a way to mobilize power to cope with the growing crisis in foreign relations, Sakuma and Yokoi reinterpreted Confucianism and thus paved the way for the Japanese reception of Western civilization. Their outlook was based, however, on the moral principles and the Heaven (*t'ien*) of Confucianism. Their successors (the leaders of modernization in the early Meiji era),[35] imbued with the ideas of Sakuma and Yokoi, embraced both the culture and the institutions of Western civilization.

PRINCIPLE/UTILITY IN CHINA

In the history of Confucianism, since Hu Yuan of the Northern Sung, the dyadic expression *t'i-yung* (principle/utility) has had a wide currency, implying contrasting but complementary qualities. Tseng

Kuo-fan (1811–1872) once applied the *t'i-yung* structure to say: "Take the establishment of one's own character as *t'i* [basic principle] and the extension of one's sincerity to the outer world as *yung* [utility] (*i tzu-li wei t'i, i t'ui-ch'eng wei yung*)." Wang Wen-shao (1830–1908) even used the expression to maintain: "Take defense as the *t'i* [basic principle] and combat as the *yung* [utility] (*i shou wei t'i, i chan wei yung*)." Thus, *t'i* and *yung* had been used in various contexts that did not necessarily share a common logical structure.[36]

Feng Kuei-fen

The first person to offer a systematic discussion on accepting Western learning by relating it to traditional Chinese thought was Feng Kuei-fen (1809–1874). His *Chiao-pin-lu k'ang-i* (Straightforward words from Chiao-pin Studio), written in 1861 and first published in 1897, was presented to the Kuang-hsu Emperor by Weng T'ung-ho in 1889, and read by many people through the 1890s. In 1898, it was presented to the Emperor again by Sun Chia-nai, and the Emperor ordered 2,000 copies to be distributed among metropolitan officials.[37]

In Mainland China, some scholars regard Feng as a landlord reformist like Wei Yuan, while others place him in the *yang-wu* group.[38] Li Tse-hou, in an effort to close the gap between the two different estimates, has regarded Feng as a bridge between the reformism of the 1830s and 1840s, and that of the 1870s and 1880s.[39] Similarly, Hu Pin wrote: "However vaguely, Feng recognized the necessity for China to learn from the West in the field of political systems, pointing the way for later reformists."[40] Both these estimates of Feng pointed out that his concern was not restricted to Western machinery and science, but included institutions. Judging from the arguments above, it may be fair to say that Feng went beyond *yang-wu lun*, if *yang-wu lun* means adopting only Western machinery and science. Many hesitate to accept this view because Feng's thought was formed as early as the 1840s and he was closely associated with Li Hung-chang, the champion of *yang-wu*.

The following letter of Li Hung-chang indicates the environment in which Feng's reformism was shaped:

What occurs to me [now] is that I met Prince Kung that year [1874] when I went to the capital and had an audience with the Emperor's casket [on the occasion of the national funeral of the T'ung-chih Emperor]. [Then] I petitioned him to build a railroad between Ch'ing-chiang and the capital to facilitate transportation between the south and the north [of China]. I vigorously pointed out the convenience of the railway. Prince Kung agreed, but he was afraid there would be no one to implement it. When he was asked if he would tell the two [East and West] Empresses Dowager, if he had the chance, he answered that even the two Empresses could not decide to implement this great a plan. Thereafter, I kept silent.[41]

Feng Kuei-fen thus developed his reformist thought in a situation in which nobody, not even Prince Kung and the two Dowagers, could advocate or implement the construction of railroads, even though they acknowledged their convenience. For Feng to have advocated adopting Western technology and machinery in those days was thus quite remarkable. In studying Feng's thought, the most important and urgent problem is how he came to open the door to receive Western machinery and technology (and to reform institutions along the lines of Western models). He insisted on introducing "barbarian" (Western) tools and machinery for China's self-strengthening and "expelling barbarians," so as to neutralize the threat of Western military power.[42] Feng advocated the introduction of Western machinery and tools (such as ships), not simply for the sake of efficiency, but with a keen consciousness of their importance to China's independence. He said that, as long as the Chinese people were not able to build, repair, and use them, Western machinery and tools remaind "of benefit to others," not "of benefit to us." To avoid this problem, the Chinese should make, mend, and pilot such importations as ships rather than hire Western technicians (or soldiers) to operate them.[43] This self-consciousness is the establishment of national identity rather than simply an adherence to traditional systems or values. It distinguishes self from others and shows a concern for national sovereignty characteristic of the *pien-fa* group of later times.[44]

Therefore, when Feng spoke of taking traditional ethics (*lun-ch'ang ming-chiao*) for the basis (*yuan-pen*) and complementing (*pu*) it with the technology of Western countries to make a nation wealthy and strong,[45] the ethics was a major part of "us" (*wo*) but not all of it. Also, the "us" in "the benefit to us" included the concept of identity induced from the concept of "self and others," as well as the Chinese ethical system itself. Apparently because of his personal experience during the Taiping Rebellion, Feng was not in favor of borrowing foreign ships and seeking foreign military help.⁴⁶ In view of China's need to learn how to operate and maintain weapons, Feng came to acknowledge the necessity of accepting the natural sciences underlying Western machinery and tools. He did go beyond advocating the introduction of Western natural sciences, because he called for institutional reforms for national self-strengthening and attempted to introduce the principles of Western political systems. When Feng wrote that "China is not as good as barbarians in placing talented persons in suitable positions," he meant to reform the Chinese examination system by adopting Western personnel recruitment systems. And, when he argued that "the relationship between the monarch and the subject in China is not so close as that in barbarian foreign countries," he may have had in mind the Western parliament, which he saw as a good channel for transmitting opinions from below to above.⁴⁷ Viewing the parliamentary system as a way to close the distance between the ruler and the ruled was a common characteristic of late Ch'ing parliamentarianism.⁴⁸ Feng considered that barbarians had achieved a closer correspondence between names and reality,⁴⁹ meaning that Western administrative systems were more effective than those of the Chinese.⁵⁰ Discussing China's shortcomings compared to the barbarians, Feng argued for "self-reflection" (returning to the self to find out what is needed) to rectify the situation.

Since the concrete way for self-reflection is given in *Chiao-pin-lu k'ang-i*, the only thing to be done is to reform the imperial government. Therefore "it need not depend on the barbarians," he said.⁵¹ It does not necessarily mean abandoning learning from Western political systems. It may have seemed to him desirable to introduce Western political systems indirectly, accepting, for instance, the underlying principles rather than the systems themselves, while advocating the direct acceptance of Western ships and machinery. The self-reflection⁵² he argued for was the same as the *fu-ku* ("returning to the ancient") he emphasized as the way to reform in his preface to *Chiao-pin-lu k'ang-i*. For him it was not the return to (or reenactment of) all things old, but the selection of those features of ancient times worth restoring. Feng observed that one could also consider selecting from the "teachings of barbarians" as well as "miscellaneous teachings," though he stressed that these selections should not deviate from the Way of the Sages in the Three Dynasties. Returning to the ancient within the limit of the teachings of the sages meant reformation through the reinterpretation of traditions. In the process, he called for the adoption of the principle of Western political systems.

The principles of the sages in the Three Dynasties, which were broad and vaguely defined, served as a conceptual boundary for his reinterpretation of tradition. Such a stance corresponds to his argument for the establishment of China's identity before accepting the good points of the West. His argument for establishing identity was not exactly due to fear that borrowing from the West might harm China's traditions, but was a way to make acceptance of the West possible in an environment in which even discussing the idea was not easy.

Feng's understanding of Western republicanism and the parliamentary system was fairly accurate, as we have seen in his arguments for the Western parliamentary system, for efficiency-centered political systems, and for efficiency in recruiting public officials as the basis for reform. He often advocated the adoption of the Western practice of decision by majority rule,[53] which he considered a fundamental principle of the parliamentary system. He rested his hope of achieving reforms based on the restoration of ancient institutions on a strengthening of imperial discipline over the bureaucracy, a forerunner of the reformist thought of the late 1890s. The *pien-fa* group of the 1890s, too, sought to achieve a constitutional system by using imperial power.

In sum, it seems to me that, although Feng advocated taking the principles of the Three Dynasties as the root, he supplemented them with foreign techniques for achieving wealth. Thus his thought differed from the so-called principle/utility formula, which assumed a fundamental antagonism between Chinese spiritual values and Western techniques. Through the process of reinterpreting Confucianism to call for a restoration of the principles of the sages of the Three Dynasties, he could juxtapose the West and the East, without seeing one as antagonistic to the other. Thus he could attempt actual reforms of the existing political system because he asserted "Chinese principle" as a precondition for accepting Western learning. If one is still tempted to call him an advocate of the principle/utility formula, it could only be in the sense that he considered "principle" as primary and "utility" as secondary.

Wang T'ao

What was the relationship between Chinese and Western learning for Wang T'ao, Hsueh Fu-ch'eng, and Ma Chien-chung, all of whom were active later than Feng Kuei-fen, and had more direct knowledge of the West? Wang T'ao wrote: "Mechanical devices [*ch'i*, tools] should be taken from the West, but *tao* [the Way] should be our own. And what is unchangeable forever is the *tao* of Confucius."[54] What Wang called learning from the West included training soldiers, manufacturing firearms, and building ships. He called these outer or branch elements, however. The inner or root element in the Chinese tradition of government, which included strengthening the discipline of officialdom, correcting the habits of the literati, upholding (good) customs, and correcting the minds of the people.[55] If the branch here meant mechanical devices (*ch'i*), the root should be the Way (*tao*), meaning good domestic administration based on the Way of Confucius. He stressed that the Way meant the ethical principles of human relations, *jen-lun*, which are universal and unique in the world. *Jen-lun* here means universal humanity, which is the same in the West and in China, and refers to the three duties and the five moral obligations in human relations (*san-kang wu-lun*), which have been given to all people from birth.[56] Such an attitude could be interpreted as meaning the absoluteness of China's ethical principles, but could also proceed to a more flexible stand, acknowledging that the West, too, has *jen-lun*. Wang eventually adopted this view.

If the West, too, possesses *jen-lun*, then it is logical to accept Western political systems, which represent the branch or exterior of *jen-lun*. Some contend that the recognition of the universality of *tao* played an important role in resolving conflicts between the goals of attaining a wealthy China and preserving a Confucian China.[57] Therefore, Wang's concern for Western political systems was serious. Although he did not call directly for a Western parliamentary system, he tried to turn public attention to the "merits and demerits of Western politics" and the "development of Western institutions." At the same time he hailed the English system of "joint sovereignty of monarch and people," and stressed that the Western political system of parliamentarianism was in accord with the spirit of governing in the Three Dynasties, thus strongly implying his support for it.[58] When he said, "The sovereign is the lord above, and the subject is the lord below" (*chün chu yü shang, min chu yü hsia*),⁵⁹ he was apparently recommending constitutionalism, or Western parliamentarianism, regarding it as applicable to Chinese as well as to foreigners. Although he was emphasizing the unchangeable Way of Confucius in comparison with "mechanical devices," he seems to have attempted to transform the Way itself by recommending those aspects of Western political systems that were compatible with the Way and also conducive to national wealth and strength.⁶⁰

It is also worth remarking that Wang had a strong inclination toward nationalism. (One scholar has called him a Confucian nationalist.)⁶¹ Wang, who had wanted to abolish extraterritoriality and to recover tariff autonomy, said that self-strengthening based on borrowed institutions should aim at transcending the West, not just catching up.⁶² From this nationalistic viewpoint, he criticized the optimistic attitude toward international law. Wang believed that international law could be useful to China only when China had a strong military force and wealth.⁶³ This distinct nationalistic tendency differentiates the *yang-wu* group from the *pien-fa* group.⁶⁴

Hsueh Fu-ch'eng

In an appeal to settle crises in foreign relations,⁶⁵ Hsueh Fu-cheng defined principle (*t'i*) as comprising morals, loyalty, filial piety, and traditional classical scholarship. He believed that, to make *yung* work, men should be recruited who were talented and knowledgeable about modern trends, students of (Western) science, capable of military command because of their thorough knowledge of military affairs for both army and navy, and talented in translation in order to communicate between West and East.

To Hsueh, the proper way of *Chung-t'i hsi-yung* meant to have an equal supply of traditional morals and learning, while recognizing the strengths of the West and learning Western technology. He proposed that, if the equal attainment of *t'i* and *yung* presented practical difficulties, less *t'i* and more *yung* was to be recommended. He saw Western and Chinese learning basically as a matter of proportion rather than as a relationship of root and branch or principal and subordinate. If *t'i* and *yung* are not considered root and branch, then equipping China with both traditional learning and Western technology is not the only possible course. In a country that had just opened its doors, "less *t'i* and more *yung*" could be recommended. This idea was peculiar to Hsueh Fu-cheng. Whether such an idea was tenable or not, it is interesting that principle/utility could be understood in such a way.

Hsueh also made remarks similar to the more standard principle/utility formula. In an essay entitled "Pien-fa" (Reform), he called for preserving the Way of the sages by adopting the learning of machinery and mathematics (science) of the West. The Way here must be identical with the "unchangeable *tao*" he mentioned in the same essay. According to Hsueh, the "unchangeable *tao*" should be preserved through the restoration of ancient ways (*fu-ku*), and changeable principles (or institutions) should be adjusted to fit the realities.[66]

Here we can see another example of the argument for the preservation of the Way through the reinterpretation of *tao*, or *fu-ku*. Hsueh did not simply wish to reinterpret existing cultural values, but wanted to find his own more basic truth in the *tao* by way of reinterpretation. Therefore, Hsueh should be regarded as concentrating not merely on safeguarding established values, but on furnishing the moral basis for accepting Western scientific knowledge. Thus, introducing Western thought is made possible culturally by preserving the Way.[67]

Hsueh stressed that scientific knowledge, which "borrows (or uses) the spirits of Nature" to "benefit the people," could not be monopolized by Westerners, but was a "public principle of heaven and earth."[68] Citing the universality of scientific knowledge, he also emphasized that it did not necessarily imply the introduction of things Western. He maintained that by adopting scientific knowledge (steam, electricity, and chemistry, and so forth), which constituted public principles, China could not only overcome her imminent crisis but could also surpass the West in the future. Here he might well be called nationalistic. He also argued that arithmetic was one kind of scientific knowledge originating from China, and he related this to the universality of public principles.[69]

Hsueh's view of Western thought and institutions was not a narrow one. Some scholars have stressed his difference from the *yang-wu* group because of his emphasis on commerce. He called merchants "the pillar of the four classes of the people."[70] Although he did not clearly distinguish which Western political systems should be applied to China, he observed that "joint sovereignty of monarch and people" was the best. Among the three Western systems of monarchy, democracy, and joint sovereignty, he preferred joint sovereignty and even praised the two-party system of Britain. In the light of such opinions, some scholars maintain that Hsueh thought it inevitable that monarchial despotism would be replaced by bourgeois democracy, since despotism could not meet the demands of a developing society. They also claim that he predicted a political revolution in Russia on the premise that feudal systems could not endure for a long time.[71] Such a claim appears to be extreme, but I agree that Hsueh's understanding of political systems was better than that of Wang T'ao.

Ma Chien-chung

Generally included in the same category with Wang and Hsueh, Ma Chien-chung argued in detail for the enrichment of the people. He recorded his view of Western political systems in a report of his life in Paris as a student. The wealth of the West, he thought, was due not only to the invention of machinery, but even more to commerce, good laws, and good administration. He added that wealth could be achieved by protecting commercial firms, and strength by winning the confidence of the people. Parliament was a system for the "transmission of opinions from the lower class (to the higher)," he wrote, speaking in a roundabout way to mean that winning popular favor was possible only through a parliament. Therefore, he said, manufacturing and military development were only trifling "branches" compared with the importance of the relationship between political systems and wealth and strength. That is, Western wealth and strength embraced both root and branch. I have already mentioned that the expressions of "transmission of opinions from lower levels" and "winning popular favor" were connected with the parliamentary system by many late Ch'ing writers. Ma, who knew more about the West than his contemporaries, discerned that international law was designed in the interest of the major powers,[72] so I think it could be said that he was as nationalistic as Wang and Hsueh.

Cheng Kuan-ying

The adoption of Western learning with the formula of principle/utility was one of Cheng Kuan-ying's proposals, but his ideas were so varied that scholars have differed in their assessments of his theories.

In his preface to *Sheng-shih wei-yen* (Warnings to a seemingly prosperous age), he developed his own logic of reform, calling for a combination of *chung* (the standard or mean of unchangeable behavior) and *shih* (contemporary conditions).[73] Thus, we have an unusual concept, *shih-chung,* a standard or mean within fluctuation. According to Cheng, *chung* was equivalent to the universal Way of the Sages, and constituted principle (*t'i*). *Shih-chung* was the changeable means (or the means of the sages), and constituted utility (*yung*). He did not adopt the common formula: Chinese learning = unchangeable Way = principle (*t'i*) versus Western learning = application to circumstances = utility (*yung*). That is, he did not directly interpret *chung* (standard or mean) as *Chung-hsueh* (Chinese learning), although the *chung* ideographs are the same. Instead he interpreted *chung* in relation to general aspects of behavioral consciousness of morals. Thus, *chung* as a universal principle of action could penetrate both Western and Chinese learning, evading the conflict between the West and China, which the logic of principle/utility is otherwise apt to generate. For this reason alone, Cheng deserves a high reputation among those late Ch'ing thinkers who struggled to define the relationship between Western and Chinese learning.

Cheng insisted that, in studying the West, China should pursue not only utility but also principle. His unique *shih-chung* formula resulted in the notion that the West also had its *t'i* and *yung*. According to Cheng, parliamentarianism, the school system, closer relations between monarch and subjects, and practical working methods were *t'i,* and shipbuilding, guns, railways, and the telegraph were *yung.* Cheng also argued, as did most of his contemporaries,[74] that Western learning originated in China, and called for the adoption of Western learning. In the preface to his *Sheng-shih wei-yen,* he advocated a return to the Three Dynasties by imitating the West. We can find here the logical basis for his idea of returning to the Three Dynasties.

In some cases, Cheng seemed to verge upon the principle/utility view that simply takes Chinese learning for the base (*chu*) and Western learning for the supplement (*fu*). But "Chinese learning" was a comprehensive and vague term to him. It included Chinese learning as the source of Western learning and current Western learning, too, as an extension of ancient Chinese learning. "Western learning," on the other hand, meant only languages. He said that the ultimate aim of the base/supplement distinction was "to have a thorough knowledge of political systems."⁷⁵ As we have seen above, Cheng did not see a confrontation between China and the West.⁷⁶ He was far from an advocate of the so-called principle/utility formula, which aimed at resolving such a confrontation.⁷⁷

Chang Chih-tung

Generally accepted as the chief representative of the principle/utility formula, Chang Chih-tung clarified his stand in his *Ch'üan-hsueh p'ien* (Exhortation to study). *Ch'üan-hsueh p'ien* was written in 1898 in an effort to cope with the radical tendency of the reformist (*pien-fa*) group in Hunan province.⁷⁸ Undeniably, the book focused on a criticism of popular rights, equality, and other Western ideas. Most scholars of modern Chinese thought agree that Chang was one of the *yang-wu* (Western affairs) group and see principle/utility reflected in Chang's *Exhortation* as a leading idea of that group. It has already been demonstrated, however, that Chang had given considerable support to the reform campaigns of K'ang Yu-wei and Liang Ch'i-ch'ao, although within certain limits.⁷⁹ Thus, there is a problem in identifying Chang simply as a part of the *yang-wu* group. I have already raised a question about whether Chang's argument for opposing popular rights and equality was closely related to the structure of the principle/utility argument. Opposition to popular rights and equality has usually been accepted as one characteristic of principle/utility, but it should be noted, among other things, that *Chung-t'i hsi-yung lun* interprets the relationship between Western and Chinese learning as a logical structure.

In view of the historical circumstances, it is unhistorical to fault Chang for excluding popular political rights from utility. One can hardly expect the advocacy of such rights under circumstances in which even partial reception of Western civilization on an extremely restricted basis was not easy. In discussing principle/utility in this early stage, the appropriate question is, instead, whether the call for Western utility involved a call for reforming institutions, as distinct from importing technology; for only after the issue of the reform of institutions was settled could the problem of popular political rights be raised.

How did his contemporaries understand Chang's *Exhortation to Study?* According to Chang Chien, conservatives like Hsu T'ung thought it supported K'ang Yu-wei.[80] Many foreign scholars held the same view.[81] Chang Chien, who sympathized somewhat with K'ang Yu-wei and Liang Ch'i-ch'ao but did not join their group, saw it as Chang's effort to find a balance between the radical and the conservative.[82] Liang Ch'i-ch'ao, however, in an essay written after the 1898 coup d'état, criticized the work's opposition to popular political rights.[83] Meanwhile, Pi Hsi-jui, who had been the head of the Nan-hsueh-hui (Southern Study Society), stronghold of the radical reformists in Hunan, said, before the 1898 coup d'état, that Chang's opposition to popular political rights was excusable in view of his position as a high official, and that the remainder of the work was admirable.[84]

As these diverse evaluations suggest, the *Exhortation* was a complex work. Although Chang advocated the consideration of "old learning" as principle and "new learning" as utility, he understood the essential point of "old (Chinese) learning" to be "practical application" (*chih-yung*).[85] Thus, a definite boundary for Chinese learning was set.

Similarly, Chang associated Western learning more with politics than with technology. He supported parliamentary government, but believed it could be adopted only after education had produced enough qualified people to operate the system. He thought it was too early to discuss the matter. The essence of the Western political system included modern schools, the study of geography, the modernization of methods of finance and taxation, weapons, the legal system, public works, commerce, and trade, all of which were to be the preconditions for parliamentary government. An appropriate economic and institutional foundation must underlie a parliamentary superstructure. Both Western and Chinese cultures were valued for their "practical use" aspects, so that the logic of principle/utility was closely associated with the reformation of Chinese "principle" itself.

Yet elsewhere in the *Exhortation* Chang identified Chinese learning as inner (governing body and mind) and Western learning as outer (governing worldly affairs). Here he was concerned not with the logical relationship between "principle" and "utility," but with their functional difference.[86] Western learning was needed so that Chinese learning might be preserved, but the foundation of Chinese learning must first be consolidated. Here principle/utility expresses the sequence of implementation. Although he saw the Way of ethics and moral discipline (*lun-chi*) as unchanging, he stressed that Western countries also had ethics of human relations which deserved attention.

Thus, Chinese and Western learning shared a moral dimension, on the premise of the universality of moral principles. If both cultures contained moral principles, then we might be able to interpret Chang's more general logic as "moral principle for principle," and "political institutions for utility."

On the other hand, Chang disparaged the radicals in Hunan who, he believed, valued only Western things, and disregarded those of China.[87] Chang appears to have been writing out of fear of the radicals' attack on the existing system from his own political consideration. But, in fact, the radicals considered China as paramount, as Chang did.

Chang Chih-tung made it clear in his *Exhortation* that he was not in favor of popular political rights (*min-ch'üan*) because he understood that the gentry's political rights were opposed to official power, which might eventually lead to justifying the practice of interference by the gentry in the areas of official jurisdiction.[88] It seems to me, therefore, that Chang's preference for a reform led by officials rather than by gentry did not characterize his principle/utility formula. For Chang, the question of whether popular political rights are included in the concept of Western learning (the *yung* of the principle/utility formula) does not necessarily change the character of the formula.

The Western Affairs (yang-wu) *Group*

The *yang-wu* group has been generally understood to mean the high-ranking officials residing for the most part outside the capital (for example, Tseng Kuo-fan and Li Hung-chang), who, acknowledging that China had something to learn from the West, advocated the acceptance of Western scientific and technological knowledge in order to strengthen military power, but had no interest in reforming institutions or in introducing Western institutions.

To clarify the relationship between the *yang-wu* group and principle/utility, I will look at the attitude of the *yang-wu* group toward institutional reform. I have already pointed out that Li Hung-chang was concerned with institutional reform,[89] particularly of the Six Boards and the examination system. Thus he declared himself a follower of K'ang Yu-wei even after the coup d'état.[90] He stressed the changeability of established laws in a memorial of 1874 on coastal defense.⁹¹ In a letter written in 1877, he said that one could learn the outlines of Western political principles and systems after about twenty years of study.⁹² Admittedly, his awareness of Western political principles does not necessarily mean a desire to imitate them fully. What ought to be noted, however, is under what circumstances Li did concern himself about Western political systems.

In a letter of November 1874 to Wen-hsiang, he called for *pien-fa* (apparently meaning partial reforms), but said that he was "dealing with Western affairs one by one" with the thought that "doing something is better than doing nothing," even amid criticism and indifference from those who were not obliged to deal with diplomacy and national defense and from "literati" ignorant of practical affairs.⁹³ About the same time, as we have seen, Prince Kung responded to Li Hung-chang's railroad proposal by saying that nobody (including himself and the two Empresses Dowager) could make the decision on his own responsibility, although he himself agreed to it.

Li complained that some people found fault with makeshift measures (which were inevitable in that environment), but the fault lay in a lack of reform of government institutions (*pien-fa*) and a lack of improvement in personnel management, the bases of wealth and power.⁹⁴ By the improvement of personnel management, Li meant the reform of the examination system,⁹⁵ but it is not certain what he meant specifically by *pien-fa*. It is probable that by 1899 he had thought of reforms involving nearly all institutions in order to advocate the reform of the Six Boards.⁹⁶ If so, Li tended toward reform on the one hand, but adopted makeshift ways in practice in order to "seek immediate stability" (*mu-ch'ien ho-chü wei-ch'ih*). This discrepancy⁹⁷ probably occurred because he was a "working official" negotiating with foreign countries and managing modern armaments. Even K'ang Yu-wei, once he became an "insider" (a man obliged to deal with national policy-making within the government), responded to a suggestion by the Emperor to set up the parliament by saying that "it could not be implemented at all while the Court was dominated by conservatives, or while the public has not been adequately educated." This position is no different from that of Chang Chih-tung in his *Exhortation.*⁹⁸

Li's remark that "all Chinese institutions and systems are better than Western, except for firearms, in which China cannot excel the West"⁹⁹ is often quoted and cannot be overlooked, although we acknowledge that his willingness to consider institutional reforms was restricted by his position as an insider. We should note, too, that he advocated adopting Western civilization primarily for military technology. The main point, however, is that his position as an advocate of Western affairs was not too rigidly opposed to institutional reform. On the contrary, it was a step toward such reform.

Parliamentary government was not unfamiliar to some of the Western affairs group. Wen-hsiang,[100] a leader of Western affairs in the 1860s and 1870s, thought a bicameral system would serve the needs of both elite and commoners, and denied that Westerners lacked civilized politics. The spirit of such a system was worth adopting, he urged the Emperor, even though China was not yet ready for the system itself.[101] China's first minister to Great Britain, Kuo Sung-t'ao, another Western-affairs champion, saw Western political systems as the true root of their strength.[102] The solution for China was to adopt the branch (technology) and then to seek the root steadily. In any event, this course should be pursued bit by bit.[103]

Thus, the difference between the Western affairs (*yang-wu*) group and the institutional reform (*pien-fa*) group lies in whether they developed their interest in Western civilization into an actual political movement, rather than whether they had an interest in Western political thought, institutional reforms, and parliamentarianism. Here again, the principle/utility formula itself fails to serve as a criterion to characterize the Western affairs group.

The Institutional Reform (pien-fa) Group

What was the relationship between Western learning and Chinese learning as far as K'ang Yu-wei, the leader of the Reform Movement, and the reform group were concerned? K'ang's veneration for Confucius, which led him to reinterpret Confucianism as a religion and make it the pillar of his reform ideology, is well known. His aim was apparently the reform of China's political system based on the Western model. But did he see his Confucian religion as part of a Chinese principle that could be counterposed to Western utility? No one will argue that his Confucian religion could not be included in *Chunghsueh*, or Chinese learning. In that case, Western learning, or *hsi-hsueh* could pertain to constitutional political systems on the Western model. If so, did K'ang consider Chinese learning and Western learning related to each other like "principle" and "utility"? Liang Ch'i-ch'ao, who faithfully propagated K'ang's thought, said in a biography of K'ang that he "made 'principle' of Confucianism, Buddhism, and Sung and Ming philosophy; and he made 'utility' of Chinese dynastic histories and Western learning."[104] Thus, although histories could be included in Chinese learning, K'ang may well be called an advocate of a sort of principle/utility dichotomy.[105] Some scholars maintain that K'ang regarded Chinese learning as the root, or the base, and Western learning as something that could be used to elucidate Chinese learning.[106]

Liang Ch'i-ch'ao, who published more articles on the Reform Movement than K'ang, came up with many phrases clearly defining the relationship between Chinese learning and Western learning. In 1896 he said: "What is worrisome today is not that Western learning does not flourish but that Chinese learning is about to perish," because "those who speak of Western learning have recently tended not only to be ignorant of Chinese learning but also to regard it as useless. . . . It is now to be feared that most of those who speak of Western learning will be as ill-informed as this if the trend is not corrected soon."[107] It appears that he thought Chinese learning without Western learning was lacking in utility, and Western learning without Chinese learning lacked a base. Writing in 1897, Liang said that people "should study thoroughly Chinese traditional learning, understanding what accounts for its essential nature, and should seek practical utility by comparing and uniting the two,"[108] thus making it possible to preserve one of the two components of the principle/utility or root/branch formula. In 1898 he wrote clearly, "There is no school that lectures on the learning of other countries while discarding all the learning of its own country. In general, Chinese learning is 'principle' and Western learning is 'utility.' These two need each other, and one is indispensable to the other."[109]

It is clear, however, that Liang did not consider principle/utility in the usual sense, in which Chinese learning represented traditional values only, and Western learning meant only machinery. In a letter to Chang Chih-tung, he wrote of "making the base the Six Classics and the Hundred Schools, and making the supplement the public principles and laws of the Westerners."[110] But we can categorize his argument as a sort of principle/utility view since it is clear that, to Liang, Chinese learning was the logical basis on which Western learning should depend. It was simply that the contents of Western learning were different from those usually recognized. If there is, in the reform group, such a close tie to principle/utility ideas, can we rightly separate them from the Western affairs group by this criterion? Or is there one principle/utility for the former group, and another for the latter?

In addition to the examples we have seen in the writings of K'ang and Liang, principle/utility arguments were common among others involved in the reform effort. The Emperor himself called for making the teaching of the sages (*i-li*) the root, while adopting elements of Western learning as needed. Grand Secretary Sun Chia-nai called for "controlling Western learning, the *yung*, with Chinese learning, the *t'i*."[111] Thus, it appears that Sun did not recognize the peculiarity of Western learning, but regarded it as depending on and affiliated with Chinese learning.[112] Sung Po-lu, the most active mouthpiece of the reformists together with Yang Shen-hsiu, also used the words *t'i* and *yang*. In a memorial calling for the reform of the examination system, Sung said that "Chinese learning is *t'i* and Western learning is *yung*.... There is no basis but for *t'i* and no efficiency without *yung*. These two are indispensable to each other, and one without the other is not sufficient." Sung was thus calling for "testing both *t'i* and *yung* by abolishing the boundary between Western learning and Chinese learning" in future examinations.[113]

Hsiang-pao (The Hsiang River journal) is one of the reformist journals that Chang Chih-tung criticized for its radicalism. In a lecture-hall regulation carried in the journal, the phrase *Chung-hsueh wei t'i, hsi-hsueh wei yung* appeared. The phrase simply meant that such books as the *Analects,* the writings of Mencius, the Ch'eng brothers, and Chu Hsi, *Wu-li t'ung-k'ao* (Comprehensive study of the five rites), *Sheng-wu chi* (Military history of the Ch'ing dynasty), and *Hsiang-chün chih* (Treatise on the Hunan Army) were considered as basic, and books on current affairs as supplementary.[114] A petition in *Hsiang-hsueh hsin-pao* said the *tao* of studying could not go beyond the boundary of the teachings of the sages, citing *Chung-hsueh wei chu, hsi-hsueh wei fu* (Chinese learning as foundation, Western learning as supplement) and *Chung-hsueh wei t'i, hsi-hsueh wei yung* (Chinese learning as principle, Western learning as utility), the phrases Sun had used.[115] The mixed phrase *Chung-hsueh wei pen, hsi-hsueh wei yung* (Chinese learning as foundation, Western learning as utility) also appeared in a memorial (19 September 1898) of Ch'ang-ch'ing, who, as a Manchu, had a positive interest in reform. In this phrase, Ch'ang-ch'ing implied the relationship of the two as root and branch, and first and last; he explained that trying to study Western learning without a thorough knowledge of Chinese learning is like looking for the branch and discarding the root.[116]

The Tao-ch'i Distinction

Tao-ch'i was another important formula conceived to make borrowing from Western technology seem compatible with maintaining Chinese tradition. *Tao-ch'i* originated in the *Book of Changes*, which describes metaphysical things as *tao* (Way) and physical things as *ch'i* (vessels). The history of Chinese metaphysical thought, however, contains many differences of opinion about which quality is primary, or whether there can be an absolute separation between them.

Tso Tsung-t'ang, a leader of the Western-affairs group, characterized Western culture and institutions in relation to Chinese learning. At the same time, he confirmed what traditional values consisted of, that is, what entity was to accept Western culture. Tso said that *tao* and *i* (techniques) were of the same origin and thus could not be separated, countering an argument, circulating in 1884, for establishing a special course to test Western techniques in the national examinations to recruit officials.[117] Although Tso used *i* instead of *ch'i*, he was basing his argument on a de facto *tao-ch'i* logic. Tso apparently used *i* to mean languages, letters, and manufacturing, placing the primary emphasis on manufacturing. He did not recognize that *i* included political systems and other components. For that very reason, however, he could see that *i* was not peculiar to the West but universal, covering manufacturing in general. Without even a crude manipulation of logic (such as maintaining that Western technology originated in ancient China), he thus got rid of obstacles to the acceptance of Western technology, for, since *tao* and *i* have the same origin, "the strengths of the Westerners" could easily be converted to "Chinese strength." Tso opposed the establishment of technical categories (*i-k'o*) in the national examinations by using this argument that *tao* and *i* had the same origin, because presumably he was afraid that there might be technical specialists who knew Western languages but were ignorant of Chinese *tao*. His objection to creating technical examination categories, however, did not develop into an objection to accepting the techniques themselves. The threat to Chinese values did not matter to him at all, partly because he did not think of *i* as involving political systems.

Wang T'ao wrote, in an essay entitled "Yuan-tao" (On the Way)[118] that, if *tao* is obstructed, *ch'i* should be appropriated to allow *tao* to attain its ends. Western technological products, such as locomotives, ships, and other vehicles, are actually embodiments of *tao*, he wrote. In his view, *tao* was "the *tao* of all the world under heaven," and "the *tao* of Confucius" as well as "the *tao* of human beings." It encompassed the ethical principles of human relations which are not subject to change. Thus, Westerners themselves could not escape beyond the bounds of *tao* common to all human beings.[119] According to this argument, apparently based on his own view of a "great unity" (*ta-t'ung*), *tao* and *ch'i* are of different origin, and, furthermore, *ch'i* is a way of realizing *tao*. If such an argument were taken a step further, *ch'i* itself could be seen to contain *tao* within it. The movement of physical phenomena becomes just a realization of metaphysical reality, which is similar to the argument of Chang Hsueh-ch'eng that *tao* could not part from *ch'i*; it is not quite the same as that of Wang Fu-chih, who said that *tao* comes from *ch'i*.

Although Wang T'ao thought that *ch'i* was to be taken from the West[120] and that *tao* was common to all the world, he did not envisage a rigid confrontation between Chinese *tao* and Western *ch'i*, because *ch'i* was thought to be a means for the realization of *tao*. The concrete contents of *ch'i* he listed as steam locomotives, ships, and other vehicles. Yet he implied more than that by Western *ch'i*, as can be seen in his essays, "Pien-fa" (Reform), "Pien-fa tzu-ch'iang" (Reform and self-strengthening), and "Ch'u-pi" (Eliminating abuses). In these essays, he listed as areas subject to reform under Western influence the general ways of governing the people, selecting officials, drilling troops, establishing schools, and legislating, implying that reform in all these fields would be helpful to the realization of *tao*.

Ch'en Ch'ih, a sponsor of K'ang Yu-wei's Reform Movement, who had won the confidence of Weng T'ung-ho,[121] unfolded his own *tao-ch'i* theory based on an assumption that Western learning originated in China. In his preface to Cheng Kuan-ying's *Sheng-shih wei-yen* (Warnings to a seemingly prosperous age), Ch'en also said that metaphysical things were *tao* and physical things were *ch'i*. To Ch'en, *tao* and *ch'i* were one, in the same sense that Wang Fu-chih regarded *ch'i* as the means of embodying *tao*. Ch'en said, however, that the *tao* and the *ch'i* of China had ceased to be transmitted because of the obscurantist policies since the Ch'in dynasty. Instead, they were transmitted to the West and were only recently reintroduced into China from the West. Ch'en, thus noting that heaven used the West to develop *ch'i*, rationalized that the acceptance of Western *ch'i* is the same as the acceptance of Chinese *ch'i*. But Ch'en expanded his notion of *ch'i* to include political and administrative systems such as policy, diplomacy, schools, parliamentarianism, military conscription, and commerce, as well as the construction of fortifications with batteries and observation balloons. In expanding the contents of *ch'i* to such an extent, he sanctioned the adoption of Western *ch'i* in his *tao-ch'i* theory.

Cheng Kuan-ying, who placed his essay on *tao* and *ch'i* at the very beginning of *Warnings*, explained in his preface his motivation in writing the essay by saying that "*tao* is the root and *ch'i* is the branch." Therefore *ch'i* is changeable, but *tao* is not. What is changeable is the [temporary] means for obtaining national wealth and power, but not the permanent essence of Confucius and Mencius. To Cheng, the principle (*t'i*) within the search for wealth and power represented institutions (for example, parliament and schools), and the utility (*yung*) meant technology (for example, ships, artillery, railroads, and electricity). Thus he called for changing the *t'i* for wealth and power, saying that only after that was done could *yung* be pursued. Cheng's explanation of why *ch'i* could have developed in the West was the same as that of Ch'en Ch'ih. Ch'en said that there was no chapter on *ko-chih* (the investigation of things) in the classical text, the *Great Learning*, nor any on *tung-kuan* (public works management) in the *Chou-li* (Rites of Chou), since *ch'i* had flowed out to the West about the time these books were written. This is certainly an argument for combining *tao* and *ch'i* which does not acknowledge either separation or confrontation between Western technology and Chinese ethics. Such logic, in effect, facilitates the acceptance of *ch'i* by stressing the existence of an unchangeable *tao*.

A *tao-ch'i* argument concerning Western learning and Chinese learning also appears in the *Wei-yen* (Words of warning) of T'ang Chen,[122] which the Court formally encouraged officials to read, together with Feng Kuei-fen's *Chiao-pin-lu k'ang-i* and Chang Chih-tung's *Ch'üan-hsueh p'ien*, on the occasion of the 1898 Reform Movement. Realizing that Western learning, referring to *ch'i*, included both political theory and technology, T'ang presented his own evidence to prove that Western learning originated in ancient China. Thus, T'ang agreed with Ch'en Ch'ih and Cheng Kuan-ying. He saw the origin of Western political theory in the *Rites of Chou* and that of Western technology in the pre-Ch'in classical philosophers; he agreed that both Western political systems and technology (which should be adopted) were not of Western origin.

Thus, he acknowledged the universality of political systems and technology, even though he required the intermediary of their Chinese origin. He managed to call for accepting Western learning, not as part of foreign culture, but through a restoration of China's own ancient heritage. This restoration was to reunite physical *ch'i* and metaphysical *tao*, which had originally been one, but later became separated, in T'ang's phrase, "to safeguard metaphysical *tao* by seeking physical *ch'i*." He thereby acknowledged the universality of Western political systems by saying that Westerners managed to include *tao* as a result of possessing *ch'i*.

T'an Ssu-t'ung, a radical at the time of the 1898 Reform Movement, is one of those who most thoroughly invoked *tao-ch'i* in relation to Western learning.[123] In discussing *pien-fa* (institutional reform), he asserted that "the *tao* of the Sages could in no way be discarded." To seek reform without discarding the *tao* of the sages, he invoked a *tao-ch'i* argument, similar to Wang Fu-chih's, namely that *tao* and *ch'i* were inseparable. He said that the *tao* of the Sages could be expressed only when there were phenomenal objects through which it could be expressed, after he finally arrived at the position that "*tao* is utility (*yung*) and *ch'i* is principle (*t'i*)," taking Wang Fu-chih's argument to an extreme. This argument that *ch'i* is the same as *tao* since *tao* can be realized only through *ch'i* is a subtle logical transformation, and may be called a utilitarian theory of value. Explaining reform on this basis, he asked: "Why will not *tao* change, if *ch'i* changes?" From this practical viewpoint he went so far as to stress the universality of *tao*, saying that neither the sages nor China could monopolize *tao* because "the *tao* of the sages is ubiquitous," indicating that there is no reason that China alone should possess it.

He apparently meant that there were no great differences between the ethics of China and those of the West, and thus he could accept Western values unreservedly. He said that China should undertake reform to recover the true *tao* (noting that contemporary Confucianism was not true) by restoring the ancient *tao* through the *ch'i* of the

West. He tended to object to the argument that the *ch'i* of the West (natural sciences) originated in China.¹²⁴ Instead, he saw that Westerners could develop their own *ch'i* because *tao* was universal. In this respect, T'an appears to be a step ahead of the others mentioned above.¹²⁵

We have seen that the *tao-ch'i* idea stresses the universal *tao* (that is, no specifically Chinese *tao* is assumed), while the principle/utility dichotomy emphasizes specific Chinese values (*chung*). Since *tao-ch'i* tends to center on an argument for the unity of *tao* and *ch'i*, it was easy for its advocates to accept Western culture and institutions as *ch'i*, thanks to the universality of *tao* itself. Some attempted to differentiate the *tao* of China from the *tao* of the West, but it appears that they did so only at the immature stage of their *tao-ch'i* argument. For example, T'an Ssu-t'ung advocated a kind of "Chinese *tao*, Western *ch'i*" before the age of thirty, stressing the unchangeability of *tao*. In his thirties, however, he moved beyond this view arriving at *"ch'i* is principle, *tao* is utility" (*ch'i-t'i tao-yung lun*).

In both the Western affairs and the reform schools of thought, principle/utility was a formula designed to link the acceptance of Western culture and institutions with the preservation of traditional values and the confirmation of Chinese identity. Different thinkers placed different degrees of value on Western culture, leading to apparent differences in their handling of the principle/utility formula. In most cases, advocates of the principle/utility related China to "principle" and the West to "utility," without fully applying the strict sense of *t'i* and *yung* as philosophical terms. They simply meant that these terms were related as the first and the last, the base and the supplement, or even the quantitative proportion of more and less. Contrary to our previous understanding, we have found that the reform group also frequently used the principle/utility formula (*Chung-t'i hsi-yung*). Whether *Chung* meant ethics or reinterpreted Confucian doctrine, it was at any rate Chinese. What was important, therefore, was not the *t'i-yung* formula itself, but the actual meaning of Western (*hsi*) and how to accept Western things. Thus, it is contrary to both the intentions of most of those who used the term and to what general readers meant by it, to consider only the formal dichotomy of *t'i* and *yung* in the sense of principle/utility as Yen Fu and Joseph Levenson did.¹²⁶

Although principle/utility thus could characterize both the Western-affairs and reform views, it cannot, on its own, account for the successive stages of the unfolding of late Ch'ing thought. It seems, rather, to be a formula that is likely to be developed when an alien culture is being forced on an indigenous one. In this respect, principle/utility could be compared with the "Eastern ethics and Western technology" of the Japanese, with the arguments of the Russian Slavophiles or the eighteenth-century reformers of Ottoman Turkey, that the machinery of the West is worth adopting but its spirit is not.[127]

If we understand principle/utility in this way, we should then reconsider the view that it was identified with Western affairs (*yang-wu*) only, and that reform (*pien-fa*) was a more advanced concept because it overcame the principle/utility formula. Another group (including Cheng Kuan-ying) who were, because of their close personal connection with eminent *yang-wu* officials, sometimes a part of the *yang-wu* group, have been described as acting as a bridge between the *yang-wu* and *pien-fa* groups. The thinking of this group should be reevaluated. In addition, it should be noted, when we discuss the unfolding of late Ch'ing thought, that advocates of Western affairs who were government officials such as Wen-hsiang, Li Hung-chang, and Kuo Sung-t'ao, as well as general advocates of *yang-wu lun*, such as Feng Kuei-fen, believed, at least theoretically, that the principles of Western political systems should be introduced, although, for various reasons, they failed to launch a movement to materialize their ideas.

In discussing whether the principle/utility argument should be seen as separate from Western affairs, it is unreasonable to focus on whether it included ideas of popular political rights (*min-ch'üan*), for these have nothing to do with its logical structure. Moreover, it is more difficult to agree with the argument that popular political rights in those contexts meant the power of the gentry (*shen-ch'üan*) as opposed to official power (*kuan-ch'üan*), and than democratic civil rights. Furthermore, although some reformers like Cheng Kuan-ying did not speak of popular sovereignty, he knew more about Western bourgeois democracy than any of the reform group who advocated popular sovereignty and, at times, actually called for the adoption of democracy.

And what of the interpretation that considers principle/utility anachronistic and reactionary (on the grounds that it was identified with Western affairs and was pitted against reform) rather than a step leading to reform? A comparison of Chinese principle/utility and

Japan's "East Asian ethics, Western technology" will further our understanding of the principle/utility formula of the Chinese Western-affairs group. Chinese principle/utility and Japan's ethics/technology are very similar in their logical structures. The proponents of both argued for reform through the restoration of the ancient Confucian ideal, for the acceptance of Western culture and institutions through a reinterpretation of Confucianism, and for the acceptance of Western learning, not as a fundamental reform of the existing order but as an effort to maintain that order. They advocated the understanding of Western learning as universal in order to facilitate the acceptance of Western learning, and they argued for native values, which they hoped would surpass Western learning and spread universally. Feng Kuei-fen's exposition of this logical structure was more systematic than that of the Japanese proponents of their formula. In particular, a concern for institutional change was more conspicuous among the Chinese advocates of the principle/utility formula. If we could say that ethics/technology enabled the Japanese to accept Western learning without discarding their own culture, "Western affairs" did the same for the Chinese.

The difference between the two, if any, was that the Japanese formula led to a successful overall reform of institutions, while the Chinese formula proved fruitless because of the failure to realize their ideas through the Reform Movement of 1898. This difference between Chinese and Japanese modern history is an important point, but the Chinese principle/utility should not be evaluated on the basis of this point alone. Therefore, it should be noted that Japanese success and Chinese failure are not exclusively attributable to the logic of their intentions of introducing Western institutions. The success and failure may have been caused instead by subsequent political movements which they hoped would realize their aspirations and ideals.

In Japan, with ethics/technology unfolding into the argument for "opening the country" (*kaikoku ron*) and paving the way for the Meiji Restoration, the Japanese could accept Western learning without defining the relationship between Western things and their own. The difference was that, after the Meiji Restoration, the ethics/technology problematique was eventually abandoned, whereas, until the May Fourth Movement, the Chinese could not be free from having to define the relationship between Chinese and Western learning.

The metaphysical/physical (*tao-ch'i*) relationship frequently discussed together with principle/utility (*t'i-yung*) was also a formula designed to resolve the question of how Chinese traditional values and Western culture and institutions were to be related to facilitate the introduction of Western learning into China. Its significance lies in that it was to resolve the conflict between Western learning and Chinese learning by stressing the universality of *tao*. According to this formula, since the West has ethical standards of its own, the West also possesses *tao*. "Phenomenal things" (*ch'i*) was also a category common to both China and the West. The essence of *tao-ch'i lun* was to accept Western phenomenal things without resistance by attempting to realize a universal metaphysical truth through such phenomenal things from the West. In this way the conflict between China and the West could be resolved.

CHAPTER FOUR

The Theory of Political Feudalism in the Ch'ing Period

From the very beginning of centralized bureaucracy in China, even before the establishment of the Ch'in empire in the third century B.C., statesmen debated the relative merits of the feudal (*feng-chien*) and bureaucratic (*chün-hsien*) governmental systems. The study of these debates is important in understanding the evolution of Chinese political thought in modern times. It is also important because the idea of "political feudalism" played an influential role in the reception of modern Western political systems in the late nineteenth century.

The *chün-hsien* versus *feng-chien* debates revolved around three issues. First, which system was *kung* (public, rule by many, just) and which was *ssu* (private, rule by few, unjust)? The *chün-hsien* system was attacked as *ssu* because it concentrated sovereignty in a single person, while the *feng-chien* system was supported as *kung* because sovereignty was shared by many. Second, which system provided greater longevity for the dynasty? Supporters of both feudal and bureaucratic systems insisted that their particular system was essential for the long life of the dynasty.

The third issue was an extension of the debate over "taking the past as a model" (*fa-ku*), that is, imitating the feudal institutions of the Chou dynasty, versus "affirming the present" (*shih-chin*), that is, accepting the present reality of centralized bureaucratic government. Writers during the Han dynasty argued that, inasmuch as the Ch'in had introduced the *chün-hsien* system and had lasted only a short time, centralized bureaucracy should not be adopted. The historian Pan Ku, for example, argued that the Chou dynasty had survived a long time even in a weakened state because it was a feudal system. Although most Han supporters of the feudal system embraced feudalism in principle, they argued for a compromise between the two systems, reflecting the influence of the bureaucratic system in their own time.

The advantages of the feudal system were also discussed in the Wei-Chin period. The central themes were, again, that it promoted the longevity of the dynasty and that the distribution of sovereignty among several people was essentially more just. Although Lu Chi in his "Wu-teng lun" used the argument of longevity, he brought up another important question: Which system is more liable to cause the people suffering? He noted that only under the feudal system was it possible to "let the people live in peace (*an-min*)." Furthermore, although he rejected private interests as being in themselves immoral, he argued that the question of how to lead private interests in a beneficial direction must be a central issue in the *feng-chien* versus *chün-hsien* debate. Lu Chi's ideas had a considerable influence on the subsequent development of the debate.

In the T'ang dynasty, the debate changed markedly. Supporters of both the feudal and the bureaucratic systems accepted the premise that what constituted good government (*li t'ien-hsia*) did not primarily involve the fate of the dynasty, but instead depended on how much it benefited the people. A just dynasty was no longer defined as divided or undivided sovereignty, but as an administration whose policies were enacted with the welfare of the people in mind. Most important of all, a new theme appeared: that the rulers must be worthy (*hsien-che*), and that this was possible only when they were selected from the literati. The recruitment of officials from among the literati amounted to shared sovereignty, making the system more "public." The concept of ruler had thus become broader than merely the prince and his lords, and included the bureaucratic officials as well.

In the T'ang, there were a few supporters of feudalism, but the supporters of centralized bureaucracy formed an overwhelming majority. In fact, they were the first supporters of the *chün-hsien* system to appear since Li Ssu of the Ch'in dynasty. Li Po-yao, Liu Tsung-yuan, and Tu Yu were representative figures. By contrast, the arguments of the proponents of feudalism were developed only in an extremely limited form. At the base of the T'ang debates lay a sense of history that recognized the change in conditions since the Chou. It was commonly acknowledged that, even if the feudal system were ideal, such a system could not be put into effect at that time.

The development of these debates continued into the Sung period. Although Chu Hsi acknowledged theoretically that the *feng-chien* system could make the empire "public," he insisted that the appointment of the unlearned sons of feudal lords to rule over the people would invite unlimited disaster. He therefore proposed a compromise between feudalism and bureaucracy by suggesting a reform of the bureaucratic system. He advocated the adoption of either the Han dynasty *chün-kuo* system (a mixture of centralized bureaucratic and feudal systems) or the T'ang dynasty *fang-chen* (autonomous military command zones) system.

In sum, it is evident that, from ancient times through the Sung, the issue of feudalism versus bureaucracy had both practical and symbolic importance in the development of Chinese political thought. Not only were concrete problems of the longevity of dynastic regimes involved, but also such intangibles as benefits to the people and the fundamental justness of government. It is not surprising that an issue that embodied such themes should have survived long after there was any practical possibility of returning to the feudal system.[1]

These debates concerning political feudalism continued into the modern period and were crucial to an understanding of the complex history of the late Ch'ing through the early Republican era. Chang Ping-lin, a political essayist of that period, wrote that "the representative system is a variation of the *feng-chien* system,"[2] indicating that the idea of political feudalism was closely associated with the introduction of modern parliamentary thought. Indeed, the traditional debates concerning the *feng-chien* system form the basis for an examination of such important questions as why the idea of local self-government, centering on representative provincial assemblies, came to play such an important role in the unfolding of the arguments for institutional reform (*pien-fa*) and for a constitution. This study will also review related questions. (1) What was the nature of the Ch'ing debates concerning political feudalism? (2) What was the understanding of local self-government in the late Ch'ing? (3) In what manner was the Chinese tradition influenced by Western thought? (4) What was the position of the gentry in both the traditional political order and in the modern reform movement? (5) How did the characteristics of the late-Ch'ing provincial assembly reflect the earlier theories of local self-government?

Only then can we consider the actual organization and activities of the provincial assemblies. This study will provide clues to the role of the gentry, as represented by this institution, in the 1911 Revolution and their advocacy of self-government as late as the Republican period. I hope that it will also aid in understanding, for example, the background for the rivalry among warlords independent of the republic's central government and the argument for a federal system of provincial self-government, thus contributing to a broader grasp of the modern transformation of the gentry.

FENG-CHIEN AS A THEORY OF INSTITUTIONAL REFORM

Major Thinkers of the Ming-Ch'ing Transition

In the aftermath of the subjugation of the Ming by the Ch'ing, scholars such as Ku Yen-wu, Huang Tsung-hsi, and Wang Fu-chih became interested in searching for an approach to a new political system. They turned to the traditional debates concerning the relative merits of the *feng-chien* (feudal) and *chün-hsien* (bureaucratic) forms of government. Generally speaking, Ku and Huang held similar ideas regarding the *feng-chien* system; Wang's position differed. We shall examine Ku Yen-wu's argument first.

In the introductory section of his treatise "Chün-hsien lun," Ku said, "Knowing why the *feng-chien* system was replaced by the *chün-hsien* system, one may well think that the *chün-hsien* system, with all its evils, should be abandoned. Is it possible then to return to the *feng-chien* system? I say it is impossible."[3]

Ku indicated that problems inherent in the *feng-chien* system led to its replacement by a centralized imperial bureaucracy. He noted, however, that the *chün-hsien* system was not without faults. Although he did not elaborate on specific shortcomings, the following comments are worthy of examination:

The failing of the *feng-chien* system was its concentration of power at the local level; the failing of the *chün-hsien* system is its concentration of power at the top. The sage-rulers of antiquity were public-minded in their treatment of all people, parceling out territory to them as fiefs. But now the ruler considers all the realm within the four seas to be his personal domain, and is still unsatisfied. He suspects everyone and personally handles every matter that comes up, so that each day the directives and official documents pile higher than the day before. On top of this he sets up supervisors and governors, supposing that in this way he can keep the local officials from tyrannizing over and harming the people. He is unaware that these officials in charge are concerned only with moving with the utmost caution so as to stay out of trouble until they have the good fortune to be relieved of their posts, and are quite unwilling to undertake anything that might profit the people. Under such circumstances, how can the people avoid poverty and the nation escape debilitation?[4]

Here Ku has indicated that the central weakness of the *chün-hsien* system lay in the fact that a centralized bureaucratic system gave the monarch absolute power, allowing him to monopolize state power and consequently to increase the suffering of the people. Ku did not, however, advocate a complete return to the feudal system. According to him, the replacement of the feudal system by a centralized bureaucracy started not in the Ch'in dynasty but during the declining years of the Chou dynasty. He believed that the collapse of the Ch'in was not due to the *chün-hsien* system itself, because the historical progression toward a centralized bureaucracy was something even the sage-kings could not have resisted. He insisted that it would be impossible to return to the outdated feudal system, but he valued some of the principles of the earlier, decentralized system, such as "treating the empire as a public domain" (*kung t'ien-hsia*), that is, dividing the land among plural rulers. Thus Ku advocated an infusion of feudal principles into the centralized state in order to cope with the shortcomings of the *chün-hsien* system. These shortcomings centered on the setting up of bureaucratic institutions to appropriate the empire for personal rule. By "the infusion of feudal principle" he meant that a number of people would rule, and that their inherent private interests as rulers would lead them to improve the welfare of their own administrative areas, thereby resulting in good government.

Following this general principle, Ku made some concrete proposals for changes in the system. He argued that the status of the county magistrate should be enhanced, since he was the official closest to the people. Ku also advocated making the magistracy inheritable, in order to correspond to the position of the feudal lord under the *feng-chien* system, while abolishing the higher provincial posts, including those of governor and governor general. In this way, he proposed to infuse the spirit of the *feng-chien* system into the *chün-hsien* system. Ku's proposal for an inheritable magistracy carried with it the condition that the post be passed on only to those whose achievements were outstanding.

Ku's proposals reveal that he had faith that local officials with the power to bequeath their posts would cherish the land and the people under their jurisdiction and thus form a good administration. He relied on the belief that it is human nature to look after one's own land and family, and he assumed that the myriad private interests, when coordinated, would bring about the greatest possible good. His prescriptions are highlighted by the elimination of the traditional rule of avoidance, which kept officials from being appointed to their home areas or to areas where their kin resided. He maintained that a magistrate should be selected from among the natives of a locality or those who live "within ten *li*," thus choosing someone who was familiar with the customs of the local people. He also proposed that a magistrate be allowed to appoint his own staff for such posts as deputy assistant magistrate, constable, jail warden, postmaster, granary-keeper, and so on. The sole exception would be the appointment of the assistant magistrate, which would remain with the Board of Civil Office. In addition, Ku suggested that the Board of Civil Office should appoint magistrates and assistant magistrates from among those recommended locally by county people, in conformity with the spirit of the local selection system used in Han times (*hsiang-chü li-hsuan chih*).

Ku Yen-wu's position reflects traditional debates on *feng-chien/chün-hsien* theories such as valuing the institutions of antiquity (*shang ku*) with due regard to present circumstances, treating the empire as a public domain, and giving first consideration to the welfare of the people. On the whole, his proposals concerning the post of magistrate appear to be in line with earlier ideas aiming toward an accommodation between centralized and decentralized models of the state. The difference is that Ku did not take the stability or the longevity of a regime into account in discussing the effectiveness of the government. He may have thought that the continuous rule of a dynasty would be the result of good administration, but this was not a focus in his arguments. Ku's position is characterized by the following points: (1) opposition to the rule of avoidance, part of the core of centralized bureaucratic machinery; (2) restriction of the central power of the bureaucracy by having local magistrates named from among those recommended locally; (3) emphasis on the welfare of people as the main goal of the government. He did not elaborate on the local elite's involvement in the selection of local magistrates, but his proposals would have meant that virtually all lower officials were appointed by the local gentry.

This is the first appearance of a theory of a local self-government, calling for the broadly defined participation of local people in local affairs. It took the form of a discussion about the pros and cons of the *feng-chien* system, and amounted to a reform program affecting the entire autocratic system. The importance of Ku Yen-wu's position should be noted, not only because many similar arguments appeared afterwards, but also because he was frequently referred to even when Western self-government theory came to be associated with traditional arguments about the two different political systems.

Huang Tsung-hsi's views on the *feng-chien* system can be found in several chapters of his famous *Ming-i tai-fang lu* (A plan for the prince). In "Yuan-chün," his chapter on the monarchy, Huang criticized the absolute power of rulers under the centralized *chün-hsien* system and went so far as to say that the most harmful person in the world was the monarch himself.[5] He did not refer directly to the *feng-chien* system, but he indicated his support for the principles of feudalism by setting the "monarchs of ancient times," such as Yao, Shun, and Yun, under the feudal system as against the later rulers under the *chün-hsien* system. Yet the chapter fails to reveal his views on *feng-chien* as a political system, speaking as it does vaguely of the mentality of the monarchs of ancient times who never treated the empire as their personal property.

In another chapter, "Yuan-fa," Huang distinguished between the laws of the Three Dynasties of earlier times and the laws of more recent times, claiming that the former benefited the empire, whereas the latter were simply a means of securing the longevity and stability of the regime. He wrote that, after the period of the Three Dynasties,

what was called the law was the law of only the ruling family, not the law of the whole empire. Thus we see that the Ch'in dynasty replaced the *feng-chien* system with the *chün-hsien* system, by which the empire was made the private property of the emperor... If they do not think deeply and reform all the institutions one by one to recover the ancient systems of *ching-t'ien* (well-field), *feng-chien*, education, and defense, the suffering of the people will not end, even if minor reforms are made.[6]

In his political discussions, Huang Tsung-hsi emphasized the restoration of those earlier systems, but in his concrete programs of reform (like Ku Yen-wu) he did not advocate a full return to political feudalism. He resembles Ku in proposing an eclectic program which attempts to reflect the original ideal of the feudal system while operating within the existing *chün-hsien* system.

In "Fang-chen," the chapter on autonomous military command zones, he said: "Today is far from the time when the feudal system was in effect. But if the current situation is taken fully into account, the *fang-chen* [autonomous military command zones] could be adopted again."[7] Huang acknowledged that both the *feng-chien* and the *chün-hsien* systems had their defects, saying that under the *feng-chien* system the strong were apt to annex the property of the weak and the orders of the emperor might not always be implemented. Under the *chün-hsien* system, on the other hand, the border regions were vulnerable to foreign invasion. Huang proposed the restoration of the *fang-chen* system of T'ang times only in border regions as a complementary means of dealing with the faults of the two systems. *Fang-chen* were administrative units with autonomy in such fields as taxation, political and ethical-religious indoctrination, the appointment of staff members, the inheritance of posts, and defense.

In his chapter on education, Huang argued for the direct participation of the gentry in politics, saying that one of the major functions of the schools should be the discussion of politics, as well as the education of scholars. His intention was that the gentry should be involved in politics through institutionalized channels instead of playing a restricted role—indirectly and individually—in the central and provincial political arena. He believed that this participation would check the possible arbitrary exercise of power under the centralized system. Following Ku Yen-wu, who emphasized the selection of officials by local elites and the political role of *ch'ing-i* (disinterested opinion) by the elite,[8] Huang recommended the re-establishment of these ancient traditions still further. In his chapter on selecting officials, Huang proposed that the prime minister, ministers of the Six Boards, chiefs of *fang-chen* regions, and governors and governors general of all the provinces, in accordance with the original spirit of the *feng-chien* system, "should be given the right to select their own subordinate officials and make trial use of them in their posts, as was the case in the probationary appointment (*she-kuan*) system of old."[9] Here he clearly suggested that the traditional rule of avoidance be abrogated.

Huang's political program, based on criticism of the traditional monarchy and the *chün-hsien* system, aimed at infusing feudal ideals into the centralized bureaucratic system. Generally speaking, it opposed centralization of power and supported local self-government. Huang's advocacy of local self-government was not as well organized as Ku Yen-wu's, emphasizing as it did the role of minor administrative units like *fang-chen* and the independent selection of staff by provincial officials as ways to restrict the centralized power of the monarch. His remarks on political discussions as a function of education apparently indicate his support for the gentry's political participation in national as well as regional affairs. In opposing the rule of avoidance and fearing that the *chün-hsien* system might be used to extend the longevity of a dynasty, Huang agreed with Ku. It is assumed that this is what Ku was referring to when he wrote in the preface to Huang's *Ming-i tai-fang lu* that he agreed with 60 or 70 percent of the opinions it contained. Huang did not, however, achieve the breadth or level of organization that Ku did in his writings on the subject. Nonetheless, it is clear that both Ku Yen-wu and Huang Tsung-hsi turned to the original ideals of the *feng-chien* system in advocating local self-government as a means to curb the arbitrary exercise of monarchal power in the *chün-hsien* system.

In their discussions of political systems, Ku Yen-wu and Huang Tsung-hsi held similar views, but the third great early Ch'ing scholar, Wang Fu-chih, differed from them in his opinions concerning the *feng-chien* and *chün-hsien* systems. In his *Tu t'ung-chien lun*, Wang supported the bureaucratic *chün-hsien* system. He asserted that the *chün-hsien* system was the result of a historical progression and could not be resisted. His discussions centered on the ways of ancient times, as in the following passage:

Wei Cheng, disputing with Feng Te-i, said that if it were true that the people of old were simple and honest but gradually came to be crafty and dishonest, by now all men would be devils. What an excellent remark! The most serious mistake the advocate of a certain theory is apt to make is to get exercised over some passing fad and fret about unlikely consequences, despising every living mortal in the world and thinking himself different from and superior to other people. Hence his mind becomes hard and merciless, and he invokes the artifice of regulations in a way that damages the harmony of nature.[10]

In the passage above, Wang clarified his opposition to the widely held belief that all the best things belong to ancient times, after which the world degenerated as time passed. He said that reforms attempting to restore earlier ways tend to be made by capricious minds, while ignoring the historical necessity for change. Referring to the Han-period discussion of limited landownership, he said that, if the system to restrict the possession of land had been humanly possible, "Wang Mang might have gone beyond Yao and Shun,"[11] indicating that it had been an anti-historical effort. Wang further stated:

The government of a period reflects the times in which it operates . . . It will spoil the whole effort if you imitate one hundred components while rejecting one. Think how much less will be accomplished if one component is adopted and one hundred rejected. It is very foolish to argue that one could successfully return to ancient ways simply by having part of our predecessors' accomplishments reflected in present-day policies.[12]

Wang was saying that it is not only ineffective but harmful to adopt even isolated elements of an ancient system, since every period has its own political institutions. Therefore, Wang claimed, it is impossible to reintroduce the *feng-chien* system, either wholly or partially.

Wang refuted the belief that the *chün-hsien* system began in the Ch'in dynasty, and expanded upon Liu Tsung-yuan's argument that the bureaucratic system is superior to the feudal system in terms of their contributions to the people's welfare and the enlisting of talented members of society into government service. It is possible, he argued, that the bureaucrats may persecute people with maladministration. The plight of the people, however, will be relieved as the bureaucrats, mostly local officials, are removed, whereas the feudal lords are never removed. It is true, he maintained, that the centralized bureaucratic system tends to shorten the ruling period of a dynastic regime, but what is affected is not the public interest but simply the power of the imperial clan.[13] The essence of his argument lies in the fact that he did not express complete support for the absolute power of the emperor. Instead, he showed a deep concern for the welfare of the people and emphasized the historical necessity of a system rather than its contribution to the stability of a dynasty. As for the issue of public versus private in judging a political system, he said:

The reason why the Ch'in dynasty has continued to be criticized generation after generation is none other than the fact that it monopolized the empire. If one returns to the *feng-chien* system in an effort to promote one's own private interests and to pass the domain on down to one's posterity forever, while repudiating the private character of the Ch'in, how can it be said that one is serving the public interest of all people?[14]

Wang was indicating here that neither of the two systems was public in essence but, if compelled to choose one, he asserted that the *chün-hsien* system was more likely to serve the public interest. He also said: "The Ch'in abolished the *feng-chien* system by replacing the feudal lords with bureaucratic officials in the hope of monopolizing the empire, but Heaven took advantage of the Ch'in's pursuit of private interest to achieve public interest."[15]

This passage is only one among many in the *Tu t'ung-chien lun* in which Wang stressed the welfare of the people. We have seen that Ku Yen-wu also distinguished between public and private based upon the people, although Ku came to different conclusions.

The historian Kung-ch'üan Hsiao, comparing Wang's views on political systems with those of Huang and Ku, said: "Huang's and Ku's arguments were reformist in nature, while Wang's resembled the criticism of a scientist or a historian."[16] Given the fact that Wang was not a reformer, it may follow that he was not inclined to argue in favor of the feudal system or its more developed version—the decentralized, local self-government system—which could have been associated with reform programs.

Yen Yuan, a scholar of the seventeenth century, expressed full support for the *feng-chien* system. Using the pen name Ssu-ku-tzu ("Man who yearns for ancient times"), Yen advocated the restoration of the *feng-chien* system and called Liu Tsung-yuan's argument for the *chün-hsien* system "brutal" (*pu-jen*).[17] Yen maintained that the *feng-chien* system could guarantee extended dynastic rule through the use of *fang-chen* command zones, good treatment for the offspring of the sages out of respect for the Heavenly Way, good treatment of meritorious subjects, and effective protection of the general public during periods of war and uprising. He believed that under the *feng-chien* system, since a dynasty is replaced by another according to the Mandate of Heaven, the transition period between dynastic regimes would involve fewer and simpler social upheavals, such as warfare, than under the *chün-hsien* system; the lives of the people would thus be affected to a lesser degree. In general, his argument lacks logic. It is simply an idealistic plea for the revival of the feudal system, referring in part to a full return to ancient systems, and having concern in part for the people's interest.

DEBATES OVER FEUDALISM FROM THE K'ANG-HSI THROUGH THE CHIA-CH'ING ERA

Chu Shu, a *chin-shih* degree-holder of the K'ang-hsi era and a contemporary of Yen Yuan, discussed the relative merits of the *feng-chien* and the *chün-hsien* systems.[18] Chu acknowledged that "a nation's existence does not directly depend upon the style of its polity, that is, whether it employs the *feng-chien* or the *chün-hsien* system." But he said that, if he were to compare the two, he would say that the evils of the *chün-hsien* system exceeded those of the *feng-chien* system. According to Chu, the *feng-chien* system was vulnerable to the annexation of the weak principalities by stronger ones; in contrast, under the *chün-hsien* system it is more likely that a nation would be invaded, that a dynastic regime would collapse, and that the people would live amid disasters and would be in danger of falling under tyranny. Like Huang Tsung-hsi, he preferred the T'ang system as a good compromise between the two. He also referred to the writings of the Sung scholars, Li Kang and Fan Tsung-yin, as well as to Ku Yen-wu's work as examples of good compromise.[19]

Agreeing with Huang Tsung-hsi, Chu Shu believed that the *fang-chen* command zones were the most effective means of protecting a nation from outside invasion. He explained that these zones took advantage of both the self-interest of the commanders and of the general public, who were determined to guard their own land. In reference to the *fang-chen* command zones, Chu wrote in favor of "taking direct advantage of the substance of the *feng-chien* system, but not necessarily calling it that." He also spoke of emphasizing the feudalistic principles within the *chün-hsien* system, as Ku Yen-wu had advocated in his "Chün-hsien lun," but his intention was somewhat different. Chu did not go so far as to advocate the infusion of the *feng-chien* ideals of *kung t'ien-hsia* (treating the empire as a public domain) into the bureaucratic system in a strict sense, but simply argued for the adoption of the *fang-chen* command zones as a complementary measure. It is clear, however, that Chu was critical of the contemporary system, exhibiting an interest in reintroducing divided rule in some of the provincial areas, and that his argument showed the influence of Ku Yen-wu.

The writings of the Yung-cheng Emperor also refer to the debate over the relative merits of the *feng-chien* and *chün-hsien* systems. His argument in favor of the *chün-hsien* system had two aims, namely the restriction of power struggles within the Imperial Court and the suppression of anti-Ch'ing thought.[20] He refuted the writings of *feng-chien* proponents such as Tseng Ching, who said: "*Feng-chien* is the Way of the Sages and the supreme method of controlling the barbarians." The Emperor also argued against Lü Liu-liang, who maintained: "The abolition of the *feng-chien* system was not in accordance with principle (*li*), but was instead necessitated by contemporary conditions (*shih*). As Confucians, we should then reintroduce the *feng-chien* system in order to ward off the despotic ruler who thinks only of private interests."[21] Lu Sheng-nan's criticism of the *chün-hsien* system for its harmful effects on the lives of the people was also attacked by the Emperor.[22]

The Yung-cheng Emperor's argument that the centralized bureaucratic system was a *fait accompli*[23] was apparently based on the T'ang scholar Liu Tsung-yuan's writings. One difference between the two is that the Emperor acknowledged that the *feng-chien* system of the Three Dynasties was "public" in nature, considering the times, while Liu did not recognize any "public" aspect to the *feng-chien* system. It should also be noted that the arguments of Lü Liu-liang, Lu Sheng-nan, and other proponents of the *feng-chien* system were presented as a kind of reform program designed to redress the centralization of power in the person of the Emperor, while claiming to be a manifestation of the Way of the Sages. These men, like Ku Yen-wu and Huang Tsung-hsi, supported a limited decentralization of power.

The argument of Kung Chien-yang (a censor of the Yung-cheng era commissioned to the Shantung circuit) deserves our attention. He advocated the establishment of a localized *hsiang-kuan* (canton-official) system. Kung never mentioned the words *feng-chien* and *chün-hsien*, but his criticism of the rule of avoidance and of the centralization of power indicated his knowledge of the debate concerning the two types of political systems. Kung proposed that four cantons (*hsiang*)— east, west, north, and south—be established under the magistrate or deputy magistrate of each department (*chou*) and county (*hsien*), and that one official be named for each canton, selected from among the local gentry, including those who held official degrees and academic titles such as: metropolitan graduate (*chin-shih*), provincial graduate (*chü-jen*), senior licentiate (*kung-sheng*), student of the Imperial Academy (*chien-sheng*), and licentiate (*sheng-yuan*), as well as local elders. Ortai, Governor General of Yunnan and Kweichow provinces, raised an objection to Kung's proposal on the grounds that it did not conform to the traditional rule of avoidance. The Governor General expressed the fear that the appointment of local people might result in poor administration, with the power of the magistrates reduced and the danger of influence-peddling by petty officials increased.[24]

Compared with earlier reformers, Kung called for the least reform possible within the category of the *chün-hsien* system. He did not go so far as Ku Yen-wu, who advocated the immediate replacement of magistrates who had been named according to the rule of avoidance, substituting local people in their place. It should be noted, however, that Kung called for the abolition of the rule of avoidance in order to deal with the defects of the *chün-hsien* system, arguing for the institutionalization of the local gentry's participation in local administration. In fact, his proposal for the appointment of canton officials, the lowest-level officials within local administration, from the literati, including *chin-shih* degree-holders, was in itself a significant reform program, since it meant that the qualifications and status of magistrates and prefects would be enhanced. It is not certain whether or not Kung was influenced by Ku Yen-wu's reform program for local administration, but similar proposals to reform the rule of avoidance by Feng Kuei-fen and Yang Hsiang-chi are clearly influenced by Ku's writings.

Yuan Mei, a poet of the Ch'ien-lung era, wrote an essay dealing exclusively with the *feng-chien* and *chün-hsien* systems.[25] A strong advocate of *feng-chien*, Yuan frequently criticized Liu Tsung-yuan's argument that local power centers could become difficult to govern by a central authority (*wei-ta pu-tiao,* lit., "the tail is too big to wag"). Yuan's position is distinct from those of other advocates of the decentralized system in that he completely disregarded the generally accepted claim that the *feng-chien* system contributed to the stability and longevity of a dynasty. Yuan emphasized instead that *feng-chien* was a system in the interest of the people, saying that "the love of the ancient sage-kings for the people was greater than their love for their own sons and daughters." He also said that the sages had established the *feng-chien* system based on the theory of the Mandate of Heaven (*ko-ming lun*), so that "the wise will flourish, while the unwise will perish," in accordance with the Mandate of Heaven. Unlike Huang Tsung-hsi, who argued for the rule of law, Yuan declared that "it is men who rule, not laws."

It appears that the merits of the *feng-chien* system as he saw it lay in the very existence of the wise ruler and the consequent beneficial effects on the welfare of the people. Underlying this view is his unique understanding of the theory of the Mandate of Heaven. Considered in light of present knowledge, the principle that the wise prosper but the unwise perish could have been applied not only to the *feng-chien* system but also to the *chün-hsien,* since revolutions took place under both. But Yuan preferred to link the merit principle only with the *feng-chien* system, seemingly because he assumed that a benevolent ruler does not necessarily arise from the *chün-hsien* system. He said:

In those times, if the emperor was not benevolent, there appeared [such eminent rulers as] T'ang and Wu to take his place. And if a feudal lord was not benevolent, there emerged [such great leaders as] Lord Huan of Ch'i and Lord Wen of Chin. In this way, if there is one benevolent leader among a multitude of states, the people can retain hope.[26]

In weighing the relative merits of political systems, Yuan did not consider their contributions to the stability and longevity of a dynastic regime. Consequently, the argument of *wei-ta pu-tiao* became meaningless to Yuan. He took a negative view of the presence of Duke Ch'i and Duke Sung under the Chou dynasty. These two lords were frequently cited by other *feng-chien* proponents as examples of the value of the *feng-chien* system in keeping royal lineages alive in succeeding dynasties.

Some of its critics blamed the *feng-chien* system for its failure to esteem sages like Confucius and Mencius (because neither sage was a descendant of a feudal lord). Yuan claimed that this low regard for these sages was not because of the political system itself, but because the Way had not yet been realized. He maintained that the decentralized system of *feng-chien* made Confucius and Mencius famous for their itinerant teaching among the feudal states. If they had been born under the *chün-hsien* system, they might have failed in the examinations and so come to nothing. (Here Yuan displayed his critical view of the examination system.)

Yuan Mei's argument differed from the views of other *feng-chien* supporters in that it did not advocate institutional reforms, but focused instead on moral standards. Yuan placed the rule of good leaders above the rule of law. As in the case of Yen Yuan, his argument for the *feng-chien* system did not develop into an institutional reform program. Thus it is possible to divide the *feng-chien* advocates into those who were motivated by moral reasons and those who argued for the reform of institutions.

Liu Hung-ao of the Chia-ch'ing era supported the *chün-hsien* system in his writings,[27] with an argument apparently based upon those of Liu Tsung-yuan of the T'ang and Su Shih of the Sung. Liu Tsung-yuan had stated that the *feng-chien* system was the inevitable result of contemporary conditions and did not, as the ancient sage-kings had wanted, make the empire a public domain. Liu Hung-ao claimed that Heaven had ordered the abolition of the *feng-chien* system which human effort could not resist. Liu Hung-ao's "Heaven" and Liu Tsung-yuan's "contemporary conditions" seem similar, but a close examination reveals a difference. Liu Hung-ao felt that, if there was a virtuous emperor, there would be a just government, regardless of the political system.

It was generally accepted, however, that there had been sages only during the early Three Dynasties period. How, then, did Liu Hung-ao deal with the *chün-hsien* system, which developed later? Liu's opinion on this point can be summed up by his observation that, under the *chün-hsien* system, a revolt is possible only when the monarch is thoroughly immoral, whereas under the *feng-chien* system even slightly immoral behavior in the monarch can lead to rebellions. Thus, he believed that the *chün-hsien* system was the less desirable of the two, but was the only realistic policy.

He was doubtful about the alleged effectiveness of the *feng-chien* system in defending the empire against the barbarians and about the value of the enfeoffment of one royal clan as a means of extending the reign of a dynasty. He also refuted Yen Shih-ku's theory of a mixed feudalistic and bureaucratic system in which the power of the feudal lords was restricted. Liu argued that feudal lords could not aid in the defense of the imperial household if they had too little power. Also, if the enfeoffed lords were unwise, the people had no way to air their grievances. In contrast, Liu claimed that under the *chün-hsien* system ill-treated people could file petitions in the court in the morning and see the officials punished the same evening. Liu may have appeared to advocate rule by men rather than rule by law, but the reverse is in fact true. Since his argument focused too much on the ideological aspects of the two systems rather than the political or institutional aspects, Liu seems to have failed to develop an institutional reform program.

DEBATES OVER FEUDALISM IN THE LATE NINETEENTH CENTURY

An argument that can be connected with traditional discussions about the *feng-chien* system appears in the writings of Feng Kuei-fen. Feng's argument was not exclusively concerned with which system, *feng-chien* or *chün-hsien*, was better, yet it related closely to the feudalistic system as we see in his "Fu hsiang-chih i" (On the reinstitution of local posts).[28] In this essay, he made an issue of the concept of division (*fen*) versus unity (*ho*) in political institutions, called for the establishment of additional indigenous local posts and the reform of the rule of avoidance, and discussed the principles of the feudalistic and bureaucratic systems, referring to Liu Tsung-yuan and Ku Yen-wu.

Feng's argument drew a great deal of attention during the late Ch'ing dynasty. A number of his proposals appeared in reform programs of that period, when local self-government and institutional reforms were the chief topics of discussion. His reform programs, which were aimed against the centralized bureaucratic system, are found in various chapters of *Chiao-pin-lu k'ang-i*. In "Fu hsiang-chih i," he wrote:

Those who reign might form a divided administration (*fen-chih*) as well as an integrated administration (*ho-chih*). Without an integrated administration, it is impossible to treat millions of people equally and unite them through a uniform policy, and so conflicts arise across the empire. Without a divided administration, it is impossible to pursue a uniform policy and hope to see it extended to millions of people, and so the empire falls into disorder.... Integrated government under the *feng-chien* system is not as stable as that under the *chün-hsien* system. Therefore, the *feng-chien* system cannot last long, but the *chün-hsien* system can endure.[29]

It seems that he recognized the superiority of the *chün-hsien* system, but went on to say: "The emperor alone cannot rule over the whole empire; he must delegate some of his administrative power to high-ranking local officials ... Even the county magistrate cannot govern his county single-handedly, but must depend on his subordinates. Such is the principle of dividing and then governing the empire."

Feng was saying that the *chün-hsien* system, though primarily an integrated system protecting the monarch's private interests, also contained the principle of divided administration, originally an ideal of the *feng-chien* system. He agreed with Wang Fu-chih that the Ch'in rulers abolished the *feng-chien* system for their private interest, and Heaven took advantage of this self-interest in order to realize public interest for the whole empire. Feng did not, however, discuss the philosophy of political systems as Wang had.

As part of his reform program, Feng made an issue of the fact that the system of divided administration by bureaucrats had not been fully translated into action. Thus, like Ku Yen-wu, he relied on the self-interest of local officials, calling for the political participation of the local gentry in their home areas as a means of carrying out the intentions of divided administration. And, as we have seen, he proposed streamlining the provincial hierarchy by establishing new local posts. The highlight of his proposal was that low-ranking officials (*kuan*) such as assistant magistrates should help the prefectural and county magistrates, and that the residents of every canton (*hsiang*) should nominate *cheng-tung* (directors-in-chief) and *fu-tung* (assistant directors) in proportion to the population of the canton. Although these directors would not be allowed to set up offices as officials, they would handle litigation, collect taxes, and generally cooperate with the magistrate's administration. They would be appointed from among *sheng-yuan* or *mu-yu*, and the functionaries below them would be selected from among the commoners.

Upon minute examination, Feng's proposal concerning a local hierarchy appears closer to Kung Chien-yang's writings than to Ku Yen-wu's. But the general principles behind his reform proposal are much the same as Ku's in that both stress the participation of the gentry in local administration and the nomination of low-ranking officials or functionaries by local residents. Feng proposed that high-ranking officials, both in the capital and in the provinces, be chosen through a formal selection process.

Specifically, he recommended that officials serving outside the capital be chosen from among low-ranking officials ranging from sub-prefects to assistant county magistrates who had been nominated by metropolitan officials or higher gentry of the respective provinces, and by the *sheng-yuan* and gentry directors in each canton.[30] He even went farther to propose the nomination and promotion of metropolitan officials by the majority recommendation of all officials. Feng advocated *ch'en shih chih fa,* or the submission of poems to inform the rulers of local conditions, in order to enable local degree-holders such as *chü-jen, kung-sheng, sheng-yuan,* and *chien-sheng* to express their opinions. He also argued for the abolition or reform of the rule of avoidance. Both these proposals followed his local self-government theory, in conformity with the spirit of divided administration.

There are a number of modern scholars who regard Feng Kuei-fen's argument in "Fu hsiang-chih i" as a combination of the Sung-Ming institution of the local covenant and the Western local self-government system, or the practices of Westerners in the Shanghai concessions.[31] Further studies are necessary before we can conclude that Feng had an understanding of and was influenced by the local self-government theories of the West. Nonetheless, it is certain that Feng's argument played an important role in the development of theories of local autonomy in the late Ch'ing period.

Yang Hsiang-chi,[32] a contemporary of Feng Kuei-fen, held views similar to those of Feng and Ku Yen-wu. Yang said, "Though it is impossible to restore the *feng-chien* system, it must be acknowledged that it was an excellent method of government." He called for introducing into the *chün-hsien* system the *feng-chien* ideal of local people taking part in local administration. His detailed recommendations included giving private secretaries (*mu-yu*) to officials and assistants to county and departmental magistrates, with the opportunity of promotion up to the post of magistrate depending on merit. This suggestion meant, in effect, that the magistrate selected his own staff members (after the *feng-chien* ideal), since private secretaries were not subject to the rule of avoidance and were employed by the magistrate. By doing so, administration would not be seriously hampered, even if the magistrate happened to be unfamiliar with the local situation under his jurisdiction. Furthermore, the machinations of the professional clerks would be discouraged. In fact, it was an important task of the local administration under the Ch'ing to incorporate the private secretaries into the official administrative system;[33] it was believed that including them in the official hierarchy could serve to improve local administration by freeing the magistrate from the expenses otherwise necessary to hire secretaries privately. In this way, the magistrate's economic difficulties would be alleviated, and he would not have to exact illegal levies. Such officially incorporated secretaries could be deputized by the magistrate to assume some of his duties with responsibilities, including certain aspects of legal procedures, unlike the common practice that exempted private secretaries from taking any responsibilities for the decisions they made.

Yang noted that the basic advantage of incorporating private secretaries into the official administrative system was that it would facilitate the original goal of the *feng-chien* system. He said: "Since the magistrate's home county is under his own jurisdiction, he is directly concerned with the good and bad deeds of the people he governs. Therefore, he will not dare to conduct cruel and dishonest policies. Since every man values those things connected to himself, the magistrate will strive to maintain close relationships with those among whom his descendants will live."[34]

Here Yang meant that the self-interest of local magistrates could be used to further the public good, conforming to the original goal of the *feng-chien* system as Ku had already advocated. Of course, his argument for the appointment of private secretaries to official posts accords with the original spirit of the *feng-chien* system. Yang's argument differs slightly from Ku's in that it does not directly mention the centralized system, but was meant to be a reform program aiming toward administrative efficiency.

Tai Wang,[35] also of the T'ung-chih period, refuted Ku Yen-wu's "Chün-hsien lun," arguing that the *feng-chien* system can be put in practice only where the *ching-t'ien* (well-field) system is already in effect and that hereditary officials are not compatible with modern bureaucratic administration. Tai believed that truly self-reliant local government was impossible under the *chün-hsien* system because of the difference in size, revenue, and expenditures among the prefectures and counties. There would be no practical way to correct illegal or unjust acts by hereditary officials if the *ching-t'ien* system were not in effect. There would also be the danger of revolts, skirmishes between counties, and conflicts among family members.

Tai meant that autonomy on the county level was impossible because of the financial inequality and weakness of the small administrative units, unlike the *fang-chen* headed by *chieh-tu-shih* in the T'ang. Tai's argument resembles Wang Fu-chih's, but it was presented as a criticism of the political system's feasibility, rather than as an objection to its principles.

Yü Yueh, who lived during the T'ung-chih and Kuang-hsu periods, advocated a mixed feudalistic and bureaucratic government. He said: "The *feng-chien* system should be implemented in accordance with the principles of the *chün-hsien* system, while the latter should be complemented by the principles of the former . . . If the two systems are used in combination, there will be no trouble."[36]

He also noted that the original *feng-chien* system contained the principles of the *chün-hsien* system within itself. He argued that this was shown in the establishment of administrative units in the area around the capital such as *hsiang* and *sui* and the appointment of some officials from outside the capital area. He thought, however, that the system had degenerated after the Spring and Autumn period. In addition, he said that the Ch'in dynasty had fallen, not because it adopted the *chün-hsien* system, but because it depended on it exclusively. Yü pointed out that, during the Sung dynasty, the presence of the Che family of Ho-tung and the Li family of Ling-wu had a significant bearing upon the destiny of the dynastic regime. Thus, he indicated that it was desirable to combine the two systems, *chün-hsien* for the interior and *feng-chien* for the border regions, as Ku Yen-wu and Huang Tsung-hsi had advocated. It appears that Yü was influenced by Ku's and Huang's arguments, at least in principle. But Yü's position cannot be determined fully, since he referred to the establishment of *fan-chen* administrative units without presenting concrete measures to implement his proposal.

During the Kuang-hsu period, Liang Ch'i-ch'ao presented an argument on this theme in the form of a commentary on the student political debates at the academy where he taught after he fled to Japan in 1898. He discussed the two systems from a purely theoretical point of view without relating them to the movement for local self-government in which he was a leader. It is difficult, since his presentation was for the education of students, to associate his position on the relative merits of the political systems with a reform program.

Liang's comments on the political discussions of Feng Ssu-luan, Feng Mao-lung, Cheng Yun-han, and other students generally followed Liu Tsung-yuan's argument, stating that the two political systems were designed to cope with different conditions, but that neither was truly "public" government (*kung-chih*), since the *feng-chien* system supported the private interests of many, while the *chün-hsien* system worked for the private interests of one person—the Emperor. The general commentary, the author of which must be Liang Ch'i-ch'ao, stated that the weakness of the *feng-chien* system lay in the fact that the people suffered from frequent wars and conflicts, unlike the *chün-hsien* system under which people lived more stable lives. He argued, however, that the *feng-chien* system would ultimately bring better conditions, since feudal states are necessarily in competition. He wrote:

Each feudal lord makes efforts to form a good administration and, in the hope of building a strong country, attempts to raise the educational level of the people. They compete with each other to recruit talented men, and as a result succeed in drawing many into public service. Freedom of both thought and speech is thus secured, and all kinds of new academic theories and techniques flower ... When the empire is united by the *chün-hsien* system, there is no longer the threat of foreign invasion. The emperor then concentrates on preventing uprisings by his own subjects. Standards for the selection of officials are established by civil service examination, which makes fools of the people (preventing them from developing their own talents freely), wastes their talents, and inhibits the development of their intelligence. This is inevitable under the *chün-hsien* system. It is therefore impossible to make an easy generalization about the merits and demerits of the two systems based on one aspect alone.[37]

The reference here to the recruitment of talented men for public office appears to describe the conditions during the period of Spring and Autumn and the Warring States. This observation, however, does not seem to match the prototype of the *feng-chien* system, and, moreover, appears to contradict the subsequent description of the ill-treatment of the people by the nobility under the *feng-chien* system. The statement that, under the *chün-hsien* system, the ruler concentrates on the prevention of internal revolts harks back to the ideas of Ku Yen-wu and Huang Tsung-hsi. Though the final statement is inconclusive, the underlying message is that the development of education and the people's intelligence is, in the end, more valuable than the people's welfare. This statement corresponds to Liang's dedication to the enhancement of the educational level of the people and to the introduction of Western thought and learning.

It is important to note here that, when Liang was serving at the Hunan Shih-wu Hsueh-t'ang (Academy of Current Affairs) before the 1898 Reform Movement, he recommended to Ch'en Pao-chen, Governor of Hunan province, that he make Hunan an autonomous province. Liang proposed the adoption of reformist policies within the limitations of the province's existing capability for autonomy, following the model of enlightened government in the West. He wanted at least to preserve Hunan, even if China should someday perish.[38] Considering the early date of his proposal, it was a daring recommendation for the times. Liang's general position seems to have been motivated by recognition of the *chün-hsien* system's inability to adapt to contemporary conditions, coupled with his aspirations for China's political and cultural development based on provincial federalism.

At first glance, the Ch'ing debates concerning the *feng-chien* and *chün-hsien* systems seem to be as diverse as those of preceding dynasties. One difference is that there were very few advocates of a combination of the two systems before the Ch'ing, when this became the dominating position. In earlier periods, arguments for the *chün-hsien* system were generally characterized by a more liberal political philosophy (than those for the *feng-chien* system), by adaptations to contemporary conditions, and by criticisms of the dominant political ideal of the past. In the Ch'ing period, however, eclecticism based on the affirmation of *feng-chien* principles took on a more progressive nature, in terms of both the reforms advocated and the critical attitude toward the centralized monarchy.[39]

Among those positions summarized in the preceding pages, supporters of the *chün-hsien* system included Wang Fu-chih, the Yung-cheng Emperor, and Liu Hung-ao, while Yen Yuan, Lü Liu-liang, Lu Sheng-nan, Yuan Mei, and Tai Wang advocated a return to the *feng-chien* system. Ku Yen-wu, Huang Tsung-hsi, Chu Shu, Kung Chien-yang, Feng Kuei-fen, Yang Hsiang-chi, and Yü Yueh could be placed in a third group; although they accepted the *chün-hsien* system as historical fact, they called for infusing the centralized bureaucratic system with the feudal system's proclivity toward local self-government. Their proposals included varying degrees of autonomy in local administration, the appointment of magistrates from among local people, independent selection by magistrates of their own assistants, the participation of the gentry in local administration, the public selection of magistrates by the local gentry, and the establishment of the *fang-chen* system. Liang Ch'i-ch'ao could also be considered a member of the third group. Thus, the majority advocated an eclectic combination of the *feng-chien* and *chün-hsien* systems, a significant difference from the philosophical climate before the Ch'ing, when one of the two systems held more attraction, depending on the period. For example, the *feng-chien* system was most popular during the pre-T'ang period, while the *chün-hsien* system held sway in the T'ang and Sung periods, as I have shown in my earlier study of the pre-Ch'ing debates on political systems.[40]

Almost all discussions of the *feng-chien* and *chün-hsien* systems during the Ch'ing period were presented not merely as philosophical debates, as in previous periods, but primarily as the basis for reform programs which would affect contemporary situations. The call for local self-government centering around local assemblies, for instance, was one such reform program around the turn of the twentieth century. In order to understand the unfolding of constitutionalism in China, we must explore the relationship between the traditional debates on political systems and the late-Ch'ing advocacy of local self-government.

LATE-CH'ING DEBATES ON LOCAL SELF-GOVERNMENT

The Boxer Rebellion motivated Empress Dowager Tz'u-hsi and her conservative supporters, who had until then stubbornly resisted reform programs, to attempt institutional reforms themselves. In the inauguration of the new administration in 1901 (influenced also by later developments such as the Russo-Japanese War of 1904–1905), the adoption of a constitution, which had been of utmost importance to the reformists, became a generally accepted goal. The only question was how and how quickly this goal could be reached. The provincial assemblies (*tzu-i-chü*), the final outcome of the local self-government theories of the Ch'ing, were a product of this period, together with the hectic debate on the parliamentary system and the constitution.

How did the traditional debates about the *feng-chien* and *chün-hsien* systems influence the constitutional programs of reform (before and after the 1898 Reform Movement) in the direction of local self-government, leading finally to the establishment of the provincial assemblies? In the early 1880s, scholars came to attach greater importance to political questions than to scientific and technological knowledge. This preference was coupled with a tendency to introduce Western scientific learning with far-fetched explanations attributing the origins of Western scientific and technological knowledge to the Chinese classics.[41] The new interest in Western political systems grew from the realization that at the root of Western wealth and power lay something more than science and technology. From the 1890s on, the parliamentary system, the core of Western political philosophy, became one of the essential items in reform programs. Aided by the explanation that it embodied the true intentions of the Chinese sages of old, the parliamentary system came to be supported by a growing number of people. As a result, from about the time of the Sino-Japanese War (1894–1895), the theory of reform became a topic in itself.[42] Among the early writings mentioning the parliamentary system were: *Ho-chung-kuo shuo* (On the United States) by Liang T'ing-nan, who had lived through the Opium War; *Ch'eng-ch'a pi-chi* (Notes from a mission of inquiry)[43] by Pin-ch'un, who toured Western countries in 1866; and *Li-tse hu-yen* (Unrestrained observations from one of limited experience), written in the late 1880s by Chang Tzu-mu. Chang spoke of Western parliaments in relation to the "intention of the sages," yet stopped short of giving them a positive evaluation.[44]

K'ang Yu-wei's first memorial to the Emperor in 1884 is noteworthy in that it was a precursor of his later political programs.[45] This memorial emphasized three principles of reform: *pien ch'eng-fa* (changing established institutions), *t'ung hsia-ch'ing* (knowing the feelings of those below), and *shen tso-yu* (taking care in selecting assistants). It did not propose a concrete reform program. "Changing established institutions" is a theoretical statement on the possibility of reform, especially of political systems. "Knowing the feelings of those below" is concerned with problems in communication channels between the ruling and the ruled. K'ang wrote, "The establishment of posts for advisory and consultant officials should be increased, and experienced and wise men should be enlisted from across the empire to collect the opinions of the people." By "taking care in selecting assistants" K'ang meant that public officials should be cautious in choosing their aides and advisers. In view of his advocacy of reform, we can assume that K'ang was suggesting that assistants be of the reformist persuasion. It is apparent that he provided the basis for ensuing arguments for the establishment of a national assembly by speaking of institutional reform and many consultant officials. The mention of "taking care in selecting officials" may reflect a desire to guarantee his faction's participation in the reform movement.[46]

K'ang's first memorial also mentions *chou-hsien* (department and county) administration. It criticizes the selection process for department and county magistrates, saying that the appointments were too easily made, considering their heavy responsibilities, and that there were no adequate advisory systems. K'ang also indicated that the procedures for selecting the magistrates were far from the "proper way of government." This memorial led finally to K'ang's local administration reform proposals, colored by local self-government theory, which included a call for raising the status of the magistrates, the participation of gentry through local parliaments, and the abolition of the rule of avoidance. His program also included a renovation of the traditional examination system.

In his *Tung-yu t'iao-i* (Itemized proposals from an eastern tour), written in 1890, Ch'en Ch'iu set forth a variety of reform programs, including the adoption of a parliamentary system.[47] In addition to the establishment of a parliament to respond to the people, Ch'en's prescriptions included the opening of *pin-kuan* (lit., "guest houses") to facilitate a talent search; the rearrangement of the hierarchy of lower-level officials, including assistant magistrates and secretaries to the prefect, by subdividing their duties; and the expansion of the private-secretary (*mu-yu*) system to help rectify general problems of administration. Underlying all these reforms was the parliamentary system, seen as a source of wealth and power, as shown in Ch'en's remarks that "the secret of the West's wealth and power lies in the streamlined communication of feelings and opinions between the upper and lower classes through the parliament," and that "all the other reforms are therefore subsidiary."

The parliament Ch'en envisioned was not for national administration and affairs, but was instead an institution to be established in each provincial administration unit to advise prefects and local magistrates. He suggested that the parliament consist of delegates from the local gentry and merchant classes, who would be chosen for the excellence of their programs to promote local interests. Ch'en proposed that the most unassuming, honest, and proficient of the parliamentary members be named private secretaries to magistrates and prefects and be given the right to deal with the details of administration traditionally undertaken by professional clerks. It is apparent that Ch'en proposed the parliamentary system as a way of reforming the administrative system, especially on the provincial level.

In *Ching-shih po-i* (Wide-reaching statecraft proposals),[48] written in 1892, Ch'en suggested that a national parliament be established in the capital, with its members selected from among the bureaucrats of the Six Boards, going a step beyond the proposals in *Tung-yu t'iao-i*. Of course, he also mentioned parliaments on the county level, which would serve to improve local administration. His explanation here of the county parliament was more elaborate than the *Tung-yu t'iao-i*, yet his conception of the local parliament was that it would be nothing more than an advisory organ for local magistrates. He also argued for increased respect for local magistrates, saying that, "if we are to speak about ways to promote wealth and power, we must first come to respect the local magistrates." As for concrete measures, Ch'en proposed that magistrates be given assistants to deal with official memorials, which would both alleviate the work load and also reduce the possibility of interference in the memorials to the magistrates. In addition, Ch'en suggested that the rank of county magistrate be raised from the 7th to the 5th grade. Also noteworthy is his statement that contemporary magistrates corresponded to the feudal lords of old, meaning apparently that the magistrate should be given prestige and autonomy comparable to that of a feudal lord.[49] Ch'en's *Chiu-shih yao-i* (Important proposals to save the nation) does not differ significantly from his *Ching-shih po-i*, published at approximately the same time, or other essays. In *Chiu-shih yao-i*, he spoke of "the opening of parliament," but he did not mention a national parliament, as in *Ching-shih po-i*.

Another important essay, which will help in our understanding of Ch'en's argument for a parliament, is "Chih-p'ing san-i" (Three proposals for orderly administration),[50] written in 1883 but not published until 1893, when it appeared in the collection called *Chih-p'ing t'ung-i*

(General discussion for orderly administration). The essay included comments on the ancient clan system, the feudal system, and the unified state. Its main point was that the *feng-chien* system can be implemented only after the ancient clan system is put in practice. By *feng-chien*, he meant a system in which the existing provincial administrative units—province, prefecture, department, and county—would be transformed into a system of feudal states governed by dukes, marquises, counts, viscounts, and barons, according to their size; political decisions would depend on the majority opinion of the bureaucrats; and the feudal lords would be given wages from the central government. His argument for the *feng-chien* system was presented as a program for reform within the framework of the existing system: The hierarchy of administrative units would continue in relationships among the feudal states, and feudal lords would be given stipends in the same manner as bureaucrats. Thus, Ch'en's program does not deviate much from Ku Yen-wu's incorporation of the *feng-chien* system into the *chün-hsien* system.

There are some scholars who claim that the argument in "Chih-p'ing san-i" was not developed further by Ch'en,[51] but it appears to me that all his later proposals, especially the *feng-chien* system, originated in this essay. For example, *Tung-yu t'iao-i*, *Ching-shih po-i*, and *Chiu-shih yao-i* all advocated the parliamentary system, particularly on the provincial level. Starting from the *feng-chien* argument emphasizing administration by majority opinion, Ch'en developed this notion into the idea of a central bureaucratic assembly and provincial parliaments. It should be noted that *Ching-shih po-i* was influenced by Feng Kuei-fen's *Chiao-pin-lu k'ang-i*, and that Ch'en's views on the clan system and the *feng-chien* system, as seen in "Chih-p'ing san-i," are very similar to Feng's.[52] Ch'en appears to have combined an affirmation of the *feng-chien* system, taking local autonomy as the basic principle of reform, with Western parliamentarian thought. His reform program, and especially his argument for the parliamentary system, was centered entirely around local administration and local parliaments.

T'ang Chen, in his *Wei-yen* (Words of warning), published in 1890, also advocated the parliamentary system.[53] Stating that "the expansion of communication" (*kuang yen-lu*) was essential in administrative reform, T'ang recommended the imitation of the Western parliamentary system, which he described as an institution that gathers the opinions of people for discussion. T'ang suggested that officials be named as advisory council members, assigned to either the upper or lower house, depending on their rank in court. The Grand Council would be responsible for selecting the members of the upper house, while the Censorate would assume the responsibility of choosing members of the lower house. At the same time, T'ang commented on the situation in the provinces by saying that there should be advisers to the magistrates chosen from among influential local gentry and degree-holders such as *chü-jen, kung-sheng,* and *sheng-yuan.* In this case, it is not clear in what manner the gentry class would participate in the "discussion," but it is certain that he was advocating the participation of the gentry in local affairs through the method of gathering opinions, a variation of the parliamentary system. Another unique feature of his argument is contained in the remark in "Tsun-hsiang lun" (On enhancing the prestige of the ministers) that the ministers and assistant ministers of the Grand Council should be selected by majority vote (of officials), following the example of the Western parliament. This idea is similar to Feng Kuei-fen's recommendation of the election of high-ranking officials.[54]

It is difficult to trace the direct influence of traditional *feng-chien* arguments upon T'ang Chen's thought, but his arguments for the parliamentary system show the influence of Feng Kuei-fen's idea, based primarily, as we discussed above, on an inclination toward the ideal of the *feng-chien* system.

Cheng Kuan-ying, a comprador-merchant from Canton who was well informed about the West, explained in *Sheng-shih wei-yen* (Warnings to a seemingly prosperous age)[55] that the purpose of a parliament was to consolidate the close relationship between the monarch and the people, as well as to win the firm support of the people by "gathering the thoughts of many people and supporting their interests." Accordingly, he suggested that members of the lower house, the organ responsible for legislation, be selected by the people, following a method based on the traditional selection system and complemented by the Western voting system. This is the first reference in Ch'ing times to popular election. As for the election of provincial parliamentarians, Cheng suggested that voting rights be extended only to those of at least thirty years of age who had been residing in the province for ten years or more, and who had a certain amount of property and education.

Cheng refuted the argument that the *i-lang* (imperial councillor) of the Han dynasty and the *tai-chien* (imperial censor) and *yü-shih* (counselor) of the T'ang and later periods were similar to parliamentarians in Western countries. He pointed out that, in traditional China, such positions were granted by the monarch, while Western parliamentarians are chosen by public election. As for the form of government, Cheng stated that he preferred neither a monarchy nor a democracy, but a combination of the two in which the monarch and the people would jointly govern the empire.

Cheng had a clear understanding of the Western parliament, and his argument was better organized than those of other contemporary observers before and after him. Although Cheng referred to the time-honored traditional selection system, and although his argument for voting rights extended only to the gentry class, it is difficult to find any clear indication that his position was based on traditional discussions relating to the *feng-chien* and *chün-hsien* systems. He did emphasize the place of registration in discussing the right to vote, but this cannot be interpreted as indicating a link with local self-government theory. I think that Cheng proposed the parliamentary system as a way to change the form of government, in contrast to other arguments for the parliamentary system, which were generally presented as part of an administrative reform program. Supporting this presumption is the fact that he openly used the phrase *chün-min kung-chu* (joint rule by the monarch and the people) which was popular among reformists in the 1890s.

Ch'en Ch'ih also discussed the parliamentary system in his *Yung-shu* (Mediocre writings),[56] written in 1893 and thus contemporaneous with Cheng's *Sheng-shih wei-yen*. In the chapter entitled "I-yuan" (Parliament), Ch'en described the parliament as a manifestation of "ancient thought" and said that it would ensure China wealth and power comparable to England and the United States by uniting the minds of ruler and ruled, making the monarch and the people one.

The parliament Ch'en envisioned consisted of two chambers, an upper and a lower house. In his formula, the upper house would be a council comprising a group of cabinet ministers or high-ranking administrators; members of the lower house would be selected from among local county officials in a series of elections by the local parliaments at the level of provincial administration—county, prefecture, and province. In other words, he suggested that the lower house, equivalent to the Western parliament, be composed of those local officials elected to the parliament by the gentry and the general public.

In what manner, then, were local officials to be appointed?[57] In his discussion of *hsiang-kuan* (local officials), Ch'en pointed out that Ku Yen-wu criticized the tendency since ancient times toward an overabundance of higher officials[58] and emphasized the need for a larger number of *hsiang-kuan*. Ch'en suggested that every unit of provincial administration (prefecture, department, county) form an assembly with two *hsiang-kuan* elected from each village, "like the Western parliamentary system." Under this program, men eligible to become *hsiang-kuan* were to be at least thirty years old with property of 1,000 taels or more. In addition to participation in administration and judicial affairs, the assembly of local officials would deal with various local affairs, including social welfare, education, and other projects to promote the national interest and help stabilize the lives of the people. Ch'en proposed that, in cases where a magistrate was so unprincipled and grasping that he completely lost the support of the people, the *hsiang-kuan* be empowered to appeal to higher authorities. Normally, magistrates were allowed to control *hsiang-kuan* at will. Ch'en also recommended that competent *hsiang-kuan* be given the opportunity for promotion to higher posts (as magistrates) directly in charge of the local populace.

Ch'en believed that such a *hsiang-kuan* system conformed to the spirit of the traditional local selection system. He called for a repeal of the rule of avoidance and for the institutionalization of political participation by the gentry. Ch'en emphasized the need for a *hsiang-kuan* system by saying that this system would restrain the power of the magistrates, who had become the modern equivalent of the feudal lords of old. They had enough power to make life difficult for the people but not enough to govern well.

Thus, Ch'en chose a compromise between the Western parliamentary system and Ku Yen-wu's proposal to strengthen the position of the local officials in order to check the excessive power of government. His support for the *feng-chien* system's goal of making a "public" world is reminiscent of traditional arguments about the *feng-chien* and *chün-hsien* systems. He stated that "the despotic Ch'in dynasty perished after only two generations, but the rule of the Three Dynasties and the period before that was long." Ch'en attributed this difference to the "private" Ch'in dynasty versus the "public" Three Dynasties. Here he must have envisioned the public character of the *feng-chien* system as comparable to the character of the parliamentary system. For Ch'en, the *hsiang-kuan* system was a demonstration of *feng-chien* principles.

After 1895, proposals for the support of a parliamentary system tended to become more elaborate and better organized. For instance, Ho Ch'i (Ho Kai) and Hu Li-yuan, both familiar with Western culture and customs, wrote as follows in *Hsin-cheng chen-ch'üan* (True explanations of the new policies):

> The founding Emperor of the Ch'in dynasty abolished the *feng-chien* system, replacing it with the *chün-hsien* system. He intended to concentrate the right to handle the affairs of the empire in one person, the Emperor himself. From today's perspective, this was an extremely foolish idea ... Considering the present situation, it is advisable to have local people govern themselves, for this will ensure that local affairs are dealt with correctly and properly.[59]

Rejecting the "private" character of the *chün-hsien* system, they advocated local self-government under the *chün-hsien* system. Their argument was based on the belief that politics should comply with the principles of public interest, as seen their remark that, "if the empire is not 'public,' it cannot be governed well ... The dynasty best known for its rulers' attempts to monopolize the empire is the Ch'in, and next to it is the Sui." Ho Ch'i and Hu Li-yuan evaluated the ancient eras of Yao, Shun, and Kings Ch'eng and K'ang of the Chou dynasty as times of "public" government. They wrote:

> During the Ch'in and Sui dynasties, all power resided with the emperor. During the period of Kings Ch'eng and K'ang of the Chou dynasty, the monarch and the people shared power. In the times of Yao and Shun, the people were the sole holders of power. Thus, the system of government during the period of Yao and Shun was excellent, but during the period of Ch'eng and K'ang it was mediocre, and in the Ch'in and Sui periods, extremely bad.[60]

Theoretically, it seems logical for Ho and Hu to have advocated a return to the *feng-chien* system, but they did not mention it directly, apparently because they recognized that even much earlier Ch'in writers, like Ku Yen-wu, were not advocating a return to the old system, but an adaptation of certain principles using methods appropriate to the times.

Ho Ch'i and Hu Li-yuan distinguished between government for public versus private interests, based on a standard of popular rights rather than governing rights. Instead of arguing for a return to the *feng-chien* system, they proposed "putting into practice the parliamentary system, which can restore popular rights. In "Cheng-ch'üan p'ien," they clearly stated that "to restore popular rights, first of all, a parliament should be established." They felt that, if one attempted to find a means by which the "intentions" of the ancient systems of Yao, Shun, Ch'eng, and K'ang could be realized within the existing centralized system, one had to agree with Ku Yen-wu's prescription calling for "an infusion of *feng-chien* ideals into the *chün-hsien* system" and "taking advantage of private-interest-oriented minds to realize the goal of 'public' government." Regarding this last point, Ho Ch'i and Hu Li-yuan wrote:

If members of a certain family are encouraged in their attachment to their own family, and if people of a local area have a particular concern for their own area, then the people may well value their own country more than any other. And it does no harm for everyone to be particularly concerned with himself. Each person recognizes that the private interests of other people are much the same, and that his own interests cannot be wholly restrained. In this way, the private interests of separate individuals may be integrated into the private interests (of all the people). Thereby, everyone can achieve his private interests, and at the same time the empire is well governed. There is no need to use the word "private" to refer to everyone pursuing his own interests; in fact, the term "public interest" may be proper in this case.[61]

Ho Ch'i and Hu Li-yuan expressed complete agreement with Ku Yen-wu's ideas, but their reform proposals differed somewhat. They advocated the establishment of modern provincial parliaments instead of a system of selecting provincial officials from among the local people, which Ku Yen-wu had supported. This is a typical example of the modern transformation of Ku's ideas.

In their program for the organization of a parliamentary system, they suggested that sixty members be selected for each local parliament on the county, prefectural, and provincial levels, and that members of all the provincial parliaments gather once a year in the capital. A minister (parliamentary leader), selected by the participants and named by the emperor, would preside over the annual meeting. Ho Ch'i and Hu Li-yuan also recommended that members of the county parliaments be elected by the commoners from among the *sheng-yuan*, those of the prefectural parliaments by *sheng-yuan* from among *chü-jen*, and those of the provincial parliaments by *chü-jen* from among *chin-shih*. The right to vote would be given to all men who were at least twenty years old, literate, and familiar with basic Confucian principles, with the exception of cripples, the blind, the dumb, and others having serious diseases.[62] In addition, they refuted the argument for naming high-ranking court officials and censors to the central parliament, saying that it conflicted with the principle of election by the people. The arguments that Ho Ch'i and Hu Li-yuan made for a parliamentarian local self-government system, influenced by the traditional *feng-chien* position, were more elaborate than those of Ch'en Ch'ih. Their proposals were characterized by the institutionalization of gentry political rights and the systematizing of gentry participation in local affairs.

Thus far I have examined the arguments presented primarily before the 1898 Reform Movement and the opinions of those not directly involved in the movement, although their treatises were published after the movement. Now it is time to turn to the arguments regarding the parliament and local self-government proposed by those men who participated actively in the 1898 Reform Movement. This movement laid the groundwork for the widespread demand for a parliamentary system during the following years, and also stimulated a consensus in support of provincial assemblies.

THE 1898 REFORM MOVEMENT AND DEBATES ON LOCAL SELF-GOVERNMENT

On 17 July 1898, Assistant Grand Secretary Sun Chia-nai presented a memorial[63] to the Emperor, which proposed to print Feng Kuei-fen's *Chia-pin-lu k'ang-i* and to distribute it to all government officials, requiring them to submit their opinions on which parts were possible to implement. The programs favored by the majority of officials would be introduced. Sun's memorial was approved the very same day, and Jung-lu, the Governor General of Chihli, was ordered to make 1,000 copies of the book.[64] One week later, the copies were distributed together with an edict calling for the officials' comments.[65] In this way, *Chiao-pin-lu k'ang-i*, which had until then been read by only a limited number of the literati, came to be known widely by the officials of those days. As a result, the book was frequently quoted in memorials calling for reform.

Even before Sun's memorial, *Chiao-pin-lu k'ang-i* had already been presented to the Emperor by Weng T'ung-ho on 6 February 1889. Weng had been impressed enough to record in his diary that the book "is appropriate to the times."[66] Feng's book could not be published on its completion for fear that it might touch on political taboos. The situation had changed so much by 1884 that it was finally published in that year (with a preface by Ch'en Pao-chen)[67] and became widely read.

Sun Chia-nai, in his memorial on *Chiao-pin-lu k'ang-i*, referred to the presentation to the Throne of two books: *Wei-yen* (Words of warning) by T'ang Shou-ch'ien, Magistrate of Ch'ing-yang county, Anhwei, and *Sheng-shih wei-yen* by Cheng Kuan-ying. After reading T'ang's *Wei-yen* in 1895, Weng T'ung-ho commented that the author was "well acquainted with current affairs," and he conferred with T'ang for a long time that day.[68] In addition, on 20 April 1895, Weng presented to the Throne Ch'en Ch'ih's *Yung shu*, together with T'ang's *Wei-yen*.[69] Yeh Ch'ang-ch'ih, in a diary entry dated 20 April 1895, noted that Cheng's *Sheng-shih wei-yen* "was a good description of the social ills of the time."[70] T'ang was ordered, on 21 August 1898, to report to the Throne in person.[71] After reading T'ang's *Wei-yen* on 28 May 1897, T'an Hsien observed that it dealt with major points under discussion.[72] Yang Hsiang-lan, a 2nd-class assistant secretary of the Board of Revenue, quoted *Wei-yen* in discussing the tax system on 20 September 1898.[73]

K'ang Yu-wei, Liang Ch'i-ch'ao, and others[74] were extremely influential around the time of the 1898 Reform Movement, but so were T'ang Shou-ch'ien, Ch'en Ch'ih, and Cheng Kuan-ying. When *Wei-yen*, published in 1890, was being written, Western learning was no longer "a target of attack," but had instead become "essential for officials."[75] During the 1898 Reform Movement, the situation had developed so far that Yang Jui, one of the "six martyrs," said that "the newly empowered group of people talk about a parliament every day, influencing the opinions of the Emperor."[76]

Those involved in the 1898 Reform Movement included a few people with an excellent understanding of the parliamentary system, such as Liang Ch'i-ch'ao, who viewed the parliament as a legislative organ designed to expand popular rights.[77] But memorials of those days generally show that the parliamentary system was seen as a reform program for administration, rather than as an alternative form of government. According to reformers, the parliament was an institution designed to bring about one or more of the following: to increase administrative efficiency by taking more men of talent into government service,[78] to build up a rich and strong nation by having the upper class and lower classes respect each other's rights and by having a just distribution of benefits,[79] to elect ministers by majority vote,[80] to understand the situation below,[81] and to broaden the communication of opinion.[82] Some proponents envisioned the provincial parliament as a lower house with the upper house functioning as a central parliament in the capital. Thus, the parliaments were not seen as independent institutions, but were to be put directly under government control, since the upper house was to be supervised by the Tsungli Yamen (Office of Foreign Affairs), and the lower house was to be under the governor general of each province.[83] The expansion of the Censorate was also considered a means of administrative reform, because it would incorporate the basic principles of both the Han dynasty *i-lang* system and the Western parliamentary system.[84]

Let us now turn to the specifics of the reform proposal formulated by K'ang Yu-wei, the leader of the 1898 Reform Movement. K'ang's first clearly defined argument for the parliamentary system appearerd in his fourth memorial of June 1895, which called for keeping in touch with the situation of the people through a parliament.[85] In his fifth memorial, submitted at the end of 1897, K'ang spoke of "executing national affairs following discussions at a national assembly," and suggested that talented men be recruited across the country to form the assembly.[86] These two memorials used the terms *parliament* (*i-yuan*) and *national assembly* (*kuo-hui*), but he made an indirect reference to the parliamentary system in his earlier, second memorial, the so-called "Kung-ch'e shang-shu" of April 1895. In the second memorial, K'ang referred to the "conference of *i-lang*" of the Han dynasty in calling for the election of one man from every 100,000 households in a prefecture, giving the "conference" of those elected the right to make decisions on national affairs by majority rule.[87] The second memorial, though it did not use the word *parliament*, was more detailed than the fourth and fifth memorials, which mentioned the parliamentary system directly.[88] The election of one man out of every 100,000 households was repeatedly advocated in K'ang's third memorial.[89]

In the fourth memorial, K'ang Yu-wei added a plan for local parliaments to the system of electing one man per 100,000 households. He suggested that assemblies be established on the provincial, prefectural, department, and county levels, and that they be allowed to submit reports to the central parliament, so that the latter would be in touch with the situation of the people as represented by the lower-level assemblies.[90]

K'ang stated his reform program most elaborately in his sixth memorial of 28 January 1898. He suggested that a "civil political bureau" (*min-cheng chü*) be established in every county, where local gentry members would gather to discuss new administrative reform.[91] In this memorial, written when the possibility of his program's being accepted was higher than at any other time, and when he should, therefore, have seriously taken into account the political effects of the memorial, K'ang, ironically, did not mention the central parliament. In earlier memorials, he had suggested that members be elected from every 100,000 households, but here he simply advocated the establishment of "civil government bureaus" at the county level. A clue to his intentions is seen in *Jih-pen pien-cheng k'ao* (A study of the political reform in Japan), written after the sixth memorial and submitted to the Throne of 19 April 1898. In his book he argued that, although it was too early to establish a central parliament, parliaments should be set up in all the lower administrative units—provinces, departments, and counties—in order to "support and propagate the virtuous will of the Emperor and to keep in touch with the feelings of the people."[92] His inclination toward local self-government was also revealed in his proposal that the heads of the "institutional reform bureaus" (*hsin-cheng chü*) be chosen from among the local people and given the right to choose their own subordinate officials.[93] (These "political reform bureaus" would be established in each *tao* or circuit, a new administrative unit which would replace the province in K'ang's scheme.) In *Jih-pen pien-cheng kao*, he also suggested that provincial administrators and magistrates be allowed to choose their own subordinates, free from the rule of avoidance.[94]

In addition, K'ang argued that provincial administrators and magistrates should be promoted in status, given more authority and a freer hand in local affairs, and that their advisers should be chosen from among degree-holders. Such an argument is contained in the first, second, fourth, and fifth memorials.[95] As we have seen, this kind of reform program apparently originated in the call to reform the *chün-hsien* system advocated by Ku Yen-wu, Huang Tsung-hsi, and Feng Kuei-fen. This sort of relationship is clearly seen in K'ang's later treatise *Nan-hai kuan-chih i* (K'ang Yu-wei's discussions of political systems), published in 1903, in which K'ang systematically reviewed parliaments at various levels of local administration. K'ang stated that, generally speaking, local self-government corresponds to the ancient *feng-chien* system and that the autonomy of the local population is demonstrated in open public discussion.[96]

It is clear, however, that the arguments for the *feng-chien* system were not the sole source of K'ang's concern for the autonomy of local administration. In *Jih-pen shu-mu chih* (Index to Japanese publications), written in 1897, he listed seven books on local self-government, including *Eikoku chihō jichi ron* (Local self-government in England) by Yonekane Mizawa, *Chihō jichi ron* (Local self-government) by Matsunaga Michikazu, and *Chihō jichi ronshu* (Collection on local self-government), edited by the German Association of Japan.[97]

K'ang Yu-wei's position resembled Feng Kuei-fen's, especially in advocating the independent selection of subordinates by local administrators, the enlistment of lower-degree-holders as advisers to the magistrates, and the establishment of "civil government bureaus" in order to give the gentry a way to handle local affairs. There are slight differences between the two, as seen in K'ang's argument for the county branch offices of the civil political bureaus, an organization influenced more than Feng's by Western ideas of the parliamentary system.[98]

As we have seen, the traditional rule of avoidance continued to be a target of criticism by Ku Yen-wu and other advocates of the ancient *feng-chien* ideals because it was contrary to the original principles of the *feng-chien* system. The initial proposal of having native people deal with affairs of their own provinces gradually developed into an argument for local self-government, centering around the local parliaments, with the gentry class as the core. Even during the 1898 Reform period, the time-honored rule continued to be a target of criticism by those who sought administrative reforms, resulting eventually in the development of local self-government theories.

A typical view along these lines was expressed in the writings of Yuan Ch'ang.[99] Yuan noted that almost all officials in Western countries were originally recruited from among gentry members of parliament. He claimed that this was the reason the Western countries had become powerful. Yuan said, though, that it was not suitable for China to adopt Western-style popular rights and parliament. Instead, he suggested the selection of provincial administrators (county and prefectural magistrates and higher officials) from among local gentry—defined as those within an area of 500 *li* in diameter—as a compromise between China's traditional systems and the "Western system of selecting government officials by voting in the parliament." He must have been referring to the provincial parliament when he said that it conformed to the spirit of the parliamentary system to select local gentry through elections to be administrators in their home areas. Recalling Ku Yen-wu's argument for "reflecting the spirit of the *feng-chien* system in the *chün-hsien* system," Yuan agreed and called for abolishing the rule of avoidance. Yuan's argument for local self-government was apparently influenced by Ku's position in the *feng-chien* versus *chün-hsien* debates.

Ho Chao-hsun, a second-class assistant secretary of the Board of Works, also requested the abolition of the rule of avoidance and praised the chapter on the abolition of the rule in *Chiao-pin-lu k'ang-i* by Feng Kuei-fen.[100] Ho claimed that, if officials of local origin governed their home areas, they would keep in touch with the situation of the general public.

Aside from the reform proposals centering around the abolition of the rule of avoidance, there were several societies formed with *chü-jen* degree-holders as key figures that inclined toward local self-government. These included Pao-Che hui (Chekiang Preservation Society), Pao-Tien hui (Yunnan Preservation Society), and Pao-Ch'uan hui (Szechwan Preservation Society), all of which were modeled after the Pao-kuo hui (Society for Preserving the Nation). Censor Huang Kuei-chun, one of the obstinate conservatives of those days, criticized these socieities, warning that they might bring about the disruption of the empire.[101] Such regional movements for political reform, initiated by local gentry and metropolitan minor officials from their respective provinces, appear to have been influenced by the general trend toward local self-government, but they were basically designed to prepare for the probable overall collapse of the imperial system.

Liang Ch'i-ch'ao also pointed out the irrationality of the rule of avoidance in connection with the suggestion of Li Tuan-fen that the gentry be given the right to supervise provincial schools. He emphasized that commissioning the local gentry to supervise schools in their own provinces was the "beginning of local self-government."[102] Liang's argument for local self-government explained his active participation in the activities of the Southern Academy as "actually having the scale of a local parliament, despite its name."[103] The Southern

Academy served as a forum for local gentry in attempting to carry out independent political reform in Hunan province and to develop the autonomy of the province in performing the role of a local parliament.[104] The theoretical background of the academy lay in the argument that the expansion of gentry rights and power should precede the expansion of popular rights. The program of study in the Southern Academy included current affairs and the discussion of the reform of administrative programs, fulfilling the purpose of the academy, which was to train local gentry to become members of provincial parliaments or members of parliaments at the department and county levels.

According to Liang, gentry participation in local self-government, by "reviving ancient principles," "adopting Western institutions," and "enhancing local power," would improve the current administrative system, which obstructed communication between the upper and lower classes. "Ancient principles" referred to the complete dependence on local officials up through the Three Dynasties period and the participation of local people in handling local affairs during the Han dynasty. "Western institutions" referred to the independent management of local affairs through the representative system. Liang thought that the excellent system of old had collapsed following the T'ang and Sung dynasties because of the imperial practice of "suspecting and checking subordinates." The rule of avoidance was then instituted, through which all the power was given to the government offices concerned, resulting in poor administration by local magistrates and an indifference among the people to local affairs.[105]

It appears that Liang's idea of local autonomy is clearly in line with the traditional criticism of the *chün-hsien* system by Ku Yen-wu, Huang Tsung-hsi, and others. The argument for increasing gentry power, which follows, can be understood to be in line with the arguments emphasizing local rule, that is, local self-government, made by advocates of the *feng-chien* system.

Parliamentary local self-government and gentry political participation were common features of reformist philosophy in the late Ch'ing period. T'an Ssu-t'ung, who, together with Liang Ch'i-ch'ao, led the radical reform movement in Hunan province, argued for the institutionalization of the functions of the gentry, for they had always dealt with local affairs in the past.[106] He also called for the establishment of parliaments in all administrative units where government offices were established.¹⁰⁷ T'an's argument also included criticism of monarchism as it had been practiced since the Ch'in dynasty, when the monarch had "monopolized the empire,"¹⁰⁸ and criticism of the *chün-hsien* system, both based on Huang Tsung-hsi's *Ming-i tai-fang lu*. It follows that T'an would advocate enhancing the status of local magistrates by having them keep their rank even after retirement, and would also support the recovery of the ancient *hsiang-kuan* system of appointing local administrators from among the native people.¹⁰⁹ Thus, it is not difficult to detect an inclination in T'an toward the *feng-chien* system as a basis for his political ideology.¹¹⁰

When we consider that the arbitrary exercise of power by the emperor since the Ch'in dynasty was an integral part of the *chün-hsien* system, it is no surprise that the reformers wanted to change the established political order and that the question of "private" and "public" as principles of political systems again became a point of debate. Liang Ch'i-ch'ao, who spoke so bitterly of despotic rulers and the *chün-hsien* system that he described them as the "enemies of the people," as T'an did,¹¹¹ declared that monarchism is "private" while democracy is "public."¹¹² This remark shows that arguments for democracy and the parliamentary system developed directly out of traditional arguments for the *feng-chien* system. Democracy here was meant to comprise the parliamentary system in general and, in part, the local self-government system based on it.

We see again, in the lectures given at the Southern Academy by Huang Tsun-hsien,¹¹³ how the case for local self-government and the parliamentary system grew directly out of traditional arguments in support of the *feng-chien* ideal instead of out of the system itself. Huang, one of the most influential proponents of the reform ideas of Liang Ch'i-ch'ao, was a leading activist in the reform movement in Hunan province where the desire for local self-government was strong. He spoke of the advantages of the *feng-chien* system and *chi-i* (listening to public opinion), a traditional practice later associated with the idea of a parliamentary system. Huang claimed that the *feng-chien* system guaranteed the extended longevity of the dynasty, because, if a great political disturbance should occur, opinions would need to be sought from the local literati, and even from the common people.¹¹⁴ He also described the *feng-chien* system in ancient times, saying that the transfer of imperial power was private, but that political systems were, on the other hand, thoroughly public in nature.¹¹⁵ Huang said that the *chün-hsien* system is not only indifferent to the welfare of the people, with all power concentrated in the hands of officials, but also so exacting that the people are oppressed merely by the existence of officials. Therefore, people tend to prefer a society where no officials exist at all to one where the officials are considered a source of trouble. Thus, although the establishment of an official post is, in itself, public in nature, the political entity as a whole is extremely private. In comparing political systems, Huang consistently applied the standards of "public" and "private," which he determined on the basis of the presence of public discussions. He concluded that the main reason for local maladministration under the *chün-hsien* system was the rule of avoidance, since the relevant regulations had been enforced from the Han dynasty onward.

In one of the lectures he gave at the Southern Academy to Hunan gentry, Huang said:

What I ask is nothing more than for you to deal with your own affairs by yourselves and to govern your local areas for yourselves. Carry out what is of benefit and change what is corrupt. The school system should be reformed, new plans for water control should be devised, commerce should be stimulated, agriculture improved, and industry promoted, and security measures ought to be discussed ... All these things are your affairs.[116]

Here, he was asking the gentry to perform their traditional functions within the institutionalized form of local self-government. Huang believed that local self-government led by the gentry would introduce the good qualities of the *feng-chien* system, in which hereditary feudal families (*shih-chia*) shared the empire among themselves, and would do away with the evils of despotic politics under the *chün-hsien* system. Huang's conception suggests Ku Yen-wu's call to infuse the ideals of the *feng-chien* system into the *chün-hsien* system. Huang argued that the benefits of listening to public opinion (*chi-i*) would gradually spread to the county, prefecture, province, and even to the central Court and would help to recover the brilliant government of the ancient republican (*kung-ho*) period, thus ushering in times of prosperity and peace. His position shows a course of development from the *feng-chien* arguments to arguments for parliamentary and local self-government systems,[117] with the ultimate goal of reviving the ideal government of the ancient republican period. Huang quoted Ku Yen-wu's argument on the *chün-hsien* system, including the famous phrase stressing the literati's responsibility for public morals,[118] and emphasized the realization of an ideal government through the institutionalized participation of the gentry in local politics. It is clear that Huang was influenced by Ku Yen-wu's argument for the *chün-hsien* system.

Yen Fu, who introduced the ideas of Darwin into the reformist philosophy of those days, severely criticized monarchism since the Ch'in dynasty in his essay entitled "P'i Han" (In refutation of Han Yu) published in 1895. He described the monarchs since the Ch'in (who were under the *chün-hsien* system) as the "great thieves of the empire."[119] In "Yuan-ch'iang" (On power), written the following year, Yen said that the monarchs since the Ch'in had treated the people like slaves.[120] In outlining ways to improve the system, he wrote:

> Ku Yen-wu said that it was impossible to free the people from private interests. The value of the government of the sages consisted in uniting the private interests of all the people and in converting these private interests into the public good. How, then, can we convince every one of the people to cherish China's interests as his own? One answer is to establish a parliament in the capital and have each prefecture and county publicly elect its own magistrates... If a sage were to appear today, he could not improve upon his proposal.[121]

Yen Fu thus spoke of the parliamentary and local self-government systems as ways of reflecting the ideal of the *feng-chien* system in the *chün-hsien* system. His arguments closely resembled those of Ho Ch'i and Hu Li-yuan. Yen spoke not only of a central parliament, but also described a local self-government system in which provincial officials would be selected through public elections, conducted in each province in defiance of the rule of avoidance. Such a proposal appears to have been heavily influenced by Ku Yen-wu's ideas of *hsiang-kuan*.[122] It is true that the public election of provincial officials did not in itself necessitate the establishment of provincial parliaments. But it would be only a matter of time before this proposal for a check on the central administration of the *chün-hsien* system developed into a call for provincial parliaments, which would deal with local affairs in compliance with public opinion. In his "Ni shang huang-ti wan-yen shu" (Ten-thousand-word memorial intended for the Emperor), drafted in 1898, Yen listed the "recruitment of local people to be officials in the provinces concerned" and the traditional system of selecting officials by local people as two of the four reforms that the Emperor should introduce after deciding to carry out general institutional reforms.[123] It seems that the "recruitment of local people" indicated the public election of provincial administrators, and the "traditional selection system" alluded to local parliaments.

A number of reformists in the 1898 Movement, besides those mentioned above, joined in advocating the parliamentary and local self-government systems. One was Wang K'ang-nien, who managed the journal *Shih-wu pao*. In "Chung-kuo tzu-ch'iang ts'e" (A plan for China's self-strengthening), Wang argued for placing parliamentarians (*i-yuan*) in all levels of provincial government as a means of checking the arbitrary exercise of power by administrators.[124] Han Wen-chü, who was a teacher at the Shih-wu Academy in Hunan, together with Liang Ch'i-chao, wrote an essay entitled "Chung-kuo chi she i-yuan lun" (Let China immediately establish parliaments),[125] in which he proposed the establishment of upper and lower houses at the provincial, prefectural, and county levels. Han suggested that members of the upper houses be chosen from among the civil and military officials and sinecurist-gentry from the province concerned as well as of other provinces. The lower houses would be composed of local gentry of lower status, such as *chü-jen, kung-sheng, sheng-yuan,* and *chien-sheng* degree-holders, both civil and military, and local commoners.

Sung Yü-jen, who was a reformist but did not participate in political activities at the time of the 1898 Reform Movement, wrote:

The parliament is the foundation of national politics, and there is a close relationship between the parliament and the school. Because of their ignorance of the foundation of politics, government officials attempt to monopolize politics, and the gentry regard themselves as having nothing to do with politics. The gentry ought to have the right to participate in discussing administration, but they have no right to participate in administration.[126]

This argument, reminiscent of Huang Tsung-hsi's discussion of the school system in "Hsueh-hsiao p'ien," is the clearest example of the coupling of the demand for the political participation of the gentry with the parliamentary system. Considering the character of the gentry class, the "discussion" of administration would naturally be associated with the establishment of local parliaments.

Thus far, I have compared the arguments[127] for the parliamentary system and local self-government presented mainly by reformists around the time of the 1898 Reform Movement with similar arguments of the preceding period. This comparison shows that traditional discussions of the *feng-chien* system, whose basic ideas facilitated the adoption of Western theories, lay in the background of the rapid spread of Western parliamentary and local self-government theories during the 1898 Reform period. Ku Yen-wu's and Huang Tsung-hsi's advocacy of institutional reforms inspired by the *feng-chien* system continued to influence the debates on the relative merits of the *feng-chien* and *chün-hsien* systems throughout the Ch'ing period, and it became popular to argue for the idea of incorporating feudal principles into the centralized system. Ku Yen-wu advocated local autonomy free from the traditional rule of avoidance. Huang Tsung-hsi called for the institutionalization of gentry participation in local administration as a way to check the arbitrary exercise of power by the monarch under the *chün-hsien* system.

The influence of Ku and Huang upon the reformists was felt not only around the time of the 1898 Reform Movement but continued into the early twentieth century with the constitutional movement. On 25 September 1908 the Ch'ing Court sanctioned sacrificial rites at Confucian shrines for Ku Yen-wu, Huang Tsung-hsi, and Wang Fu-chih. Until then, most of their books had been forbidden, but the situation had changed so radically that sacrifices for their souls were given state approval. This event occurred two years after the decision to begin official preparation for a constitution, and two months after decrees for the implementation of provincial assemblies (*tzu-i-chü*) as a foundation for constitutionalization.[128] Meng Sen, one of the most active leaders of the constitutional movement, commenting on the sanctioning of rites for the pioneer advocates of reform, said that this honor would facilitate the constitutional movement. Apparently, he anticipated official toleration of the anti-monarchism found in the works of these great scholars.[129]

Ku Yen-wu, Huang Tsung-hsi, and Wang Fu-chih exerted such a strong influence on those who followed them that, when the constitutional movement led by the gentry reached its peak, the Ch'ing authorities were obliged to grant them official recognition. Their influence was not limited to classical learning, as is shown by repeated memorials by the Board of Rites calling for the official sanction of sacrificial rites for the three scholars at Confucian shrines.[130] It is well known that Huang's ideas were accepted by late-Ch'ing reformists and revolutionaries such as Liang Ch'i-ch'ao and Ch'en T'ien-hua as an argument for popular rights. Another important but little-known fact is that the writings of Ku Yen-wu and Huang Tsung-hsi were a powerful influence on the formation of self-government theories advocated by the constitutional movement, a movement that preceded the decision to allow sacrificial rites in their honor. Their direct influence on the constitutional movement is clearly seen in "Ku T'ing-lin *Jih-chih lu* chih ti-fang tzu-chih shuo" (Local self-government theory as seen in *Jih-chih lu* of Ku Yen-wu), an essay in *Tung-fang tsa-chih*, published in May 1906. According to the author of the essay:

Although the local self-government system is not one that has been practiced in China since ancient times, Huang Tsung-hsi in his *Ming-i tai-fang lu* has already presented an argument conforming to the spirit of the system. He calls for respecting the people while restraining the monarch. Proposals for local selection of officials, local management of financial affairs, local enlistment of soldiers, and public discussions at schools . . . closely resemble the local self-government system of the West.[131]

He also referred in the same article to Ku Yen-wu's argument for revitalizing the spirit of the *feng-chien* system under the *chün-hsien* system and insisted that, though Ku's concrete prescriptions were not identical to the contemporary, Western local self-government system, there was no real difference between the two in spirit. The author gave a detailed explication of Ku's "Chün-hsien lun," expressed strong opposition to the rule of avoidance between officials from North and South China, enforced since the Ming dynasty, and emphasized the old *hsiang-kuan* system by relating it to the modern local self-government systems in Japan and Prussia.

At about the same time, even Hu Ssu-ching, who persisted in his unpopular opposition to a constitution, was observing that modern political thinkers advocated local self-government theories, including the *hsiang-kuan* system, election of "public people," the concentration of all the people's power, and the sharing of the duties of the empire. He pointed out that these thinkers were influenced by the argument for the *hsiang-kuan* system of Ku Yen-wu.[132] It is unnecessary to relate numerous other examples of such arguments associated with the late-Ch'ing constitutional movement. Clearly, in the background of the acceptance of Western local self-government theories as the basis of the constitutional movement[133] lay the traditional arguments of Ku Yen-wu and Huang Tsung-hsi.

We go too far, however, if we claim that local self-government and the parliamentary system were based completely on traditional arguments for the *feng-chien* system. The existence of the gentry class itself in Chinese society was instrumental in bringing the ideas on local autonomy of the early thinkers into play. Any reform program, however, had to depend on the gentry class for its successful implementation, as long as there was no fundamental change in the traditional society, that is, as long as there was no newly rising class which could take charge of sweeping reforms. Indeed, almost all the reformist memorials collected in *Wu-hsu pien-fa tang-an shih-liao* and *Wu-hsu pien-fa* assumed gentry participation in the implementation of their reform programs in education and industry and, to a certain degree, even in the area of defense. Under the traditional system in which a magistrate and a few officials governed a large territory, local administration was complemented by unofficial gentry participation. Gentry support, of course, was even more important for political reforms than for general administration. Since reform programs required their participation, the gentry gradually began to demand public status and power.

In the early-Ch'ing period, pioneer reformists such as Huang Tsung-hsi and Pao Shih-ch'en[134] were already asking for direct political participation by the gentry. They advocated the infusion of the spirit of the *feng-chien* system into the *chün-hsien* system, which meant introducing local self-government conceived in terms of the autonomy of the local gentry. It is apparent that modern theories of self-government and the parliamentary system, together with traditional arguments on the *feng-chien* system, guaranteed political participation by the gentry. The demand for gentry political participation was inevitable in the reform of the traditional Chinese political system. The leaders of the 1898 Reform Movement, recognizing this situation, attempted to build a new force to stand against the conservatives by institutionalizing gentry participation.

The local gentry, comprising former officials and qualified aspirants, were a part of the ruling class, together with incumbent officials, because they took part in maintaining the existing social order. But they were distinguished from incumbent officials by the non-bureaucratic character of their social participation and their interests and rights as a ruling class outside officialdom. The gentry also included some subgroups, such as the lowest degree-holders, the *sheng-yuan*. Because of their unique role in society, how the *sheng-yuan* group related to the upper levels of the gentry class in the process of reform or in the implementation of local self-government programs is a study worth pursuing.[135]

The interests of the lower-level gentry often coincided with those of the upper-level gentry, for example, their demands for political participation. But there was some doubt about how they would act if their attempts for political participation failed and their interests subsequently collided. The conflict between the conservatives and reformists during the 1898 Reform period partly reflected the relationship between incumbent officials and the local gentry. That is, the reformist group, composed of lower-level officials in the central government (mostly sinecurists), the local gentrymen, and those who had recently attained official posts, generally showed the characteristics of the local gentry strongly. They did not necessarily share the same viewpoint with the upper levels of the gentry, and thus their conduct could differ, within certain limits, from those of the upper class, including high-ranking officials and other entrenched bureaucrats, whose official titles were closely associated with their status and livelihood.

It should also be noted that nearly all the late-Ch'ing arguments for the parliamentary system and local self-government were presented as part of administrative reform programs, and thus were not associated directly with the promotion of popular rights. Even among those who clearly recognized and argued for the distinction between administrative power and legislative and political power, there were many who came to represent local self-government and local parliaments as part of administrative reform programs, or as a supplement to local administration, on the grounds that the time was not ripe for their full realization. This is partly due to a poor understanding of modern local self-government theories, but at the same time it seems to be the inevitable result of the process of combining the spirit of traditional reforms centering around *feng-chien* ideals with modern demands for more changes.

The advocates of local self-government were pointing the way to a parliamentary system and, in particular, to local parliaments in which the principles of local self-government would be applied. The growing demand for self-government throughout the Ch'ing period was finally realized in the opening of provincial assemblies in 1909.

CHAPTER FIVE

The Late-Ch'ing Provincial Assembly

On 14 October 1909, provincial assemblies were established in the capital of every province except Sinkiang. The assemblies were set up in response to the constitutional and self-government movements and were influenced by the theory of *feng-chien*.[1] By combining the traditional idea of *feng-chien* with a modern purpose, the gentry demonstrated how tradition can play a role in the process of modernization.[2]

In order to understand the role of the provincial assemblies in the constitutional movement in the late Ch'ing and the turbulent period of revolution that followed, we need to look at the sequence of events that led up to the establishment of the assemblies: what discussions took place, what preparations were made, and where the leadership was centered. The way in which the gentry confronted the challenges of the late-Ch'ing period furnishes an important clue to understanding the tenacious character of the gentry in modern Chinese history.

DEBATES ON THE ESTABLISHMENT OF THE PROVINCIAL ASSEMBLY (1900–1907)

Progressive arguments for a parliamentary system and local self-government based primarily on the idea of *feng-chien*, discussed in the previous chapter, began to appear in the wake of the 1898 Reform Movement. During the time of the Boxer Rebellion in 1900, Sun Yat-sen wrote a letter concerning this issue to the Governor of Hong Kong. In a political program attached to the letter, Sun urged that a national as well as provincial parliaments be organized, with representatives selected on the basis of county constituencies. Each provincial parliament would constitute a government independent of the central government and have rights of taxation. The provinces would be governed by people selected by the provincial parliament. This proposal, related to the independence movement of Kwangtung and Kwangsi, was probably not widely known to the public at the time. Nevertheless, it is significant in its explicit proposal for parliamentary local self-government, and it shows the influence of Ho Ch'i (H'o Kai), a renowned reformist in Hong Kong, who had earlier expounded a detailed discussion of local self-government based on the *feng-chien* idea.[3]

At about the same time, Wang K'ang-nien, an influential Shanghai journalist, was insisting on the establishment of a "national constitution" and a "national assembly" in response to the independent action of governors general of the southeastern provinces in the days of the Boxer Rebellion, analogous to the Kwangtung-Kwangsi independence movement.[4] In an earlier article, "On the Way to Make China Strong" (1896), Wang had argued for the creation of a central parliament as well as local parliaments in each province, prefecture, department, and county throughout China. His proposal of 1900 was thus a continuation of his persistent advocacy of parliamentarianism and local self-government.

A more forceful argument appeared in 1901 in an essay entitled "Pien-fa p'ing-i" (Ordinary proposals on reform), by Chang Chien, a powerful member of the Kiangsu gentry.[5] Drawing somewhat on Japanese institutional experience, Chang called for "instituting assemblies at the central and local levels." He quoted Japanese regulations to the effect that the right to elect or be elected was limited to those with property or reputation and observed that the man with property or reputation in Japan was equivalent to a member of the Chinese gentry. Huang Tsun-hsien in the following year also made a similar appeal for the adoption of the Japanese system of local assemblies.[6]

As we saw earlier, Huang, who had a full understanding of the political systems of England and Japan, based his arguments for local self-government on the traditional *feng-chien* system. He proposed that the local assemblies follow "first the Japanese practice and then the British." Like those of Chang, his remarks seem to imply the restriction of candidacy to the gentry class.

Huang's concern for local assemblies was related to a desire to limit imperial power. He said, in effect, that local assemblies might serve to share official power so that sovereign power and the people's power would become equal. Seeking to use local autonomy to restrict monarchical sovereignty, Huang envisioned the system of local assemblies as creating a kind of federalism. Huang's argument for the separation of powers on the local level projected elements of the traditional *feng-chien* concept onto the *chün-hsien* power structure. In this respect, it would be safe to say that the arguments of Sun Yat-sen and Wang K'ang-nien show a basic similarity to that of Huang Tsun-hsien. In a similar vein, Hunanese students in Japan in 1903 called for self-government in Hunan; like Huang, they urged that "(central) bureaucratic power be balanced by the power of the people."[7]

In 1903, K'ang Yu-wei, who conceived of local self-government as the modernized extension of the *feng-chien* tradition, argued for setting up assemblies at every local level to "help the officials govern" and "get in touch with the feelings of the common people."[8] These assemblies would continue in modified form the gentry tradition of mutual consultation. Only citizens (*kung-min*), whose qualifications differed from those of commoners, were to be considered eligible to vote. The concept of "citizen" differed slightly from the older concept of "gentry": it signified rather than status the performance of public duty. To be classified as a citizen, however, one had to be a resident for years, over twenty years old, of good family, without a criminal record, with a willingness to help the poor and the ability to pay an annual tax of 10 yuan.[9] K'ang clearly considered local self-government and the establishment of local assemblies as extensions of the traditional activities of the gentry. Voting rights did not belong to commoners. It should be noted that K'ang failed to propose restrictions on the power of the central governmental powers; rather, he took local self-government as a measure for supplementing government from the county.

The idea of local self-government continued to be a popular component of political reform up through 1904. Later arguments, however, differed from earlier ones in centering predominantly around the issues of advancing the people's rights and establishing constitutional government. Articles to this effect were published in *Tung-fang tsa-chih* (Eastern miscellany) and *Ta-kung-pao* in 1904, publications sympathetic to the constitutional movement. These articles were inspired directly by the formal petition submitted by Sun Pao-ch'i, Minister to France, for the establishment of a constitution, which was followed by similar petitions by several governors general and governors in 1905.[10]

The arguments in favor of a constitution were strengthened by the Russo-Japanese War, which broke out on 9 February 1905. When Japan sank Russia's Baltic fleet near Tsushima Island, the victory of "constitutional Japan" over "autocratic Russia" tended to support the arguments of the constitutionalists. For instance, Chang Chien (a typical proponent of constitutionalism at this time) made this connection explicit in a letter to Yuan Shih-k'ai, Governor General of Chihli: "Japan's victory over Russia is also the victory of constitutionalism over autocracy. Which is the one thoroughly autocratic state in the world today? If one autocratic state were to confront many constitutional governments, what chance would it have?"[11]

Chang thought it was time for constitutionalism in China. In May 1904, with the help of friends, he drafted a memorial to the Throne to this effect for Chang Chih-tung, Governor General of Hu-kwang, and Wei Kuang-t'ao, Governor General of Liang-Kiang.[12] The following month, at the request of Chang Chih-tung, he sent a letter (just cited) to Yuan Shih-k'ai, an old acquaintance of Chang Chih-tung. Yuan approved the idea in principle.[13] That summer Chang Chien, with the help of Chao Feng-ch'ang, a private secretary to Chang Chih-tung, printed the Japanese constitution and forwarded it to the Empress Dowager who responded favorably.[14] He printed copies of his *Jih-pen hsien-fa i-chieh* (Exposition of the Japanese Constitution) and *Jih-pen i-hui-shih* (History of the Japanese Diet) and sent them to T'ieh-liang (appointed President of the Army Ministry the following year), who was later to become a strong proponent of constitutionalism and would play a key role in getting the Ch'ing Court prepared to promulgate a constitution. Chang also discussed the constitution issue with him personally.[15]

After the battle of the Sea of Japan, the constitutional movement began to gain ground. On 4 June 1905, Yuan Shih-k'ai, Chang Chih-tung, and Chou Fu (the new Governor General of Liang-Kiang) jointly submitted a memorial calling for a constitution. They urged the establishment of constitutional government within thirteen years.[16] Just as the constitutional movement was moving up to the level of governors general and into the Imperial Court, the government on 16 July 1905 despatched a delegation (including Hsu Shih-ch'ang, Tai Hung-tz'u, and Tuan-fang) to Japan and Europe to investigate the constitutional governments of foreign countries,[17] which implied that the government was considering the adoption of a constitution in the near future.

In the course of trying to influence public opinion, the arguments about local self-government took a new turn. What was sought was not simply organizational reform or the streamlining of administrative efficiency, but a constitutionalism aimed at the overall reform of the political structure itself.[18] Its proponents argued that constitutional government required local self-government and provincial assemblies and that these were the major tasks of the constitutional movement.

After commenting on the bicameral legislatures in foreign counties, Sun Pao-ch'i, who had initiated the constitutional debates, said in his letter to the Bureau of Government Affairs:

In each provincial capital and prefectural and county seat, a measure to comply with the people's wishes is needed. In imitation of the old institution of the village school, a public forum called a Kung-i t'ang (Hall of Public Discussion) should be established there. The size of the gentry electorate for each institution must be decided on the basis of the size of each area. In general, a Kung-i-t'ang in a provincial capital would embrace the gentry of the prefecture and counties in that province, one in a prefectural seat would embrace the gentry of its counties, and one in a county seat would embrace gentry in the villages. Public matters like education, agriculture, industry, commerce, and public works should be carefully discussed and decided by both local officials and the Kung-i-t'ang gentry in order to garner wide support. Decisions would then encounter no opposition. The present level of the people is such that only after ten years of this kind of experimenting could new regulations for elections by instituted and the will of the people upheld.[19]

Sun Pao-ch'i emphasized here the functional importance of local self-government as a step toward constitutionalism, and he institutionalized the traditional role of gentry in his picture of self-government.

In the preface to his *History of the Japanese Diet,* Chang Chien argued: "Today only three out of all the countries of the world have failed to establish a constitution. Of these, Russia has a system of local self-government, so we might say that it has a semi-constitutional government."[20] Chang's logic that Russia's institution of local self-government qualifies it as semi-constitutional concurs with Sun Pao-ch'i's argument and shows that both these prominent leaders of the late-Ch'ing constitutional movement considered local self-government to be of prime importance in that movement. In view of the attitudes of these leaders, it would seem that the Ch'ing constitutional movement was to go far beyond the mere adoption of a constitution or a responsible cabinet to the point of advocating local self-government as well.

Thus, two major concerns in the constitutional movement evolved. One was to facilitate the establishment of a constitution and the opening of a national assembly. The other was to first establish local self-government by setting up provincial assemblies. An article entitled "Li-hsien chien-shuo lu" (A rudimentary discussion of constitutionalism), which was reprinted in *Tung-fang tsa-chih* in October 1905, pointed out: "The system of local self-government is closely allied with the system of constitutional government. If a constitution is to be sought, the reality of local self-government should also be pursued. Self-government can only be realized through the efforts of the people and should not be guided by officials."[21]

In the next issue of *Tung-fang tsa-chih,*[22] Lu Tsung-yü spoke of a parliamentary system composed of both a bicameral parliament and a local assembly. Lu believed that the formal establishment of the legislative body would not work out in practice, however, because the Chinese people were not yet enlightened. Referring to the example of the Germans, who opened provincial meetings prior to the establishment of a national parliament in order to acquaint the people with politics, Lu recommended that the traditional gentry associations at the local level (such as the *Shen-tung-chü* in Shantung province or the *hsiang-she* in Shansi province) be institutionalized as the first step toward the formation of a local assembly. The local assembly would be responsible for rural militia, defense, elementary education, strict enforcement of the mutual surveillance system, conscription, the construction of roads, and irrigation, as well as some new administrative affairs like conscription or sanitation, which were outside traditional gentry functions. Another article which appeared two issues later in *Tung-fang tsa-chih*, entitled "Lun li-hsien teng i ti-fang tan-chi wei chi-ch'i" (The argument in favor of a constitution should be based on local self-government) stressed just what its title proposed. The main thrust of the article was to recommend the institutionalization of the traditional functions of local gentry and the development of this policy as the foundation of a future national assembly.[23]

Shen Chia-pen, a Vice-President of the Board of Punishments who was later appointed a member of the National Assembly, emphasized the need for local self-government as a part of the constitutional system in a memorial submitted at this time and printed in the same issue of *Tung-fang tso-chih*.[24] He also spoke of institutionalizing certain traditional gentry organizations like the *hsiang-she* (rural covenant) system of Shansi, which he likened to the Japanese system of issues later entitled "Lun chin-jih chi chien-she hsien-fa yen-chiu-hui" (Set up promptly a constitution study society) continued the same line of argument more assertively: "Local self-government is the most important element of the constitutional system. Without it, the constitutional system is nothing but an outward form or a mere formality."[25] Many other articles were written in a similar vein at the same time.[26]

In May 1906, *Tung-fang tsa-chih* began to publish the writings of Liang Ch'i-ch'ao, who had initiated the constitutional movement in Tokyo.[27] That the articles of an influential leader under prosecution and unable to return to China could be printed openly in a leading magazine within the country shows the strength of the desire for a constitution. Liang's manifesto for his Political Information Institute,[28] published in November 1907, presented as four points in the platform of this association the establishment of local self-government, the proper division of governmental power between local and central governments, the introduction of a parliament, and the institution of responsible government. Liang advocated the immediate establishment of provincial assemblies as an important step. "The Chinese people are now accustomed to the words *local self-government* but neither the government nor the people are taking positive steps to bring it about," as he stated in his article. "This is the reason why we are actively advocating local self-government and are hoping to see it through." The Ch'ing government had by this time announced that provincial assemblies would be established, but the regulations were still to be made public.

It is clear that the arguments in favor of local self-government and provincial assemblies were now widely known and had become an inseparable part of the constitutional movement. The government had already decided to promulgate a constitution in the future, but what was its position regarding local self-government and provincial assemblies? First, it announced in July 1905 that a group of ministers would be sent to Europe to investigate the practice of constitutional government there. Then, on 18 November, the Ch'ing government ordered the Committee of Ministers (Hui-i cheng-wu-ch'u) to prepare an outline of a constitution upon the delegation's return.[29] Finally, a week later, the government established a Committee for the Investigation of the Principles of Modern Politics and Government and had the committee recruit men of talent to compile occasional reports on foreign political institutions that were compatible with the contemporary Chinese political system.[30]

On 18 September 1905, all ministers stationed in foreign countries were notified that they should consult with the delegation that was to be sent abroad to observe foreign constitutional systems.[31] These ministers in response recommended that the government take three preliminary steps: (1) state clearly the government's principle intention; (2) put the institution of local self-government into practice; and (3) introduce legislation regarding public gatherings and the press. Here again, the introduction of local self-government was emphasized as a primary prerequisite to constitutionalism. In their exposition of local self-government, the ministers proposed to get rid of the traditional rule of avoidance and institute the local election of "indigenous officials" (*hsiang-kuan*). The regulations for such local officials were to be prepared in accordance with the practice of local self-government as it was carried out in foreign countries.[32] Here we find that the link between the rule of avoidance and the practice of the *hsiang-kuan* system was based both on the *feng-chien* tradition of local self-government and the modern Western idea of constitutionalism.

What were the findings of the ministerial Mission to Investigate the Practice of Constitutional Government in Foreign Countries, which lasted from 12 December 1905 to 12 July 1906? Observing the British form of government, the ministers, including the influential Manchu noble Tsai-tse, concluded: "The self-government of London is the starting point of the British constitution. Britain established constitutionalism before other countries, and its system of local self-government is approved of and copied by other countries."³³ The statement continued:

> While it is true that the essence of the British system lies in the strength of its navy and army and the operation of its industry and commerce, *its unique character in fact lies in its system of local self-government*. Within this system, each county [*fu* in Chinese] is divided into several hundreds [*hsiang*] and each hundred into several parishes [*ch'ü*]. Parishes and hundreds have chiefs and heads and counties have county magistrates, all of whom are elected from within their respective units. Accordingly, local customs and local opinions are known to them. They are in charge of housing, sewage, roads, industrial development, schooling, emergency help, and charity, and they are able to take care of even the most niggling details. Although the regulations are strictly enforced, the people do not feel that they are treated harshly, *because these men are overseeing the affairs of their own local areas*. Taxes are high, but the people do not complain, because the levies are used for local needs. Since this organization is subordinated to the central government, the latter is able to scrutinize and encourage these officials and may help financially. By enhancing the people's livelihood and bettering their way of life, this system is profoundly in tune with the old system of the *Chou-li*. Although this is certainly an efficient way to manage domestic affairs, there is some complexity and ambiguity regarding the division of responsibility, which makes it difficult to apply the plan to the Chinese political system. Thus, a model has to be developed for China to follow by choosing the best parts, and discarding the deficiencies, of other constitutional systems.³⁴

The high status and authority of the authors of this recommendation in favor of a modified adoption of the British system ensured that their findings would have critical influence upon whatever future course the Ch'ing Court might take. Perceiving that Britain's strength came from its local self-government system, they urged the government to introduce a similar policy. They also made it clear that Great Britain's system ran counter to the traditional rule of avoidance, which was criticized by most of those who advocated the restoration of the *feng-chien* ideal within the *chün-hsien* system throughout the Ch'ing. They suggested, too, that the institutionalization of the function of China's traditional gentry on the local scene would be the basis for adopting the British system. It is interesting to note their observation that with self-government the common people would not resist an increase in taxes. One is reminded of Sun Pao-ch'i's memorial which touched upon the usefulness of the system in meeting the expected financial problems that would result from a policy of preparation for a constitution. The Ch'ing officials and the nobility feared an outburst of resistance against an increased tax, which did come about later, furthering the collapse of Ch'ing rule.[35] The view that people would not complain about higher taxes because those taxes would go to meet local needs[36] reaches beyond the classic formula of representative government that demands "no taxation without representation." The high officials of the Ch'ing induced the dynasty to secure the "institutionalized cooperation" of the gentry, which, along with the system, would be able to secure from the people the needed revenue for the new expenditures.

The mission urged China to be selective in imitating British local self-government. This was not only because of the complexity involved in the division of responsibility in British practice, but also because local self-rule might also weaken the power of the central government. The imperial relatives and the noblemen of the Manchu Court were strongly attached to the idea of a powerful central government, viewing it as the only way to save the Ch'ing dynasty from crisis. Thus, the mission had to consider how to deal with opposition at court to decentralization when they put forward their proposal. They did so by looking to France for a model for local self-government.

> In Britain, the people's ability to govern themselves comes first; overall control by the central government comes later. In France, the government first establishes its overall authority and then allows the people to present their opinions [through the local self-government system]. It would seem desirable for a large, heavily populated country to centralize its government and not diffuse it.[37]

Concentration of power in the central government and a high degree of public enlightenment are taken here to be the main premises for local self-government.

Tsai-tse and his companions were somewhat ambiguous about the relation between local assemblies and the authority of local organization. Of the British system they said merely: "The county officials come from among the local people," a statement that reveals their lack of understanding regarding the process of popular participation in local self-government in Britain. Reporting on the Belgian system,[38] however, for the first time they mentioned that there were assemblies of gentry leaders in the provinces and counties in addition to governors. When discussing the provincial assemblies, they said that the provincial gentry discussed provincial affairs in their meetings, and that their functions were similar to the traditional ones of the Chinese gentry, such as extending charity and organizing relief.

Tsai-tse described in detail the authority of the provincial governor, emphasizing his power to prorogue a provincial assembly. Thus, he suggested that, when local self-government was introduced to China, the provincial governor appointed by the central government should be empowered to control the local assembly. A provincial meeting could deal only with the affairs of its own province and was forbidden to intervene in the affairs of another province. At a practical level, Tsai-tse and his colleagues feared that provincial assemblies might form an interprovincial federation and encroach on the powers of the central government. (This threat to the central government was realized later.)

Tuan-fang, another high official who investigated Western constitutional systems and was as influential as Tsai-tse in the process of realizing constitutional government,[39] emphasized in two memorials the importance to political stability of setting national policy with regard to constitutional government and the need to undertake governmental reorganization as a preparatory step to implementing constitutionalism.[40] In Shanghai on the way to Peking, he met Chang Chien and discussed "the Constitution" with him. Upon reaching Peking, he urged in his memorials that China imitate Japan's way of introducing constitutionalism. Emphasizing the necessity of a parliament, he suggested that assemblies be established on the provincial level as practice organs for the formal national and provincial assemblies to be set up in the near future. He proposed a period of fifteen to twenty years as a preparatory stage in promulgating a constitution. He pointed to the need to clarify the division between central and local authority in order to check the broad power of provincial governors, and proposed the establishment of a "Congregational Assembly," a transitory organ similar to the later Central National Assembly (Tzu-cheng-yuan). He also urged the establishment of provincial assemblies as part of local administrative reform.

THE ESTABLISHMENT OF THE PROVINCIAL ASSEMBLIES (*TZU-I-CHÜ*)

After the ministerial delegation returned in July 1906, the constitutional question became widely discussed. Upon their return, the Empress Dowager called Tai Hung-tz'u and Shang Ch'i-heng once, Tsai-tse twice, and Tuan-fang three times to ask their opinions on constitutional government.[41] They all extolled its benefits and pointed out the danger to China of not adopting this course. The Empress Dowager was said to have been persuaded. In addition, as mentioned, Tsai-tse and Tuan-fang submitted formal memorials regarding the necessity of constitutional government and the method of putting it into practice.

Some Grand Councillors, including Hsu Shih-ch'ang, who insisted on the introduction of local self-government as a preparatory step to constitutional government, also memorialized, expressing their own opinions but agreeing ultimately with the views of the delegation, which they summarized in a ten-point proposal. The Empress Dowager then ordered Prince Ch'un (Tsai-feng), the Grand Councillors, the Grand Secretaries, other ex-officio members of the Committee of Ministers, and the Governor General of Chihli province, Yuan Shih-k'ai, to discuss the proposal. This conference was held at Lang-jun-yuan in the palace of Prince Kung and at the Office of Foreign Affairs on 26 and 27 August respectively.

One of the topics of the heated discussion at the Lang-jun-yuan conference was how to implement local self-government. T'ieh-liang, then President of the Board of War, took the position that, if China were to become a constitutional monarchy with local self-government, the hegemony of bad gentry who traditionally obstructed the proper management of local administration could become worrisome. Yuan Shih-k'ai agreed that this might be a problem, but felt that good local officials would keep those bad gentry from spreading their influence. Yuan and Tuan-fang argued that the local administrative system be rectified before formally introducing local self-government, and this view seemed to prevail at the conference.[42] All agreed that local self-government had to precede constitutional government, although many recognized the threat that wicked gentry might pose. They merely suggested that good officials be permitted to impose restrictions on the wicked gentry, though, in view of the situation at the time, this was an impossible task. Finally, most of the preliminary discussions about constitutional government in the Ch'ing Court centered on local self-government as the foundation of constitutional government.[43] All that was left to be decided was how that policy was to be carried out.

On 28 August, after the Lang-jun-yuan conference had ended and the participants met the Empress Dowager with a recommendation for a constitution, the Imperial Court announced preparations for a constitutional government. Its first move was to reform government institutions in the central and local administrations. An Office for Revising Government Institutions (Cheng-chih pien-ts'uan-kuan) was set up. Sun Pao-ch'i and Yang Shih-ch'i, who had been the first to discuss constitutional government and local self-government openly, became its directors. The members in the drafting department were Chin Pang-p'ing, Chang I-lin, Wang Jung-pao, and Ts'ao Ju-lin. They were for the most part students who had been studying in Japan or who had otherwise been exposed to new ideas.[44] The work in the newly created Office for Revising Government Institutions culminated in two edicts, one ordering each province to prepare measures to reorganize local administration and the other announcing the reorganization of the central government.[45] The former stated that it was too soon to introduce the practice of local self-government because the people were not ready for it. As an alternative to preparing for self-government, ir recommended relocating magistrates and increasing the number of their assistants, noting the need to reexamine their competence as a precaution against possible evil practices. Obviously the edict reflected T'ieh-liang's warning.

In response to these edicts, "A memorial by Prince Ch'ing and others"[46] was presented on 6 November, proposing the plan to reorganize provicial administration. In the memorial which was approved by the Throne, it was proposed to increase the number of administrative assistants to the magistrate as a base of local self-government. Further, Article 6 of "Regulations on the Local Administrative System in Each Province," included in this memorial, stated:

Each provincial governor general or governor must institute a council (*hui-i-t'ing*) where he regularly convenes his ranking subordinate officers to discuss important matters and make decisions about policy implementation. For local issues, he may select, in addition, upright members of the local gentry to join in the deliberation.[47]

Here we see an embryonic stage of local self-government in which the gentry are allowed to participate in local matters in a meeting with officials. On 15 November, a memorial to the Emperor was presented by Prince Ch'ing and others:

Now that we are revising the provincial administrative organization, we, your ministers, are of the opinion that local self-government is the seedbed for the gradual growth of constitutionalism. Departments and counties are the foundation of the empire. If we wish thoroughly to implement self-government, all the lower officials below the rank of magistrate should be local gentry with whom the magistrates cooperate. In this way we may gradually revive the ancient idea of locally appointed officials.[48]

The Office for Revising Government Institutions also recommended that the lower-level native officials be selected by examination from those who had received a modern education, and that they could qualify for promotion to a position as high as county magistrate or higher (contrary to traditional practice). Once this recommendation had been imperially authorized,[49] the rule of avoidance, which had been the custom for a thousand years, ceased to operate, and the traditional argument concerning native officials became enmeshed "formally" with the argument in favor of local self-government. It was a historic change for Chinese society. Although no clear schedule was officially announced as to how and when local self-government would be implemented, the desire for its realization had grown among the people. There was a strong demand for a constitutional government, and the Ch'ing Court had been obliged to respond to that demand.

According to our present information, the first time that the term *tzu-i-chü* (provincial assembly) was used was in a memorial submitted on 10 June 1907, by Ts'en Ch'un-hsuan, the Governor General of Kwangtung and Kwangsi, in response to an imperial edict asking for the opinions of provincial governors in relation to the reorganization of local administration. Ts'en insisted that the establishment of a local assembly in each province was necessary to local self-government, and he proposed a series of steps toward the institution of a constitutional government, with a "national assembly" (*tzu-cheng-yuan*) in the capital, a "provincial assembly" (*tzu-i-chü*) in each province, and a "deliberative council" (*i-shih-hui*) below the provincial level.[50]

The provincial assembly he proposed was to be composed mainly of "the gentry and merchants"—those whom he considered "well-versed in the principles of government"—from each prefecture and department, who would later become officials. Even those with actual posts in a provincial capital were to participate in the provincial assembly, the governor of the province acting as chairman. The content of the memorial, particularly in reference to the appointment of the provincial assemblymen from the gentry as officials, which seems to have been drafted by his private secretaries, Yao Shao-shu and Kao Feng-ch'i,[51] was reactionary compared to those adopted later. It was similar to the proposals submitted earlier by Tsai-tse and T'ieh-liang, but reached further in the sense that it articulated the idea of a provincial assembly in which not only the gentry but also the merchants participated.

The terms *national assembly* (*tzu-cheng-yuan*) and *provincial assembly* (*tzu-i-chü*) are used for the first time in Ts'en's memorial to mean central and local parliaments. Usually, when an organization is being established, its function is discussed and not its fixed name. But, in this case, names for these new organizations were also proposed, probably of Ts'en's own devising.

One source indicates that the Office for Revising Government Institutions had already prepared articles regarding the national and provincial assemblies.[52] Such articles would have been merely an outline in preparation for the introduction of local self-government and, therefore, somewhat different from the articles as they were finally published, but the names of the two organizations were probably adopted at that time, though tentatively. Ts'en's use of the terms *national assembly* and *provincial assembly* and his proposal about the provincial assembly probably reflect to some extent the contents of drafts made by the Office for Revising Government Institutions.[53] It seems that both Yao Shao-shu and Kao Feng-ch'i were acquainted with Western politics, and that they might have had some close connection with members working in the Office for Revising Government Institutions.

There are two pieces of evidence that support my conclusion that Ts'en's memorial first publicized the term *provincial assembly*. First, an imperial edict issued on 10 June 1907 ordered provincial governors and governors general "to discuss the establishment of a provincial assembly as proposed by Ts'en Ch'un-hsuan."[54] Second, a memorial of the Ministerial Council for Government Affairs (Hui-i cheng-wu-ch'u)[55] mentioned the term *provincial assembly*, referring also to Ts'en's memorial.

Ch'eng Te-ch'üan, Governor of Heilungkiang province, was one of the governors who responded to Ts'en's memorial. He agreed that, if the nation had a national assembly, each province must have its own organization to gather and discuss public opinion, which he argued was "the root of constitutional government."⁵⁶ The implication was much more progressive than Ts'en's proposal, in that Ch'eng did not mention the appointment of assembly members as officials.

Following Ts'en's memorial, Yuan Shih-k'ai presented a memorial on 28 July in which he urged further preparations for the adoption of a constitution. In it he discussed the ten key points of constitutional government:

In the debates of recent years over railroads and mines, petitions to the Throne protesting the loss of rights were quite common. I now request that we give some direction to these developments by first [as a measure to do so] establishing councils in the departments and counties and assemblies in the provinces, then ultimately a national assembly. Through these organizations we may make use of the abilities of the people. . . . I request that local self-government be instituted. Local self-government does not encroach on bureaucratic authority, and there is good reason to believe that the people elected with a majority would not be from the undesirable element in the villages. I request that local self-government be introduced properly and maintain that we shall see miraculous results within ten years.⁵⁷

Yuan included some points that had been previously raised: (1) a fear about the quality of the elected members, which T'ieh-liang had dealt with at the Lang-jun-yuan meeting; (2) a worry that local self-government might turn out to be an obstacle to the bureaucratic power of the central government, to which the investigation ministers, including Tsai-tse, had already responded; (3) the recognition that a mechanism to institutionalize gentry power was needed to bring the gentry under some control to cope with the current problems facing the Ch'ing Court, since the movement for the recovery of rights had been collectively launched by the gentry; and (4) a perception of the value of linking this mechanism (that is, the provincial assembly) to the constitutional structure of the national assembly in the capital. Yuan's proposals were in line with the current mood, and can be considered basically identical to the constitutional arguments among Manchu noblemen like Tsai-tse. Once everyone accepted these arguments, the decision to establish provincial assemblies would be easier. It is no exaggeration to say that the regulations later promulgated for the provincial assemblies largely reflected the arguments that Yuan made in this memorial. He had expanded on the arguments made earlier by Ts'en Ch'un-hsuan and was the first to make the points about gentry control and a link to the national assembly.

Because of his influence as Governor General of Chihli, and given the power of his arguments, Yuan's memorial was to have a considerable impact on the establishment of the provincial assemblies.[58] It also fixed the terminology for the provincial and national assemblies.

The Office for the Investigation of the Principles of Modern Politics and Government (K'ao-ch'a cheng-chih-kuan), which was inaugurated on 25 November 1905, when the investigation mission was dispatched to foreign countries, was reconstituted under the name of the Office to Draw up Regulations for Constitutional Government (Hsien-cheng pien-ch'a-kuan) on 13 August 1907.[59] In an edict of 19 October 1907, the Emperor finally made it public that provincial assemblies were to be installed promptly in each province.[60] This question having been resolved, the next question then was what form this local self-government and these provincial asemblies would take. This matter was left to the constitutional office.[61]

The edict of 19 October outlined the general idea that the provincial assemblies would: (1) aid local security by acting as a conduit for public opinion; (2) provide members for a future national assembly; (3) encourage officials and gentry to cooperate with each other; (4) discuss local affairs, though the final decisions would be subject to the veto of the governor general or governor; (5) refer important decisions to the governor, who would ask the Emperor for guidance; and (6) not only report their resolutions to the governor but also to the national assembly, which would review their reports. All these points were included in the regulations for the provincial assemblies and for the election of the assemblymen, which were promulgated on 22 July 1908.[62]

The edict of 19 October outlined the general idea that the provincial assemblies would: (1) aid local security by acting as a conduit for public opinion; (2) provide members for a future national assembly; to draw up any detailed regulations.[63] It is no wonder, therefore, that one local official, Governor Feng Hsu of Anhwei, proposed his own regulations for the assemblies.[64] And, in some other provinces, provincial assemblies were installed independently without waiting for any detailed regulations and without elections. In order to clear up the confusion, the Office to Draw up Regulations for Constitutional Government sent a directive to each province to make it clear that a preparatory office should first be set up, that any provincial assembly established independently without elections should be renamed the

Provincial Assembly Preparatory Office (Tzu-i-chü ch'ou-pan-ch'u), and that provincial assemblies should be established by these preparatory offices within a year.[65]

Other examples show how the local gentry responded to the edict asking for a "prompt installation." Chang Chien and other Kiangsu gentry gathered at the Constitutional Preparatory Association (Yü-pei li-hsien kung-hui) in Shanghai, a center of the constitutional movement of Kiangsu gentry, on 19 December 1907. They promulgated their own draft regulations for an assembly,[66] and, in accordance with these regulations, established a Kiangsu province assembly (without any elections).[67] Hupeh and Chihli saw the creation of similar groups, a Provincial Assembly Inaugural Bureau (Tzu-i-chü ch'uang-pan-chü) in the former and a Provincial Assembly Preparatory Office (Tzu-i-chü ch'ou-pan-ch'u) in the latter;[68] a committee of the Chihli office even drafted articles for its provincial assembly.[69] In Kiangsi, a similar Provincial Assembly Preparatory Office was organized and a public meeting was held by "all-province representatives." How the representatives were selected is not known.[70] In Kwangtung, a provincial assembly was installed and its articles drafted.[71] In Kwangsi, a provincial assembly was installed and its chairman and vice-director were appointed by the Governor. The assemblymen were selected from the "good gentry."[72] Fengtien followed suit, installing a provincial assembly and setting up an election office within it.[73]

These "provincial assemblies" which were established independently in compliance merely with the outline given by the central government, before the official promulgation of regulations in 1908, promptly went to work. The assembly in Shansi passed a regulation prohibiting the smoking of opium. In Chihli, the assembly issued a public notice regarding mining affairs in Luan-chou.[74] In Kiangsu, the new provincial assembly officially passed resolutions on the collection and transmission of the land tax in silver, the problems of using copper coinage, and the collection of revenues to meet the expenses of local self-government.[75] The variety of regulations was a natural outcome of the confusion arising from a directive that called for the prompt establishment of assemblies without providing any procedure for their creation.

Meanwhile, the constitution office in the capital drew up two sets of regulations: one regarding the organization of the provincial assemblies, and the other the election process. Because both sets of regulations were written using modern terminology, many local officials were not able to understand them and could not put them into operation.[76] Officials who had worked in the capital, with a knowledge of Western law or government, returned students from Japan, or graduates of new-style institutes who had some knowledge of modern law and political affairs were invited by governors general to serve on preparatory committees and to put these regulations into effect.

The names of the members of these preparatory offices in twelve provinces (excluding Szechwan) are known.[77] According to the Emperor's edict, both the officials and the gentry were to participate in the formation of the assembly. In practice the distinction between these two became blurred, except in the cases of senior provincial officials of the respective provinces, such as provincial treasurers, provincial judges, or circuit intendants. A report from Kiangsu province, which clearly distinguished official and gentry statuses, is an exception. In this report, however, we find Chiang Ping-chang, a second-class compiler of the Hanlin Academy, listed as gentry. In Kwangsi province, two second-class compilers and one expectant magistrate,[78] all of whom were natives of Kwangsi, and who had been sent from Peking, similarly participated in the establishment of the provincial assembly. Metropolitan officials were regarded as gentry when they behaved as members of a pressure group, particularly metropolitan officials who were from the same province.[79] Sheng Yun, the Governor General of Shensi and Kansu, adopted a different strategy and sent a telegram to Kansu natives in the capital to request the selection of Kansu gentry from the metropolitan officials serving in the capital to assist the Governor in preparing the assembly. In either case, it is apparent that, if an official in the capital went back to his home province, he was classified as gentry.[80]

There were a substantial number of expectant officials among members of the preparatory office. Public opinion at the time was not in favor of this component,[81] since their presence gave the impression that the officials were more powerful than the gentry, despite the Emperor's edict ordering officials to cooperate with the gentry. Yet, the status of an expectant official was ambiguous. Although he was assigned to a province and nominally was an official, in practical terms he was not necessarily treated as an official in that province unless he had an actual provincial post or actual designation, especially if he were active in his own native province with the nominal status of expectant official. As we shall see, many members of the preparatory offices were elected to the provincial assemblies and most of them were second-class compilers in the Academy (despite the regulation in the articles that an official was disqualified from election). In addition, one of the members of the Hupeh Provincial Assembly was an expectant circuit intendant assigned to Kiangsi and two members of the Hunan Provincial Assembly were expectant circuit intendants assigned to Hunan province. These expectant officials were treated as officials.

The inclusion of officials in the preparatory office, especially three senior provincial officials, stemmed from the provisions of the regulation. Most of those, except the senior provincial officials, who were involved in the suffrage census or in making inquiries about the candidates' qualifications and who managed the voting process, were either enlightened gentry or officials who were serving as gentry. It would be safe to say that the gentry dominated most of the preparatory process for the provincial assembly. In Szechwan,[82] the Governor was forced to change his policy of supporting the dominance of officials in the preparatory process because the gentry refused to cooperate. In Hupeh, the Governor neglected the role of the gentry in the preparatory process. In an investigative hearing, the gentry called the General Secretary of the Preparatory Office to account. When the gentry's concern with participation in the provincial assembly increased, two positions (associate chairman and councillor) in the office were secured for them.[83]

The keen concern for the ratio of participation between officials and gentry is well demonstrated in Szechwan and Hupeh. In referring to the general process of preparation in each province as of September 1908, *Tung-fang tsa-chih*[84] classified provinces such as Chihli, Shansi, Kwangsi, Kiangsi, and Shantung as led by officials and the other provinces, such as Chekiang, Kiangsu, Fukien, and Kwangtung, as led by gentry and the people. In those provinces that were gentry-led, the gentry initiated independently the organization of the Preparatory Office and called upon the governor for its official installation. Clearly, those gentry who led the preparation were in the forefront when the coalition among the provincial assemblies from various provinces was formed later and developed into a petition movement to establish a national assembly without delay. The gentry from Kiangsu and

Chekiang, in particular, had shown their strength in the movement to protect the railway concession.[85] Even in the provinces where officials dominated the process, the actual preparation for the provincial assembly was largely guided by the gentry.

The quota of provincial assemblymen in each province was set at 5 percent of the quotas for students (*sheng-yuan*) in the prefecture, department, and county schools within the province, quotas which were based on the degree of cultural advancement of the provinces. (These quotas are listed in the first column of the table at the end of this chapter.) There was a supplementary quota in certain provinces based on the amount of grain the province contributed, that is, every 30,000 *shih* of grain tribute warranted an extra assemblyman. In addition, there was a special quota for Manchu bannerman.

Within these quotas, assigned first by province, the qualified constituents were counted (these are listed in the second column of the table), and their ratio to the assigned quota was used to determine the numbers selected per prefecture, department, and county. The method of election was similar to the Japanese dual electoral system. In each primary election, a certain number of people were elected who, in turn, elected the final candidates. The number elected in this final election was one-tenth the number in the primary. It worked out that there were about a thousand voters per assemblyman (see the third column of the table). Yet not all those eligible to vote participated in the elections. According to contemporary reports, between 40 and 70 percent of Kiangsu voters went to the polls.[86] In the Fukien countryside, only 10 to 20 percent voted as against 40 percent in the cities.[87]

The elections were held in 1909, between 20 February (Fukien) and 17 July (Kwangtung).[88] Descriptions of the election process are rare, but fortunately we do have one from a prefecture of Chihli province. Shun-t'ien prefecture had 21,073 eligible voters[89]; voting records reveal that 18 successful candidates received a total of 1,227 votes.[90] There were 9 unsuccessful candidates who, among them, received 315 votes. (At least 39 votes were required for election, so one can assume that each of the 9 averaged 35 votes apiece.) What is striking in this case is the gap between total voter turnout (1,542) and the total number of those eligible to vote (21,073). (There may have been some scattered votes for candidates other than these 27, but their number would have been insignificant.) Shun-t'ien was the prefecture in which Peking was locted and had what was probably one of the more highly educated electorates. The low turnout there suggests what may have happened in areas with less educated populations.[91] A foreigner's estimate confirms the low turnout elsewhere.[92] It probably reflects an indifference or a lack of understanding of the institution of elections. The fact that officials in the capital had to be mobilized for the preparation for the provincial assemblies because of the scarcity of intellectuals educated in modern ways among the resident gentry testifies to the absence of an informed electorate.

In contrast to indifference and low participation in some areas, there were also reports of bribery and heated electioneering. The contests in the southern part of Kiangsu and Kwangtung were particularly intense. A newspaper reported that, in Kwangtung, the son of a board vice-president, "who was notorious for squeezing rural people by every possible means," was elected by intimidation and bribery.[93] In Fukien, the election results of two districts (*ch'ü*) in Hou-kuan county, Fuchow, were declared void because of irregularities on the part of those supervising the polling booth.[94] In Kiangsu, several were found to be voting by proxy in a county in Yangchow prefecture in the northern part of Kiangsu.[95]

In 1910, Censor Ou-chia Lien wrote an angry memorial to the Emperor, castigating irregularities in elections.[96] "One vote was sold for 10 taels here or 100 taels there," he said. "Elected in such a manner, who would call the successful candidates assemblymen? They will gather together to discuss public affairs only in their own self-interest. The ideas of one or two people will claim to represent the opinions of everyone. Who will believe that they are representatives of the people?" In the Hangchow by-election one vote was considered worth 50 taels.[97] In Anhwei, some who were unqualified voted, and the result was known before the officials opened the ballot box.[98] In An-su county, Chihli, votes were decided by village fights.[99] No wonder there were disputes over election results in many places.[100]

How could there be such contention when the general attitude toward elections was so apathetic? It appears that there were a few people determined to make their way through the political waters into the provincial assemblies. To understand why there was corruption in the election and why certain people directed their ambition in this direction, it may be helpful to investigate the composition of the provincial assemblies. It is not enough to say that election bribery was common both in China and the West.[101]

CHARACTERISTICS OF THE NEWLY ESTABLISHED PROVINCIAL ASSEMBLIES

On 22 July 1908, the election regulations for provincial assemblies were promulgated in response to the rather vague imperial order of the previous October for their establishment. The articles made it clear that each province was to establish an assembly within one year from the proclamation, though the actual opening date was set for 14 October 1909. According to Chang I-lin, who worked in the Office for Revising Government Institutions, the articles were drafted there. A report in the *Times*, however, insisted that it was prepared by three returned students from Chekiang who had studied in Japan.[102] None of the four members of the Office's drafting department came from Chekiang.[103] Their role may have been to draft the guidelines for the provincial assemblies contained in the imperial edict of 19 October 1907. And their ideas may have influenced Ts'en Ch'un-hsuan to write his memorial to the Emperor.

According to the *Times*, the regulations were made by returned students who, like most modern intellectuals at this time, relied on Japan as the source of new knowledge. Whether or not the four returned students the *Times* referred to actually drafted the regulations, it is probable that the writers of the regulations were returned students from Japan serving in the Office for Drawing Up Regulations for Constitutional Government. A modern education was obtained either by going abroad or by studying at schools run by Japanese-educated teachers. Even high officials, eager to observe the practice of foreign constitutional governments, learned about legal and political institutions through reading Japanese books.[104] We should bear in mind that Liang Ch'i-ch'ao actually drafted Tuan-fang's memorials of 1906.

Most discussions on local self-government or local assemblies that emerged out of the arguments about provincial assemblies relied on Japanese systems of local self-government. As we have seen in Tuan-fang's first memorial to the Emperor, the model of a constitutional system which called for both local self-government and a provincial assembly derived from Japan. There was general agreement between officials and the public with regard to the importance of local self-government not only as an essential part of constitutional government but as its very foundation.

K'ang Yu-wei's argument during the 1898 Reform Movement and Chang Chien's later argument emphasized the same point. An editorial in *Tung-fang tsa-chih* in 1907, which took its argument from Gneist or Bluntschli and insisted on the importance of local self-government for the preparation of constitutional government, recalled some historical examples. The writer argued that German constitutional government originated in local parliaments, and that the Japanese form grew from prefectural meetings.[105] Tuan-fang, who recommended imitating the Japanese experiment in the process of establishing a parliament,[106] pointed out that the term *local self-government* (*ti-fang tzu-chih*) itself came from Japanese (*chihō jichi*).[107] He built his argument from this terminological link and argued for the adoption of that system. Thus, we can see that the Japanese example of local self-government had a profound influence on Ch'ing institutions.

The regulations for the provincial assemblies presented by the Office to Draw Up Regulations for Constitutional Government followed the Japanese example.[108] Dual election and voter qualifications also followed Japanese practice. For example, in the commentary on the draft regulations, the committee clearly stated that it had followed Japan in setting the minimum age for candidates at thirty. The Ch'ing government followed the Japanese example with an eye to keeping bureaucratic control (by means of government-initiated local assemblies) over the civilian movement to urge the government to establish a national parliament promptly, and over parliamentary and party politics later.[109]

The most specific section in the regulations is Article 3, which deals with the qualifications of voters and candidates. Candidates had to be at least thirty years old; voters had to be male, at least twenty-five years old, and listed as permanent residents of the province. Both voters and candidates had to meet one of the following criteria: they had to (1) have served in a school or other public sector for at least three years; or (2) have graduated either at home or abroad from a middle school or university; or (3) hold a traditional title of at least *kung-sheng*, or *sheng yuan*; or (4) have served in a bureaucratic post of the civil 7th rank or military 5th rank or higher and have no record of prosecutions; or (5) have business capital or real estate in the province valued at 5,000 yuan; or (6) in the case of non-natives, have resided in the province for ten years of more and have business capital or real estate worth 10,000 yuan.

Certain categories of people were specifically disqualified from voting: profiteers, convicted criminals who had been sentenced to imprisonment or harsh punishment, dishonest businessmen, bankrupts, opium users, the insane, persons of base occupation (entertainers, servants, and so forth), and illiterates. Provincial officials, private secretaries, soldiers, clergymen, and students could neither vote nor become candidates; primary-school teachers could not become candidates.

In their use of the *sheng-yuan* quota of each province as the criterion for determining the number of members in the provincial assemblies, the election regulations were already designed from the gentry's viewpoint. Article 3 simply reinforced that position. The list of voters for the provincial assemblies prepared at the time favored the gentry with four of its voting qualifications: (1) public service, (2) a degree from either a traditional or a modern school, (3) bureaucratic rank (with actual positions and no record of prosecution), and (4) property. Given the traditional educational and public-service roles of the gentry class, it is clear that, even without a degree and bureaucratic rank, the mere reference to "public service" was meant to indicate the gentry class as a whole. The bureaucratic-rank qualification (limited to those who had held actual positions) seems to have been intended to exclude those who purchased nominal titles, though purchased ranks that led to actual positions (for example, those of "expectant officials") were included within this category.

The educational qualification, though it included graduates of modern schools, did not depart from the traditional concept of the gentry. Many *sheng-yuan* were involved with these new modern-style schools; conversely, many with foreign educations, such as Chin Pang-p'ing and Ts'ao Ju-lin, had received the traditional titles of *chü-jen* and *chin-shih*. The qualification based on assets may seem to diverge from the traditional concept of the gentry. The distinction between real estate and business capital seems to have separated merchants from non-merchants. In the case of non-merchants, if they were landlords relying on land for income, they were likely to have purchased at least the title of *chien-sheng*. The likelihood increased if they were interested in public affairs. Although it is not correct to assume that the gentry were necessarily landlords, generally speaking most landlords were indeed gentry. The merchant category was the only exception, but it is doubtful whether many relied on the minimum qualification of 5,000 yuan alone, since it was common for them to purchase official titles. In Chang P'eng-yuan's investigation into the social background of provincial assemblymen (see below), only six members in Shensi and one in Shantung were qualified on the grounds of their assets.[110]

Given the incompleteness of the data, it is doubtful whether the presence of people of property in the assemblies varied significantly from one province to another (except perhaps in Shansi and Anhwei, where merchants were prominent, or in the modern commercial city of Shanghai). The fact that there were 6 men of property in Shensi alone raises some doubt about the authenticity of the data in the provincial gazetteer. How is it that fully 10 percent of the 63 assemblymen in Shensi province (excluding quotas for Manchu bannermen) were in the category of merchants who had no traditional degree? Was Shensi province so noted for its commerce in those days compared with other provinces? According to Chang's report, one man was qualified on the basis of his holding 5,000 yuan of property in Kweichow, but he was also listed in the record as holding the title of "military *chü-jen*." In those days, most men were reluctant to reveal the extent of their property, so it is unlikely that this man would appear on the voters' list as the possessor of assets worth 5,000 yuan instead of under his title of military *chü-jen*. Therefore, I doubt that the editor of the Shensi gazetteer got the assets of the 6 from the voters' lists. Thus, one may very well treat the qualifications in the articles as applicable uniquely to the gentry.[111]

The dual-election system was intended to remove the "defects of reckless and random choice," according to the commentary on Article 2. "Wicked profiteers," for instance, a category singled out in the edict of September 1907 were excluded from voting. Who decided whether someone was a wicked profiteer or not? Local officials alone were authorized to judge these matters. Such restrictions had earlier been voiced by T'ieh-liang at the Lang-jun-yuan meeting: they indicate a traditional disapproval of "those who defy the fundamental principles of society, rebels against proper teachings, pettifoggers, and wicked gentry who engage in conspicuous evil," according to the commentary on Article 6. It was the job of local officials to decide who among the gentry were wicked. To some extent, T'ieh-liang did not need to worry on this score, since there were existing procedures (at least nominal ones) to identify and isolate immoral elements among the gentry. In practice, however, it is doubtful how much power local officials had to judge the degree of wickedness of the gentry.

The most thorough investigation of the social background of the men elected to the assemblies is Chang P'eng-yuan's study of constitutionalists and the 1911 Revolution.[112] According to Chang, the majority of the candidates belonged to the gentry.[113] Many of them were students (with a Japanese or a modern-Chinese education) and enlightened intellectuals; he was able to identify positively nearly 100 students with a Japanese education, and just under 50 who had graduated from schools of either law or politics.[114] For two reasons, Chang believed, however, that the actual proportion was far greater: lack of data, and the omission of educational backgrounds for candidates who also held traditional titles, which were still more highly respected than education.

"Research centers for self-government" (*tzu-chih yen-chiu-so*), which appeared in various areas after the Emperor's decree on the government's preparation for constitutional government, provided short-term training in constitutionalism.[115] We are not given the percentage of members who took the courses, though it is probable that many members in the provincial assemblies, besides those who received a foreign education or a domestic modern-school education, had some knowledge of modern political institutions.

Whether the men who took part in preparing for the provincial assemblies were classified by their traditional titles or by their modern education, they were enlightened intellectuals who had been exposed to modern legal and political practices. Most of them were elected to the provincial assemblies and actively participated in their activities, usually in leadership positions.[116] Many of the enlightened intellectuals were considered outstanding at the time for their legal and political knowledge.[117] Some studies show that this enlightened group, because of its strength in the provincial assemblies, became active in the movement to urge the government to open a national assembly without delay.[118]

The most significant group action of the gentry in the late Ch'ing was the movement to protect railway rights. In the Soochow-Hangchow-Ningpo railway dispute case there were 11 names of provincial-assembly members among the 113 in 11 prefectures of Chekiang province who signed a protest petition.[119] Ten provincial assembly members participated among the 68 founders of the Kiangsu Railroad

Association, which worked for the Kiangsu side of the railway.[120]

We have seen that the constitutional movement was led primarily by returned students, journalists (such as Meng Sen, Editor of *Tung-fang tsa-chih*, and Ti Pao-hsien, Editor of the newspaper *Shih-pao*), and graduates of domestic modern schools. In the provincial assemblies, too, they took the lead.[121] In November 1910, a conservative censor named Wen Su reported as follows:

> The provincial assemblies and local self-governing associations are the foundation of the parliamentary system. Those qualified for membership, however, are few. The reason is that local officials, when they are unable to determine the qualifications of a voter, delegate authority to the investigators (of the preparatory office). The investigators are all untrustworthy figures from a journalistic or modern-school background. The prominent people in the rural areas are ashamed of mingling with them. Because of this reluctance, ordinary people are suspicious [about the elections]. Consequently, they let the investigators decide who is qualified to vote. Since there was no surveillance, the good have been mixed with the bad.[122]

If the search for qualified candidates was already under the control of enlightened intellectuals from a journalistic or modern-school background, it is not surprising that an imperial censor would seek to correct such "defects" in favor of the conservative gentry who were skeptical of the locus of leadership in the provincial assemblies. Wen Su recommended that actual officials holding posts and gentry with a degree of at least *kung-sheng* or *chü-jen* be granted double voting rights and the priority of being selected in the case of a tied vote. He also recommended privileges for those who paid a higher-than-average tax.

Wen's assertion that "prominent people in the rural areas" were reluctant to join "untrustworthy figures from a journalistic or modern-school background" tallies with a memoir written by a contemporary participant by the name of Chung Ts'ai-hung.[123] The memoir records the case of an old Hanlin scholar's refusal to serve as a member, although he was elected. It also tallies with the assertion of Sheng Hsuan-huai, famous for being attacked as the man in charge during the Chekiang railway dispute, that "southern gentry are happy to act in accordance with the opinions of journalists and students [of the modern schools]."[124] Those involved in newspapers and modern schools increased their influence during 1907 and 1908. The enlightened intellectuals were particularly active because the conservative gentry avoided participation in the provincial assemblies, thereby permitting them to take the lead away from the conservative upper gentry. The provincial assemblies had become the rallying places for the enlightened sector. J. O. P. Bland maintained that the members of the provincial assemblies were professional politicians with a background in Western education.[125] Charles Tenney, secretary to the American Consulate Office, observed correctly that "the educated minority forming the constitutional party ... possess superior ability and energy, and, moreover, control the provincial assemblies and the Senate [i.e., National Assembly]."[126]

Chang P'eng-yuan in his investigation of the social background of the provincial-assembly members followed Chung-li Chang's division of the gentry into upper and lower class, arguing that the lower class was in the majority.[127] This view needs to be qualified. If we look more closely at the assemblies in Shantung and Szechwan, for example, we might come to a different conclusion. In Shantung, among 97 members (excluding 7 unconfirmed out of the original 104), 52 were lower-stratum gentry (holding *sheng-yuan, ling-sheng, fu-sheng,* and *tseng-sheng* titles). In Szechwan, among 114 (excluding 13 unconfirmed out of 104), 54 belonged to the lower stratum (*sheng-yuan* and *lin-sheng*).[128] Thus, the lower-degree-holders were certainly no less numerous than the upper stratum; but, considering the numerical majority the former occupied within the gentry class as a whole,[129] we find (at least in this context) a conspicuous predominance of the upper stratum. If we divide the gentry into those who were former officials with actual posts and those who held *chü-jen, kung-sheng, sheng-yuan,* and *chien-sheng* degrees, as the Tientsin self-goverment regulations do, we must conclude that there were fewer representatives from the upper (official) stratum. Yet, we have to keep in mind that half of the chairmen, vice-chairmen of the provincial assemblies, and members of the preparatory committees were holders of the *chin-shih* degree.[130] Although the *chin-shih* were in an overall minority, their influence was great. The strength of the upper stratum varied widely between provinces and even within each province.[131] Nonetheless, the leaders of the constitutional movement and the provincial assemblies are better characterized by the education they received than by their degrees or titles. That is, the leadership of the gentry relied less on the authority of higher degrees than on the content of the education they received and the activities that resulted from it.[132]

The conservative gentry hesitated to participate in the provincial assemblies, not only because they wished to avoid the "untrustworthy figures from a journalistic or modern-school background," but because of bad elements ("wicked gentry") within their own ranks. As another imperial censor said: "Among those elected there were many untrustworthy village types. The upright gentry feel ashamed of mingling with them."[133] The problem did not go unnoticed in the Regulations of the Provincial Assembly, and T'ieh-liang once worried about it, but, as I mentioned earlier, the authorities could not deal effectively with the bad sector. Some of the "wicked gentry" succeeded in getting elected to some assemblies. The troubles these men caused were to be found originally on the county rather than the provincial level. During the discussion about the establishment of local self-government organizations in prefectures, departments, and counties, the matter naturally became serious.[134] On the provincial level, too, there were certain areas in which these "wicked gentry" could play a significant role. Some tried to obstruct the passage of resolutions to prohibit semi-official gambling.[135] For example, one elected assemblyman was prosecuted on the grounds that he had received bribes during the process of deliberating a bill in the Kwangtung Provincial Assembly prohibiting gambling. He was, in fact, the secretary of a merchant involved in a gambling case.[136] Another member of the Kiangsi Provincial Assembly had worked for ten years as an arbitrator of petty disputes, which was a common occupation for corrupt gentry, and he succeeded, at great expense, in getting himself elected.[137]

Out of five Hupeh assemblymen who were to fill the vacancies left by the assemblymen transferred to the National Assembly, one man, Liu Pang-chih, held the title of expectant circuit intendant assigned to a province. He was called "the most influential person among the gentry associated with the provincial government" because he was Director of the Bureau of Training, Director of the Military School, and Director of the Army Special Primary School. As a result of holding these posts, he managed to become a member of the provincial assembly. He even became a standing member of the provincial assembly.[138] The expression *the most influential person among the gentry* could be read, depending on the situation, as "wicked gentry." When he amassed so much power through various positions, why would he need to become a member if not to increase his own power? For him, the position of member in the provincial assembly meant another "official" (*kuan*) post. Thus, when the anti-constitutionalist Hu Ssu-ching made the following statement, it was not without some justification:

Once the traditional principle of personnel administration ceased to work, every elected person aspired to become an official in his local area. With the abolition of the examination system, every *chü-jen* and *kung-sheng* hustled to find some official position. Even though the members of both the National Assembly in the capital and the provincial assemblies in the provinces were not registered in the list of officials, they all received salaries and hence were regarded as the same as officials.[139]

He went on to blame the members and the chairmen of the self-government associations for including "wicked gentry and bad *chien-sheng*" in their midst.

Chang P'eng-yuan has noted that many assemblymen had had careers as government officials.[140] Among the 63 chairmen and vice-chairmen, 40 had served as officials either in the capital or locally, most in middle-level ranks. Chang's data regarding the pre-election posts of the assemblymen, however, are incomplete, except for one or two provinces.[141] In Fengtien, only 2 of 31 assemblymen (53 including the expectant assemblymen) were officials with actual posts.[142] In Hupeh, the pre-election careers of 35 out of 97 (excluding the general secretary but including expectant members) have been identified.[143] Nineteen were expectant officials. Even though there were far more expectant officials than officials with actual posts in the late Ch'ing, one can detect a movement of expectant officials into the provincial assembly, which agrees with Chang's observation that membership was viewed as the ultimate goal of the candidate official.

There is some evidence to support this view. As we have seen, a proposal was fielded to appoint provincial assemblymen as officials. Some argued that those elected to the self-government body should be "rewarded with an official position."[144] Thus, assemblymen like Liu Pang-chih of Hupeh naturally viewed membership in the provincial assembly as an "actual position" that had a considerable influence over local administration. As Hu Ssu-ching pointed out after the abolition of the examination system, there was a serious question about what was going to happen to the people who formerly had sought official posts through the system.[145] Without resorting to the favor of the governor or the additional purchase of posts, these people hoped to find posts through election to the provincial assembly.

Hu Ssu-ching castigated the assemblymen for even receiving a salary. The data in Hunan show that, as in Hupeh, the expense allowance (*kung-fei*) for chairmen was 100 yuan, for vice-chairmen 80 yuan, and for standing members and general secretaries 60 yuan.[146] When the Hupeh Assembly followed the model of the Shantung Provincial Assembly in which the expense allowance was increased on condition that "they do not assume other positions," the amount was changed to 150 yuan for chairmen, 120 for vice-chairmen, and 70 for standing members and general secretaries. These allowances are comparable to the salary of Chang I-lin, who received 60 yuan as an outstanding private secretary to the Governor of Chihli.[147] The members were also given an extra expense allowance during the session.

Granted that he based his investigation of the numbers of voters on incomplete data, Chang estimated the ratio of voters to total population as 0.42 percent. Aside from the three provinces where information is lacking, these calculations are close to those of Chung-li Chang, who found the ratio of gentry to total population in the late nineteenth century to be 0.39 percent.[148] Their provincial figures are also close, especially for Anhwei, Shansi, and Kwangsi.[149]

THE AUTHORITY OF THE PROVINCIAL ASSEMBLY

Section 6, Article 21 of the Regulations of the Provincial Assembly described the authority of the assembly as follows: (1) approval or rejection of projects relevant to the interests of the province; (2) deliberation on the provincial budget; (3) settlement of accounts of the budget for the province; (4) decisions concerning the tax laws and bond issues of the province; (5) decisions concerning the financial obligations or welfare burden of the provincial population; (6) revision of particular regulations in the province; (7) affairs relating to concessions within the province; (8) election of national assemblymen (from the provincial assemblymen); (9) decisions in response to requests from the National Assembly; (10) decisions in response to requests for advice from the governor; (11) settlement of disputes among lower self-government associations; and (12) decisions regarding appeals or recommendations from lower self-government associations.

Article 28 gave the provincial assembly additional authority to denounce officials or gentry to the governor general or governor for accepting bribes or for other illegal acts.

The authority of the provincial assembly was naturally limited to its own province. Without the establishment of a local self-governing body, and no distinction set clearly between national and local taxes, however, the local provincial assemblies had difficulty interpreting the definition of "the approval or rejection of projects relevant to the interests of the province." Many problems arose in dealing with various agenda related to the regulation because of the different interpretations of whether a particular project was national or provincial. The Office to Draw Up Regulations for Constitutional Government wrote to each governor: "There have been many projects dealt with in the provincial assembly which are actually within the jurisdiction of the central government. The distinction between national and provincial jurisdiction can be made only after the appropriate regulations have been fixed. Since such regulations have not yet been established, the governor is temporarily authorized to make such judgments."[150]

The Office acknowledged that there had been disputes over the rights, duties, and jurisdictions of the provinces:[151] whether, for example, the burden of bond issues would be partially borne by the people of a province, or the contracting of foreign loans would be done independently on the provincial level. Yet, one may read the ambiguous phrase *the approval or rejection of projects relevant to the interests of the province* as a way of helping the new administration to expand projects like educational and sanitary facilities and to promote the formulation of traditional gentry functions discussed earlier. To the Ch'ing nobles and high-ranking officials like Tsai-tse, Lu Tsung-yü, and Yuan Shih-k'ai, it was supposed to be what was called "supplementing the insufficiency of bureaucratic administration."

For the gentry themselves, local self-government was something they had desired for a long time. An argument that appeared after the proclamation of the Regulations of the Provincial Assembly defined the gentry as longstanding representatives of local self-government. It stated that "Chinese local self-government in the past was in accord with a natural tendency and existed in practice but was not called by that name. . . . Now, in instituting this system, we are carrying out an earlier practice, not creating a new one."[152]

The establishment of the provincial assemblies was in a sense a response to T'an Ssu-t'ung's question, "What is the sense of dealing with the affairs of a local area without having the people deliberate them themselves?"[153] It was this kind of argument that led to the establishment in Hunan of the Southern Study Association prior to the 1898 Reform[154] and the Political Association after the failure of the 1907 Reform. In Hunan, the Provincial Assembly grew directly out of the Political Association.[155] Ridiculing the franchise as "silk-gowned voting power," Bland considered that each provincial assembly, under the pressure of members desirous of monopolizing influence and political power, performed a nationwide function of protecting the interests of middle-class intellectuals who had governed locally for centuries.[156]

In addition to the institutionalization of the traditional functions of the gentry in local administration, new functions were added to the provincial assemblies. For example, the power to deliberate on taxes and the issuance of bonds, the power to examine the financial burden for the people of the province or to grant and receive concessions, and so on, could be considered extensions of the already existing traditional functions. But deliberating on a budget and the settlement of a budget were new activities which encroached on some of the powers of the governor. The authority to prosecute corrupt officials, described in Article 28, could contribute to strengthening the power of the gentry.

When the constitutional movement incorporated the traditional argument for local government, the provincial assemblies were pressured to develop their activities far beyond the limits set for a pure form of local self-government. We need only refer, as an example, to the petition movement for the prompt opening of a parliament in coordination with the provincial assembly in each province. Since the assembly itself was an elective institution, the provincial assembly was a significant development in Chinese history. Whereas some Western observers were afraid the provincial assembly would have an "autocratic-bureaucratic" character,[157] others lauded the establishment of the assembly as a sort of "bloodless revolution."[158] The following statement, which appeared in a summary of events for the 9th month of the 1st year of Hsuan-t'ung (1909) in *Tung-fang tsa-chih*, expressed a common feeling about the importance of the provincial assemblies: "On the 1st day [of the 9th month], the session of each provincial assembly opened. It means for China the dawn of a new age when the people are allowed to deliberate questions of government."[159] The desire of the gentry since the late Ming and early Ch'ing to exercise their power institutionally and to participate in politics as a class and not as individuals was on its way to fulfillment. Although one may not agree that this was a "bloodless revolution," the traditional gentry did take over new functions, and leadership within the gentry class shifted from the conservative gentry with high degrees and high rank to the enlightened intellectuals. Clearly, a new era had arrived.

The most troublesome area lay in the relationship between the authority of the governor and that of the provincial assembly. The anti-gubernatorial stance of the provincial assembly was related to its inherent tendency to oppose centralized power, which eventually led to revolution.[160] The memorial outlining the regulations of the provincial assembly, written by the Office to Draw Up Regulations for Constitutional Government, discussed the relationship between the local executive and the assembly as follows:

Constitutional regimes in foreign countries use a bicameral system, in which the lower house in the capital has a direct link to local parliaments. In federal systems, each state has its own parliament and the national government controls the fundamentals only. With a vast land expanse and a large population, China has been divided into provinces, and the administration of each province has been under the control of its governor. Local government is not directly related to central government as it is in foreign countries. The present *chün-hsien* system, however, is different from the *feng-chien* system. The governor is under the direction of the central government in every particular, and the relationship is different from that of a federal government where each state has its own laws and implements them independently. The provincial assembly was established as the pivotal connection between local self-government and centralized power in the capital. Through this relationship, each provincial administration is expected to reflect public opinion without jeopardizing the power of the central government.[161]

This statement shows that the Office to Draw Up Regulations for Constitutional Government had great difficulty in defining the relationship between the governor, the central government, and the provincial assembly, partly because the position of the governor in the late Ch'ing was a peculiar one. In those days, the Court was also determined to increase its centralized power at the expense of the governors' authority while encouraging the practice of local self-government.[162] A governor's authority was, in fact, dual. According to the constitutional office, the governor was competent enough to "preside over administrative matters in his own province," yet, in spite of the decentralizing tendency, the governor "operates under the direction of the central government in every particular."[163] In fact, the institution of the governorship was directly related to the emperor, and the governor possessed authority, automatically or by request, to participate in decision-making about national policies. Public policies within a given province were not implemented simply by conforming to orders coming from the central government, but were initiated by the governor himself and implemented after acquiring the approval, or sometimes even post-facto approval, of the central government. Sometimes, a specific governor was authorized to deal with affairs involving the national interest, such as foreigners or foreign governments. As a matter of fact, the central government used to follow the practice, although it was not founded upon institutional arrangements, of asking routinely for the opinion and agreement of the governors when it made some important policy decisions.

That the governor had wide discretionary power over financial as well as military matters certainly helped to strengthen his position. Without discretionary power over financial matters, the office would not have succeeded in building large-scale factories for military armaments or the training of army personnel in each province during the late Ch'ing period. Because of these peculiar characteristics some governors were privileged to stay in office for an unusually long period. For example, Chang Chih-tung was the Hu-kwang Governor from 1887 to 1907 and Li Hung-chang the Chihli Governor from 1870 to 1895 and again from 1900 to 1901.

The ministers who investigated constitutionalism in Europe feared that the French or Belgian type of local assembly would tend to decentralize the government. The Ch'ing Court did not want the power of the provincial assembly extended in a similar way; it wanted to pursue the policies of both centralized administration and local self-government simultaneously. The argument in favor of local self-government had its source in the traditional concept of *feng-chien*, and in reality the members of the assembly represented the power of the gentry on the local level. This emphasis on the local level, or on the existence of the gentry as distinct from the officials, would lead to both anti-officialdom and anti-centralization as it did, for example, in the antagonism between the gentry and the officials dramatized in the Rights Recovery Movement.[164] The central government tried to resist these tendencies.

The conclusion might be drawn that the central government gave the governor authority for this reason. As we have seen, it granted the governor, who theoretically was not responsible to the local assembly, power of supervision over the provincial assembly and the power of approval over the resolutions passed in the assembly (Section 8, Article 46). The governor was also given discretionary power to act as judge over the differences in interpretation of a bill and other means of controlling the general operation of the provincial assembly. Discretionary power over differences in interpretation was particularly significant to the extent that the provincial assembly, as the product of the constitutional movement, was expected to become the instrument of the constitutional movement. It would be unfair, however, in this connection, to ignore the counter-tendency built into the imperial structure to curb the ever-powerful offices of the governor, which made it possible to utilize the provincial assemblies as a means of reducing the authority of the governor.

At the same time, in response to the fear that its own authority might be weakened as the constitutional movement advanced, the central government advocated the policy of centralization, representing it as characteristic of Western-style polities. An editorial appearing in a 1907 issue of *Tung-fang tsa-chih* criticized the move as follows:

> The recent infiltration of Western influence into the East has no precedent and is so powerful that, in accordance with general opinion, we are forced to reform our institutions. This has caused considerable trouble for the high-ranking officials around the Emperor who have racked their brains to come up with a plan to preserve their power. The only alternative acceptable to the Court, which is thereby hoping to revitalize itself, is what Westerners call the centralization of power. This move is, in reality, no less than the transfer of the military and financial power of provinces to the central government. The centralization of power is, in fact, diametrically opposed to local self-government.[165]

The argument clearly points to contemporary concern about this dilemma, a concern that resulted, partially, in a considerable reduction of the governors' authority in the Regulations of the Provincial Assembly. Yü Shih-mei, a member of the second group of ministers to investigate and draft a constitution, presented a memorial to the Emperor on 21 June 1909, condemning the Office to Draw Up Regulations for Constitutional Government for broadening the authority of the provincial assembly to be much wider than the Prussian model.

That caused some vitriolic controversy at the time.[166] The authority of the provincial assembly described in Article 21 (summed up in the twelve kinds of authority listed above) was attacked because it was considered "limitless." Articles 22, 23, and 24, which gave a National Assembly (with the participation of representatives of the provincial assemblies) final discretionary power over any disputed bills in the provincial assemblies, were also condemned. Attention was drawn to clauses that allegedly rendered the provincial assembly powerful, such as its authority (1) to audit and approve financial matters; (2) to appoint and to impeach the governor, and (3) to deliberate statutory bills. The second point was a source of considerable controversy. The Office to Draw Up Regulations for Constitutional Government and Liang Ch'i-ch'ao argued that it was necessary to include the power to appoint and to impeach in the articles of the provincial assembly.[167]

The authority of the provincial assembly over whatever projects were approved or rejected was an ambiguous formula which might have resulted in the restriction of the governor's authority over tax laws, public debts, concessions, and burdens of the people in the province, the nature of which could be extended to the nation in practice, thus reducing the power of the governor and the central government as well. Article 28, giving the assembly the power to prosecute and denounce officials or gentry to the governor in a given province for their illegal acts, would have had the same effect. The right to approve the budget intruded on the governor's traditional "independent power over finance," and, at a time when the distinction between national and local taxes was yet to be made, the governor's authority in this area was further undermined.

If we consider how bills were to be initiated (Article 25), both the provincial assembly and the governor had a right to introduce legislation, except for the latter's exclusive right to initiate budget bills. These provisions meant that the governor was under considerable restraint, in contrast to the enormous power he had wielded in the past. The Office to Draw Up Regulations for Constitutional Government suggested subtly that "the establishment of the provincial assembly is the pivotal connection between the local government and the centralization of power." The real implication of this sophisticated statement can be fully understood only when the Regulations of the Provincial Assembly are carefully scrutinized in relation to given conditions.

Since the beginning of the New Policy in 1901, the traditional argument for local self-government—the incorporation of the *feng-chien* ideal into the present system, the removal of the rule of avoidance, and the strengthening of the power of the gentry—was combined with modern arguments for a Western-style parliament to support the idea of local self-government. After 1904, these arguments were advanced as a part of the discussions about a constitution. High officials who were despatched abroad to observe constitutional systems related their recommendations to the need to improve traditional local administration and to institutionalize the power of the gentry. They concluded that a constitution was not only desirable but possible. Their observations also convinced them that, in order for the Ch'ing government to prepare for and control the constitutional process, local self-government was indispensable. In addition to institutionalizing the traditional functions of the gentry, local self-government was considered essential to mobilize the energy of the gentry in implementing the new order.

There seemed to be a consensus on the introduction of local self-government as a preliminary move toward a constitution. A number of opinions in favor of local self-government were both expressed within court circles and published in fora such as *Tung-fang tsa-chih*. The Lang-jun-yuan meeting, where T'ieh-liang, Yuan Shih-k'ai, Hsu Shih-ch'ang, and others gathered in response to the report from the Ministers for Investigating and Drafting a Constitution culminated in a statement declaring the intention of preparing a constitution and reforming government institutions as a preparatory step. The Office for Revising Government Institutions was set up for this purpose, providing a preliminary step toward establishing a provincial assembly as the parliament for each province. With the support of powerful officials such as Ts'en Ch'un-hsuan, Yuan Shih-k'ai, and Ch'eng Te-ch'üan, the establishment of the provincial assemblies was officially proclaimed on 9 October 1907.

On 11 August 1908, the regulations and election laws for the provincial assembly were proclaimed, and preparation for the assemblies went forward under the leadership of enlightened intellectuals, that is, gentry who had been educated in Japan or in modern schools at home. A majority of the preparatory members became members of the provincial assemblies and monopolized the positions of chairman and vice-chairman. The rapid development of modern schools and journalism also helped in the preparation of the assemblies. The gentry thus institutionalized its traditional functions and was expanding its activities. At the same time, the leadership of the gentry class in the assemblies passed from the grand old gentry to men who were the possessors of the new knowledge rather than the traditional degrees.

There were the so-called "wicked gentry," the profiteers who participated in elections along with the enlightened intellectuals. They brought corruption to the election process in the midst of a prevailing skepticism and indifference. Yet both groups represented the gentry class.

The election laws differed to some extent from those of Japan (where the amount of property tax was the criterion for election) in that the electorate was composed of the traditional gentry class. The difference between the two countries may be attributable to the difference in the character of their social structures, Chinese society being a "gentry-official order."

In the formal plan, about 1,000 gentry voters were to elect one member for the assembly, but the actual number turned out to be much smaller, and a considerable number of those elected were mere expectant officials without actual posts. As the traditional rights of the gentry became institutionalized, membership in the provincial assembly was considered to be a bureaucratic position of a kind. The reason for electoral irregularities in the midst of general apathy was attributable to this holdover from the past.

The Ch'ing Court aimed to secure support from the gentry class in exchange for the realization of their traditional aspiration, that is, the formalization of their traditional functions. The central government, then, tried to have the time-honored aspiration for constitutionalism proceed in a controlled fashion. If affairs went as the government wished, the power of the provincial governors general and governors, which represented in a sense a centrifugal tendency in the late Ch'ing, would be restricted to some extent (through the provincial assemblies) and the provincial assembly, too, would be under the control of the central government. In reality, however, the provincial assembly opposed the governors general and governors and, in so doing, opposed the central government of which the governors were deputies. The provincial assemblies even went so far as to organize an alliance to press the central government for the prompt establishment of a parliament, which was clearly beyond their jurisdiction. In fact, the central government preferred to lead up to the establishment of a central parliament; it would take years for the preparatory plan to take effect.

The modern Western political theory of local self-government undoubtedly played an important role in the establishment of the provincial assembly. What I have attempted to clarify is how this modern theory applied to the Chinese and how it became institutionalized. We have looked at the process of establishing the provincial assembly from the perspective of gentry power. The introduction of the provincial assembly greatly modified the traditional official-gentry relationship. A new relationship developed in line with the radical transformation occurring within the old order.

The pressure on China of modern Western theory was of great importance, but it was effective only within the context of Chinese historical tradition. There is a danger of overestimating outside forces. It would be unrealistic to think of this movement as a break in the continuity of Chinese history. Change in China becomes an actuality but only when it is rooted in Chinese history. The "new" China developed not as a result of foreign influence but in keeping with its own historical evolution.

The Quotas and Electorates for Provincial Assembly Elections 1909

Province	Assemblymen Quota	Qualified Electorate	Voters per Assemblyman
Fengtien	50	52,679	*1,053
Kirin	30	15,362	512
Heilungkiang	30	4,446	144
Chihli	140	162,585	1,101
Kiangsu	121	162,472	2,772
Anhwei	83	77,902	938
Kiangsi	106	(120,025)	*(1,295)
Chekiang	114	90,275	792
Fukien	72	50,034	694
Hupeh	80	113,233	1,415
Hunan	82	100,487	1,225
Shantung	100	119,321	1,193
Honan	96	(90,527)	*(943)
Shansi	86	53,669	*622
Shensi	63	29,055	*461
Kansu	43	9,249	*215
Sinkiang	(30)	---------	------
Szechwan	105	191,530	*1,824
Kwangtung	91	141,558	1,555
Kwangsi	57	40,284	710
Yunnan	68	(47,005)	*(691)
Kweichow	39	42,526	1,090

* My own calculation.

Notes: The quotas for assemblymen are taken from "Ko-sheng tzu-i-chü chang-ch'eng fu an-yü (The regulations of the provincial assemblies with commentary), in *Cheng-chih kuan-pao.* no. 226. According to the second article of Section 2, Kiangsu province, in accordance with its student quota, was to have 89 members. This number is less than the 114 assigned to Chekiang, whose cultural advancement was not significantly different. The authorities may have regarded Kiangsu as more populous than Chekiang and increased the number of the Kiangsu assemblymen in accordance with the amount of grain tribute. Cf. Chang P'eng-yuan, *Li-hsien-p'ai,* p. 16. The regulations give a figure for Kiangsi of 97. Later the Office to Draw Up Regulations for Constitutional Government decided to change that number to 106 in response to the claim put forward by the Governor of Kiangsi that the quota had been miscalculated. See "Telegram of the Kiangsi Government to the Office to Draw Up Regulations for Constitutional Government," in *TFTC* 6:5–237. Chang P'eng-yuan was mistaken when he gave the number 93. (See Chang P'eng-yuan, "Ch'ing-chi tzu-i-chü i-yuan," pp. 13, 226.) The numbers for the three northeastern provinces were allocated at random, since no fixed numbers of students had been set and the governorships had only recently been established. Sinkiang province could not establish an Advisory Council because the educational level of its people was considered too low to operate a provincial assembly.

The numbers of voters per assemblyman are taken from the following sources: Fengtien: *Tung-tang tsa-chih* (*TFTC*) 6.3:101–106; Kirin: *TFTC* 6.3:107–108; Heilungkiang: *Cheng-chih kuan-pao* 722:307 (the *Hei-lung-chiang chih-kao* compiled in 1932 gives the number 155; I do not know where this figure came from); Chihli: *TFTC* 6.6:231–232; Kiangsu: *TFTC* 6.3:101–106 and 6.4:174; Anhwei: *TFTC* 6:5:236 and *Cheng-chih kuan-pao* 705:487–480; Chekiang: *TFTC* 6.5:234; Fukien: *TFTC* 6:4:175; Hupeh: *TFTC* 6:5:233; Hunan: *TFTC* 6.6:293–294; Shantung: *TFTC* 6:6:234; Shansi: *TFTC* 6:6:236; Shensi: *TFTC* 6:6:235; Kansu: *TFTC* 6:6:236; Szechwan: *Cheng-chih kuan-pao* 649:521–528; Kwangtung: *TFTC* 6.7:351–353; Kwangsi: *TFTC* 6.6:236; Kweichow: *TFTC* 6.6:231–232.

Since I do not have the number of voters in Yunnan, Kwangsi, or Honan, I have used the estimated number of gentry in these provinces in the post-Taiping period as given by Chung-li Chang in *The Chinese Gentry*, p. 164. Chang's figures for the gentry in the provinces other than the three above correspond roughly with those given in the sources above.

CHAPTER SIX

The Soochow-Hangchow-Ningpo Railway Dispute

When foreign powers intensified their thrust into China after the Sino-Japanese War, the Chinese launched a movement to recover their lost economic rights. Local gentry led several campaigns, paving the way for the constitutional movement and the formation of a national capitalist class. These campaigns were directed against the concessions for the development of mines and for the construction of railways granted to foreigners. Their aim was to abrogate foreign concessions and use Chinese capital to carry out development projects.

One of the most successful of these efforts involved the Soochow-Hangchow-Ningpo Railway. From 1905 on, the leaders of the movement to recover the railway concession in Chekiang and Kiangsu demanded that the preliminary Sino-British contract of 1890 be canceled and a British loan turned down. A sharp clash followed between the local Chinese gentry on one side and the British and the Imperial Court on the other.[1]

The movement was led by Chang Chien and T'ang Shou-ch'ien, two prominent leaders of the local gentry of Chekiang and Kiangsu provinces. They were concurrently leaders of the constitutional movement, which was going on at the same time. The railway dispute appears to have been related to the growing movement for a constitution, and to the activities of the provincial assembly, a representative institution of the gentry. A study of the dispute should give us some insight into the nature of nationalism and regionalism as well as constitutionalism in China in the late Ch'ing period. Since the dispute in Chekiang and Kiangsu was a precursor of the railway-rights preservation movement in Szechwan (a major factor leading to the 1911 Revolution), this study should also help us understand how the Chinese gentry stratum responded to the 1911 Revolution.[2]

THE BACKGROUND OF THE DISPUTE

The idea of a railway linking Soochow, Hangchow, and Ningpo had been suggested as early as 1895 by Chang Chien, a noted leader of Kiangsu province. In a draft memorial for the Governor General, Chang pointed out that a railway line with a great deal of traffic in the area to be served would be profitable, and that the topography posed few problems for the construction of a relatively short line.[3] He noted that a number of foreign companies were interested in the construction of such a line.[4] A group of Hangchow gentry-merchants, headed by Circuit Intendant Lin Wei-chen, petitioned[5] the Chekiang Governor, proposing the construction of a 40-*li* commercial line (between Kung-ch'en-ch'iao and Chiang-kan cha-k'ou), as part of the Soochow-Hangchow-Ningpo railway. In addition to Lin, a certain Kao with three others was also interested in the railway construction in Kiangsu and Chekiang.[6]

These moves did not result in any concrete plan and came to an end on 15 October 1898, when Sheng Hsuan-huai, Director General of the Imperial Chinese Railway Administration, signed a preliminary contract with the British and Chinese Corporation[7] to construct the Soochow-Hangchow-Ningpo line. Article 3 of this contract stipulated that, after the signing of the preliminary contract, Jardine, Matheson & Co. would conduct an "immediate" survey of the probable route and the Imperial Chinese Railway Administration would make the necessary arrangements for the protection of the British surveyors. Article 4 stated that, if local difficulties should arise, they should be "put right" by Chinese authorities.[8]

The contract was not translated into action for some time, however, since the British goal in signing it was to secure a concession in China ahead of other competing powers, not necessarily to start work immediately.[9] A movement soon developed, therefore, from the Chinese side to construct the lucrative line with their own capital and engineering. In 1899, an official named Hsu Ch'i petitioned for the suspension of the Hangchow-Ningpo line project, but the central government turned down the proposal on the grounds that a contract had already been signed with Britain.[10]

In 1903, four years later, Ch'ien Chin-sun, together with fellow Chekiang gentry, suggested the construction of a railroad that would link Shanghai to Hangchow and Hu-shu via a route that went through Cha-p'u, along the coast of Hangchow Bay, in collaboration with German investors. This proposal for a parallel line that covered almost the same territory as the Soochow-Hangchow-Ningpo railway[11] was apparently designed to hold in check the British concession. The proposal was rejected by Sheng Hsuan-huai for fear it might result in a waste of capital and a British protest.

Undisturbed by the rejection, however, the Chekiang gentry, led by Li Hou-yu,[12] an influential merchant-gentryman of Shanghai, applied for a line[13] similar to that proposed by Ch'ien. Faced with these moves by the gentry, Sheng notified Byron Brenan (the British Consul General in Shanghai, who was acting as agent for the British and Chinese Corporation) on 24 May that, "unless within six months from the date of this letter surveys are made, estimates prepared, and a final agreement concluded," the Soochow-Hangchow-Ningpo railway concession would be withdrawn by China and the preliminary contract would be canceled.[14] Sheng reasoned that, since other Chinese merchants were moving to construct a railway that would link Soochow, Hangchow, and Ningpo, he could wait no longer. Brenan replied on 31 May. He declined to comment on the call for a survey within six months,[15] maintaining only that the conclusion of a formal agreement at an early date was up to the Chinese. According to Sheng, when a contract on the Shanghai-Ningpo line was signed on 9 July, he again notified the British orally of the Chinese plan to abrogate the preliminary contact if the British did not begin work within a time limit.[16] Chinese concern seemed to have subsided for the time being.

The movement to recover economic rights spread to other parts of the nation. In 1904, Chang Chih-tung led a successful movement to recover the American Canton-Hankow railway concession.[17] Beginning in April 1905, efforts to reclaim foreign mining concessions were launched in Wenchow and three other prefectures in Chekiang province.[18] In May of the same year, an American corporation offered the Chekiang Governor a loan for the Chekiang-Kiangsi line. The proposal aroused such a protest among the gentry in Hangchow and other prefectures of Chekiang that it was rejected.[19]

The success of the gentry's rights-recovery movements involving the Canton-Hankow line and the Chekiang-Kiangsi line no doubt encouraged the Chekiang gentry, who had failed to get permission to construct the Soochow-Hangchow-Ningpo line, to renew their efforts to exclude foreigners from the construction of the Soochow-Hangchow-Ningpo railway.[20] As a result, the Chekiang Railway Company was established on 3 August 1905, by about 160 Chekiang gentry, including such leading constitutionalists as Wang K'ang-nien, Chang Yuan-chi, and T'ang Shou-ch'ien, and Shanghai capitalists such as Yen Hsin-hou and Shen Tun-ho. At its inaugural meeting, T'ang was chosen as Director General and Liu Chin-tsao as Vice-Director. The participants at the meeting decided to call for the abrogation of the 1898 Sino-British preliminary contract on the Soochow-Hangchow-Ningpo railway, and telegraphed the decision to Sheng Hsuan-huai.[21] Huang Shao-ch'i, a Sub-Chancellor at the Hanlin Academy from Chekiang province, reported to the Board of Commerce the establishment of the company and the selection of its staff members. In compliance with commercial law, its charter was also reported to the board.[22] Other high-ranking Chekiang natives in the Peking government supported the establishment of the company, including such renowned gentry as Wang Wen-shao, a former Grand Councillor, Ko Pao-hua, a former Minister of the Board of Punishment, Ch'en Pang-jui, a Vice-Minister of the Board of Revenues, and Shen Chia-pen and Hu Yü-fen, two Vice-Ministers of the Board of Punishment.[23] From the names of supporters and promoters of the company one can easily gather that the company reflected the wishes of most of the Chekiang gentry. Within ten days after its establishment, the subscription for its shares totaled 2 million yuan,[24] reflecting the strong support among the people of Chekiang for the native-financed company. The formation of the Chekiang Railway Company was quickly approved by the Imperial Court on 23 September 1905.

In an effort to realize its goal, the company had Chu Hsi-en, a Chekiang-born Censor in Peking, memorialize the Throne in September, requesting an outright abrogation of the British Soochow-Hangchow-Ningpo railway concession. Chu argued that the preliminary contract should be annulled because seven years had passed since its signing, which was generally accepted in the West as the length of time after which a contract could legally be annulled. He also argued that Sheng Hsuan-huai himself should be responsible for its negotiation with the British company. The memorial was approved and Sheng Hsuan-huai was given an imperial order, on 23 September 1905, to negotiate the contract's abrogation together with the Chekiang Governor.[25]

On 3 October, Sheng informed the British and Chinese Corporation of the imperial order and called for a conference, for which he failed to receive a positive response. On 28 December, he again urged the British to discuss the matter, pointing out that the contract stipulated that it could be revised if any difficulties arose.[26] He argued, too, that it should be canceled, since his earlier call for the start of a survey within six months had been ignored. The British rejected Sheng's request, first saying that a local protest does not constitute a difficulty as stipulated in the contract and that the initial survey had already been done between October 1898 and March 1899.[27] On 12 January 1906, in answer to the second communication, the British argued that Sheng did not qualify as a negotiator since he was currently official intendent of the Shanghai-Ningpo Railway Corporation and that he, therefore, could not be regarded as representing the formal position of the Chinese government.[28] Sheng replied that he was under an imperial order to negotiate about the issue, and that the alleged survey had not been reported nor presented to the Chinese for discussion.[29]

Continuing to ignore Sheng as a negotiator, the British began to seek direct communication with the Chekiang Governor.[30] They probably perceived that it would be unfavorable to deal with Sheng because of his earlier call for a survey within a six-month period. In spite of their earlier claim to Sheng that the initial survey had already been done, the British asked the Governor of Chekiang to negotiate so they could embark on a survey as stipulated in the preliminary contract. The Governor, however, turned down the request, saying that the contract was signed by Sheng and the British and that Sheng had already called for its annulment.[31]

Faced with the Governor's firm attitude backed by the gentry-led local movement, the British now approached the Board of Foreign Affairs in Peking, notifying them that the interests of both countries would be hurt and bilateral relations would deteriorate if the Chinese government continued to drag its feet.[32] In October, the new British Minister, John Jordan, urged the Board of Foreign Affairs again to conclude a formal contract and let the British embark on a survey for the sake of good diplomatic relations. The board counter-proposed the signing of a formal contract for the Canton-Kowloon railway that would leave room for compromise and further consultation.[33] Thus, a difference of opinion between the central government and provincial authorities on the railway problem began to surface.

Late in 1905, the Chekiang gentry began a survey between Chiang-kan and Hu-shu, the first portion of the Soochow-Hangchow-Ningpo line; they held a groundbreaking ceremony in November of the following year.[34] After concluding a formal contract on the Canton-Kowloon line on 7 March 1907, a British-Chinese negotiation was held between Wang Ta-hsieh, a Vice-Minister of the Board of Foreign Affairs, and the British and Chinese Corporation. The two sides tentatively agreed that the Chinese would undertake the construction of the railway with a British loan. A final agreement was soon reached by the British and Vice-Minister Liang Tun-yen, who succeeded Wang when the latter was appointed Minister to Britain.

The agreement consisted of eight terms, stating in part that the British corporation would supply a loan of £1.5 million for railway construction beyond the available funds raised by the merchant gentry of the Chekiang company. The Chinese would control and manage the line, and the Chinese capital that had already been collected, not the railroad itself, would secure the loan in order to prevent the British from interfering in the construction project.[35] Thus, the negotiations put China in control of the railway's administrative and financial matters during and after the construction of the railway, but left considerable financial profit to the British. The agreement did not satisfy the gentry who were determined to recover their lost rights from foreign powers, since it compelled them to accept a foreign loan. Endorsed by the Emperor, the agreement was made public on 20 October 1907.

The imperial announcement expressed confidence in the involvement of the British, saying that a foreign loan was necessary, since Chinese funds were not enough for the construction of the projected line. The agreement also included some measures to placate those involved in the railway project, including the assurance of a subscription by the Chekiang gentry to the flotation of a British loan.[36]

Before the imperial announcement was made public, the Chekiang gentry continued their efforts to annul the preliminary contract of 1898. In November 1905, for example, Fan Kung-hsu, a former compiler at the Hanlin Academy, petitioned the Chekiang Governor, calling on him to memorialize the Board of Foreign Affairs to have Sheng Hsuan-huai proceed with the demand to annul the preliminary contract. In February 1906, a strong message calling for the abrogation of this contract was cabled to the Peking government in the name of both the Director and Vice-Director of the Chekiang Railway Company, and a petition in the name of the Chekiang people was sent to the Board of Commerce. In May, Sun Pao-ch'i, a Chekiang official in Peking, petitioned the Board of Commerce to push on with the Chinese demand.[37]

In April 1906, in Kiangsu province, apparently influenced by the movement in Chekiang, Lu Jun-hsiang and 256 other gentry inaugurated the Kiangsu Railway Company in order to undertake the construction of the part of the Soochow-Hangchow-Ningpo railway passing through their own province. Wang Ch'ing-mu was elected as its Director, and Chang Chien, Wang T'ung-yü, and Hsu Ting-lin were chosen as Vice-Directors.[38]

Because the loan agreement was made, in spite of the strong protests of the Chekiang gentry, a new movement to turn down the loan developed. News of the forced British loan set off widespread protest rallies. On 22 October 1907, two days after the imperial announcement of the loan agreement, a mass rally was held in Hangchow to express the Chekiang people's opposition to the loan, and on 24 October, the railway companies in both Kiangsu and Chekiang jointly issued a strong statement against the loan.[39]

In an effort to cope with the growing anti-loan movement, the Board of Foreign Affairs invited local leaders of the movement to Peking and gave them access to official documents. On 29 November 1907, the board called on both provinces to send their representatives.[40] The railway companies in the provinces were critical of this move. But in the respective meetings of their shareholders, on 12 December and 14 December, the two companies chose delegates to go to Peking, not to discuss the loan issue as the Board of Foreign Affairs wanted but to call for the construction of the Soochow-Hangchow-Ningpo railway with their own capital.[41] Both companies chose Wang Wen-shao, a former Grand Councillor from Chekiang, and others to represent them in Peking. Hsu Ting-lin, Yang T'ing-tung, Lei Fen, and Wang T'ung-yü, the leading constitutionalists, were chosen to represent the Kiangsu side, and Chang Yuan-chi, Sun T'ing-han, and Sun I-jang to represent Chekiang.[42]

The delegates met with Yuan Shih-k'ai, Minister of the Board of Foreign Affairs in Peking. At the meeting, Yuan proposed that the British loan be received, not directly by the provincial railway companies, but by the Board of Posts and Communications, to be secured by mortgaging revenues from other national railways. In a separate move, the Board would "reloan" 10 million yuan to the two companies.[43] The delegates agreed to the proposal. A loan agreement of 24 articles to that effect was concluded on 6 March 1908 between the Board of Posts and Communcations and the British. A loan agreement between the Board and the delegates was effected, which was reported to and approved by the Throne on 15 April.[44]

The Sino-British loan agreement stipulated the following: (1) the Chinese government would receive the British loan and be responsible for the construction and management of the railway; (2) the loan would be repayable after ten years; and (3), if a chief engineer should be necessary before the repayment, he should be British.[45]

The loan agreement between the Board and the railway companies regarding the Kiangsu-Chekiang railway made it clear that the railway would be a fully commercial one, and stipulated that the railway companies in the two provinces would borrow 7.5 to 10 million yuan from the Board of Posts and Communcations, adding, however, that they would not be subject to any British interferences. The agreement also stated that the first 800,000 yuan would be paid within seven months after the signing of the pact, and the rest within the next twelve months, with the time limit extendable up to twenty-four months in case of emergency. It added, however, that the pact itself would lose its effect if the time schedule were not met. The railway's name was changed to the Shanghai-Hangchow-Ningpo Railway, with the northern terminus changed from Soochow to Shanghai.[46] The

Board of Posts and Communications established a bureau in Shanghai for the construction of the railway, and named Shih Chao-tseng as its chief director and Chou Chin-chen as its secretary.[47]

At first glance, it may seem strange that the local gentry's representatives agreed to the compromise, for, despite the pledge to prevent any British interference in the railway construction, they actually accepted the British loan. Furthermore, the recent anti-loan movement had been extremely violent. To understand this change of posture, we must re-examine the role played by the Director General of the Imperial Chinese Railway Administration, Sheng Hsuan-huai, in the negotiations to abrogate the preliminary contract. The public believed that Sheng Hsuan-huai had made the British agree to "tacitly" nullify the preliminary Sino-British contract, and this belief had been used as an argument for canceling it. As they came to know that the British in fact had not agreed, even "tacitly," they could no longer stand firm with the demand to nullify the preliminary contract.

Sheng said in a reply to central government officials from Chekiang province in September 1905[48] that, because there had been no response from the British to his second notification (of 3 July 1905) more than two months previously calling for the contract's annulment, China might announce that it would construct the railway independently, taking advantage of Britain's silence. If several more months should pass before the British made any claim, he said, it could be regarded as a "tacit" agreement of the British to the contract's abrogation, leading to nullification.[49] From his letter, the public might have hastily assumed that the British had "tacitly" agreed to the abrogation. Later, on 28 December 1905, Sheng wrote to the British corporation[50] stating that the preliminary contract should now be nullified because two and a half years had passed since he first notified them, on 24 May 1903, that China would cancel the contract unless surveys were made and estimates prepared within six months. Sheng did not mention, however, that the British had responded to this letter on 31 May 1903, though they failed to comply with his demand. In fact, Sheng himself did not say directly that the British had ever agreed "tacitly" to the abrogation. But the misunderstanding was no doubt due to his failure to report that the British had actually responded to his letter. When Sheng's letter to the British alone was circulated without any explanation, the public might have been reminded of their earlier mistaken assumption that the British once agreed "tacitly" to abrogate the preliminary contract, and might have presumed that the British agreed this time, again tacitly, to the abrogation by failing to respond.[51]

According to T'ang Shou-ch'ien, the Director of the Shanghai Railway Company, who denounced him, Sheng never told the Chekiang gentry in Shanghai that there was actually a British response when he left Shanghai for Peking in late 1906 to clarify, under the orders of the Emperor, if there really was a "tacit" British agreement to the abrogation.[52] If T'ang's accusation was true, Sheng seems to have glossed over the true picture in order to curry favor momentarily with the people of Kiangsu and Chekiang. Since the spreading report of the British "tacit" agreement was providing a reason for the nullification of the contract, the Board of Foreign Affairs decided, on 29 November 1907, to invite representatives of the gentry of Kiangsu and Chekiang to view the diplomatic documents; the Board felt obliged to defend the British position in order to foster good diplomatic relations.[53] To the Kiangsu and Chekiang delegates who came to Peking, Liang Tun-yen, an Acting Vice-Minister of the Board of Foreign Affairs, revealed the testimony of J. O. P. Bland, the representative of the British corporation, that the British had already responded (to Sheng's letter) and thus had never agreed "tacitly" to the abrogation.[54]

In the meantime, Sheng, answering an imperial order of 11 December demanding clarification of the affair, acknowledged that he had received a response from the British corporation on 31 May 1903, but said that, although the reply had not answered his question, it did not seem that the British appeared to have agreed "tacitly" to the abrogation.[55] After Sheng's explanation, the Kiangsu-Chekiang gentry's representatives could no longer demand the contract's nullification, and thus had to agree to the proposition of the Board of Posts and Communications that the Board would accept the British loan, and that it would reloan the fund to the local railway project in question. The indignation of the Kiangsu-Chekiang gentry now switched from the Board of Foreign Affairs to Sheng Hsuan-huai. His testimony in Peking had been carefully planned by Yuan Shih-k'ai to break the brunt of the gentry's attack by deflecting it from the board to Sheng.[56]

Three days after the signing of the loan agreement on 6 March 1908, however, Sheng was promoted to the position of Vice-Minister of the Board of Posts and Communications. But two days after that, he was named to serve concurrently as the High Commissioner in charge of commercial negotiation in Shanghai. The abrupt removal of Sheng from actual duty as the Vice-Minister in Peking to a nominal minor post in Shanghai appears to have been a punitive move by Yuan Shih-k'ai to call him to account in the face of the gentry's rising indignation.[57]

THE MOVEMENT TO ANNUL THE SINO-BRITISH LOAN AGREEMENT

The British loan was approved by the Throne on 20 October 1907. As soon as it was announced, several anti-loan movements on the part of both the railway companies and the local populace, led by the Chekiang gentry, broke out almost simultaneously. As already mentioned, a mass rally was held in Hangchow on 22 October,[58] and the railway companies sent a letter to the Liang-Kiang Governor General on 24 October, in which they expressed their strong opposition to the loan.[59] A hunger strike against the loan led to the deaths of Wu Kang, a student at the Chekiang Railway School (on 23 October), and of T'ang Hsu, a Vice-Engineer-in-Chief of the Chekiang Railway Company (on 26 October). The power of their protest intensified the movement.[60]

The gentry coordinated large-scale activities against the loan. A total of 113 people representing all eleven prefectures in Chekiang province, headed by former Grand Councillor Wang Wen-shao, jointly memorialized the Chekiang Governor, calling on him to transfer their memorial against the loan to the Throne.[61] The gentry representatives also telegraphed the Grand Council on 18 November, urging it to refuse the loan and asking it to memorialize the Throne against the loan.[62]

Other activities of the gentry included a coordinated memorial from Chu Fu-shen, a Sub-Chancellor at the Hanlin Academy, and other Chekiang-born officials in Peking on 3 November.[63] In October, November, and December, a series of similar memorials were filed separately by Chu Fu-shen and Censors Hsu Ting-ch'ao, Chao Ping-lin, and Chiang Ch'un-lin.[64] These efforts exerted a great influence on the central government as well as on provincial authorities.

On 22 October, one day after the announcement of the Sino-British loan agreement reached Hangchow, a Chekiang Citizens' Anti-Loan Association was formed at a meeting in Hangchow attended by about 200 Chekiang gentry.[65] A former Kiangsu magistrate,

Wang T'ing-yang,[66] was elected as its chief secretary. The prospectus of the society[67] claimed that the loan would encroach upon Chinese sovereignty and increase the financial burden of the Chinese people. In the society's first meeting, Wang said that they would engage in the anti-loan movement as Chinese nationals, stressing that it was not to protect the interests of the local companies' shareholders. The society, therefore, called for the collaboration of all gentry, merchants, students, and soldiers. The movement now became more than purely a railway problem, and began to represent a growing conflict of interest between the central government and the local populace within a context of growing nationalism.

On 31 October, teachers and students of the Chekiang High School in Hangchow held an anti-loan rally on their school campus and convened a meeting of representatives from all schools in their province. One hundred and eighteen representatives of the schools in Chekiang gathered in the Hangchow school on 6 November and inaugurated the Chekiang Academic Circles Anti-Loan Association (later renamed the Anti-Loan Association of the Chekiang Federation of Schools). The association held its first formal meeting on 23 November, and two more in December. Other schools in Ningpo, Hu-chou, and various cities and towns followed suit.[68]

The Chekiang Citizens Anti-Loan Association sponsored an anti-loan mass rally two days later on 25 November at a temple in Hangchow, at which Wang Wen-shao was elected president by delegates from all eleven prefectures in Chekiang. Wang agreed to accept the position on condition that "all the members abide by the law."[69] In the meeting, such radical ideas as the refusal to pay taxes and the proclamation of the independence of Chekiang were proposed by some members of the Tokyo-based T'ung-meng-hui, but they were rejected by the moderate members.[70] The society played a central role in the anti-loan movement across the province, becoming a standing body as proposed by Wang T'ing-yang. The Academic Circles Association offered to be a supplemental body of the society. Branches were established in Yü-yao, Te-ch'ing, Chia-hsing, and Ningpo. Other anti-loan rallies were held in Ningpo, Chia-hsing, Hu-chou, Hsia-shih, Wenchow, and Shanghai, led by merchant-gentry or intellectuals. These rallies supported the demand of the anti-loan society in Hangchow. In addition, the society sent speakers, including Wang T'ing-yang, T'ao Ch'i-piao, and Ho Lang-hsien, to various other gatherings.[71]

In Peking, Chekiang students at different schools filed an anti-loan memorial through the Censorate, led by Ch'eng Chün-sun, a teacher at the Metropolitan University. They also planned to form a national student organization for the anti-loan movement.[72] Surprised by such a move, the Ch'ing Court expelled Ch'eng Chün-sun from Peking and ordered students not to engage in political activity.[73]

In Kiangsu province, meanwhile, the gentry joined in the anti-loan movement and organized the People's Public Association for Railways and Mines[74] when they gathered on 29 October to form the provincial assembly. In another gathering on 1 November, the Kiangsu gentry formed the Kiangsu Railway Association after discussions in the provincial assembly. The first convention of the Kiangsu Railway Association was held in Shanghai on 9 November with about 2,000 people attending; a second convention was held two days later.[75] Both were chaired by Ma Liang, the leader of the association.[76] The association resembled the Chekiang Citizens Anti-Loan Association against the railway loan, since its provisional charter stated that members of the association should do their best to promote the anti-loan movement because it was their responsibility as citizens (*kuo-min*) of their country.

In Soochow, another anti-loan rally was held at nearly the same time as the Kiangsu association's inauguration; 800 to 900 merchants, gentry, and students attended. One speaker argued that the people should cooperate with the Kiangsu Railway Company in the anti-loan movement, but maintained that the people should keep an eye on the railway company lest it take a passive attitude. The speaker warned against the conciliatory attitudes that could be expected of the railway's shareholders. The Kiangsu Railway Company might take a passive attitude about their economic interests since the part of the projected railway traversing Kiangsu was far shorter than that passing through Chekiang, and the construction cost of the Kiangsu section was set at only a quarter of the Chekiang section, which was estimated at 30 million yuan.[77]

What was the reaction of the shareholders? As already mentioned, on 20 October, the Ch'ing government had taken special measures to satisfy them. They had announced that the Chinese would be allowed to participate in the flotation of the British fund for the loan, and that the status of the Chinese workers engaging in the construction of the railway would be guaranteed.[78] A message the Board of Foreign Affairs sent to the Governor of Chekiang stressed that the merchant-gentry would not sustain any losses.[79]

These measures, however, failed to satisfy the shareholders of the two railway companies. The Kiangsu and Chekiang railway companies sent a letter to a provincial administrator on 24 October, calling on him to memorialize the Throne against the loan, reasoning that allowing Chinese to join in the British flotation of the railway stocks was putting the cart before the horse. Moreover, it would be inconsistent for the government to solicit them to join in the British loan since the government considered that the shareholders did not have enough money; collections already fell far short of what was needed for the construction of the railway.[80]

This anti-loan movement was accompanied by the subscription of domestic capital for the railway. As one of the protest letters said, "What we need to do now is to protest against the loan publicly, while collecting the capital privately."[81] Subscriptions for the railway's stocks were accepted in almost all of these rallies. As of early November, the nominal subscriptions accepted by the Kiangsu Railway Company totaled 10 million yuan,[82] and by the Chekiang Railway Company a little more than 22 million yuan.[83] Railway stocks were even subscribed to by people in the lowest classes of society, such as carters, butchers, entertainers, and sedan-chair bearers.[84] As Wang Wen-shao, the ex-Grand Councillor representing 113 Chekiang gentry observed in a memorial to the Throne, "All the people seem to have gone crazy to the extent that even coolies, peddlers, servants, women, and young boys are stirred up to subscribe to railway stocks, cutting down on clothes and food."[85] Actual sales of railway stock fell far short of subscription figures, however. In the case of the Kiangsu Railway Company, the number of shares actually sold, as reported to a shareholders' meeting on 13 November, amounted to no more than 600,000 shares.[86]

Merchant anti-loan movements were also extensive. The Shanghai Merchants Association, headed by Li Hou-yu, filed protests with the Board of Agriculture, Industry, and Commerce and the Board of Foreign Affairs.[87] About 1,000 merchants of Shanghai's Southern City also held a protest rally on 12 November, and Shen Mao-chao (Shen Man-yun) as the representative of the Southern Shanghai Merchants Association presented a protest letter to the Chekiang Governor.[88] In addition, protests against the loan were lodged by merchant associations in more than a dozen prefectures of the two provinces.[89] Slightly more common were joint protests with groups of gentry and students.[90] Regional protest rallies were held in Shao-hsing, Ningpo, Hu-chou, and seven other areas.[91] Chekiang merchants living in Shanghai also held anti-loan meetings, as did merchants from outside Chekiang who were resident in Hangchow.[92] It is not clear yet who led the regional rallies, but presumably they involved a combination of merchant-gentry and students.

The prospectus of the Chekiang Citizens Anti-Loan Association, published on 22 October, called for the association of all "citizens" (*kuo-min*), by which it meant gentry, merchants, students, and soldiers.[93] The prospectus stated that all groups should be united to cope with the imminent threat to the local interest. This indicates clearly that the movement was particularly understood as a conflict between the central government and local interests. Among the four groups, the participation of soldiers in collective actions was negligible, though a few of them, including some of the New Army in Hangchow and even the Manchu banner garrisons in Hangchow, joined in the subscription for railway construction in response to the association's appeal.[94] The people clearly felt that their interests were pitted against those of the central government.

It is significant that the coordinated movement of the merchant-gentry and students won broad support at the grass roots. As we noted above, ordinary people responded passionately to the subscription for railway stocks, but the important point is that their activities were collective and on a large scale. For example, more than 200 sedan-chair bearers of Hangchow subscribed 100 odd lots of railway stocks and sent a petition to the Governor.[95] But because this lowest class of society was participating, there was a fear that the anti-loan movement would become violent. The official reply of the Chekiang Governor to the petition stated that the petition included rather "inappropriate wording," which testifies to this fear.[96] The circuit intendant of Shanghai, referring to the spread of anonymous leaflets which contained subversive wording, presumably by a member of the Society to Prevent the Destruction of the Nation (Pao-wang hui), called on the authorities of the Kiangsu Railway Company to do their best to keep the peace and to prevent these groups from getting violent. He suspected, judging from the wording, that the members of the society came from the lower classes (*fei-shang-liu she-hui*).[97] A French correspondent, reporting on Chinese anti-loan movements, wrote that about 6,000 laborers staged an outdoor protest against the British loan, and that about 2,000 beggars, actors, and monks also joined in the protest rally.[98] The people were so enraged over the loan that their anger could easily have led to an outbreak of violence. The subscription for railway stocks, however, served as a safety valve. It is understandable that the Chekiang Governor urged the sedan-chair bearers of Hangchow to save their pennies to pay for railway stocks but otherwise keep to their social station and carry on with their livelihood (*an-fen ying-sheng*) and not conspire to make trouble.[99] In Ningpo, gentry and merchants petitioned the Chekiang Governor to memorialize, noting that it was hard to reason with the workers of Ningpo because they were especially rude. For the moment, however, they had succeeded in calming them down and keeping control by persuading the workers to subscribe to railway stocks.[100]

The response of women to the movement also suggests that the consciousness of crisis was widespread among the people. A Women's Association for the Preservation of Railway Rights (Nü-chieh pao-lu-hui) was formed on 7 November in Shanghai.[101] Another Women's Citizens' Anti-Loan Association (Nü-kuo-min chü-k'uan-hui) appealed to the people to join in its anti-loan movement, circulating pamphlets written in the vernacular.[102] A rally for women to promote the subscription of railway stocks was held in Shanghai on 8 November by more than 40 woman leaders, most of whom were primary-school teachers.[103] Anti-loan rallies were also held in women's schools in Sung-chiang, Ch'ang-chou, and Ningpo.[104]

These mass movements naturally led to activities other than simply collecting subscriptions for railway stocks and sending protest letters. In a meeting of the Chekiang Citizens Anti-Loan Associations, a strike was discussed, but it was not realized because of the strong opposition of leaders.[105] In an anti-loan meeting of about 300 people in Shao-hsing, an agreement was made to boycott classes in school and to suspend business activities if the government persisted in its plan for the British loan.[106] A resolution adopted at a rally in Hangchow of the Chekiang Citizens' Anti-Loan Association threatened to boycott some miscellaneous taxes, including those for training soldiers, if the government continued to force them to accept the loan.[107] Presumably in compliance with the resolution, Hangchow merchants declared that they would not pay housing taxes but would purchase railway stocks with the money.¹⁰⁸ It was because of these moves that T'ang Shou-ch'ien, who led the anti-loan movement in Chekiang, pleaded with the people to refrain from such radical activities as the boycott of taxes.¹⁰⁹ Some journals in Shanghai, however, encouraged the people to boycott taxes as a protest, pointing out that it was the rule in Western constitutional countries not to pay taxes without representation.¹¹⁰

An editorial in the daily newspaper *Chung-wai jih-pao* recommended that "the people of Kiangsu and Chekiang work out their own self-protective measures promptly, if the Court throws away Kiangsu and Chekiang like an old shoe . . . and perform what they think right by blood and iron." A group of Chekiang people in Japan, in a telegram to an anti-loan rally in Hangchow, said: "Even if the government is going to ruin Chekiang, [we the people of Chekiang] could not go to ruin by ourselves. You [participants at the meeting] may as well keep [Chekiang's] 'independence' until death, and boycott taxes."¹¹¹ A contemporary comment on the policy of the Board of Foreign Affairs included in *Chiang-Che t'ieh-lu feng-ch'ao*, a collection of documents pertaining to the railway dispute published early in 1908, argued, "The Court ignored public principles. Accordingly, subjects no longer have an obligation to obey orders of the Court."¹¹² The railway issue thus came to the verge of repudiating the Manchu Court.

Despite radical arguments put forward in this agitated atmosphere, the Chekiang Citizens Anti-Loan Association decided in its Hangchow rally to use peaceful rather than radical means, as T'ang pleaded with the people.¹¹³ But the petition of 113 Chekiang gentry representatives shows that this was only a temporizing measure. They said they could prevent the outbreak of a riot "for the time being," but could not guarantee that a riot would not occur in the future.¹¹⁴ The judicial commissioner of Chekiang, in a telegram to Prince Ch'ing on 2 November said: "The people of Chekiang are all united in anger. Their indignation has mounted so high that a man killed himself a few days ago in rage over this issue. I cannot speculate how the situation will develop if the revolutionaries take advantage of this opportunity to rise in revolt."¹¹⁵ In a message cabled to the Board of Foreign Affairs, a Manchu general-in-chief in Hangchow said, "All of Chekiang province is trembling with fear . . . It seems that a great revolt is imminent. That is why [even a Manchu general] like me cannot say a word."[116] After receiving these reports, the Grand Council ordered the Liang-Kiang Governor General and the Governors of Kiangsu and Chekiang to make a careful investigation; the Grand Council feared a possible revolt by "revolutionary bandits" who mingled with the people to take advantage of the railway issue.[117]

In fact, at this time secret societies were active in the Kiangsu-Chekiang area. According to reports by the Liang-Kiang Governor General and the Governors of Kiangsu and Chekiang in January 1908,[118] salt smugglers and some other secret society members in prefectures along the border between the provinces were becoming daily more threatening; 67 separate incidents involving them were reported. In places such as Hai-yen, Hsia-shih, Hai-ning, and T'ung-hsiang, where the anti-loan movement was strong, "bandits" fought government troops, damaging church and school buildings. In T'ung-hsiang, people helped the "bandits" to enter the prefectural town and joined them in the destruction of shops and likin tollgates. The government sent the troops of General Chiang Kuei-t'i from Kansu to suppress the insurgents.[119] No evidence is available that the activities of "bandits" or secret societies were directly related to the anti-loan movements, but the outlaws probably took advantage of the unrest created by the anti-loan movements. An editorial in the Shanghai newspaper *Shih-pao* (Eastern times) claimed that the British loan increased the influence of the anti-Manchu revolutionary movement, and speculated that a growing number of people would join in revolutionary activities owing to the railway dispute. As the editorial pointed out, the loan issue was coming to a province where unrest was prevalent after mass arrests in Chekiang in early July (of 1907) in the wake of Hsu Hsi-lin's attempted assassination of the Governor of Anhwei, and the arrest of Ch'iu Chin and others in late July for their roles in plotting an uprising in Shaohsing. Social unrest was also provoked, according to the editorial, by the government's plan to allot land to Manchu bannermen in Chekiang (where many bannermen were stationed). The editor also pointed out that discontent with the government was growing, too, because of the alleged insincerity of the Ch'ing Court in going ahead with constitutionalism. The editorial claimed that the people of Chekiang had come to realize that the Court had abandoned them.[120] Presumably, this social unrest contributed to the fervor of the anti-loan movement.

Newspapers in Shanghai played a role in stirring up popular sentiment against the railway loan. A considerable number of anti-loan editorials in *Shih-pao, Chung-wai jih-pao* (Universal gazette), *Shen-chou jih-pao* (North China daily news), *Hsin-wen-pao* (Daily news) and *Shen-pao* (Shanghai daily news) were collected in *Feng-ch'ao*, the documentary collection mentioned above. Minister Yuan Shih-k'ai of the Board of Foreign Affairs, in response to Chang Chih-tung's fear that the anti-loan struggle might become heated, said that such rumors were spread by newspapers and should not be believed.[121] Sheng Hsuan-huai also made fun of the gentry in the southern provinces for their alleged following of the guidelines set by the opinions of newspapers and students; he criticized T'ang Shou-ch'ien, charging that he curried favor with reporters and students.[122] There is little doubt that newspapers played an important part in influencing the attitudes of the people to the railway dispute.

THE MOVEMENT TO ABROGATE THE LOAN DEPOSIT AGREEMENT AND OPPOSE THE DISMISSAL OF T'ANG SHOU-CH'IEN

The anti-loan movement in Chekiang and Kiangsu provinces slowed down temporarily with the conclusion of the Loan Deposit Agreement between railway companies of the two provinces and the Board of Posts and Communications, but not all the questions were settled. On 6 July 1908, the British Consul urged the prompt selection of a British chief engineer according to Article 17 of the loan agreement between the Chinese government and Great Britain.[123] This clause influenced in a significant way the later development of the railway dispute:

> The construction process and the right to manage this railway will be entirely in the hands of the government of China. The Board of Posts and Communications may allow the chief director of the railway bureau to select and appoint one British engineer-in-general for the construction... After construction is completed the government of China is to employ an engineer-in-general. During the term of the loan this engineer-in-general should be a British national.[124]

On 22 October 1908, a chief engineer was appointed after a long delay. The British Consul, however, lodged a protest with the Board of Foreign Affairs, accusing the railway companies of the two provinces of deliberate negligence in assigning duty two months after the arrival of the Director of the Shanghai-Hangchow-Ningpo Railway Bureau (Shih Chao-tseng) and a British Chief Engineer in Shanghai.[125]

It is apparent that the two provinces were resisting even after their reluctant acceptance of the Loan Deposit Agreement. The Chief Engineer, appointed on 6 July, managed to conclude an employment contract with the companies only on 14 November.[126] The companies, however, still were not cooperating with the Director or the Chief Engineer. The Shanghai-Hangchow-Ningpo Railway Bureau, under the sponsorship of the Chinese government, could not even be established until late November of 1908.[127] The Director and the Chief Engineer began their work in early December only after the protest of the British Consul had forced the Board of Foreign Affairs and the Board of Posts and Communications to intervene.[128]

Disputes about the implementation of the Loan Deposit Agreement continued. The terms of the agreement stipulated that the agreement would be nullified if the necessary amount of money (that is, between 7.5 and 10 million yuan) was not delivered and deposited in twenty-four months. By February 1910, twenty-four months had passed and only 1.8 million yuan had been forwarded to the company, less than a quarter of the minimal amount.[129]

We do not have enough evidence at present to explain why the delivery of the loan deposit was delayed, but we can assume from the following remarks that the Chinese government was waiting for the companies to give in. T'ang Shao-i, Minister of the Board of Posts and Communiations, mentioned that the agitation in Chekiang and Kiangsu would subside for lack of capital,[130] and an English reporter noted: "The native capital is exhausted, and shareholders, seeing no prospect of any return, have recently been offering their shares for sale at 70 percent devaluation."[131]

Since the Board of Posts and Communications intended to spend the money not on construction but on the purchase of bonds of the Chekiang and Kiangsu railway companies, the Board seems to have had no intention from the beginning of carrying out the agreement. In April 1910, the Board suggested to the British and Chinese Corporation that they could put an end once and for all to the railway question by taking advantage of the company's difficulties. The idea is said to have been discussed as early as the winter of 1909,[132] so it is not likely that they would have willingly delivered the loan deposit to the company. A statement of Liu Chin-tsao that Liang Shih-i, inspector of the Railway Bureau of the Board of Posts and Communications, deliberately witheld the money would bear out this conclusion.[133]

Despite their acceptance of the Loan Deposit Agreement, the Chekiang and Kiangsu railway companies were not entirely content with it, for they claimed that the agreement was accepted because "the anti-loan movement had failed to achieve its purpose."[134] Some suggested that the loan not be used,[135] and this became another roadblock in carrying out the agreement.

The intention of the Board to buy the bonds of the Chekiang and Kiangsu railway companies, as mentioned above, and to nationalize the railway itself coincided with the British view of what should be done. In his communication to the Chinese government in June 1910, the British Consul demanded that the Chinese government retrieve all its own rights on the basis of Article 17 of the Loan Agreement.[136] Another inquiry of March 1911 from the British Consul strongly protested that the Board of Foreign Affairs and the Board of Posts and Communications had deceived the British government by putting the railway under the management of merchant (gentry) and concluding the Loan Deposit Agreement with the provincial railway companies contrary to the Loan Agreement.[137]

The Board of Posts and Communications, after deciding to purchase initially the shares of the Kiangsu Railway Company, asked the British government to allow 2 million yuan to be used for that purpose, which could be allocated from the sum already loaned. The Chinese government needed the consent of the British in order to use the loan in a way not specified in the agreement. Britain, however, was obstinate and would not consent to the request unless the Chinese government "retrieved the whole railway," as stipulated in Article 17.[138]

In a shareholder's meeting held in June 1910, the Chekiang Railway Company decided to abrogate the Loan Deposit Agreement on the ground that the Board of Posts and Communications had failed to fulfill its obligations under the agreement.[139] A year later, on 30 March 1911, the Kiangsu Railway Company, too, held a special meeting of shareholders at which they argued that the Loan Deposit Agreement was no longer valid, and voted for the elimination of the Shanghai-Hangchow-Ningpo Railway Bureau and for the resignation of the British Chief Engineer within a month. They also voted to spend 600,000 yuan of the amount of the loan received so far to compensate for various losses the company had incurred. The Board of Foreign Affairs asserted in opposition that the decision was contrary to the Loan Agreement, and stood firmly against approval.[140]

On 9 May 1911, the doomed railway-nationalization policy was announced, advocating the construction of major railways by means of foreign loans.[141] With this new policy, officials rejected categorically the people's demands to turn down the foreign loan. The struggle against the Loan Deposit Agreement ended in the 1911 Revolution which flared up five months later.

Another important outcome of the Chekiang-Kiangsu railway disputes was the dismissal of T'ang Shou-ch'ien from the post of Director of the Chekiang Railway Company. In February 1911, on the eve of the doomed railway nationalization, the Governor General of Chihli province asked Chang Chien, Cheng Hsiao-hsu, and T'ang Shou-ch'ien, the three most prominent leaders of the Chekiang and Kiangsu gentry, whether the foreign loan should be accepted, alluding presumably to the fund to nationalize the railways. Cheng endorsed the idea without reservation, and Chang was in basic agreement, though he questioned where it should be used, but T'ang was decidedly against it. "We should not take the loan. If we take it, the nation will be ruined (*wang-kuo*)."[142] Since T'ang was one of the most radical anti-loan nationalists, the Ch'ing Court made persistent efforts to prevent him from dealing with the Chekiang Railway matter. In August 1909, the Ch'ing Court had appointed T'ang as provincial judge of Yunnan province (he had already refused to accept the appointment of acting Liang-huai salt controller)[143] and ordered the Chekiang Railway Company instead to elect a new chief director.[144] The company, however, held a general meeting in September 1909 and decided that T'ang should retain the post. They argued that there were no grounds for the government to order the reelection of the chief director of the Chekiang Railway Company because chief directors of other companies usually retained their posts, even though appointed by the government to other posts, and that T'ang was needed to push the movement for the abrogation of the Loan Deposit Agreement.[145] T'ang's appointment to the new post was widely understood at the time as a device to separate him from the Chekiang Railway Company and to lay the groundwork for the Board of Posts and Communications to monopolize the Chekiang and Kiangsu railway companies.[146]

T'ang declined to take the new post in Yunnan and turned down a subsequent appointment as commissioner of education in Kiangsi in December of the same year (this decision was officially acknowledged on 27 February 1910).[147] After the government failed to separate T'ang from the railway dispute, the Chekiang Railway Company decided at a shareholders' meeting of June 1910 to send T'ang to Peking to negotiate the abrogation of the Loan Deposit Agreement. As he was leaving for Peking, an imperial edict was announced on 17 August 1910, ordering Sheng Hsuan-huai to return to his original post as Junior Vice-President of the Board of Posts and Communications.[148] The gentry of Chekiang and Kiangsu were not pleased with the edict. They felt that returning Sheng to his original post was not adequate, since his fault of misleading the anti-loan movement, and thereby causing the Loan Deposit Agreement to become the only alternative, was too grave. Furthermore, they realized that, since Sheng was hostile to the gentry of Chekiang and Kiangsu provinces,[149] his return to the key post in the Board of Posts and Communications would be harmful to the movement.

The gentry's reaction is reflected in T'ang Shou-ch'ien's censure of Sheng in 22 August 1910, which was unusually bitter and emotional. He charged Sheng with being the person chiefly responsible for accepting the foreign loan, as well as the main enemy of the anti-loan movement. He also accused him of seeking to enrich foreign countries at China's expense and amassing a private fortune in public service. Unless the Grand Council canceled Sheng's return to the Board of Posts and Communications and transferred him to a post unconnected with the railway issue, T'ang threatened to resign his directorship of the Chekiang Railway Company. He even said: "If I were relieved of the directorship, I would consider myself fortunate in not having to be humiliated by the instructions Sheng Hsuan-huai the arch-villain would give. [If the Grand Councillors find that I am wrong], I would prefer to be beheaded and gibbeted as an apology to Sheng on the charge of censuring a high official."[150] The Grand Council chose to accept his resignation. The decision was announced on 23 August in the form of an imperial decree, which made it clear that T'ang was "dismissed" from the directorship because he had attempted to become famous by making outrageous statements.[151]

This decision amounted to a direct confrontation between the government and the gentry of Chekiang and Kiangsu. It sparked another anti-government movement, epitomized by a statement, "The people are going wild."[152] Even after T'ang voluntarily resigned his post of chief director, the Board of Directors of the Chekiang Railway Company sent a telegram to the Board of Posts and Communications and to the Board of Agriculture, Industry, and Commerce, expressing its opposition to the government decision.[153] The telegram pointed out that, according to commercial law, the shareholders had the exclusive right to elect and dismiss the chief director. Therefore, the government had no authority to dismiss a director of a business corporation. It also said that, if the government should dismiss the director, who had been elected by the merchant shareholders and was respected by the people of Chekiang province, private merchant-run companies (in China) could no longer exist.

At a special shareholders' meeting of the Chekiang Railway Company held in Shanghai on 11 September 1910 which drew more than 1,200 people, it was decided that representatives of the company should visit the Provincial Governor in Hangchow the next day to hand him petitions asking that he memorialize the Throne for them. They arrived in Hangchow on 12 September and handed in their petitions the following day.[154] The Provincial Assembly stepped in and asked the Governor to open a special session in order to discuss the situation. A protest meeting was also held in Ningpo; tens of thousands of people gathered and telegrams were sent by overseas Chinese.

The Governor memorialized in response to these pressures, pointing out that "the people are going wild" and there was a danger of making things worse unless the government acted appropriately. It would be advisable, he thought, to let T'ang keep his railway post and redeem himself, even though his wrongdoing was recognizable. The government rejected the Governor's suggestion in its reply of 16 September and warned him that he would be asked to take the responsibility if he failed to prevent a disturbance.[155] On 24 September, the Board of Posts and Communications made final the government's opinion, which was that railway companies needed special supervision because they were involved with the interests of the state, and that, accordingly, the director and the vice-directors of such a company must be under the supervision of the government, although elections in other companies did not need government approval. The ultimate right of appointment and dismissal, therefore, was put in the hands of the government.[156]

The Chekiang Railway Company rejected this position at another shareholders' meeting. The company sent a petition to the Board in which they reiterated that commercial law could not be superseded by an administrative order and tried again to abrogate the Loan Deposit

Agreement. They dispatched six officers to Peking to defend their views before the Board.[157] When the delegates arrived in Peking they handed an explanatory note to the National Assembly in which they pointed out that, since the Chekiang Railway Company had been approved in the Loan Deposit Agreement as "completely under merchant management,"[158] it should not be treated differently from other private companies. They visited the Board and were told by Shen Yun-p'ei, Acting Senior Vice-President, that the Loan Deposit Agreement was no longer valid because it had not been followed as agreed.[159] Sheng Hsuan-huai (who always sided with the British company), also hinted that the agreement would be nullified after all.[160] As far as T'ang's dismissal was concerned, however, they failed to change the government's decision.[161]

The incident of T'ang Shou-ch'ien's dismissal became the main topic in the Provincial Assembly. When the anti-loan movement began, there was no unified or institutionalized channel through which the opinions of the gentry could be gathered and expressed. But such an organization was now established; it would not only represent the interest of the gentry but also function as a channel for their opinion.[162] Eleven of the 113 gentry who had signed the anti-loan plea as representatives of eleven prefectures of Chekiang province became members of the Chekiang Provincial Assembly. The assembly asked the Governor to open a special session, but he refused on the pretext that the regular session would be held shortly.[163]

As soon as the regular session was opened on 5 October,[164] a representative, Chang Ch'uan-pao, made a move to change the agenda and deal with the Chekiang railway question first, which was unanimously approved by the members. The Vice-President of the assembly, Ch'en Shih-hsia, then spoke, saying that the Provincial Assembly, in order to perform its duty as a representative of public opinion, should intervene in the Chekiang railway question, upon which the fate of the whole Chekiang people depended. (Ch'en Shih-hsia was one of the four students in Japan who had decided to return to China in order to contact the Chekiang Citizens Anti-Loan Association.)[165] The Assembly, thereupon, decided to send a petition opposing the dismissal of T'ang to the Governor and ask him to memorialize the Throne for them.

The main points of the petition emphasized the principle of democratic constitutionism that the ruler as well as the ruled was subject to law, and argued that the Chekiang railway question should be treated as being within the rights of Chekiang province as specified in the provincial assembly charter. The Governor refused to accept the demand of the assembly to submit a memorial. His reasons were that he had already submitted a similar memorial (in response to the petition of the shareholders of the Chekiang Railway Company) that had been denied, and that the Board of Posts and Communications had already explained why T'ang was dismissed, and that such a demand for a memorial was outside the jurisdiction of the Provincial Assembly.

After this incident, the Provincial Assembly turned into a stage for the anti-government struggle. There was a report that most of the members became frustrated and were of the opinion that the assembly should be dissolved.[166] The Provincial Assembly voluntarily suspended the session as a sign of protest, but the Governor ordered its resumption. After some disputes between the two sides, the session was resumed through the good offices of the National Assembly; but, because the Provincial Assembly still clung to the discussion of the Chekiang railway question, the Governor suspended the session and even threatened to dissolve it. The reason was that the Provincial Assembly was exceeding the limit of its authority, and that it did not obey the Governor's earlier order to open the session (according to the Regulation of the Provincial Assembly, the Governor was authorized to open and suspend the assembly), and that it was displaying an unrepentent attitude. The Provincial Assembly responded that there was no need for "repenting" because it had done nothing wrong, and reiterated that its demand for a memorial from the Governor was not exceeding the limit of its authority because it was connected with the "province's own rights," which the assembly was authorized to discuss in accordance with the regulations of the Provincial Assembly. Thus, the dismissal of T'ang not only intensified centrifugal trends but also deepened the anti-government mood.[167] This new development prevented the Ch'ing Court from using the constitutional movement to strengthen centralization.[168] The Chekiang Provincial Assembly was strongly supported by other provincial assemblies, which were also confronting the central government on the railway question.[169]

THE CHANGING ATTITUDE OF THE GENTRY CLASS

One of the most conspicuous characteristics of the disputes during the period from the anti-loan movement in the late Kuang-hsu years to the protest against T'ang Shou-ch'ien's dismissal on the eve of the 1911 Revolution is the intensification of the conflict between the central government and the local gentry. Caught between local interests and the diplomatic concerns of the central government, local gentry launched an anti-imperialist (nationalistic) movement for the recovery of privileges lost to foreigners. "Nationalistic localism," or localism that sought to enhance national consciousness and not merely preserve local interests, became the main current of the movement. The gentry who led the movement were enlightened intellectuals, not traditional local gentry whose concern usually never went beyond the interests of their own areas.

The Chekiang Citizens' Anti-Loan Association and the Kiangsu Railway Association, which led the Chekiang and Kiangsu railway companies in the anti-loan and the agreement-abrogation movements, were not commercial organizations like the railway companies, but public organizations on a provincial scale. We have already noticed that the associations tried to draw together four groups—the gentry, the merchants, the intellectuals, and the army—to compose the citizenry (*kuo-min*). Teachers as well as students of Western-style schools were included among the "intellectuals." For example, the anti-loan meeting held at Hangchow High School on 26 October 1910, which led the anti-loan student movement of the whole province, was presided over by Wu Lei-ch'uan, the Superintendant of Hangchow High School who held the rank of compiler of the 2nd class in the Hanlin Academy.[170] One hundred and ten representatives of schools in Chekiang province participated in a United Anti-Loan Meeting of Chekiang Schools on 2 November, a meeting presided over by the same Wu Lei-ch'uan.[171] T'ao Hui-fu, director of a normal school, conducted an anti-loan meeting in Chia-hsing.[172] It is noteworthy that T'ao and Wu were gentry schooled in the new style of Western learning.

The members of the Provincial Assembly constituted another segment of this group of new enlightened intellectuals. As already noted, 11 of the 113 people who had signed the anti-loan plea became members of the Chekiang Provincial Assembly. Wang T'ing-yang, an active leader of the anti-loan movement, was elected from Chin-hua prefecture.¹⁷³ They came from six of the province's eleven prefectures, representing about one-half of all the prefectures, although they numbered only about 10 percent of the total membership in the assembly.¹⁷⁴ Among those who were also active in the anti-loan movement, Ch'en Shih-hsia (Vice-President of the Provincial Assembly) and Shao Hsi were elected as members.¹⁷⁵ The Kiangsu Provincial Assembly showed a similar tendency. Ten of the 68 people who had established the Kiangsu Railway Association became members of the Provincial Assembly; they represented half of the ten prefectures and the one independent subprefecture. Noted constitutionalists and active leaders of the anti-loan movement, such as Lei Fen, Ma Liang, Meng Chao-ch'ang, and Huang Yen-p'ei, were included.¹⁷⁶ Other members of the Kiangsu Provincial Assembly, including its President, Chang Chien, participated in the anti-loan movement.¹⁷⁷

Enlightened intellectuals among the gentry class thus found a common ground in the Chekiang-Kiangsu railway disputes and then proceeded to form the provincial assemblies.¹⁷⁸ Those who worked for newspapers and those who had received their education at Western-style schools played a leading role, not only in the constitutional movement, but also in the creation of the provincial assembly. The wholehearted support of these people was also significant in the Chekiang-Kiangsu railway disputes. When Sir John Jordan returned to China in 1906, after an eight-year absence, to serve as the British Minister in Peking, he found a "new generation" growing up in China.¹⁷⁹ He was supposedly surprised that this new generation now began to realize that there was a new arena outside the traditional dynastic order which allowed a common participation in national or provincial interests beyond the conventional differences in social stratifications. With anti-imperialistic nationalism in the air, superficial as it was, they even demanded "no taxation without representation." To them, however, the constitutional movement to secure representation meant defending their established prestige or interests in a new way, as an activist expressed it:

Now, at the moment when the constitutional principle is beginning to take hold and the preparation for the provincial assembly is in full swing, our people suddenly become frustrated [over the railway dispute]. If we timidly lower our heads and do not protest, in keeping with our traditional servility, how can we hope to achieve a constitution? Is it not clear that we would return to the miserable condition of slavery? Then we gentry would not be members of a representative body, no matter how much we might wish to be.[180]

In the same vein, Yao Tzu-liang, executive officer of the Soochow Anti-Loan Association, stated, "When the goal of the anti-loan movement is achieved, the constitution can truly be realized."[181] They recognized that the anti-loan movement and the constitutional movement both sprang from the same root. The constitutional system meant for the gentry the extension of "the rights of the people" (*min-ch'üan*), as opposed to "the rights of the government" (*kuan-ch'üan*).[182] Hence the expression "suppressing the spirit of the people" (*i-ya min-ch'i*)—which Chang Chien stated as one of his reasons for turning against the Ch'ing Court after the 1911 Wuchang Uprising—simply meant "stifling the opinion of the gentry." The term *people's party* (*min-tang*), which was frequently used during and after the revolution, should also be understood from this viewpoint. The concept of "gentry right" is at the heart of this term.[183] The constitutional system, which presupposes the concept of "citizen" (*kuo-min*), evolved as a conceptual goal for the protection of "the rights of the people." The practical reality of "citizenship" was in turn realized by protecting local interest against the central government. The crux of the Chekiang railway dispute lay in who took charge of the local railways, which the gentry invested in and the local interest depended upon. Ma Liang said: "The foreigners once demanded the partition of China, but now they, having changed their tactics, confuse the Chinese people by means of agreements, and embolden the ambition of the Ch'ing Court by their active support for the theory of centralization. And they try to gain their own profit by sowing seeds of dissension among the Chinese in internal as well as in foreign affairs."[184] Bland, the British and Chinese Corporation's representative in China, testified to the truth of Ma Liang's point of view when he said that the hope for centralization had vanished completely as a result of the railway disputes.[185] Therefore, the more deeply the "national consciousness" (consciousness as the *kuo-min*) was felt, the stronger was the tendency toward centrifugal regionalism. Bland continued:

The results of the Shanghai-Ningpo Railway agreement were particularly significant, for the program of provincial autonomy (and as a direct consequence, the anti-Manchu movement) received herein its final impetus of enthusiasm.[186]

With this remark, Bland observed that provincial leaders, after the railway disputes, were able to ignore the authority of the central government with impunity and that the Ch'ing Court had no way of dealing with such disobedience. That Sheng Hsuan-huai and Bland took the conclusion of the loan agreement as a sign of the complete "victory" of provincial gentry over the Ch'ing Court[187] meant that regionalism in its confrontation with the central government had made significant progress. In other countries, nationalism usually developed on the basis of internal (national) unity. In late-Ch'ing China, however, nationalism in the sense of the unity of "citizens" (*kuo-min*) was promoted through the anti-imperialist movement, which was conducted on the basis of regionalism and in opposition to the central government. The movement against the central government in Chekiang and Kiangsu developed further into the movement against the Loan Deposit Agreement and against the dismissal of T'ang Shou-ch'ien. Conflicts with the Ch'ing Court thus continued up to the time of the 1911 Revolution. The attitude of the Chekiang and Kiangsu gentry toward the Revolution, therefore, can be accurately understood only if we take into account the general trends of that period arising out of the Chekiang-Kiangsu railway disputes.

The anti-loan movement, which gave an impetus to internal nationalism, waged as a protest against the authority of the Ch'ing Court, could not fail to become an external anti-imperialist nationalism because the movement itself resulted from the pressure of Britain's imperialism. The anti-imperialist character of the movement is reflected in a telegram sent to the Peking office by the Chekiang Railway Company. In view of its emotional tone, it may have been written by T'ang himself:

The Board of Foreign Affairs, covetous of the loan commission, intends to hand Chekiang province over to others without even considering the principles already sanctioned in the name of the Emperor, the commercial law enacted by the government, the dignity of the country, and the people's wish. Should the people of Chekiang province, controlled by the Board, follow in the footsteps of ruined countries like Egypt, India, Korea, and Vietnam?[188]

The same anti-imperialist sentiments can be seen in the remark of Yao Tzu-liang, Executive Officer of the Soochow Anti-Loan Association: "If the anti-loan movement does not succeed, the fate of China would be the same as that of India or Korea."[189] "How can the Court ignore its promise to the Chinese people, and assign greater importance to its promise to the foreigners?"[190] asked an editorial in *Shihpao*. Here the interests of the Ch'ing Court and Britain were regarded as the same. A similar idea was clearly expressed by Ma Feng-po, who was invited as a guest to a meeting of fellow Chekiang provincials in Shanghai on 6 November: "The present [Chinese] government is a government of foreigners. [Therefore,] we do not have to follow its orders."[191] This logic, in fact, is not at all different from that of the revolutionaries who advocated the overthrow of the Ch'ing.[192]

It is not surprising, therefore, to discover that Chang Chien and T'ang Shou-ch'ien observed the rapid decline of the authority of the Ch'ing dynasty, although they were always careful to keep the movement from developing into a violent revolt. T'ang said:

There is a rumor that a riot might break out in Hangchow. If such an incident happens, it should be considered as initiated by the Board of Foreign Affairs, stirred up by government edicts, and "tacitly" agreed to by the eminent elders [like Sheng]. If I and Liu Chin-tsao [Director and Vice-Director of the Chekiang Railway Company] were to try putting down the riot, we would not be confident of success even if we tried our utmost.[193]

T'ang Shou-ch'ien here admits not only the possibility of a violent revolt but also the validity of such a revolt. The same attitude is inherent in the petition memorial to the Throne that shareholders of the Chekiang Railway Company sent to the Chekiang Governor in protest against the dismissal of T'ang Shou-ch'ien:

We would rather take "the blame of disobedience" [which alludes to revolt] by sacrificing our lives to keep our qualification as citizens [*kuo-min*] who enjoy constitutionalism than to lose that qualification by obediently following [government orders].[194]

"A certain Chekiang native living in Shanghai," who sent his opinion on the anti-loan matter to *Chung-wai jih-pao*, showed a similar resolve:

If there is no positive result [even after having made an appeal to the government] to the last, it means that the government will throw away Chekiang and Kiangsu like old shoes. Then we will have to prepare quickly some "self-protective" measures.[195]

Chang Chien spoke again of "a certain Chekiang native," with whom he discussed the petition for the prompt opening of the parliament, and he quotes him as saying: "If we consider the present circumstances of government and society, there seems to be no absolute guarantee that the nation will not collapse." Chang does not identify this "Chekiang native," but, since there was no other person except T'ang Shou-ch'ien whom Chang could possibly regard as a representative figure of Chekiang province at that time,[196] it is almost certain that T'ang himself was the one who dared to admit the inevitability of the downfall of the Ch'ing dynasty.

At one point in the anti-loan movement, T'ang expressed the anxiety he felt about his actions:

Because the superiors have strayed from the proper path, the inferiors are giving way to disorder. I have become like a gambler who has to make his final bet, or like someone who is locked in a jar. My hardship is infinitely beyond that of high government officials.[197]

When the last bet is lost, the game is over. The Chekiang and Kiangsu gentry made their last bet with the protection of the Chekiang-Kiangsu railway rights, but, when the final outcome was almost decided, the Wuchang Uprising broke out and they had to withdraw from the game and race to support the rebels.

Chang Chien, who was taking a more moderate line than T'ang, said: "Even if the petition [for the prompt opening of the parliament] does not succeed, we should let future generations know that, on the day when the Ch'ing falls, we did our best for the dynasty."[198] He recognized that "the immediate realization of a constitution may not prevent the downfall of the Ch'ing, but people suffer less when a constitutional regime collapses than when an autocratic regime does."[199] Thus, he admitted the inevitability of the Ch'ing's collapse. As Chang Chien became gradually aware that the Ch'ing would fall, one of his aides, Liu Hou-sheng, predicted:

During the last couple of years, what some of the nobility in the Court have done is sufficient to make the members of all the provincial assemblies in the country feel a deep frustration. The day when those members despair is the day when the base of the Ch'ing dynasty is shaken.[200]

In Chekiang and Kiangsu provinces, the course the railway dispute took brought the provincial assemblies as well as the gentry class face to face with the fact that the Ch'ing Court was "turning its back on constitutionalism by suppressing the people's vigor,"[201] and that what was created under the name of constitutionalism was nothing but a "disguise."[202] Furthermore, the incident of T'ang Shou-ch'ien's dismissal made the Provincial Assembly perceive that, in order to protect local rights, opposition to the government must be continued.

When we read the proclamation of the Hupeh Revolutionary Army in full knowledge of these circumstances, we realize more clearly the significance of the policy of centralization and railway disputes, including the Chekiang and Kiangsu railway disputes. The proclamation, announced in the name of Li Yuan-hung, Governor General of Hupeh province, read:

[The Ch'ing Court] has carried out centralization under the cloak of constitutionalism ... Today the Court gives a city to a "friendly nation" or sells a mine. Tomorrow it will sell a railway. If we, the people, happen to argue that such activities are wrong, the Court calls this "interference" and says that we "deserve death." Moreover, they forfeit not only the railway that we were taking charge of but also the capital that we collected.[203]

Revolution was precipitated by an anti-government, anti-centralization impulse for self-protection and hence expressed in the form of provincial "independence".

In Chekiang province, as in other provinces, the New Army raised the banner of revolution. An army general was ousted, and T'ang Shou-ch'ien was made the new Governor of Chekiang province. He was considered the one who could deal with the situation because he had succeeded in "controlling the people during the railway dispute."[204] T'ang also became president of a civil organization which was established by the Hangchow gentry immediately after the Wuchang Uprising. Though self-protection was said to be the purpose of the organization, it was, in fact, to respond to the Revolution.[205] It is well known that T'ang, with Chang Chien and Ch'eng Te-ch'üan, Governor of Kiangsu, later played an active role in creating the provisional republican government.[206]

In the midst of the disturbance caused by the 1911 Revolution, T'ang Shou-ch'ien and Chang Chien made a decisive contribution not only to turning the tide but also to keeping order. They influenced Shanghai and Soochow in achieving independence, and were effective in other provinces where the people were watching developments.[207] Furthermore, they jointly sent a telegram, urging the soldiers of northern China to support the Revolution.[208] They played a pivotal role in creating as well as maintaining the Nanking provincial government. Their main stage was Shanghai, which had been one of the centers of the anti-loan movement. Although it was within the administrative jurisdiction of Kiangsu province, Shanghai shared common interests with Chekiang province, so Shanghai and Chekiang acted together. T'ang and Chang, but especially T'ang, were able to play leading roles because of the Soochow-Hangchow-Ningpo railway dispute, which dragged on until the eve of the Revolution. The disputes made it possible for the gentry of those areas to stand together to support the Revolutionary Army against the Ch'ing government.

It should be remembered that the two provinces, Chekiang and Kiangsu, produced more government officials and gentry than any other province during the Ch'ing period. For example, Chekiang province was first in the number of local magistrates, followed by Kiangsu. As for the number who gained *chin-shih* status in the Ch'ing, Hangchow prefecture was first nationwide with 1,004 *chin-shih*, Shaohsing sixth, Chia-hsing seventh, and Hu-chou eighth (all of these are in Chekiang province). In Kiangsu province, Soochow was second in the county, and Ch'ang-chou fourth. The total number of Chekiang *chin-shih* was 2,405, more than half of the total number of *chin-shih* in the Ch'ing.[209] Since the Ch'ing political system was based upon the gentry-official hierarchy, it is not surprising that the two provinces became the center of political influence in the country, that the gentry of these provinces were closely affiliated, and that their leaders exerted a nationwide influence.

As we have seen, the Chekiang and Kiangsu gentry, though pessimistic about the prospects for the dynasty, could not leave the gambling table until they made the last bet. The feeling of unity pervasive among the gentry class was one reason for their persistence. Although they had wide support from the gentry in general and from common people in the anti-loan movement and spoke of "the citizenry" (*kuo-min*), they had only a limited feeling of unity with the people. This difference is typically reflected in "The Opinion of the Anti-Loan Assembly of the Soochow Railway Shareholders in Nanking."[210] In this "Opinion," the shareholders (probably the holders of small amounts of stock) criticized executive board members for their contempt for wealthy merchants (probably commoners) and for not being eager to solicit them to buy stocks. They called for an election to replace the thirteen members of the company's executive board because they treated the shareholders like slaves and disdained any advice the shareholders gave them. The "Opinion" concluded that the executive members were no different from the "corrupt government of the modern age," implying the Ch'ing government.[211] This expression of the commoners' discontent with the small group of the upper gentry class who constituted the executive board indicates that the movement was not completely unified even among the shareholders.

The active merchants in Shanghai were cool toward the anti-loan movement.[212] An anti-loan meeting held on 8 November in the Southern City, with 1,000 people present, registered only 7,000 share pledges.[213] Two days earlier, at a meeting of Chekiang residents of Shanghai, the merchant group of the Southern City had promised to invest 5,000 yuan, while the merchant group of northern Shanghai pledged 250,000 yuan.[214]

According to a source that tells us about the general composition of the Southern Shanghai Merchants' Association in 1911, most of the 56 members seem to have been small-scale companies dealing in or producing daily necessities. Only 6 of them appear to have been large-scale industries—a waterworks company, two banks, a transport company, a flour company, plus one other.[215] Among the members of the Southern City who were active in the anti-loan movement, only Li P'ing-shu, Shen Man-yun, and Yeh Hui-chün are mentioned in the documentary collection on the anti-loan movement, the *Chiang-Che t'ieh-lu feng-ch'ao*.[216] The first two were managers of modern industries in the Southern City, and the third, Yeh Hui-chün, ran a rice store; this does not sound like a modern-style business but was probably a rice mill with modern facilities. Yeh seems to have been an influential merchant, for he was First Executive Director of the Southern Shanghai Merchants and Students Association in 1911, then Vice-President of the National Confederation of Merchant Associations (Ch'üan-kuo shang-t'uan lien-ho-hui), which had been organized in March 1911.[217]

Most of the activists among the merchants of the Southern City were thus running large modern businesses, as were most of the executive members and the large shareholders of the Chekiang and Kiangsu railway companies, who came from the gentry class and were powers in modern industry.[218] The directors of the Chekiang and Kiangsu railway companies once defined the enforcement of the loan as an act of nipping modern-style Chinese industry (*shih-yeh*) in the bud.[219] The differences between the gentry "industrialists," presumably the very executive members of the railway companies who were criticized for being contemptuous of (traditional) rich merchants, and those who were running traditional small or medium businesses made it difficult to unite as businessmen or as citizens.[220]

The leading gentry group of the anti-loan association sought a non-violent course in dealing with the government. For instance, when Wang Wen-shao became President of the National Anti-Loan Association, he took the post on condition that there would be no resort to armed revolt. This non-violence was the basic difference between the Chekiang-Kiangsu railway dispute and the Szechwan railway protection movement, which finally developed into the Revolution. T'ang Shou-ch'ien and other leaders, however, were well aware that Chekiang and Kiangsu were on the verge of rebellion. The active participation of lower-class people was welcomed, but possible armed revolt was checked, and the activities of small merchants who were not from the official-gentry class were limited. The Chekiang and Kiangsu gentry who led the anti-loan movement and the Soochow-Hangchow-Ningpo Railway Agreement abrogation movement did not allow these movements to go any further.[221]

The armed riots of secret societies were intensified by the railway disputes, but they were not connected with the mainstream of the anti-loan movement because the movement had held violence in check. The leaders of the movement could maintain a moderate posture because they achieved some success. Even Sheng Hsuan-huai called the exclusion of direct foreign control of the Chekiang-Kiangsu Railway a "victory";[222] and provincial officials were sympathetic to their cause. This was in contrast to the railway protection movement in Szechwan, also led by the gentry, which eventually became violent.

The gentry of the late Ch'ing, who failed to create a sense of unity with the masses, opposed the Ch'ing and obtained the support of the people by means of local interest and the principle of people's rights. They were not in a position to destroy the Ch'ing dynasty, although they realized that the end was inevitable. As they hesitated, the New Army began the revolt that finally brought the dynasty down. Not until after this uprising did the gentry join the New Army and offer their leadership and influence. Then and only then did they abandon the hope of negotiating a peaceful solution with the Ch'ing Court.

CONCLUSION

Let us conclude this discussion with a brief look at the position of the Ch'ing Court and of Yuan Shih-k'ai, who actively promoted the introduction of the foreign loan as Minister of the Board of Foreign Affairs, and who represented the opinion of the Court.

The weak Ch'ing government needed support from foreign powers, especially from Britain, so it had to handle the Chekiang and Kiangsu railway disputes in the way Britain wanted. Given the strong opposition from its own people, the government faced a dilemma. The British government was afraid that its diplomatic pressure would increase the opposition of the gentry and the people, and that, as a result, the Ch'ing government would be weakened. The British sometimes backed down, but they did not always make concessions because they knew that their support was essential to the Ch'ing government. So they used a skillful application of the "stick-and-carrot" policy.[223] During the Chekiang and Kiangsu railway disputes, Britain changed from denying abrogation of the preliminary contract to offering the loan indirectly, but never gave up its demand for the supply of the loan and for the appropriation of the Kiangsu-Chekiang railway by the central government.

The Ch'ing Court justified its actions by appealing to the "principle of diplomacy," which is that, "when the strong nation [Britain] keeps the faith (*hsin-i*), the weak nation [Ch'ing] cannot be faithless."[224] This was, however, a logic of submission: "Faithfulness" is often interpreted on the basis of the reality of power.

Yuan Shih-k'ai, who earned a strong position by winning the confidence of the foreign powers during the Boxer Rebellion, was the Minister of the Board of Foreign Affairs. As such, he would be likely to show a cooperative attitude toward the powers, as the *Shen-chou jih-pao* (North China daily news) in a report of 15 November observed: "Of all the high officials in the Board of Foreign Affairs, only Yuan Shih-k'ai supported the introduction of the foreign loan, because he hoped thereby to improve China's diplomatic relations with Britain and also heighten her credibility among the powers."[225]

This passage clearly shows that the Board of Foreign Affairs was greatly influenced by Yuan himself in its attempt to solve the disputes as the British wanted them solved. The "submissive faithfulness" of Yuan Shih-k'ai stands diametrically opposed to the attitude of Chang

Chih-tung, who took the lead in the Kwangtung-Hankow railway recovery movement.[226] We can see the difference also in their responses to the Chekiang-Kiangsu railway disputes. It was reported that Chang, having noticed the violent reaction in Chekiang and Kiangsu provinces, worried about a possible catastrophic incident and appealed for a more considered policy, while Yuan ignored the fear that such an incident might occur, regarding it as a mere fabrication of the newspapers. Chang was quoted as responding to Yuan by asking how all the Chekiang people could be manipulated by the press.[227]

If such a story is true, it will help us to understand Yuan Shih-k'ai, who later took full advantage of the 1911 Revolution and attempted to become the Hung-hsien Emperor. It helps us to know what he thought about the importance of the mass media, the force of nationalism, and the degree of gentry power when it maintains a connection with provincial interests.

Sheng Hsuan-huai, a representative figure among the comprador-style officials in the late Ch'ing, also pointed out that the officials and gentry of southern and central China were manipulated by the mass media and the student movement.[228] Although he was politically opposed to Yuan, his attitude toward the railway disputes was similar to Yuan's. Referring to the activists of the anti-loan movement in Chekiang and Kiangsu, he said: "Having achieved a victory over the Ch'ing Court in the Soochow-Hangchow-Ningpo railway incidents, they became arrogant and held meetings too often."[229] This statement also shows how ignorant Sheng was of the growing nationalism. It is, therefore, not surprising that, to Sheng, the Chekiang-Kiangsu railway dispute did not become a "lesson" but a pretext for the nationalization of the railway—"the construction of the railway under the supervision of the central government with the help of the foreign loan."[230] When the Ch'ing Court stiffened its attitude during the Chekiang-Kiangsu railway dispute, the attitude of the people toward the Ch'ing Court also hardened. Chekiang and Kiangsu were fortunately spared the violence that in Szechwan and other provinces brought on the Revolution.

Notes
Bibliography
Glossary/Index

NOTES

Preface

1. With the exception of the chapter "Chinese 'Principle' and Western 'Utility,'" which was published as an article in *Tongbang hakchi*, Vol. XVIII (Seoul, Yonsei University, 1978), the articles mentioned here are all included in my book *Chungguk kŭndaesa yŏn'gu: Sinsach'ŭng ŭi sasang kwa haengdong*. This book contains eleven articles, republished with some revisions, on the history of modern China, especially of the Ch'ing, which appeared originally between 1963 and 1972 in various journals.
2. This article was published in December 1966 in *Chindan hakpo*, in the combined Volumes XXIX-XXX. The main points of the articles can be found in the introduction to "The Theory of Political Feudalism in the Ch'ing Period," in this book.
3. The division of the upper and lower gentry made in Chapter 2 of this book is not effective for understanding the activities on the provincial level after the constitutional movement began.
4. A part of my study on the Reform Movement of 1898 was introduced to American readers by John Schrecker in *Reform in Nineteenth-Century China*, ed. Paul Cohen and John Schrecker (Cambridge, East Asian Research Center, Harvard University, 1976). Thirteen of my papers in Korean on the Reform Movement of 1898 were included in my book *Chungguk kŭndae kaehyŏk undong ŭi yŏn'gu—Kang Yu-wi chungsim ŭi 1898 nyŏn kaehyŏk undong*.

5. With the exception of "Chinese 'Principle' and Western 'Utility'," the articles were introduced in considerable detail to Western readers in *Oriens Extremus* 23.1:123–132 (1976).

1. *The* Jehol Diary *and the Character of Ch'ing Rule*
"*Yŏlha ilgi* e pich'in ch'ŏngjo t'ongch'i ŭi cheyangsong"

1. Kim Sŏng-ch'il, "Yŏnhaeng sogo." [This process is also described in Arthur W. Hummel, ed., *Eminent Chinese of the Ch'ing Period*, p. 394. –Trans.]
2. "Jidai kikō mokuroku," ed. Nakamura Eiko, in *Seikyū gakusō*. Sungkyunkwan University in Seoul has published selections from various diaries of travel to Peking in two volumes under the title *Yŏnhaeng-nok sŏnjip*. [Cf. John K. Fairbank, ed., *The Chinese World Order*, p. 27 –Trans.]
3. *Yŏlha ilgi*, p. 39. This edition of *Yŏlha ilgi* is included in *Yŏnam sokchip*, published by Kim T'ae-yŏng in 1901. There are also the complete edition published by the Kwangmun-hoe in 1911, based on the volume owned by Yu Chin-ch'ŏl; the edition published in 1932 as a separate volume of *Yŏnamjip* by Pak Yŏng-ch'ŏl; and the photocopy of a manuscript edition published in Taiwan in the *Chung-hua ts'ung-shu* series. For annotations, there is Kim Sŏng-ch'il, *Yŏlha ilgi yŏkchu*. There are also many extant manuscript editions. Of the editions already cited, the Kwangmun-hoe edition is the best. The citations here refer to the most commonly used edition, the Kyŏnghŭi Press copy of the Pak Yŏng-ch'ŏl edition. According to Hsu Yü-hu, *Ta-lu tsa-chih* 13.6 (1956), the *Chung-hua ts'ung-shu* edition is based on an original manuscript, but we cannot hastily accept this conclusion.
4. In the movement to "restore the orthodoxy of literary style," King Chŏngjo noted that, beginning with Pak Chi-wŏn and followed by Pak Chae-ga and Yi Tŏk-mu and others, the Yŏnhaeng-nok (China-travelogue) style "aimed at introducing novelty and embellishing with colorful details" and "imitated the fictional style of miscellaneous writings and short stories of the Ming and Ch'ing." The movement was initiated by the Emperor's fear that this style would become popular and spread the liberal views it expressed. Because he said this kind of writing should be done in a pure and orthodox style, that is, the *ku-wen* style, it was called the "restore the orthodoxy of literary style" movement. As part of this movement, King Chŏngjo forbade written conversations or the exchange of poetry and letters with the Chinese, and prohibited the buying of any books other than "orthodox philosophy" (that is, the works of the Ch'eng-Chu school), so the movement for literary orthodoxy would cause problems only in the literary sphere. Chŏngjo feared that writers who went beyond the orthodox framework would denigrate Chu Hsi as some Chinese did. He ordered Pak Chi-wŏn to take responsibility for the popularity of the *Yŏlha ilgi* style and to write works in the *ku-wen* style and present them to the King. Cf. the Pak Yŏng-ch'ŏl edition of *Yŏnamjip*, chüan 2, "A Letter to Pak Chi-wŏn by Nam Kong-ch'ŏl," attached

to Pak's letter to Nam Kong-ch'ŏl. On the movement, see Takahashi Tōru, "Kosaiwo no buntai hansei."
5. The year after his meeting with Pak, Yin was sentenced to death by strangulation. See Arthur W. Hummel, *Eminent Chinese of the Ch'ing Period*, pp. 921–922; also *Ch'ing-tai wen-tzu-yü tang* 2.6:581–686; Wang Hsien-ch'ien, *Tung-hua hsu-lu*, chüan 93 (*keng-shen*, 4th month, 46th year of Ch'ien-lung).
6. For example, corruption in the bureaucracy is thought to have become widespread in the Ch'ien-lung reign; David S. Nivison, "Ho-shen and His Accusers: Ideology and Political Behavior in the Eighteenth Century," in David S. Nivison and Arthur F. Wright, eds., *Confucianism in Action*. The degeneration of the spirit of the *mu-yu* (private secretaries), who occupied an important position in the Ch'ing administrative structure, began in the late Ch'ien-lung period. See the chapter "Ch'ŏngdae maguje wa haengjŏng chilsŏ ŭi t'ŭksŏng," in *Chungguk kŭndaesa yŏn'gu*.
7. Quoted in Fujitsuka Chikashi, "Richō no gakujin to Kenryū bunka," p. 290.
8. Kim Ch'ang-ŏp, *Kaje yŏnhaeng-nok*, p. 228.
9. *Yŏlha ilgi*, p. 207. What seems to have made Pak think this way was the treatment of a Korean emissary by the Board of Rites of the Ch'ing dynasty. *Yŏlha ilga*, p. 240, stated: "The Ch'ing Board of Rites in general does not deal with any fundamental matters, but only tries to please the Emperor temporarily. As a result, they deceive their ruler and invite the scorn of foreigners [like the Koreans]. If the Board of Rites is like this, one can guess how it is with the other boards," and concluded: "From matters like these one can infer the situation of China as a whole."
10. *Yŏlha ilgi*, p. 226.
11. Ibid. Pak saw the tendency of the Chinese to praise the Imperial Court without taking into account the severity of execution of the laws and the strictness of imperial regulations. He reasoned that some Chinese believed that an exchange of views with foreigners constituted rebellion. For example, Pak wrote (*Yŏlha ilgi*, p. 253) that, if the Chinese uttered thoughts opposed to the government in their speech to foreigners, they were considered rebels by the present government, because their behavior made the Chinese lose face in their native land.
12. *Yŏlha ilgi*, p. 226. A similar kind of taboo is found in Ch'ien Yung, *Lü-yuan ts'ung-hua*, chüan 17: "In the first year of the Yung-cheng period [1723], Hsu K'uan-ch'ing wrote a poem stating: '[Though] the bright (*ming*) moon shines on me as if to show its concern about me, the cool (*ch'ing*) breeze blows by me as if it cared for nobody.' An enemy of Hsu's secretly denounced him, taking this poem as proof of a rebellious intent."
13. *Nakyang-nok*, Chapter 2.
14. Kim Ch'ang-ŏp, p. 19.
15. Ibid., p. 227 (7th day, 2nd month, 52nd year of K'ang-hsi). Kim Ch'ang-ŏp also saw that the reason for summering in Jehol was not simply to escape the heat but to encourage military arts and a simple lifestyle.
16. Hong Tae-yong, "Kyebang ilgi," Chapter 2 (29th day, 3rd month, 54th year of K'ang-hsi), in *Tamhŏn yŏn'gi*.

17. *Yŏlha ilgi*, p. 41.
18. Ibid., p. 232.
19. Ibid., p. 251.
20. Ibid., p. 232.
21. Ibid., p. 227.
22. *Yŏlha ilgi*, p. 233. At the conclusion of this section, Pak displayed his self-confidence by saying: "Those who have not gone out for thirty years and who worry about the troubles of the empire ought to remind themselves of my words today."
23. Ibid. There is a similar view in Yu Tŏk-kang, *Nakyang-nok*, Chapter 1.
24. *Yŏlha ilgi*, p. 199; ibid., p. 254, records a similar view.
25. Ibid., p. 210.
26. Ibid., p. 254.
27. Ibid., p. 253.
28. See *Ta-i chüeh-mi lu* 4:24a–b. He accused the men before the K'ang-hsi period who uttered anti-Ch'ing opinions only of having "lost their chastity," which meant disloyalty to the Ming. But he brought different accusations against dissidents who were born after the K'ang-hsi period. See also Ch'ien Mu, *Chung-kuo chin-san-pai-nien hsueh-shu shih*, Chapter 2.
29. Hong Tae-yong, "Kŏnjŏng p'ildam," in *Tamhŏn yŏn'gi*.
30. It is difficult to judge how deep the "longing for a Chinese ruler" was among the Chinese literati. The author's view is that a generation later, when the much stronger Western barbarian threat appeared, the *ssu-Han* psychology was extremely weak. But, even in the Ch'ien-lung period, the scholars had to face reality, which dampened the *ssu-Han* feeling.
31. *Yŏlha ilgi*, p. 253.
32. Ibid., p. 260.
33. Ibid., p. 265. The opening quotation is from the *Analects* 8.9; Arthur Waley, tr., *The Analects of Confucius*, p. 134.
34. Ibid., p. 204.
35. Ibid., p. 209. Wang Hu-ting pointed at a hairnet that Pak was wearing (which was worn in China, too, in the Ming dynasty) and said: "That style began when Ming T'ai-tsu borrowed it from the Taoists," and at the same time he wrote, pointing to Pak's head, "He bound up the heads of all the people in the empire in those nets" and laughed. Pak retorted: "Why do you shave yourself bald like that?" Wang was silent, and hung his head. Then he blotted out all the words he had just written.
36. *Yŏlha ilgi*, p. 262.
37. Ibid., p. 263.
38. Pak added his own commentary to this passage on Wang Mang. He wrote: "These words of Wang Hu-ting are directed at a hidden target. They are not simply a general historical discussion. Though he praises the legitimacy of the Ch'ing domination of China vigorously, in the course of the discussion he sometimes reveals his real feelings. Here, particularly, in speaking of rebels who succeed and fail, he is referring to his own feelings."
39. Hsiao I-shan, *Ch'ing-tai t'ung-shih* 2:695–794.

40. *Yŏlha ilgi*, p. 264.
41. Ibid., p. 216. Elsewhere (p. 264) Pak praised Shih K'o-fa's argument as absolutely correct.
42. Ibid., p. 196.
43. E.g. Yano Jin'ichi, *Kindai Shina shi*, pp. 166–168; Inaba Iwakichi, *Shina kinseishi kōwa*, pp. 62–63.
44. [The Ch'ien-lung Emperor called the printed edition of the *Ssu-k'u ch'üan-shu* the Assembled Pearls (*chü-chen*) edition. In fact, the Assembled Pearls Bureau was a separate organization set up to publish only certain rare editions, not the entire project. I am grateful to Kent Guy for this information. –Trans.]
45. *Yŏlha ilgi*, p. 254. The same view is also found in Yi Tŏk-mu, *Angyŏp-gi*, p. 372.
46. *Yŏlha ilgi*, p. 258.
47. Yano Jin'ichi, *Kindai Shina shi*, p. 168.
48. Pak's observations may reflect the narrow range of people with whom he came in contact. Unlike Pak Chae-ga, Yi Tŏk-mu, and Yu Tŏk-kong, who met the most prominent scholars of their time, such as Chi Yun, Sun Hsing-yen, and Juan Yuan, Pak met almost nobody who could even be called a scholar. See Fujitsuka Chikashi. We should also bear in mind that Han Learning flourished at a time after Pak's visit, that is, after the completion of the *Ssu-k'u ch'üan-shu*, in the late Ch'ien-lung and Chia-ch'ing periods.
49. *Yŏlha ilgi*, pp. 254–255.
50. Ibid. On p. 254 it is stated that refutations of Chu Hsi were "extremely fashionable."
51. *Ta-i chüeh-mi lu* 1:1a, 4:1a–17b. The appropriate edicts are found in *Ta-Ch'ing Shih-tsung shih-lu* and *Tung-hua hsu-lu* for the 5th day, 7th month and 12th day, 9th month of the 7th year of Yung-cheng.
52. Chao-lien, *Hsiao-t'ing tsa-lu*, chüan 8.
53. Yu Tŏk-kong, *Yŏndae chaeyu-rok*.
54. Yamanoi Yū, "Minmatsu Shinsho ni okeru keisei chiyō no gaku," esp. p. 141.
55. See my "Ch'ŏngjŏ ŭi hwangje t'ongch'i wa sasang t'ongje ŭi silje: Chŭngjŏng moyŏk sakkŏn kwa *Taeŭi kangmi-rok* ŭl chungsim ŭro."
56. Joseph R. Levenson, *Confucian China and Its Modern Fate*, Vol. I: *The Problem of Intellectual Continuity*, pt. 2, Chapters 3, 4, esp. pp. 53–58.

2. The Sheng-yuan–Chien-sheng *Stratum* (Sheng-Chien) in Ch'ing Society
"Ch'ŏngdai 'saenggamch'ŭng' ŭi sŏngkyŏk"

1. Chung-li Chang, *The Chinese Gentry: Studies on Their Role in Nineteenth-Century Chinese Society*; Kung-ch'üan Hsiao, *Rural China: Imperial Control in the Nineteenth Century*; Sakai Tadao, *Chūgoku zensho no kenkyū*; Robert M. Marsh, *The Mandarins: The Circulation of Elites in China, 1600–1900*; Ping-ti Ho, *The Ladder of Success in Imperial China: Aspects of Social Mobility*,

1368–1911; T'ung-tsu Ch'ü, *Local Government in China under the Ch'ing;* Chung-li Chang, *The Income of the Chinese Gentry.*
2. *Gentry* is commonly used by Western researchers to translate *shen-shih* or *shih-ta-fu,* but there are criticisms of this usage. Cf. Marsh, pp. 40–41; T'ung-tsu Ch'ü, pp. 313–314, 318; Ping-ti Ho, p. 40. The main reservations about the term concern the linking of the examination system and the school system, and the question of landholding, i.e., whether the gentry should necessarily be regarded as landlords. The Japanese equivalent of the gentry is *kyōshin.* There is a similar ambiguity in that term.
3. Marsh, pp. 33–70. Cf. T'ung-tsu Ch'ü, p. 313.
4. Sakai Tadao, pp. 77–82.
5. Distinctions among the gentry are described in the next section.
6. See my "Ch'ŏngdae maguje wa haengjŏng chilsŏ ŭi t'ŭksŏng," pp. 145–146, 165–166.
7. For several examples, see Yuan Shou-ting, "Chü-kuan t'ung-i," and Hsieh Chin-luan, "Chü-kuan chih-yung," in Miao Ch'üan-sun, ed., *Hsu pei-chuan chi,* chüan 42, *shou-ling* 2; chüan 44, *shou-ling* 5.
8. Italics mine. Hsieh Chin-luan in *Mu-ling shu,* chüan 1.
9. T'ung-tsu Ch'ü, pp. 172, 319.
10. Ch'en Hung-mou, "Tzu-hsun ti-fang li-pi yü," in *Mu-ling shu,* chüan 2.
11. Huang Liu-hung, *A Complete Book Concerning Happiness and Benevolence,* tr. Djang Chu, p. 471.
12. Ibid., p. 150.
13. In *Kuo-ch'ao ch'i-hsien lei-cheng (ch'u-pien)* 217: 34a–35b, it is stated, for example, that the former county magistrate, Chang Hsi-i, was called Chang Hsiang-shen.
14. All degree-holders from *chü-jen* down to *sheng-yuan* had privileges similar to those of 7th- to 9th-rank officials and could participate in the official ceremonies held by administrative authorities. Of course they had other privileges as well.
15. Chung-li Chang, in *Chinese Gentry,* pp. 125–126, stated that, in a given time in the early nineteenth century, of a total of 18,000 civil *chü-jen,* about 8,000 attained a *chin-shih* or an official post. Compare this with a total of 530,000 *sheng-yuan* at that time.
16. Ping-ti Ho, p. 27; Chung-li Chang, *Chinese Gentry,* pp. 24–25.
17. T'ung-tsu Ch'ü, pp. 174, 322.
18. Ping-ti Ho, pp. 33–34.
19. Chung-li Chang, *Chinese Gentry,* p. 107.
20. For details on their institutional status and special privileges, see Rinji Taiwan Kyūhan Chōsakai, ed., *Shinkoku gyōseihō* 3: 381–385; Miyazaki Ichisada, *Kakyō;* Chung-li Chang, *Chinese Gentry,* pp. 32–51; Kung-ch'üan Hsiao, *Rural China,* pp. 124–139; T'ung-tsu Ch'ü, pp. 173–175.
21. Feng Kuei-fen, *Hsien-chih-t'ang kao,* chüan 9, includes all below *chü-jen* in the *chin,* i.e. *shih,* as is usual. The "T'ien-chin-fu tzu-chih-chü shih-pan tiao-ch'a chien-chang" of the late Kuang-hsu period states that *shen* includes "all former officials who have served in a post, no matter what grade," and that *shih* in-

cludes "*chü-jen, kung-sheng, chien-sheng, sheng-yuan,* and students of modern schools (above high or primary grades)." See *Tung-fang tsa-chih* 4.4:172–176 (1907). But, as will be explained below, *chin* often refers exclusively to *sheng-yuan.*
22. There are few examples of "wicked *chin*" (*sheng-yuan*) and "vicious *chien*" (*chien-sheng*), but, for one instance, see Liu Ping-chang, "Tsun-ch'a Chiang-hsi cheng-shou ting-ts'ao shu," which states, "Wicked *chin* (*sheng-yuan*) and vicious *chien* (*chien-sheng*) mistreat the commoners, engross the grain tribute, resist taxes and manipulate the officials." For examples of the term *chin-sheng,* see Jen Ch'i-yun, "Yü Hu i-hou shu"; Feng Kuei-fen, "Chün-fu i," in Sheng K'ang, ed., *Huang-ch'ao ching-shih wen hsü-pien,* chüan 36 (also included in Feng Kuei-fen, *Hsien-chih-t'ang kao* 10:1a–6a); Huang Liu-hung, *Fu-hui ch'üan-shu,* 21:6b–11a.
23. *Mu-ling shu,* chüan 2. Yuan Mei, "Ta men-sheng Wang Li-ch'i wen tso-ling shu," in *Huang-ch'ao ching-shih wen-pien* 21:23–27.
24. Yueh Yuan-sheng, *Ch'ien-ch'u-tzu wen-chi,* chüan 5, and Yen Mao-yu, *Ti-chi lu,* quoted in Sakai Tadao, pp. 81, 82.
25. T'ung-tsu Ch'ü, pp. 171–172.
26. See note 21 above.
27. T'ung-tsu Ch'ü, p. 172.
28. Ch'ü criticizes Ho's distinction and use of the term *ruling class* because it is unclear whether it corresponds to the traditional term *shen-chin* (Ch'ü, p. 318), and he criticizes Chang's terms *upper* and *lower* because it is not clear from the sources what these terms correspond to (Ch'ü, p. 320).
29. Chung-li Chang, *Chinese Gentry,* pp. 7–8.
30. Ibid.
31. Ping-ti Ho, pp. 34–41. On pp. 38, 39, Ho explains *chin-hu* (i.e., *shih*) as "holders of the first degree" (i.e., the *sheng-chien* class).
32. Ping-ti Ho, p. 28, called the *sheng-yuan* "undergraduates" because they were subject to the yearly examinations of the provincial director of education and could not become officials; the *kung-sheng* were called "graduates" because they were different in this respect from the *sheng-yuan.*
33. According to T'ung-tsu Ch'ü (p. 318). Ping-ti Ho, in his article, "Aspects of Social Mobility in China, 1368–1911," in *Comparative Studies in Society and History* 1.4:330–359 (June 1959), used the term *ruling class* instead of *gentry.* T'ung-tsu Ch'ü, in *Local Government,* used *official class* instead of *ruling class.* The index of the book under *ruling class,* however, refers to officialdom, nobility, *chin-shih, chü-jen,* and *kung-sheng* as if they had the same meaning. Ch'ü saw the scholar gentry as a middle stratum (neither a ruling class nor a subject class) which did not participate in the governmental structure but held rather wide-scale authority, special privileges, and the power of a ruling class. He regarded them as an elite, distinct from the masses. Because they were potential officials, they could also be called a potential ruling class (Ch'ü, p. 172).
34. Kung-ch'üan Hsiao, *Rural China,* pp. 505–506.
35. We discuss in the following section the *sheng-chien* class as a whole, but main-

ly the *sheng-yuan* component of it, because of the availability of sources. *Chien-sheng* differed from *sheng-yuan* in many ways because they attained their degrees by the unorthodox route, but, for those aspects discussed here, there were no great differences.
36. Ku Yen-wu, "Sheng-yuan lun," part 3, *T'ing-lin wen-chi* 1:17–22.
37. Ping-ti Ho, pp. 32–34; Chung-li Chang, *Chinese Gentry*, pp. 11–13, 102–111.
38. Wu Jung-kuang, "Yang-min."
39. On the local participation of the gentry in public works, Chung-li Chang, *Chinese Gentry*, pp. 51–69, is quite detailed. On their income, see Chung-li Chang, *Income*, pp. 43–109.
40. Chung-li Chang, *Chinese Gentry*, pp. 43–51, on gentry exploitation of their privileged position; T'ung-tsu Ch'ü, pp. 185–190, on exploitation and unlawful activities; also Kung-ch'üan Hsiao, *Rural China*, pp. 132–137, 318–320, 437–438, 598–599.
41. T'ung-tsu Ch'ü, pp. 172, 174, 322.
42. (*Ch'in-ting*) *Hsueh-cheng ch'üan-shu* 31:589–603, "Ch'ü-pieh liu-pin"; *Li-pu tse-li*, chüan 59, "I-chü ch'ing-li-ssu, chüan-na."
43. Pak Chi-wŏn, *Yŏlha ilgi*, in *Yŏnamjip*, p. 165.
44. Other conditions are relevant to ideal government: complete payment of taxes, equalization of tax burdens, elimination of deficits, promotion of culture (encouraging the scholarship of the literati, aiding the construction and repair of academies), just settlement of lawsuits, capture of thieves, suppression of disturbances, control of water (dike-building, irrigation, and repair of reservoirs), repression of abuses of clerks, famine relief, elimination of customary fees, etc.
45. Lu Shih-chi, "Ts'ang-chou chih-hsien Hsu-kung Shih-tso hsing-chuang," in *Pei-chuan chi* 102:21a–23a; *Kuo-ch'ao ch'i-hsien lei-cheng (ch'u-pien)* 229:4a–6a, "Hsu Shih-tso." P'eng Ch'i-feng, "Hsu Shih-tso mu-chih-ming," pp. 6a–9b, has the same content.
46. Wang Chih, "Shen-shih"; Yuan Mei, "Ta men-sheng Wang Li-ch'i wen tso-ling shu"; Yuan Shou-ting, "Chü-kuan t'ung-i."
47. T'ung-tsu Ch'ü, p. 321.
48. Kao T'ing-yao, *Huan-yu chi-lueh*, pp. 7a–7b, 8b–9a.
49. See note 46 above.
50. Fa K'un-hung, "Lai Yen-wu chiao-yü Li chün i-shih," in *Pei-chuan chi* (1893), *Hsiao-kuan* (*hsia*), 112:8b–9b. The biography of the same person (a Yung-cheng *chü-jen*) by Han Meng-chou "Li hsien-sheng Kuan-ying chuan," 112:8a–8b, stated, "In this region, as administration has long been cruel, they follow the wishes of their superiors and treat the *shih* abusively," indicating the prevalence of the practice of abusing the lower gentry. See also Tien Lan-fang, "Kiangsi Fu-chou-fu t'ui-kuan T'ang hsien-sheng Wei-jan mu-piao," in *Pei-chuan chi* 88:2b–3b; Kuo Shan-yun, "Yeh P'eng-yun mu-chih-ming," in *Kuo-ch'ao ch'i-hsien lei-cheng (ch'u-pien)* 234:45a–46b.
51. These decrees and edicts are all found in *Ta-Ch'ing hui-tien shih-li* (1908 ed.), chüan 383, *li-pu*, hsueh-hsiao, "Ch'uan-ch'eng yu-lieh."
52. *Shinkoku gyōseihō* 3:381–533.

53. Feng Kuei-fen, *Chiao-pin-lu k'ang-i* 1:2b–5b.
54. Miao Chia-yü, "Ch'ung-yang k'o-wen" 26:26a–33b.
55. Cf. Kung-ch'üan Hsiao, *Rural China*, pp. 68–69.
56. *Hu-pu tse-li* (1791), chüan 12; Kung-ch'üan Hsiao, *Rural China*, p. 601.
57. Po Ching-wei, *Li-hsi ts'ao-t'ang chi*, chüan 1; Kung-ch'üan Hsiao, *Rural China*, pp. 178–179.
58. Kung-ch'üan Hsiao, *Rural China*, p. 191, citing *T'ung-kuan hsien-chih* and *Po-pai hsien-chih*, which record an edict of 1690.
59. Chung-li Chang, *Income*, pp. 43–73, is particularly detailed.
60. T'ung-tsu Ch'ü, p. 340.
61. *Ta-Ch'ing hui-tien shih-li*, chüan 172, "Ts'ui-k'o chin-ling."
62. Kung-ch'üan Hsiao, *Rural China*, pp. 132–134.
63. Feng Kuei-fen, *Chiao-pin-lu k'ang-i*, pp. 182–184.
64. T'ao Shu, "Yen-chin chin-kun pao-ts'ao so lou-kuei p'ien," in Sheng K'ang, ed., *Huang-ch'ao ching-shih-wen hsu-pien*, chüan 36.
65. T'ung-tsu Ch'ü, pp. 170–171.
66. According to the *Hsueh-shih lu* cited in Kung-ch'üan Hsiao, *Rural China*, pp. 137–139, when the tax-collection offices were far away (in some cases the clerks deliberately kept the number of tax-collection offices small and cut short the time period for collection), they themselves might profit by proxy remission. There were cases where lineages without wealthy members entrusted payments to fellow villagers, or where the county magistrate, to ensure success in tax collection, made wealthy households responsible for the collection of the entire quota in the township (*tu*) or ward (*t'u*) to which they belonged.
67. Chung-li Chang, *Chinese Gentry*, pp. 48–49; T'ung-tsu Ch'ü, p. 187, gives details.
68. Chung-li Chang, *Chinese Gentry*, pp. 45–46; T'ung-tsu Ch'ü, pp. 185–186.
69. *Ta-Ch'ing hui-tien shih-li*, chüan 383.
70. *Kuo-ch'ao ch'i-hsien lei-cheng*, (*ch'u-pien*), 230:23a–25b, "Feng Ta-shan"; T'ao Shu, "P'u-ch'a ts'ao-an ch'ing-hsing p'ien," in Ch'en Tai-lin, "Ch'ing yen-ko cheng-ts'ao chi-pi shu," in *Huang-ch'ao ching-shih-wen hsu-pien*, chüan 36; Kung-ch'üan Hsiao, p. 136; Kojima Shinji, "Taihei tengoku," pp. 129–130, 141–142.
71. Chung-li Chang, *Chinese Gentry*, p. 46; Miyazaki Ichisada, "Yōsei jidai chihō seiji no jitsujō," pp. 4–11; Kojima Shinji, pp. 129–130, 141–142.
72. Ono Kazuko, "Shinsho no shisō tōsei o megutte," p. 105; Meng Sen, "Tsou-hsiao an," pp. 434–452.
73. Kung-ch'üan Hsiao, *Rural China*, p. 507.
74. *Ta-Ch'ing mu-tsung i-huang-ti shih-lu* 44:45a–48a (27th day, 9th month, 1st year of T'ung-chih). See also Kojima Shinji, p. 129.
75. Kung-ch'üan Hsiao, *Rural China*, pp. 433–434.
76. Kojima Shinji, p. 142, describes this, citing Wang Shih-to, *I-ping jih-chi*.
77. Li Chien-nung, *Chung-kuo chin-pai-nien cheng-chih shih*, pp. 271–272.
78. Kung-ch'üan Hsiao, *Rural China*, pp. 506–507; Kojima Shinji, p. 108; Ku Yen-wu, "Sheng-yuan-lun," part 3, *T'ing-lin wen-chi*, chüan 1.

79. In Chung-li Chang, *Chinese Gentry*, p. 70, there is a different emphasis. Chang wrote: "In normal times the main interests of the government and gentry coincided, and they cooperated in keeping the wheels of society turning and maintaining the status quo. Sometimes, when their interests diverged, the gentry criticized or even opposed and blocked official actions but without any serious threat to the central government . . . But . . . as the strength and efficiency of the central government declined, the gentry took over more and more of the government's functions and authority, and reached a position where they could choose whether to support the government or directly challenge its authority." He referred to gentry who supported the Taipings and to the ability of Tseng Kuo-fan and Li Hung-chang to build up their own armies and political machines. Chang's explanation applies to the case of "great gentry" (*shen*) who were closest to central authority, but the *sheng-chien* who led tax-resistance movements could not easily take over the government's authority or independently promote changes in the existing government. On the contrary, the village-level anti-government movements led by the *sheng-chien* tended to ally themselves with a section of the *shen* or with the external revolutionary force.
80. *Ta-Ch'ing hui-tien shih-li*, chüan 383.
81. Ibid., chüan 389, *li-pu, hsueh-hsiao*, "Hsun-shih kuei-t'iao."
82. (*Ch'in-ting*) *Hsueh-cheng ch'üan-shu*, chüan 26, "Cheng-chieh shih-hsi," pp. 461–496.
83. Ch'en Hung-mou, "Tzu-hsun ti-fang li-pi yü," and Ch'eng Han-chang, "Hsun-fang ko-t'ing chou-hsien ti-fang ch'ing-hsing cha," in *Mu-ling shu* 2:30–35.
84. *Ta-Ch'ing hui-tien shih-li*, chüan 383.
85. Sun I-yen, "Liang hsien-sheng mu-piao."
86. Wang Hui-tsu, "Chih shih-tzu kan sung chih fa," in his *Hsueh-chih i-shuo*, chüan 2; *Ping-t'a meng-hen lu*, entry for ting-wei (1787).
87. T'ao Shu, "Yen-chin chin-kun pao-ts'ao suo-lou kuei p'ien," in Sheng K'ang, ed., *Huang-ch'ao ching-shih wen hsu-pien*, chüan 36, *hu-cheng* 6, *fu-i* 3.
88. Fang Tsung-ch'eng, "O-li yueh" (1868), in ibid., chüan 25, *li-cheng* 8, *shou-ling*.
89. Wang Fang-hsi, "T'iao-ch'en ting-ts'ao li-pi su," in ibid., chüan 36, *hu-cheng* 8, *fu-i* 3.
90. Chung-li Chang, *Income*, pp. 136–143; T'ung-tsu Ch'ü, pp. 170–171.
91. Ibid.; Wang Chih, "Shen-shih"; *Ta-Ch'ing hui-tien shih-li*, chüan 392; *Huang-ch'ao wen-hsien t'ung-k'ao* 71:1a–1b (edict of 1735); Huang K'o-jun, "Pi-su"; Chung-li Chang, *Income*, p. 142; Ping-ti Ho, p. 36.
92. Lo Erh-kang, *T'ai-p'ing t'ien-kuo shih-kao*, p. 38.
93. See my "Ch'ŏngjo ŭi hwangje t'ongch'i wa sasang t'ongje ŭi silje."
94. Kondo Hideki, "Shindai no ennō to kanryō shakai no shūmatsu."
95. Kung-ch'üan Hsiao, *Rural China*, p. 198.
96. Lu Shih-chi; Yü Yueh, "Hsien Jen-f'u hsiung chia-chuan"; Muramatsu Yuji, "Shindai no shinshi—jinushi ni okeru tochi to kanshoku"; *Kuo-ch'ao ch'i-hsien lei-cheng (ch'u-pien)*, chüan 230, *shou-ling* 16, "Hsia Chao-hsin," p. 2a.

97. Chung-li Chang, *Income*, pp. 142, 146.
98. Chung-li Chang, *Chinese Gentry*, p. 138.
99. Ibid., pp. 71–141.
100. Ping-ti Ho, pp. 92–125.
101. T'ung-tsu Ch'ü, p. 173.
102. Examination strikes were conducted not only for selfish gain but also for the welfare of the local area, or out of Confucian idealism. A famous example is the strike of the students of Kwangchow in 1841 after the San-yuan-li struggle against the British. The students struck out of anger at the collaboration of the Kwangchow prefect (who supervised the examinations) with the British military. See Hatano Yoshihiro, "Ahen sensō ni okeru tai-Ei kyōkō ron no imi suru mono," in *Kōza kindai Ajia shisō shi* (1960), and Kung-ch'üan Hsiao, *Rural China*, pp. 492–498.
103. *Ta-Ch'ing hui-tien shih-li*, chüan 383.
104. Araki Toshikaze, "Yōsei ninen no hikō jiken to Ten Bun-kyō."
105. See note 103 above.
106. Pan I-k'uei, "Pan shih ssu-hsueh po-ho chuan," and "Pan Ch'un-te chuan," in *Pei-chuan chi* 112:10a–10b.
107. Mo Yu-chih, "Wai-chiu Fu-t'ang hsien-sheng mu-chih-ming." Uprisings of *sheng-yuan* against their oppression by clerks and runners are found in T'ao Yuan, "Chang Chin-yü chuan" and Chao Kuang-kuei, "Tung Hsiang chuan," in *Pei-chuan chi*, chüan 89 and 111; Hsu Tzu-ling, "Ying-shang chiao-yü: Ts'ao chün mu-chih-ming," in *Hsu pei-chuan chi* 46: 7a–7b.
108. Kung-ch'üan Hsiao, *Rural China*, pp. 247–248.
109. Kao T'ing-yao, *shang*, p. 6a.
110. T'ung-tsu Ch'ü, p. 177.
111. *Ta-Ch'ing hui-tien shih-li*, chüan 383.
112. Wang Feng-sheng, "Shen-shih"; Chou Hao, "Yü Wang Ch'un-hsi shu," in *Huang-ch'ao ching-shih wen-pien* 22:43.
113. *Ta-Ch'ing hui-tien shih-li*, chüan 383.
114. Chung-li Chang, *Chinese Gentry*, p. 8, found a distinction between school and examination systems in the biographical section of gazetteers. T'ung-tsu Ch'ü, p. 322, noted the limitation on the right to strip gentry of their rank. Only *chin-shih* and *chü-jen* required the emperor's approval to be stripped of rank; lower ranks could be stripped by governors and governors general or by school officials. This is a basic distinction between the school system and the examination system.

3. Chinese "Principle" and Western "Utility"
"Chungch'e sŏyong non'go"

1. See Wang Erh-min, "Ch'ing-chi chih-shih fen tzu ti Chung-t'i Hsi-yung lun." On p. 54, Wang said it was generally understood that *Chung-t'i hsi-yung lun* was initiated by Chang Chih-tung because Liang Ch'i-ch'ao had given the phrase the status of a "concept of the times" in his *Ch'ing-tai hsueh-shu kai-lun*. But Chang Chih-tung used the phrase *chiu-hsueh wei t'i, hsin-hsueh wei*

yung (old learning for principle, and new learning for utility), not *Chung-hsueh wei t'i, hsi-hsueh wei yung*, in *Ch'üan-hsueh p'ien*. It appears, however, that Liang was not wrong when he said that Chang used the term *Chung-t'i hsi-yung*, since Chang referred to *Chung-hsueh* as *chiu-hsueh* and *hsi-hsueh* as *hsin-hsueh* here and there in *Ch'üan-hsueh p'ien*. Nonetheless, I think it is incorrect or ambiguous, or at best insufficient, to interpret Chang as saying that "principle/utility" was based on the understanding that the West had no scholarly disciplines except for geological surveying, navigation, manufacturing, and troop training. As we shall explain in the latter part of this chapter, Chang did not say in *Ch'üan-hsueh p'ien* that the West had no scholarly attainments that China should learn except natural sciences and military affairs.
2. No one has ever questioned whether we can call the administration of Western affairs a "movement." Is it proper to call it a "movement" in the same way that we speak of the so-called "reform *(pien-fa)* movement"? In my opinion "self-strengthening" efforts are worthy of the term "movement."
3. Min Tu-ki, "Musul pyŏnbŏp undong ŭi paegyŏng e taehayŏ: t'ukhi ch'ŏngnyup'a wa yangmup'a rŭl chungsim ŭro," p. 147.
4. Huang I-feng and Chiang Feng, "Chung-kuo yang-wu yun-tung yü Jih-pen Ming-chih wei-hsin tsai ching-chi fa-chan shang fa pi-chiao."
5. Hsia Tung-yuan, "Lun yang-wu p'ai."
6. Feng Yu-lan, "Liang Ch'i-ch'ao ti ssu-hsiang," p. 134.
7. See Wang Erh-min, pp. 51–53. The *t'i-yung* formula of almost all advocates of *Chung-t'i hsi-yung lun* was not based on a strict definition, but was a somewhat vague, inclusive concept.
8. Kondō Kuniyasu, "Shinmatsu hempō to Tan Shi-tō no shisō: hempō to seijin no michi," p. 44.
9. Li Tse-hou, "Lun shih-chiu shih-chi Chung-kuo kai-liang-p'ai pien-fa wei-hsin ssu-hsiang ti fa-chan," pp. 39–40, 49, 52–53.
10. This was essentially the argument of Li Tse-hou described above. Onogawa Hidemi, *Shinmatsu seiji shisō kenkyū*, pp. 3, 7, 30, 281.
11. Chester T'an, *Chinese Political Thought in the Twentieth Century*, pp. 215–216.
12. The ten professors, in their declaration, included even the Reform Movement led by K'ang Yu-wei and Liang Ch'i-ch'ao in the category of "principle/utility," criticizing it as no more than a political imitation.
13. Hu Shih et al., *Hu Shih yü Chung-hsi wen-hua*, p. 129.
14. It is understandable that, in the frequent comparisons between the *yang-wu* movement in China and the Japanese Meiji Restoration, the Chinese campaign tended to be compared unfavorably to the Japanese model, just because the former failed while the latter succeeded. I think, however, that it is not proper to compare the two according to the same criteria, since the Meiji Revolution started a step ahead by virtue of the modernization efforts of the Bakumatsu period (which may be said to be a Japanese version of the *yang-wu* movement), while the *yang-wu* movement is comparable to the *bakufu* modernization efforts. The Meiji policy of sweeping modernizations in every field was a result of gradual developments in political thought during

the preceding period. For example, *tōdō seigei ron*, a formula similar to *yang-wu lun*, as we shall show in the latter part of this chapter, provided a platform for the launching of the Meiji Restoration. Therefore, because it was regarded as fulfilling a historical mission, the Japanese formula has received a positive appraisal. Despite its structural similarity with *yang-wu lun*, however, *Chung-t'i hsi-yung lun*, in the same sense as *yang-wu lun*, has been given a negative evaluation. There is a difference between the two formulae, as far as their social and political utilities in the context of historical development are concerned, but I think there is no reason for giving *yang-wu lun* a different appraisal from that of *tōdō seigei ron*, at least in regard to their logical structures.

15. Nomura Kōichi, "Shinmatsu kōyō gakuha no keisei to Kō Yū i gaku no rekishiteki igi," in *Kindai Chūgoku no seiji to shisō*, pp. 85–86.
16. This line follows the verse calling for clarification of the ways of Emperors Yao and Shun as well as full use of the Western arts of machines and tools, which Nomura left out, probably to emphasize the freshness of Yokoi's argument. Ibid., pp. 85–86.
17. Ibid. Nomura differentiated the "principle/utility" of Chang Chih-tung from those of the so-called advanced intellectuals, such as Cheng Kuan-ying, without detailed explanation, and simply added that there was a difference in nuance between them. Considering that this means that "principle/utility" varies from person to person, it appears that Nomura's understanding of it is open to criticism. If the difference exists only in nuance, is it necessary to differentiate one from the other?
18. Hsueh Fu-ch'eng, "Pien-fa" (Reform), *Ch'ou-yang ch'u-i*.
19. Hsueh Fu-ch'eng, "Hsi-fa wei kung-kung chih li shuo."
20. The history of thought properly considers not only those ideas that are preserved in written records, but also those that conditioned or induced certain actions, bringing about certain results. Therefore, although the logical structures of any two concepts may be similar, their roles in their historical contexts may not be the same. It would be too much to say, however, that, in studying a concept, it is unnecessary to conduct a basic study of its logical structures.
21. Toriumi Yasushi, "Recent Trends in the Studies on Modernization in Japan"; Uete Michiari, "Meiji keimō shisō no keisei I, II, III"; Minamoto Ryōen, "Bakumatsu ishin no seishin jōkyō"; Toyama Shigeki, "The Meiji Restoration and the Birth of Modern Intellectuals."
22. Minamoto Ryōen, p. 457.
23. Uete Michiari, I, 58.
24. Hereafter, I am citing or explaining the opinions of Uete, unless otherwise indicated.
25. Another explanation of *tōdō seigei ron* by Uete is also worthy of note. See especially Uete Michiari, II, 59–60. Uete said, "Shōzan did not intend to make a definite distinction between the morals (*dōtoku*) of the East and the technology of the West. But he appears, at first glance, to have thought of such a distinction, as he spoke of *tōyō dōtoku, seiyō geijutsu*, and of making

longitude the teaching of the sages of China, and latitude Western learning of every art. He did his best to accept Western scientific knowledge. However, his primary goal of studying Western scientific and technological knowledge was to help the theories of *ko-wu ch'iung-li*, systematized by the Ch'eng brothers and Chu Hsi, live up to the needs of those days. His intention was not to replace traditional science and technology with the Western . . . That is, he understood modern natural science (of the West) to be an extension of *ko-wu ch'iung-li*. It means, on the other side of the coin, that natural science was understood as the basis for all learning and all patterns of thought. His notion of *tōdō seigei* may have been premised unconsciously on the traditional view that morals are the root (*pen*), and that techniques and arts are the branches (*mo*). However, his attitude toward natural science shows a tendency to reverse the traditional root-branch relationship." Uete understood Sakuma Shōzan's *tōdō seigei ron* as a formula to facilitate the introduction of Western scientific knowledge, in which the acceptance of Western sciences was just the realization of traditional principles. In this respect, it seems to me that Shōzan's argument was no different in its essence from those of Chinese advocates of *Chung-t'i hsi-yung lun:* that Western learning originated in China and that the acceptance of Western science was merely the restoration of the Way of the Sages. Is it proper to conclude, however, that Shōzan took Western natural science as the foundation for all learning and further for all patterns of thought? I agree that "Shōzan understood that behind the military power of Western nations lay natural scientific knowledge, and attempted to absorb [Western culture] from its roots." (Uete p. 56.) It seems to me, however, that Sakuma never went beyond this. Uete's conclusion that Sakuma adhered to the end to identifying the "principle" (*li*) of Neo-Confucianism or the teachings of the *Book of Changes* with the natural scientific laws of the West is questionable.

26. In the case of Feng Kuei-fen, the merits of the parliamentary system were adopted to serve as the principle of reform in the operation of political systems. In "Chih yang-ch'i i," for example, Feng said that the relationship between the monarch and the people (in China) was not as close as in barbarian nations, alluding to the merit of the Western parliamentary system. He meant that the parliamentary system prevented the estrangement between ruler and subject. In addition, he tried to introduce the "public recommendation" (*kung-t'ui*) system in various fields of government, which seems to have been adapted from the election system or majority rule. See Chapter 4 in this volume.

27. Ch'en Hsu-lu, "Kuan-yü *Chiao-pin-lu k'ang-i* i-shu chien lun Feng Kuei-fen ti ssu-hsiang." In this article, p. 115, Ch'en reported that, in a manuscript draft of the *Chiao-pin-lu k'ang-i,* preserved in the Shanghai Library, Feng said, "Various barbarian books show that, in America, the president rules the nation, and that political power is transmitted not to [the president's] son but to the wise. People reportedly write down the name of their favorite candidates on ballots and throw them into the ballot box, and the one who wins the most ballots rises to the presidency. The state governors are elected

through the same procedures. Therefore, the nation became wealthy and powerful, gradually surpassing in national strength even Russia, England, and France. Who dares say that there is no man [of greatness] among the barbarians?" (Of course, extant copies of Feng's *Chiao-pin-lu k'ang-i* do not contain these remarks.) Feng added, however, that the American election system was not practical for the Chinese, but he apparently thought that it was so good that it was a source of the nation's wealth and power. Therefore, he praised the U.S. system in connection with the principle of conceding power to the wise, a political ideal of the Chinese, and denounced monarchism, in which the monarch hands over power to his son as inferior to democracy. Thus Feng's understanding of Western political systems was surprisingly accurate. If Feng's remarks are compared with Sakuma's statement quoted here, it appears that Feng understood the essence of democracy far better than Sakuma.

28. Uete said that this relativism marked the beginning of the destruction of Confucian thought and political doctrine, but did not mean that the door was then open to modern social and political thought. However, according to what Uete quoted, the political scientist Maruyama Masao said that a clue can be found in Sakuma Shōzan to an effort to understand the social and political systems of Western nations. Whichever side we are on, the positive attitude of Sakuma is noteworthy.
29. Uete Michiari II, 64–65.
30. According to Chinese terminology, material culture (*ch'i*) is distinct from metaphysical (*tao*). See the discussion of *tao-ch'i-lun* later in this chapter.
31. This "practical learning" (*jitsugaku*) in the Kumamoto area where Yokoi came from was influenced by Yi T'oegye of Korea and Otsuka Taiya who propagated the teachings of Yi T'oegye. See Uete Michiari III, 843.
32. In China, Feng Kuei-fen was the first man who advocated reforms by restoring the institutions of the period of the Three Dynasties. A clear description of Feng's argument is seen in the preface to *Chiao-pin-lu k'ang-i*.
33. See note 26 above.
34. In "Shou p'in-min i," in *Chiao-pin-lu k'ang-i*, Feng Kuei-fen said that he would even reject the old traditional laws (of the sages) if they were not good and imitate the laws of the barbarians only if they were good, and would introduce Western institutions such as welfare programs, educational programs for the poor like those of the Netherlands, and the primary education system like that of Sweden. Pointing out the excellence of Western laws, he said that their attraction reminded him of the old saying *Li shih erh ch'iu chu yeh* ("Having lost the rituals, seek them among the uncivilized peoples"). Apparently, he thought that these Western institutions conformed to the laws of the sages of the Three Dynasties. Feng added that the institutions of Sweden and the Netherlands were originally supposed to deal with secondary matters. However, as observed in contemporary circumstances, they were actually based on the recognition of fundamental issues. He meant that the Western systems corresponded more to the spirit of the Three Dynasty laws compared with the Chinese situation of the later period, when there were numerous

beggars and illiterate people but inadequate measures to cope with them.
35. Nakamura Keichoku, in "Shōzan sensei shisō hyōgen," pp. 469–470, pointed out the fallacy of *tōdō seigei*, recognizing that Western morals (*dōtoku*) and techniques and arts (*geijutsu*) were not separable but were two sides of one coin. Katō Hiroyuki attributed the difference between the East's poverty and the West's wealth to the difference in morals between the two sides of the world.
36. Hu Yuan of the Northern Sung advocated *ming-t'i ta-yung*. Such scholars as Shao Yung, Ch'eng I, Ch'eng Hao, and Chang Tsai used the idea as a speculative category. Chu Hsi used it as an important concept for the reinterpretation of the Confucian classics, as seen in *Chung-yung chang-chu, Chu-tzu yü-lei, Lun-yü chi-chu*. See Shimada Kenji, *Shushigaku to Yōmeigaku*, pp. 7–8. For both Tseng Kuo-fan's and Wang Wen-shao's usage, see Wang Erh-min, pp. 51–52.
37. Ch'en Hsu-lu, pp. 117–118.
38. Ibid., p. 115.
39. Li Tse-hou, p. 21.
40. Hu Pin, *Chung-kuo chin-tai kai-liang-chu-i ssu-hsiang*, p. 64. See also Onogawa Hidemi's unclear distinction between Feng and the thought of the 1890s reformists, p. 20.
41. Li Hung-chang, "Fu Kuo Chün-hsien hsing-shih" in *P'eng-liao han-kao*, p. 12a.
42. Feng Kuei-fen, *Chiao-pin-lu k'ang-i*, pp. 69a, 71a, 73a–b, 74b.
43. Feng Kuei-fen, "Chih yang-ch'i i," pp. 74–75.
44. On the political background of the 1898 Reform Movement, see my "Musul pyŏnbŏp undong ŭi paegyŏng e taehayŏ."
45. Feng Kuei-fen, "Ts'ai Hsi-hsueh i," pp. 69a–b.
46. Ibid.
47. Feng Kuei-fen, "Chih yang-ch'i i."
48. See my *Chungguk kŭndaesa yŏn'gu*, pp. 246 ff.
49. Feng Kuei-fen, "Sheng-tse li-i." Feng appears to have been advocating the reform of government institutions and systems from this viewpoint, as is seen in a statement in his "Sheng-tse K'ang-i," p. 146: "The present age, it is said, has three evils: clerks, complicated regulations, and the quest for profit."
50. Feng Kuei-fen also said that "the land (of China) does not bring in as many benefits as that of the barbarian (country)," which is interpreted as referring to the development of mining and industry in the Western countries accompanying the increase of scientific and technological knowledge.
51. Feng Kuei-fen, "Chih yang-ch'i i," p. 71b.
52. Feng Kuei-fen, "Preface," in *Chiao-pin-lu k'ang-i*.
53. Feng Kuei-fen, "Chung ju-chia i," pp. 119, 120, 121; "Kung ch'u-chih i," p. 17; "Kuang-ch'ü shih i," p. 133; "Chung hsiang-kuan i," pp. 36, 53.
54. Wang T'ao, "I-yen yuan-pa," in Cheng Kuan-ying, *(Tseng-ting) Sheng-shih wei-yen (cheng-hsu-pien)*.
55. Wang T'ao, *T'ao-yuan wen-lu wai-pien* 2:3b.
56. Wang T'ao, "Pien-fa," in ibid., 1:1a.

57. Paul A. Cohen, *Between Tradition and Modernity: Wang T'ao and Reform in Late Ch'ing China*, p. 235.
58. See Cohen, pp. 220–221, 225, 229; and Wang Wei-ch'eng, "Wang T'ao ti ssu-hsiang," pp. 41–46.
59. Cohen, pp. 220–221.
60. Cohen, p. 235, said that Wang T'ao differed from those who advocated the introduction of (Western) ways to help preserve old values (their beliefs), because he insisted that the *tao* itself should be transformed for the preservation of China.
61. Cohen, p. 231.
62. Wang Wei-ch'eng, p. 43.
63. Ibid.
64. See my "Musul pyŏnbŏp undong ŭi paegyŏng e taehayŏ."
65. Hsueh Fu-ch'eng, "Ch'iang-lin huan-tz'u chin-ch'en yü-chi shu," in *Yung-an ch'üan-chi: Hai-wai wen-pien* 2:17b–18a.
66. Hsueh Fu-ch'eng, "Pien-fa," p. 47a.
67. Huang Tsun-hsien, who is considered part of the reform group together with K'ang and Liang, made a similar remark, in *Jih-pen kuo-chih* 32:22b, regarding the way of preserving the unchangeable *tao*. "As for the saying 'Heaven and the Way are both unchangeable,' will it not end in totally abandoning our knowledge and learning from others? . . . [Westerners] take advantage of their superiority in certain things to cheat and oppress us every day. We cannot sit around idly for a single day discoursing on the Way. So those who seek methods of preserving our Way must avail themselves of every means to use [the Westerners'] methods to accomplish that end."
68. Hsueh Fu-ch'eng, "Pien-fa"; and Hsueh Fu-ch'eng, "Hsi-fa wei kung-kung chih li shuo," pp. 3a–b.
69. In *Jih-pen kuo-chih* (just after the sentence quoted in note 67 above), Huang Tsun-hsien said in the same vein that *ch'i-yung chih-wu* (physical mechanisms) were not only for their inventors, and that *ko-chih chih hsueh* (empirical study) of the Westerners should not be rejected as the "learning of others," since it apparently contained the intention of the (Chinese) ancients. Huang also said that the Chinese could surpass Westerners by far within a few years, reinstating the prosperity of the Three Dynasties and rising above all nations, only if they adopted the methods of the Westerners in addition to the talent and wisdom of China.
70. Hsia Tung-yuan, p. 48; Huang Tzu-t'ung, "Hsueh Fu-ch'eng ti ssu-hsiang," p. 53.
71. Hsueh Fu-ch'eng, "Tsai-lun O-lo-ssu li-kuo chih shih," pp. 12a–12b. Regarding Hsueh's views on political systems, see Hu Pin, pp. 66–67.
72. "Jen Chi-yü," and "Ma Chien-chung," in *Chung-kuo chin-tai ssu-hsiang lun-wen-chi*, p. 8.
73. Cheng Kuan-ying, preface, p. 1b.
74. See Ch'üan Han-sheng, "Ch'ing-mo ti Hsi-hsueh yuan ch'u Chung-kuo shuo." Hsueh Fu-ch'eng and Huang Tsun-hsien were of the same opinion.
75. Cheng Kuan-ying, "Hsi-shih p'ien," in *Sheng-shih wei-yen*, p. 15a–b, and "Tao-ch'i p'ien," in *Sheng-shih wei-yen* pp. 1a–b.

76. Li Tse-hou, p. 40, said that *chu-Chung fu-hsi lun* was identical to *Chung-t'i hsi-yung lun* of the *yang-wu* group, but this appears to be inaccurate.
77. Onogawa Hidemi said in *Shinmatsu seiji shisō kenkyū* that Cheng Kuan-ying did not consider seriously the fundamental reform of institutions, although he thought the base for reorganization was a parliament (*i-yuan*). His argument, however, is obscure to me. For one thing, the word *fundamental* is ambiguous. Some may doubt even whether it is appropriate to describe as "fundamental" or "basic" the policies of K'ang Yu-wei at the time of the 1898 Reform Movement. Onogawa said that Cheng was not as thoroughgoing as Ch'en Ch'iu, because Cheng advocated the establishment of a parliament along with the preservation of other existing institutions (while Ch'en sought reforms related to the foundation of new institutions) by stressing the importance of the Six Ministries and calling for the restoration of the (ancient) system of the Three Dukes. But which is more fundamental: Ch'en's calling for the appointment of incumbent officials as members of parliament, or Cheng's idea of selecting parliamentarians from among the people and having newspapers supervise the parliament? "I-yuan," in Cheng Kuan-ying, *Sheng-shih wei-yen*, chüan 4.
78. Chang Chih-tung, "Chang Hsiao-ta shang-shu tien chih Hsu hsueh-shih shu," in *I-chiao ts'ung-pien* 6:1a.
79. See my "Musul pyŏnbŏp undong ŭi paegyŏng e taehayŏ"; and "Musul-kaeyok undong gua sang'hae ei sang'in gurup."
80. Chang Chien, *Chang Chien jih-chi*, p. 201, quoted in Ch'en Hsu-lu, p. 120.
81. Hung-ming Ku, *The Story of a Chinese Oxford Movement*, p. 37.
82. Chang Chien, *Chang Chien jih-chi*.
83. In "Shang Yueh-tu Li Ch'uan-hsiang shu," which Liang wrote after the suppression by Chang Chih-tung in 1900 of T'ang Ts'ai-ch'ang's uprising, which he supported. Liang quoted a saying by "a knowledgeable man of Tientsin": "Ten years from now all the world will turn away from this book [*Ch'üan-hsueh-p'ien*] in disgust, although it may already have been reduced to ashes." (Liang Ch'i-ch'ao, *Yin-ping-shih wen-chi* 5: 62.) Ku Hung-ming, who was a personal secretary to Chang Chih-tung and was conservative, also said (*The Story of a Chinese Oxford Movement*, p. 38) that *Ch'üan-hsueh-p'ien* was originally intended as a declaration of opposition to the Jacobinism of K'ang Yu-wei.
84. P'i Hsi-jui, "Shih-fu-t'ang jih-chi."
85. Kobayashi Takeshi said that *Chung-hsueh* (Chinese learning) which should be *t'i* (principle) had come to lend direction to *chih-yung* (utility). *Kangakuhen to Yokukyō sōhen* (*Ch'üan-hsueh p'ien* and *I-chiao ts'ung-pien*), in *Chūkogu tetsugaku shi no tempō to mosaku*, p. 831.
86. Chang Chih-tung, ed. Kimura Eiichi, "Chang Hsiao-ta shang-shu tien chih hsu hsueh-shih shu," in *I-chiao ts'ung-pien* 6:1a.
87. Chang Chih-tung, *Ch'üan-hsueh-p'ien*, in *Chang Wen-hsiang-kung ch'üan-chi* 202:11b–12a.
88. Ibid., 23a.
89. Min Tu-ki, "Musul pyŏnbŏp undong ŭi paegyŏng e taehayŏ, pp. 142–145.
90. Sun Pao-chüan, *Jih-i-ch'i jih-chi*, winter of 1899, quoted in Ting Wen-chiang,

ed., *Liang Jen-kung hsien-sheng nien-p'u ch'ang-pien ch'u-kao*, p. 101. In a lettter of 1900 to Li Hung-chang, Liang Ch'i-ch'ao said that Li had called upon him in exile to study Western learning closely and to improve his skill, in the hope that he could one day concentrate on national affairs. Liang Ch'i-ch'ao, *Yin-ping-shih wen-chi* 5: 55. "Chih Li Hung-chang shu," which K'ang Yu-wei wrote probably in 1900, also pointed out Li's approval of reform ideas. (K'ang Yu-wei, *K'ang Nan-hai wen-chi kao-pen*.) A similar statement is seen in "Shang Yueh-tu Li Ch'uan-hsiang shu erh-shou," *Ch'ing-i-pao* 57: 3705 (1900).

91. Min Tu-ki, "Musul pyŏnbŏp undong ŭi paegyŏng e taehayŏ," p. 143.
92. Li Hung-chang, "Fu-kuo chün-hsien hsing-shih," *P'eng-liao han-kao* 7:12a, *Li Wen-chung kung ch'üan-chi* 14:31b–326b.
93. Li Hung-chang, *P'eng-liao han-kao* 14: 31b–326b, *Li Wen-chung kung ch'üan-chi*.
94. Li Hung-chang, "Fu Liu Chung-liang chung-ch'eng," *P'eng-liao han-kao* 16: 30a–b.
95. Min Tu-ki, "Musul pyŏnbŏp undong ŭi paegyong e taehayŏ," pp. 143–144.
96. Ibid., pp. 142–143.
97. Ibid., pp. 145–146.
98. Regarding K'ang's retraction of his argument for the establishment of parliament, at least in its outlook, see Huang Chang-chien, *Wu-hsu pien-fa-shih yen-chiu*, pp. 560–566.
99. Li Hung-chang, "Chih Tsungli Yamen shu," in *Ch'ou-pan i-wu shih-mo*, T'ung-chih reign 25:9.1.
100. See Ŏm Yŏng-sik, "Munsang ŭi yangmu sasang"; and Wang Chia-chien, "Wen-hsiang tui-yü shih-chü ti jen-shih chi ch'i tzu-ch'iang ssu-hsiang."
101. *Ch'ing-shih kao* 173:4b.
102. Kuo Sung-t'ao, "Fu-chien an-ch'a-shih Kuo Sung-t'ao t'iao-i hai-fang shih-hsuan." In "Fu Yao Yen-chia," he said: "All wealth and power has its basis. The accumulation of *jen-hsin* [human will], *feng-su* [public morale], and *cheng-chiao* [political principles] are exactly that basis. Is it appropriate to seek wealth and power only by preserving those qualities as they exist in the present day?" Ibid., p. 309.
103. Kuo Sung-t'ao, "Chih Li Ch'uan-hsiang shu," in Kuo Sung-t'ao, *Yang-chih shu-wu i-chi* 13:21a (1894).
104. Liang Ch'i-ch'ao, *Yin-ping-shih wen-chi* 6:62; K'ang Yu-wei, *K'ang Nan-hai hsien-sheng chuan*.
105. Ichiko Chūzō, "Hōkyō to hempō," p. 232.
106. Itano Chōhachi, "Kō Yū-i no taidō shisō," p. 173. Itano defined K'ang's thought as "principle/utility."
107. Liang Ch'i-ch'ao, *Yin-ping-shih wen-chi* 1:126; 3:2–3. A concrete reference to this relationship is seen in Liang Ch'i-ch'ao, "Hsueh-hsiao yü-lun." That is, he criticized such advocates of *yang-wu lun* as Cheng Kuan-ying, who did not cultivate Confucian culture and pass through the examinations, and negotiated between high-ranking officials and merchants. Such persons did not know about the Chinese situation and political customs, though they might have a considerable amount of knowledge about Western political systems. (See my article in *Tongyang sahak yŏn'gŭ* 11:85.)

108. Liang Ch'i-ch'ao, *Yin-ping-shih wen-chi* 3:2–3.
109. See Liang Ch'i-ch'ao, "Wu-hsu cheng-pien chi," section 1, p. 56; *Wu-hsu pien-fa*, ed. Chung-kuo shih-hsueh-hui, 4:489.
110. Liang Ch'i-ch'ao, in *Wu-hsu pien-fa* 4:17.
111. Sun Chia-nai, "Tsou-ch'en ch'ou-pan ta-hsueh-t'ang ta-kai ch'ing-hsing che," p. 312.
112. Sun Chia-nai, "I-fu k'ai-pan ching-shih ta-hsueh-t'ang che."
113. Sung Po-lu, in *Wu-hsu pien-fa* 2:348.
114. *Hsiang-pao lei-tsuan*, pp. 25b–27a.
115. *Hsiang-hsueh hsin-pao*, pp. 309–317.
116. Kuo-chia tang-an-chü, ed., *Wu-hsu pien-fa tang-an shih-liao*, p. 311.
117. Tso Tsung-t'ang, *Tso Wen-hsiang kung ch'üan-chi, shuo-t'ieh*, p. 1b.
118. Wang T'ao, "Yuan-tao," *T'ao-yuan wen-lu wai-pien*.
119. Wang T'ao, "I-yen yuan-pa," and the above-mentioned "Yuan-tao" and "Pien-fa shang."
120. Wang T'ao, "I-yen yuan-pa."
121. Min Tu-ki, "Musul pyŏnbŏp undong ŭi paegyŏng e taehayŏ," pp. 101–147.
122. T'ang Chen, *T'ang Chih-hsien hsien-sheng wei-yen*, pp. 10a–12b.
123. T'an Ssu-t'ung, "Ssu-wei i-hu t'ai tuan-shu: Pei pao Yuan-chang" and "Shang fu-tzu ta-jen shu erh," also called "Hsing-suan hsueh-i," in *T'an Ssu-t'ung ch'üan-chi*, pp. 292, 390.
124. Such a position is seen in "Hsing-suan hsueh-i," but it is not firmly rooted. For instance, there is no strong objection to such a view even in "Tuan-shu." Here T'an Ssu-t'ung maintained that all Western institutions had originated in China, but he also said that accomplishment was not restricted to the Chinese sages of the past. The Chinese, therefore, should recover their own past by learning quickly from the West.
125. See Chang Te-chün; "T'an Ssu-t'ung ssu-hsiang shu-p'ing," esp. pp. 31–35.
126. In "Shang chin shang huang-ti wan-yen shu," which he wrote during the 1898 Reform Movement period, Yen Fu said that *pen* (the root) is unchangeable *tao* (the Way), while *chih* (institutions) are changeable *fa* (methods). In 1902, however, he argued the logical fragility of the "principle/utility" formula, because it denied the validity of the "principle" within Western learning itself. Yen Fu, "Yü *Wai-chiao-pao* chu-jen Lun chiao-yü shu," in *Yen Chi-tao shih-wen ch'ao*, pp. 240–241. He likened *Chung-t'i hsi-yung lun* to an unreasonable effort to combine the functions of oxen and horses, saying that the ox has its own function (of carrying cargo), as the horse has its own function (of running quickly to a distant point). Regarding the date of this "Lun chiao-yü shu" (A letter on education), see Benjamin I. Schwartz, *In Search of Wealth and Power: Yen Fu and the West*, p. 49. Meanwhile, Levenson attributed the failure of *Chung-t'i hsi-yung lun* to its own logical structure, in *Confucian China and Its Modern Fate*, Vol. I.
127. J. Gernet, *Le Monde Chinois*, p. 514. As Benjamin Schwartz has already pointed out, there should be serious reconsideration of how helpful the dualistic formula of tradition versus modernity (or *Chung-t'i* vs. *hsi-yung*) will be in explaining the development of Chinese thought, not only in the twentieth

century but also in the nineteenth, if we identify *Chung-t'i* with tradition, and *hsi-yung* with modernity. Cf. B. Schwartz, "The Limits of Tradition versus Modernity as Categories of Explanation: The Case of the Chinese Intellectuals," pp. 79–85. See also Mihashi Fujio, *Osuman Toruko shiron*, p. 327.

4. The Theory of Political Feudalism in the Ch'ing Period "Ch'ŏngdae pon'gŏn-non kŭndaejŏk pyŏnmo"

1. The above discussion is an abstract of my "Chungguk ŭi chŏnt'ongjŏk chŏngch'isang: ponggŏn kunhyŏn nonŭi rŭl chungsim ŭro," in *Chungguk kŭndaesa yŏngu*. Lu Chi's "Wu-teng lun" is found in *Wen-hsuan*, chüan 54. For Chu Hsi's views on *feng-chien*, see *Chu tzu yü-lei*, chüan 260–275 ("Feng-chien k'ao"); also chüan 63, 108, 134.
2. Chang Ping-lin, "Yü Ma Liang shu," in *Chang-shih ts'ung-shu*.
3. Ku Yen-wu, "Chün-hsien lun."
4. Ibid., tr. *Sources of Chinese Tradition*, ed. Wm. Theodore de Bary, pp. 556–557. In *Jih-chih lu* (the version compiled and annotated by Huang Ju-cheng) 9:16b–19b, Ku said the same thing, adding that the local administrators under the *chün-hsien* system tended not to make an effort to promote the well-being of the people and that real administrative power, originally in their hands, was likely to be appropriated by the professional clerks.
5. Huang Tsung-hsi, *Ming-i tai-fang lu*, p. 2b.
6. Ibid., pp. 6b, 7b–8a.
7. Ibid., p. 24a.
8. Ku Yen-wu, "Ch'ing-i," *Jih-chih lu chi-shih* 13:11b–13a.
9. Huang Tsung-hsi, p. 22a.
10. Wang Fu-chih, *Tu t'ung-chien lun* 20:411, in his discussion of T'ang T'ai-tsung.
11. Ibid. 5:75, discussing Han Ai-ti.
12. Ibid. 21:430–431, discussing T'ang T'ai-tsung.
13. Ibid. 1:1, discussing Ch'in Shih-huang.
14. Ibid. 1:1–2.
15. Ibid.
16. Hsiao Kung-ch'üan, *Chung-kuo cheng-chih ssu-hsiang shih*, p. 631.
17. Yen Yuan, "Feng-chien," *Ts'un-chih p'ien*, in Hsu Shih-ch'ang, ed., *Yen Li i-shu*.
18. Yao Ch'un, ed., *Kuo-ch'ao wen-lu*, chüan 6.
19. Ku's essay which Chu cites here is not "Chün-hsien lun" in *T'ing-lin wen-chi* but "Fan-chen" in *Jih-chih lu* 9:28a–33a.
20. See my "Ch'ŏngjŏ ŭi hwangje t'ongch'i wa sasang t'ongje ŭi silje."
21. Lü Liu-liang, *Ssu-shu chiang-i*, quoted in Ch'ien Mu, *Chung-kuo chin-san-pai-nien hsueh-shu shih*, p. 77.
22. Min Tu-ki, "Ch'ŏngjŏ ŭi hwangje t'ongch'i wa sasang t'ongje ŭi silje."
23. *Ta-Ch'ing shih-tsung shih-lu* 83:49.
24. Ortai's memorial dated 19 June, the 7th year of the Yung-cheng Emperor's reign, in *Yung-cheng chu-p'i yü-chih*. Though the original memorial by Kung has not been found, its outlines are revealed in Ortai's memorial. Fei Chin-wu and the Yung-cheng Emperor also objected to Kung.

25. Yuan Mei, "Tsai shu feng-chien-lun hou," p. 9.
26. Ibid.
27. Liu Hung-ao, "Feng-chien lun," pp. 19a–20b.
28. Feng Kuei-fen, "Fu hsiang-chih i," pp. 33–38.
29. Ibid.
30. Feng Kuei-fen, "Kung ch'u-chih i," p. 17.
31. Kuo T'ing-i, "Chin-tai hsi-yang wen-hua chih shu-ju chi ch'i jen-shih." See also note 27 above. F. O. Lojewski, "Reform within Tradition: Feng Kuei-fen's Proposal for Local Administration."
32. Yang Hsiang-chi, "Ni-ts'e" 7, in 27:4a–6a.
33. See my "Ch'ŏngdae maguje wa haengjŏng chilsŏ ŭi t'uksŏng."
34. Yang Hsiang-chi, 27:6a.
35. Tai Wang, "Ku chih-fang chün-hsien lun po-i."
36. Yü Yueh, "Feng-chien chün-hsien shuo," pp. 32a–33a.
37. *Ch'ing-i-pao ch'üan-pien*, 2.8:3–10.
38. Liang Ch'i-ch'ao, "Shang Ch'en Pao-chen shu," reprinted in *Wu-hsu pien-fa* 2:533–535.
39. See note 1 above. Studies in Japan of the arguments involving the *feng-chien* and *chün-hsien* systems include Fujiwara Sadamo, "Shindai no hōken shisō to hōkensei no zanzon," pp. 20–24; and Kiyoda Kenzō, "Shina hōkenron shi kōryaku."
40. See note 1 above.
41. Onogawa Hidemi, pp. 75–76.
42. Ibid.
43. Kuo T'ing-i, "Chin-tai hsi-yang wen-hua chih shu-ju chi ch'i jen-shih." Pin-ch'un's description of the British Parliament in his "Ch'eng-ch'a pi-chi," published in 1869, was relatively detailed and perceptive. See particularly the entries for the 18th and 24th days of the 4th month, 5th year of T'ung-chih, p. 26b.
44. Onagawa Hidemi, p. 77.
45. K'ang Yu-wei, "Shang Ch'ing-ti ti i-shu."
46. Regarding K'ang's first memorial, Tikhvinskii said: "K'ang's first memorial included the basic call of the reform group or *wei-hsin-p'ai:* (1) to strengthen the nation by renovating the national administrative system; (2) to have learned and competent representatives of the people (selected from among the enlightened intelligentsia of the bourgeoisie and landlord class, regardless of their status and financial capabilities) to participate in the national administration, thereby putting a restriction on the autocratic power of the monarch under the Ch'ing polity and to replace obstinate and conservative government officials with the supporters of reform . . . These programs were never proposed by the advocates of 'Western affairs' (*yang-wu*), for it was believed that they would, if realized, restrict the power of the Ch'ing Court and feudal bureaucrats to a considerable degree." S. L. Tikhvinskii, *Chung-kuo pien-fa wei-hsin yun-tung ho K'ang Yu-wei*, pp. 41–44. Tikhvinskii's conclusion seems a bit far-fetched. In fact, the most conspicuous difference between the *wei-hsin* (*pien-fa*) faction headed by K'ang and the rival party lay

in their opinions as to who should be included in the *pien-fa* movement, and the problem of leadership. The *wei-hsin* group called for institutional reforms along the lines of the Western parliament in order to attain these goals. With regard to their goals and action in this respect, see my "Kang yu-wi kaehyŏk undong (1898) ŭi kibon panghyang; kŭ chihyang kwa chuajŏl" (The cardinal aim of K'ang Yu-wei's Reform Movement [1898] and the course of his frustration), in *Chungguk kŭndae kaehyŏk undong ŭi yŏn'gu*.

47. Ch'en Ch'iu, "Tung-yu t'iao-i," in *Chih-p'ing t'ung-i*, quoted in Onogawa Hidemi, p. 90.
48. Idem., *Chih-p'ing t'ung-i*, reprinted in *Wu-hsu pien-fa* 1:218–219.
49. Ibid., p. 200.
50. Onogawa Hidemi, pp. 86–87.
51. Ibid., p. 90.
52. Ibid., p. 88.
53. T'ang Chen, "I-yuan," in *Wei-yen*, chüan 1, reprinted in *Wu-hsu pien-fa* 1:177–178.
54. Feng Kuei-fen's *Chiao-pin-lu k'ang-i* was first published in 1884; T'ang's *Wei-yen* was published in 1890.
55. The following discussion of Cheng Kuan-ying's ideas comes from Cheng Kuan-ying, "I-yuan," *Tseng-ting Sheng-shih wei-yen cheng-hsu pien* 4:2a–3a, reprinted in *Wu-hsu, pien-fa* 1:55–58.
56. Ch'en Ch'ih, "I-yuan," in *Yung-shu, wai-p'ien*, chüan hsia, reprinted in *Wu-hsu pien-fa* 1:245–247.
57. Ibid. "Hsiang-kuan," reprinted in *Wu-hsu pien-fa*, 1:234–235.
58. Ku Yen-wu, "Hsiang-t'ing chih chih," *Jih-chih lu chi-shih* 8:10a.
59. For the quotation from *Hsin-cheng chen-ch'üan* I have depended on Hsiao Kung-ch'üan's *Chung-kuo cheng-chih ssu-hsiang shih*, pp. 798–802. *Hsin-cheng chen-ch'üan* is a collection of articles written by Ho Ch'i and Hu Li-yuan between 1898 and 1890, published in 1901. For their personal careers, see Hsiao Kung-ch'üan, *Chung-kuo cheng-chih ssu-hsiang shih*, p. 795.
60. Ibid.
61. Ibid.
62. *Wu-hsu pien-fa* 1:190–198. Their description of the method of electing members of the county parliaments is somewhat ambiguous. In the introductory part of the essay, they spoke of the selection of members both by the *sheng-yuan* group and by the commoners. They also indicated that those eligible to participate in the selection of members of the county parliaments were not necessarily to be *sheng-yuan*, saying instead that all healthy and learned adult males should be given the right to vote. There is no contradiction here if they were including *sheng-yuan* among the commoners. On the other hand, it is probable that the selection by *sheng-yuan* alone of members of the county parliaments out of a pool of *sheng-yuan* who would run for the positions was presented as part of a series of multiple elections to choose members of the prefectural parliaments from among *chü-jen* by *sheng-yuan* and members of provincial parliaments from among *chin-shih* by *chü-jen*.

63. Sun Chia-nai, "Ch'ing ch'ih shua-yin *Chiao-pin-lu k'ang-i* pan-hsing shu," reprinted in *Wu-hsu pien-fa* 2:430.
64. An imperial edict dated 29 May 1898, reprinted in *Wu-hsu pien-fa* 2:40.
65. An imperial edict of 25 July 1898, reprinted in ibid., p. 43.
66. Weng T'ung-ho, *Weng T'ung-ho jih-chi*, the entry for 6 February 1889.
67. Hsiao Kung-ch'üan, *Chung-kuo cheng-chih ssu-hsiang shih*, p. 822.
68. Weng T'ung-ho, the entry for 9 March 1895.
69. Ibid., the entry for 17 April 1895.
70. Yeh Ch'ang-ch'ih, *Yuan-tu-lu jih-chi ch'ao*, the entry for 20 April 1895, reprinted in *Wu-hsu pien-fa* 1:527.
71. An imperial edict of 21 August 1898, reprinted in *Wu-hsu pien-fa* 2:57.
72. T'an Hsien, "Fu-t'ang jih-chi hsu-lu," reprinted in *Wu-hsu pien-fa* 1:536.
73. Kuo-chia tang-an-chü, Ming-Ch'ing tang-an-kuan, ed., *Wu-hsu pien-fa tang-an shih-liao*, p. 421. In a memorial dated 1st day, 3rd month, 24th year of Kuang-hsu (21 April 1898), Yuan recommended seven people including T'ang to be members of the forthcoming special department for the economy. (Yuan Ch'ang, "I fu chi-yü shih-chien t'iao-ch'en," in *Yü-hu wen-lu*.) In regard to this memorial by Yuan, see my essay entitled "Musul pyŏnbop saryo yŏngsŭp," *Paeksan hakpo* 8:561. Chang Pai-hsi, a member of the Imperial College of Inscriptions, in his memorial of 5th day, 2nd month, 23rd year of Kuang-hsu (17 March 1897) recommended T'ang, together with Yang Jui (Ku-kung po-wu-yuan, Chün-chi-ch'u tang-an, Cheng-li tang-an mu-lu; kuang 535). T'an Ssu-t'ung, after taking Liang Ch'i-ch'ao with him to serve at the Shih-wu Academy in Hunan, recommended T'ang to succeed Liang as chief editor of *Shih-wu-pao* (T'an Ssu-t'ung, "Chih Wang K'ang-nien shu," p. 354).
74. Liang's view of the parliament is seen in such essays as "Lun chün-cheng min-cheng hsiang-shan chih li," *Shih-wu-pao* (5 September 1897), and "K'ai i-yuan lun," *Shih-wu-pao* (23 February 1898).
75. T'ang Chen, *Chung-hsueh*, in his *Wei-yen* 1:12b.
76. Yang Jui, "Yang ts'an-cheng kung chia-shu," reprinted in *Wu-hsu pien-fa* 2:572.
77. As to Liang's thoughts about popular rights, see Chang P'eng-yuan's *Liang Ch'i-ch'ao yü Ch'ing-chi ko-ming*, especially Chapter 3. Liang's contemporaries saw him as "exerting himself to propagate democracy and parliamentarianism" (13 June 1898, a memorial by Huang Chun-lung, reprinted in *Wu-hsu pien-fa tang-an shih-liao*, p. 253). The Southern Academy, in which Liang actively participated, had as its goal the promotion of gentry power as a step toward promoting popular rights (Liang Ch'i-ch'ao, "Shang Ch'en Pao-chen Hu-nan ying-pan chih shih," reprinted in *Wu-hsu pien-fa* 2:552).
78. A memorial by Kao Shih-fen, a Peking *sheng-yuan*, in 7th month, 20th year of Kuang-hsu, reprinted in *Wu-hsu pien-fa tang-an shih-liao*, p. 192. Hsu Chih-ching, a member of the Hanlin Academy, called for "opening wide the door" (for the talented) by appointing retired officials as advisers. (*Wu-hsu pien-fa tang-an shih-liao*, p. 176.)
79. A memorial by Ch'eng-ch'in, a Mongolian *sheng-yuan* belonging to the Bordered White Banner, of 7th month, 24th year of Kuang-hsu, ibid., p. 187.

A few sentences (before and after the phrase *shang-hsia hsiang-ch'uan*) were quoted from Cheng Kuan-ying's *Sheng-shih wei-yen* (specifically, "I-yuan"). By the phrase *shang-hsia hsiang-ch'uan*, however, he meant that the parliaments should undertake administrative functions, such as dealing with military affairs and promoting trade and manufacturing.

80. A memorial of the 4th day, 8th month, 24th year (19 September 1898) by Lo Ch'eng-jang, a member of the Hanlin Academy, ibid., p. 197.
81. A memorial by Ch'en Shih-cheng, dated the 14th day, 8th month (29 September 1898), ibid., p. 197; K'ang Yu-wei, "Shang Ch'ing-ti ti i-shu," 8th day, intercalary 5th month (30 June 1895), reprinted in *Wu-hsu pien-fa*, 2:184.
82. A memorial by Yu K'un-p'ei, a *chü-jen* of Kweichow, dated 4th day, 8th month (19 September 1898), reprinted in *Wu-hsu pien-fa tang-an shih-liao*, pp. 172–173.
83. A memorial by K'uo-p'u T'ung-wu, Sub-Chancellor of the Grand Secretariat and Vice-President of the Board of Rites, dated 3rd day, 7th month (20 August 1898), reprinted in *Wu-hsu pien-fa tang-an shih-liao*, pp. 172–173.
84. Ts'ai Chen-fan, "Tsou ch'ing shen-kuan ting-chih i ch'eng hsin-cheng che," reprinted in *Wu-hsu pien-fa* 2:388.
85. *Wu-hsu pien-fa* 2:176.
86. Ibid., p. 184.
87. Ibid., p. 152.
88. In the first memorial, reprinted in *Wu-hsu pien-fa* 2:129, K'ang advocated increasing the number of "advisory officials" (*hsun-i chih kuan*), calling on the wise and experienced from across the nation in order that the government might better grasp the situation among the people. It appears that he did not identify *i-lang*, selected in proportion to the population of the concerned locality, with the "advisory officials" called in by the Emperor. The first memorial does not, however, present a concrete program to call in such advisory officials.
89. K'ang Yu-wei, "Shang chin shang huang-ti ti-san shu," *Ssu shang-shu chi*, chüan 2, in *Hsi-cheng ts'ung-shu*, published in 1897. The third memorial comprises the second memorial and a further elaboration. Huang Chang-chien presumed that the original text of the third memorial presented to the Emperor might not have included the part regarding *i-lang*, claiming that it violated the political taboos of those days. See Huang Chang-chien, *Wu-hsu pien-fa shih yen-chiu*, p. 594. The argument about *i-lang* does not seem to go against any political taboo of the period, so I disagree with Huang's conclusions here.
90. According to *Wu-hsu tsou-kao*, there was a memorial entitled "Hsieh-shang pien-shu yin-liang ch'i yü-ting k'ai kuo-hui ch'i ping hsien hsuan ts'ai i-cheng hsu-min shang-shu che," which was allegedly presented to urge the opening of the parliament. There is a question as to whether the memorial included in *Wu-hsu tsou-kao* is exactly the same as the original one presented by K'ang. See Huang Chang-chien, pp. 262–263. In the memorial K'ang spoke of ordering local officials to select one man in each prefecture to congregate at the Palace in Peking, but the organization he envisioned was comparable to a conference of advisers rather than to a Western parliament.

91. As to the difference in content between the original and the versions of the sixth memorial we have at present (seen in "Tsung-li ko-kuo shih-wu yi-k'uang teng che," in *Wu-hsu pien-fa tang-an shih-liao*, p. 8, and *Wu-hsu pien-fa* 2:202), see Huang Chang-chien, pp. 541–546. Here I follow the version in *Tang-an shih-liao*.
92. *Jih-pen pien-cheng k'ao*, chüan 6, *an-yü* (commentary), contained in the microfilm (M.C. 192) of the handwritten text of *K'ang Nan-hai wen-chi*, kept in Taipei by Chung-yang yen-chiu-yuan, Chin-tai-shih yen-chiu-so. As to *Jih-pen pien-cheng k'ao*, see Huang Chang-chien, pp. 561, 570.
93. See note 91 above. The memorial was abridged in the *Tang-an shih-liao*. A reference to *tao* is seen in the allegedly transmitted version contained in *Wu-hsu pien-fa* 2:202. There are minor differences between the two versions of the memorial, but no major discrepancy in their contents.
94. *Jih-pen pien-cheng k'ao*, chüan 1, commentary on the events in March, the first year of the Meiji government in Japan.
95. *Wu-hsu pien-fa* 2:128, 151, 182, 201.
96. K'ang Yu-wei, *Nan-hai kuan-chih i*, pp. 3–7, 19–20. His preface was written in January 1903.
97. *Jih-pen shu-mu chih*, chüan 5. This book, published by the Ta-t'ung shu-chü of Shanghai, does not carry the year of publication, but K'ang's preface indicates that it was written in 1897.
98. In Chapter 8, entitled "K'ang Nan-hai chih Chung-kuo cheng-ts'e," of his *K'ang Nan-hai chuan*, in *Ch'ing-i-pao ch'üan-pien*, chüan 8, and *Yin-ping-shih wen-chi*, Liang Ch'i-ch'ao described K'ang's programs for local government by saying that he thought "the size of the provinces in China today too large and that it would be wise to reduce them and replace them with the present *tao* (circuits), in which a parliament would be established as an institution affiliated with the central government. Each *tao* would form a small government in itself." K'ang's proposal, however, placed the civil government bureaus (*min-cheng-chü*) to be established at the county level in a position comparable to the Western local parliament, rather than the *hsin-cheng-chü*, which were to be established at the circuit (*tao*) level. In the preceding part of the same chapter, Liang also said that K'ang had advocated the early opening of local parliaments. In addition, Liang said K'ang thought that old autonomous practices could serve as a foundation for local self-government. But it seems to me that K'ang did not speak of old practices oriented toward local autonomy until the time of the 1898 Reform Movement. It was only after the Reform Movement, in *Hsin-min tsung-pao*, no. 7, that K'ang argued for the first time that "civil self-government" (*kung-min tzu-chih*) should be implemented, based on the old practices of the villages. Sun Yat-sen argued instead that the Chinese were grounded in civil rights, citing the old communal, autonomous practices, such as participation (primarily by the gentry) in litigation, defense, road repairs, and education. Sun's intention was to support his position calling for revolution, as against the arguments for enlightened monarchism or gradual reform programs centering around the education of the people. Sun Yat-sen, "Po pao-huang-pao shu," reprinted in *Ko-ming wen-hsien*, 1953, no. 3.

99. Yuan Ch'ang, "I fu chi-yü shih-chien t'iao-ch'en," 3rd month, 24th year of Kuang-hsu.
100. A memorial by Ho Chao-li, a 2nd-class assistant secretary of the Board of Works, 7th month, 24th year of Kuang-hsu, reprinted in *Tang-an shih-liao*, pp. 188–190.
101. Huang Kuei-chün, "Chin-chih yü-yen che," of intercalary 3rd month, 24th year of Kuang-hsu, reprinted in *Wu-hsu pien-fa* 2:464–466.
102. Liang Ch'i-ch'ao, "Wu-hsu cheng-pien chi," p. 61.
103. Ibid.; and Ting Wen-chiang, p. 37.
104. Liang Ch'i-ch'ao, "Shang Ch'en Pao-chen shu," in *Wu-hsu pien-fa* 8:272–278. See Min Tu-ki, "Ch'ongmal sinsa ŭi ŭigi ŭisik kwa kaehyŏk," in *Chungguk kŭndaesa yŏn'gu*.
105. Liang Ch'i-ch'ao, "Shang Ch'en Pao-chen shu lun Hu-nan ying-pan chih shih" (November 1897), reprinted in *Wu-hsu pien-fa* 2:553–555; *Wu-hsu cheng-pien chi* 8:249–262.
106. T'an Ssu-t'ung, "Shang Ou-yang Pan-chiang shih shu," no. 10, *T'an Ssu-t'ung ch'üan-chi*, p. 307.
107. Ibid., no. 2, p. 293.
108. Examples of the criticism of centralized monarchism include T'an's *Jen-hsueh*, in his *T'an Ssu-t'ung ch'üan-chi*, pp. 53, 56–58; and "Shang Ou-yang Pan-chiang shih shu," no. 12, *T'an Ssu-t'ung ch'üan-chi*, pp. 322–324.
109. T'an Ssu-t'ung, "Ssu-wei i-hu t'ai tuan-shu," *T'an Ssu-t'ung ch'üan-chi*, p. 408.
110. "Shang Ou-yang Pan-chiang shih shu," no. 12, *T'an Ssu-t'ung ch'üan-chi*, p. 324.
111. T'an Ssu-t'ung, *Jen-hsueh*, in *T'an Ssu-t'ung ch'üan-chi*, p. 58; Liang Ch'i-ch'ao, "Hsueh-t'ang jih-chi p'i," reprinted in *Wu-hsu pien-fa* 2:549.
112. Liang Ch'i-ch'ao, "Yü Yen Yu-ling hsien-sheng shu," in *Liang Jen-kung nien-p'u ch'ang-pien ts'ao-kao*, p. 74.
113. *Hsiang-pao lei-tsuan*, p. 310.
114. Ibid.
115. Ibid. This is basically identical to Ku Yen-wu's argument that the feudal lords increase the public welfare by acting in their own private interests.
116. Ibid.
117. In "Tung-hai kung lai-han," in *Hsin-min ts'ung-pao*, no. 13 (July 1902), which was written after the 1898 Reform period, Huang definitely called for establishing parliaments, with members chosen by popular election, from the central government to the lower administrative units of prefecture and county.
118. Ku Yen-wu, *Jih-chih lu chi-shih* 13:5b.
119. *Wu-hsu pien-fa* 3:81.
120. Ibid., p. 58. As to the date of its publication, see Hashimoto Takakatsu's "Gen Fuku no chūsei hikaku bunka ron," *Tōhōgaku* 41:5.
121. *Wu-hsu pien-fa* 3:59.
122. In a commentary (*an-yü*) for section 9, chüan 10 of his *Fa-i*, published in 1906, Yen clearly praised the merits of the *feng-chien* system, expressing regret over the early demise of the feudal system in which divided rule was valued as a basic principle and "public law," or *kung-fa*, could be realized, and he

deplored the results of the *chün-hsien* system. Chou Chen-fu, *Yen Fu ssu-hsiang shu-p'ing*, p. 40.
123. See Chou Chen-fu, pp. 93–94.
124. *Shih-wu-pao*, August 1896.
125. *Ching-shih wen t'ung-pien*, chüan 37.
126. Sun Yü-jen, *Ts'ai-feng chi*, chüan 1, in Ch'i-lu Chu-jen, ed., *Shih-wu t'ung-k'ao* 21:1a–1b.
127. Chang Ping-lin, who supported the position of the *pien-fa* group during the 1898 Reform period and spoke of enhancing the rights of the people, later came up with a unique argument that the representative system could not be a means of promoting popular rights. He said that the representative system was a variation of the *feng-chien* system, and that constitutionalized, monarchic polity was close to it (see note 2 above). This reflects a trend in which people generally thought of the *feng-chien* system in relation to a parliament. Chang also proposed the combination of the *feng-chien* and *fan-chen* systems to form a new political entity, suggesting a revival of the spirit of the *fan-chen* system by making all areas except around the capital into *fu-yung* (subordinate areas). Chang Ping-lin, *Chiu hung-shu* and *Hsin hung-shu*. See Onogawa Hidemi, p. 424.
128. Chu Shou-p'eng, "Kuang-hsu ch'ao tung-hua lu," *Shih-erh ch'ao tung-hua lu*, p. 5975.
129. In "Kuang-hsu san-shih-ssu nien chiu yueh ta-shih chi," in *Tung-fang tsa-chih* (October 1908), Meng Sen, commenting on the enshrinement of the three early-Ch'ing scholars, said: "Though some ministers did not hesitate to conceal their uneasiness in supporting the idea of the enshrinement of the three scholars because of writings such as 'Yuan-chün' by Huang, the Prime Minister, nonetheless, supported the idea. The enshrinement may have had a favorable influence on the future of the constitutional movement."
130. The full text of the Board of Rites memorial can be seen in Chu Shou-p'eng, as cited in note 128 above. The memorial records the details of the attempt (since the Tao-kuang reign) to get government approval for the enshrinement of the three early-Ch'ing scholars.
131. *Tung-fang tsa-chih*, pp. 111–119. This essay by an unknown author was transcribed from *Cheng-i t'ung-pao*, 1906, no. 2.
132. Hu Ssu-ching, "Lun ti-fang tzu-chih," 12, in his *T'ui-lu ch'üan-shu* 3:19a.
133. *Tung-fang tsa-chih*, p. 112.
134. See Pao Shih-ch'en's argument for enhancing the morale of the people, thoroughly grasping the feelings of the people, and having students and various degree-holders discuss administrative, judicial, and other affairs. Hsiao Kung-ch'üan, *Chung-kao cheng-chih ssu-hsiang shih*, p. 659.
135. Refer to Chapter 2 in this book. In Chapter 5, I discuss the response of the lower-degree-holders to the provincial assembly.

5. *The Late-Ch'ing Provincial Assembly*
"Ch'ŏngmal chaŭiguk ŭi kaesŏl kwa kŭ sŏngkyŏk"

1. In Chapter 4 of this volume, I point out the importance of the *feng-chien* argument not only within the history of ideas but also within the Reform Movement.
2. In the present chapter, theories of local self-government refer exclusively to those arguments centering on the establishment of a local assembly in each province (*sheng*). They do not include various local self-governing organizations or local assemblies on a level lower than the province. Debates about self-government were directly linked to the debates on the parliamentary system, and the provincial assembly was the focal point of discussions, in contrast to district assemblies in cities (*ch'eng*), towns (*chen*), or counties (*hsien*).
3. *Kuo-fu ch'üan-shu*, pp. 358–359. There is a controversy over the authorship; Schiffrin has asserted that it was written by Ho Ch'i. See Harold Z. Schiffrin, *Sun Yat-sen and the Origins of the Chinese Revolution*, pp. 179 ff and pp. 207–209. True or not, it is quite possible that Sun was under the influence of the argument that both Kwangtung and Kwangsi provinces should develop into an independent unit, a view championed by Ho Ch'i. See Chapter 4 of this volume.
4. Wang K'ang-nien was the publisher of *Chung-wai jih-pao* (Universal gazette). See his "Lun pao tung-nan i ch'uang-li kuo-hui," *Chung-wai jih-pao* (Shanghai, 7–8 June 1900), quoted in Li Shou-k'ung, "T'ang Ts'ai-ch'ang yü tzu-li chün," p. 97.
5. Chang Chien, *Cheng-wen lu*, in his *Chang Chi-tzu chiu lu* 2:52–59.
6. Huang Tsun-hsien, "Tung-hai kung lai-han," *Hsin-min ts'ung-pao*, cited in Ting Wen-chiang, p. 160.
7. *Yu-hsueh i-pien* 12:7–12, 18 (November 1903), quoted in Wu Hsiang-hsiang, *Sung Chiao-jen–Chung-kuo min-chu hsien-cheng ti hsien-ch'ü*, p. 13. For further discussion of Hunan self-government, see Chapter 4 of this volume.
8. K'ang Yu-wei, *Nan-hai kuan-chih i*. See his introduction, written in February 1903, pp. 3–7.
9. This is the formal requirement for a citizen (*kung-min*) defined by K'ang Yu-wei. Supporting his basic premise that "enlightened knowledge" makes the difference between the gentry and the people, K'ang Yu-wei described the citizen elsewhere in the same source as follows: "How is it that the nations of Europe and America today have precise laws and have attained wealth and power? It is because the citizen works for the state. Everyone has the right to participate in politics through discussion and has an obligation to express concern over the state of his country. Such a man is worthy of being called a citizen. Everyone treats the state as if it were his own family, recognizing that the gain and loss of the state are his as well." K'ang Yu-wei, *Nan-hai kuan-chih i*, p. 4. Here *kung-min* is regarded as the same as gentry in social and political function.
10. The writer of "Tsou-ch'ing li-hsien chih feng-shuo," *Tung-fang tsa-chih* 1.5 (8

July 1904) said: "In the last few months arguments in favor of constitutional government are being heard everywhere. Some relate it to the telegram from a certain minister stationed in a foreign country and a memorial signed by certain governors general. Everyone—at home and abroad, in power and out—says that constitutional government can be expected." In "Lun Chung-kuo li-hsien chih yao-i," reprinted in *Tung-fang tsa-chih* (hereafter *TFTC*) 1.5 from the 18 June issue of *Ta-kung pao,* the following argument was presented: "What is the new problem, just beginning to emerge, for the present Chinese government? It is the problem of establishing a constitutional system.... The Ambassador to France, Sun Pao-ch'i, is said to have written a memorial to the Emperor recommending the introduction of a constitution, and some governors general have followed Sun's lead by submitting memorials in favor of constitutional government." Sun's letter to the Bureau of Government Affairs (Cheng-wu-ch'u) is in *TFTC* 1.7 (14 September 1904). Yü Shih-mei asserted that "Sun Pao-ch'i, the Ambassador to Germany [sic], was devoted to the study of political systems and was talented and enlightened. He was among the first who memorialized to request the creation of a constitution." See Yü's "K'ao-ch'a Ying Te Jih san-kuo hsien-fa ch'ing-hsing che," *Kuang-hsu ch'ao tung-hua lu* 211:5762–5764.

11. Shen Tsu-hsien et al., *Jung-an ti-tzu chi,* pp. 151–152; Chang Chien, *Se-weng tzu-ting nien-p'u,* p. 56. The necessity for a constitutional system is emphasized in the same vein in "Ch'ing ting-kuo shih i an ta-chi che" by Tuan-fang, on his return after observing foreign constitutional systems (pp. 6:34a–b). Cf. I-min, "Kai-ko chih tung-chi an-tsai?" in *Cheng-lun* 1:3–4 (1907).
12. Chang Chien, *Se-weng tzu-ting nien-p'u,* pp. 56–57; Chang Hsiao-jo, *Nan-t'ung Chang Chi-chih hsien-sheng chuan-chi,* pp. 138–139.
13. Shen Tsu-hsien et al., p. 152; Chang Chien, *Se-weng tzu-ting nien-p'u,* p. 156.
14. Chang Chien, *Se-weng tzu-ting nien-p'u,* p. 156.
15. Ibid., p. 57. See also Chang Chien's preface to the latter work reprinted in *Wen-lu,* in his *Chang Chi-tzu chiu lu,* p. 2203.
16. Kuo T'ing-i, *Chin-tai Chung-kuo shih-shih jih-chih* 2:1231; Li Shih-yueh, *Chang Chien ho li-hsien-p'ai,* p. 44.
17. *Ta-Ch'ing Te-tsung shih-lu* 546:5018, entry for *i-mao,* 6th month, 31st year (15 July 1905).
18. In "Ku T'ing-lin *Jih-chih lu* chih ti-fang tzu-chih shuo," *TFTC* 3.5:112, we find the expression that "there have been a lot of elaborate arguments in favor of constitutionalism in recent times, but the foundation of constitutionalism lies with local self-government." Cf. H. M. Vinacke, *Modern Constitutional Development in China,* p. 69.
19. *TFTC* 1.7 (September 1904).
20. Chang Chien, preface to *Jih-pen i-hui-shih,* included in *Chang Chi-tzu chiu-lu,* p. 2203.
21. "Li-hsien ch'ien-shuo lu," *TFTC* 2.9.:51 (October 1905), reprinted from *Chung-wai jih-pao,* 11 July 1905.
22. Tsung-yü, "Li-hsien ssu-i," *TFTC* 2.10:165–169 (November 1905), reprinted from *Chin-pao,* 16 August 1905.

23. *TFTC* 2.12:216–218 (January 1906), reprinted from *Nan-fang pao*, 21 September 1905.
24. Ibid., pp. 219–220.
25. *TFTC* 3.2: *Nai-wu* 27–33 (March 1906), reprinted from *Shih-pao*, 14 January 1906.
26. The following articles deal with the topic: "Lun kuo-chia yü wei li-hsien i-ch'ien yu k'o-i-hsing pi-i-hsing chih yao-cheng," *TFTC* 2.12:203–216 (January 1906), reprinted from *Chung-wai jih-pao*, 20 September 1905; "Lun li-hsien tang yu yü-pei," editorial in *TFTC* 3.3:42–47 (April 1906); "Kuo-min i-wu pien," *TFTC* 3.4:87–93 (May 1906), editorial reprinted from *Nan-yang jih-jih kuan-pao*, 26 February 1906; "Lun kuo-jen i chih cheng-fa chih ta-yao," *TFTC* 3.5:109 (June 1906), reprinted from *Shih-pao*, 22 April 1906; "Lun ti-fang tzu-chih wei yü-pei li-hsien chih ken-pen," *TFTC* 4.1 (March 1907), reprinted from *Pei-yang kuan-pao*, 29 November 1906.
27. Liang Ch'i-ch'ao, "Lun min-ch'i," *TFTC* 3.4 (May 1906); idem., "Lun chu-chang ching-cheng-che tang chih fa-chih," *TFTC* 3.5:1–17 (June 1906); Chang P'eng-yuan, *Li-hsien-p'ai yü hsin-hai ko-ming*, p. 59.
28. *Cheng-lun*, no. 1 (November 1907).
29. *Kuang-hsu ch'ao tung-hua lu*, p. 5416, entry 22nd day, 10th month, 31st year.
30. *Ta-Ch'ing Te-tsung shih-lu*, 550:5061, entry for 10th day, 12th month, 31st year.
31. Ibid., 548:5039, entry for 20th day, 8th month, 31st year.
32. "Ch'u-shih ko-kuo ta-ch'en hui-tsou ch'ing hsuan-pu li-hsien che," in *Chung-hua min-kuo k'ai-kuo wu-shih-nien wen-hsien* 1.8:484.
33. Tsai-tse et al., *K'ao-ch'a cheng-chih jih-chi*, pp. 48b–49a, entry of 30 March 1906.
34. Ibid., p. 71b. This portion also appeared under the title "Ch'u-yang k'ao-ch'a cheng-chih ta-ch'en Tse kung teng tsou tsai Ying k'ao-ch'a ta-kai ch'ing-hsing che" in *TFTC* 3.8:180–181 (September 1906).
35. Violent assaults against newly established institutions during the reign of Hsuan-t'ung (1909–1911) are well recorded in Yamashita Yoneko, "Shingai kakumei no jiki no minshū undō," pp. 141–147. Cf. Hazama Naoki, "Santō Raiyō bōdō shoron."
36. The Japanese experience with "local parliaments" was considered the model for China, particularly in the relationship between the central government and provincial assemblies. For the similarity in the process of their institutional acceptance, see Kamekakegawa Hiroshi, "San shimpō jidai to jichisei no seitei," and Irie Toshio, "Fukenron," p. 469. Chang I-lin, "Ni-fu chün-chi chang-ching nei-ko chung-shu Yin K'o-ch'ang," in *Hsin-t'ai-p'ing-shih chi*, pp. 44–45, emphasizes the effectiveness of "local self-government" in surveying and tax collection.
37. Tsai-tse et al., *K'ao-ch'a cheng-chih jih-chi*, p. 80a, entry of 18 May.
38. Ibid., pp. 121b–127a.
39. "Li-hsien chi-wen", in *Hsien-cheng ch'u-kang*, an occasional issue of *TFTC*, January 1907, reprinted in *Hsin-hai ko-ming* 4:14. According to this report, Tuan-fang was received by the Emperor three times and Tsai-tse twice; Tuan-fang memorialized the Emperor three times and Tsai-tse once.

40. These two memorials are in Tuan-fang, *Tuan Chung-min kung tsou-kao* 6:28a–43b, 43a–68b. Although they are not dated, they seem to correspond to the second and the third ones mentioned in the following passage from *Hsien-cheng ch'u-kang:* "Minister Tuan-fang memorialized the Emperor three times: first, delineating the constitutions of other countries; second, arguing the necessity of constitutional government; and, third, asking that this system be drawn up in detail." According to *Jen-kung nien-p'u ch'ang-pien ch'u-kao*, pp. 205–206, Liang was largely responsible for preparing Tuan-fang's memorials on constitutionalism. The fact that Tuan-fang and Tai Hung-tz'u, another of the ministers sent to Europe, met Chang Chien is confirmed in *Se-weng tzu-ting nien-p'u*, p. 59. Tuan-fang's recurrent emphasis on clearly demarcating the authority between the central and local governments and on putting local self-government into practice is in keeping with one of the three objectives of the Cheng-wen-she as stated in Liang's "Cheng-wen-she hsuan-yen," *Cheng-lun*, no. 1 (November 1907).
41. The description of the ministers' audience with the Empress Dowager (and formally with Emperor Kuang-hsu) is derived from *Hsin-hai ko-ming* 4:14.
42. Chang I-lin, *Hsin-t'ai-p'ing-shih chi*, p. 472.
43. Yuan Shih-k'ai, T'ieh-liang, Tsai-tse, and Tuan-fang played the key roles in writing the "Proclamation for Preparing a Constitutional Government," as confirmed in *Hsien-cheng ch'u-kang*. Evidence is also found in a memorial to the Emperor by an obstinate anti-constitutionalist, Hu Ssu-ching. His memorial is cited in Liu Chin-tsao, *Ch'ing-ch'ao hsu wen-hsien t'ung-k'ao* 999: 11497.
44. Chin Pang-p'ing, from I county, Anhwei, studied at Waseda University in Japan and later became Secretary General of the National Assembly. Ts'ao Ju-lin, from Shanghai, and Lu Tsung-yü, from Hai-ning county, Chekiang, also studied at Waseda University. Chin, Ts'ao, and Lu returned in 1905. Chin and Ts'ao became *chin-shih* and Lu a *chü-jen* through the civil examination for students who had studied abroad. Chin and Ts'ao were appointed *chu-shih* (second class secretaries) and Lu was appointed *nei-ko chung-shu* (a secretary of the Grand Secretariat). Chang I-lin, born in Soochow, was not educated in Japan but was active as Yuan Shih-k'ai's *mu-yu* and had some modern knowledge. Wang Jung-pao, also from Soochow, studied at Hōsei University in Japan. He became a secretary at the Board of the Interior and later a member of the National Assembly. For the above information, I have consulted the biographical index in *Ch'ing-chi hsin-she chih-kuan nien-piao*, *Ajia jimmei jiten*, and Kuo T'ing-i, *Chin-tai Chung-kuo shih-shih jih-chih*, Vol. II.
45. *Ta-Ch'ing Te-tsung huang-ti shih-lu* 564:5168–5169.
46. *Kuang-hsu ch'ao tung-hua lu*, pp. 5688–5690, entry for 27th day, 5th month, 33rd year.
47. The council (*hui-i-t'ing*) remained, after the introduction of the provincial assemblies, as the advisory body under the governors. Both local officials and the representatives from the provincial assemblies participated. See notes 40 and 41 above. Cf. the commentary on Article 12 in the "Joint Memorial

Pertinent to the Regulation of Provincial Assemblies, with Commentaries and Election Regulations" in *Cheng-chih kuan-pao*, no. 226, 10:397–418.
48. *Kuang-hsu ch'ao tung-hua lu*, pp. 5688–5690, entry for 27th day, 5th month, 33rd year.
49. *Kuang-hsu ch'ao tung-hua lu*, pp. 5670–5671, entry for 29th day, 5th month, 33rd year.
50. Shen T'ung-sheng, ed., *Kuang-hsu cheng-yao* 33:20a–24a; *Ta-Ch'ing Te-tsung huang-ti shih-lu* 572:5245–5246, entry for *ping-yin*, 4th month, 33rd year.
51. Hu Ssu-ching, "Kuo-wen pei-ch'eng," included in *T'ui-lu ch'üan-shu*, pp. 28b–29a. Chao Ping-lin also supported Hu Ssu-ching's statement in his *Kuang-hsu ta-shih hui-chien* 12: 9a–9b.
52. Chang I-lin, *Hsin-t'ai-p'ing-shih chi*, p. 472. Chang I-lin was a member of the drafting committee in the Office for Revising Government Institutions.
53. The term *tzu-i* (the Chinese term for provincial assembly, which means, literally, "advisory discussion") is found in "Hsin-she tung-san-sheng tsung-tu ch'i-i hsing-sheng kung-shu kuan-chih pien-fa" prepared by the Board of the Interior in April 1907, before Ts'en memorialized advocating the establishment of the office of *tzu-i*. See *Kuang-hsu cheng-yao* 33: 13a–20a. The term *tzu-i* found here presumably was borrowed from the term used in the draft prepared by the Office for Revising Government Institutions.
54. *Ta-Ch'ing Te-tsung huang-ti shih-lu* 572:5245–5246.
55. *TFTC* 5.1:7–10 (February 1908).
56. *Cheng-chih kuan-pao* 65 (29 December 1907).
57. *Ta-Ch'ing Te-tsung huang-ti shih-lu* 575:5268, entry for 19th day, 6th month, 33rd year.
58. I have deduced that the members of the drafting committee in the Office for Revising Government Institutions, such as Chin, Ts'ao, Chang, and Wang, drafted the outline of the charter of the provincial assembly. Chin, Tsao, and Chang were once under Yuan or they had close relations with Yuan. See *Jung-an ti-tzu chi*, pp. 153, 168; see also Chang I-lin, pp. 44–45. We cannot exclude the possibility that they tried to convey their idea to the Throne through Yuan.
59. *Ta-Ch'ing Te-tsung huang-ti shih-lu* 576:5274, entry for 5th day, 7th month, 33rd year.
60. Ibid., 579:5305–5306, entry for 13th day, 9th month, 33rd year.
61. Unfortunately, we do not have complete data concerning the composition of the Office to Draw Up Regulations for Constitutional Government or the proclamation process by which the charter of the Advisory Council was proclaimed, but we do know that the committee included Yang Tu, known as a man of talent among his contemporaries, and Lao Nai-hsuan, who later on became a national assemblyman by appointment. Cf. Chang I-lin, p. 475.
62. *Cheng-chih kuan-pao* no. 266, 10:393–418 (24 July 1908). Suematsu Kaiichirō, a Japanese expert, was invited into the northeastern provinces in 1907 to set up a Local Self-Government Bureau where regulations on local self-government were prepared. After the provincial-assembly regulations applicable to all provinces universally were proclaimed, the Japanese expert was sent back to his country. Suematsu Kaiichirō, *Chihō jichi seido yōgi*, p. 1.

63. The framework of the regulations of the provincial assembly, in light of the above, may have been made by the Office for Revising Governmental Institutions. It seems that time was too limited for the Office to Draw Up Regulations for Constitutional Government to prepare the framework. It was only two months after the committee was set up that the edict urging prompt establishment of the provincial assemblies, giving only an outline of the assembly, was issued.
64. Cf. note 62 above.
65. *Cheng-chih kuan-pao* no. 277, 10:539 (4 August 1908).
66. Mo Pei, ed., *Chiang-Che t'ieh-lu feng-ch'ao* 1:139.
67. *Cheng-chih kuan-pao* no. 225, 10:263–264 (13 June 1908).
68. Ibid. no. 146, 5:353 (26 March 1908).
69. *TFTC* 5.4:266 (May 1908).
70. Ibid. We do not know how the "all-province representatives" were selected; they may have been chosen by the provincial governor.
71. *TFTC* 5.4:266 (May 1908).
72. Ibid. The assemblymen referred to here were presumably selected in the same way as those in Kiangsi.
73. *TFTC* 5.2:140–141 (March 1908).
74. Ibid., 5.4:266 (May 1908).
75. Chang Hsiao-jo, *Nan-t'ung Chang Chi-chih hsien-sheng chuan-chi*, p. 141. The date the author gave, "the autumn of the 34th year of Kuang-hsu" should be "the autumn of the 33rd year."
76. For example, it is said that the Governor General of Hukwang, Ch'en Kuei-lung, was ridiculed for his memorial which stated: "I originally established a provincial assembly (*tzu-i-chü*), but, because of the low level of the people, it was corrected to the Office for Establishing a Provincial Assembly." *TFTC* 5.9:64 (October 1908).
77. These names are reported in *Cheng-chih kuan-pao*, nos. 322 (12:431), 359 (14:36), 375 (14:303), 395 (15:124), 434 (16:328–29), 437 (16:392), 443 (16:500), 447 (16:594), 452 (17:109–11), 460 (17:250); Tuan-fang, *Tuan Chung-min kung tsou-kao* 13:40a–41a.
78. Cf. Chao Ping-lin, *Chao Po-yen chi* 1:24a; *TFTC* 5.10:103 (November 1908).
79. On the role of metropolitan officials acting as gentry in their native provinces, see Chapter 6 in this volume.
80. Column on constitutionalism in *TFTC* 5.11:129 (December 1908).
81. Column on constitutionalism in *TFTC*, 5.10:102 (November 1908).
82. *TFTC* 5.12:164 (January 1909).
83. The record of monthly events for the 9th month, 34th year of Kuang-hsu (September/October 1908), in *TFTC* 5.10:89–97 (November 1908).
84. The record of monthly events for the 8th month, 34th year of Kuang-hsu (August/September 1908), in *TFTC* 5.9:73 (October 1908).
85. See Chapter 6 in this volume.
86. *Chung-wai jih-pao*, 13 April 1909, cited in Li Shou-k'ung, "Ch'ing-mo chih tzu-i-chü."
87. *Shun-t'ien shih-pao*, 25 April 1909.

88. As reported in *TFTC* 6.4 (May 1909) and 6.5 (June 1909). Elections were held on 19 May in Yunnan; 23 May in Chekiang; 18 June in Hunan, Szechwan, and Honan; 2 July in Kwangsi; 17 July in Kwangtung; 29 April in Fengtien; 20 February in Fukien; and 20 February and 2 March in Kiangsu.
89. *TFTC* 6.5:231–252 (May 1909). An edict of 7 July 1907, mentioned Chihli and Kiangsu as two "enlightened" provinces; see *Ta-Ch'ing Te-tsung shih-lu* 574:5257–5258, entry for *tung-ssu* day, 5th month, 33rd year.
90. *Cheng-chih kuan-pao*, no. 653, 517–518 (22 August 1909).
91. Chang P'eng-yuan, *Li-hsien-p'ai*, p. 18. U.S. State Department Records relating to the Internal Affairs of China (1910–1929) 893.00/351/2, state that the number of qualified citizen voters of Kwangchow was about 1,600, but that actual voters numbered 399. (Li Shou-k'ung also cited this information without footnote, in "Ch'ing-mo chih tzu-i-chü," p. 192.) However, according to "The Constitutional Column" in *TFTC* 6.7:351–353 (August 1909), voters of Kwangchow actually numbered 55,538 and allocated members of the provincial assembly numbered 35. (The number of voters in all of Kwangtung province was 141,558 and allocated members of the assembly, 91.) The prefectures with the smallest number of voters were Yai-chou with 1,091 voters and Ch'ao-chou with 1,173. If the number of qualified voters of Kwangchow the U.S. Consul reported were to be convincing, the figure of the capital prefecture could only be comparable to the smallest figures in the province. Actually, Kwangchow could produce one assemblyman per 1,555 qualified voters. Another example of erroneous figures is the following: When Meribeth Elliott Cameron mentioned the election of the provincial assembly in Shantung in *The Reform Movement in China, 1898–1912*, p. 122, the figures she gave for the number of those "who went to the polls" were actually the figures for all qualified voters.
92. *The North China Herald*, 12 June 1909.
93. See "The Constitutional Column," in *TFTC* 6.4:71 (May 1909); see also "Comments on Current Events," in *Chung-wai jih-pao*, 23 August 1909, cited in Li Shou-k'ung, "Ko-sheng tzu-i-chü lien-ho-hui yü hsin-hai ko-ming," p. 323.
94. *TFTC* 6.4:172.
95. Ibid.
96. *Huang-ch'ao hsu wen-hsien t'ung-k'ao* 400:11516.
97. *Min-hu-pao*, 6 June 1919, cited in Chang P'eng-yuan, *Li-hsien-p'ai*, p. 18.
98. *Cheng-chih kuan-pao*, no. 762, 27:475.
99. *Min-hu-pao*, 6 June 1919, cited in Chang P'eng-yuan, *Li-hsien-p'ai*, p. 19.
100. *Hsien-cheng hsin-chih*, cited in Hu Sheng-wu and Chin Ch'ung-chi, *Lun Ch'ing-mo ti li-hsien yun-tung*, p. 34.
101. Chang P'eng-yuan, *Li-hsien-p'ai*, p. 18.
102. *The Times*, 15 October 1909; Cameron, p. 120.
103. See note 44 above. Did the *Times* report mean men from Kiangsu province instead of Chekiang? Three of the four members of the draft committee in the Office for Revising Government Institutions came from Kiangsu province.
104. Yang Tu-sheng, a member of Tsai-tse's entourage, entrusted Sung Chiao-jen with the translation of *Eikoku seidō yōran* (A handbook of institutions of

the United Kingdom). Cf. Sung Chiao-jen, *Wo chih li-shih,* pp. 96–97.

105. "Lun ti-fang tzu-chih wei yü-pei li-hsien chih ken-pen," *Pei-yang kuan-pao* 18 November 1906, reprinted in *TFTC* 4.1 (March 1907). "Prefectural meetings" (*fukenkai*) in Japan refers to the system of incomplete self-government laid out in the *Fukenkai kisoku* of 1878. This was the first law in Japan allowing local parliaments. The prefectural system (*fukensei*) as an administrative local self-government body was not put into practice until 1890. For information about the prefectural system in Japan, see the essays by Kamekakegawa Hiroshi and Irie Toshio previously cited.

106. Tuan-fang, *Tuan Chung-min kung tsou-kao* 6:36b–37a.

107. "Liang-chiang tsung-tu Tuan-fang teng tsou ti-fang tzu-chih hsien chiu sheng-ch'eng she chü ch'ou pen che,"*Cheng-chih kuan-pao,* no.103, 4:6–7 (11th day, 1st month, 34th year), Mou Shu-tzu emphasized the imitation of the Japanese example in an article, "Lun ko-sheng ch'ing-yuan kuo-hui tai-piao chi-ying ch'ou-pei ti-fang tzu-chih," pt. 4, *Shun-t'ien shih-pao,* 29 September 1908.

108. The commentary on the fifth article cited the Representative Law of Japan as the source. It is the same eligibility as prescribed in the regulations governing the Japanese prefectural system. Cf. Irie Toshio, p. 476.

109. These tendencies are set out in a memorial by Yü Shih-mei, a member of the second group of investigators of Western constitutionalism in *Kuang-hsu ch'ao tung-hua lu,* entry for *jen-wu* day, 10th month, 33rd year (29 November 1907), p. 5763. For details, see Nagahama Masatoshi, *Chihō jichi,* pp. 11–18.

110. Chang P'eng-yuan *Li-hsien-p'ai,* pp. 295–297. Chang said that, "if the circumstances of Shensi province, which was not a particularly wealthy province, were like this, the provinces along the coast and in the southeastern area must have been better" (ibid., p. 31). But this is not a problem of poor and rich. Even if we had a complete background survey, the rich provinces did not necessarily produce rich merchant representatives. In addition, Chang himself said that the people who represented an industrial-commercial community in the constitutional movement were, in fact, the gentry, not the merchants (ibid., p. 72).

111. At that time, Bland, the well-known China hand, criticized the article on suffrage in the Regulations of the Provincial Assembly, calling it a "silk-gowned franchise," that is, a suffrage limited to gentry. J.O.P. Bland, *Recent Events and Present Policies in China,* p. 125. Another observer at the time, speaking in a different context about the qualifications of assemblymen, said that they had a Confucian viewpoint in which the ideal was the close relation between politics and morality. Paul S. Reinsch, *Intellectual and Political Currents in the Far East,* p. 239. In favoring the gentry, the qualifications for suffrage in China contrasted strongly with Japanese election procedures, in which voting eligibility was tied to tax liability. Kamekakegawa Hiroshi, pp. 162–163, and Saka Chiaki, "Chihō jichi no kaiko to tembō," p. 139.

112. Chang P'eng-yuan, *Li-hsien-p'ai,* pp. 247–312. See also my review of Chang P'eng-yuan's book in *Yŏksa hakpo* 47:156–157 (1970), in which I was able to add new findings pertinent to the career of the assemblymen. The names of the assemblymen are given in lists printed in *Cheng-chih kuan-pao* and *TFTC* 6.5 (June 1909).

113. Chang P'eng-yuan, *Li-hsien-p'ai,* pp. 26–28.
114. Ibid.
115. Ibid., p. 30.
116. Of the four members of the preparatory office representing the gentry in northern Kiangsu, two (Chiang Ping-chang and Wang T'ung-yü) were elected to the provincial assembly. Chiang had returned to administer a modern school prior to the preparation and became involved with the preparatory office; he was first an expectant member for Soochow, and later became a full member and served as Vice-Chairman. Wang was elected but resigned, and Liu Yung-ch'ang substituted for him. All had been among the twelve men voluntarily involved in preparations for a provincial assembly before the proclamation of the assembly regulations. In the southern section of Kiangsu province, four (Chang Chien, Hsia Yin-kuan, Hsu Ting-lin, and Ch'iu Chi-heng) out of the five gentry representatives on the preparatory committee were elected to the provincial assembly; Chang became Chairman and Ch'iu Vice-Chairman. In addition, many of Chang's personal friends (Yang T'ing-tung, Meng Sen, Lei Fen, Wang T'ung-yü, and Meng Chao-ch'ang) were elected. See Liu Hou-sheng, *Chang Chien ch'üan-chi,* pp. 177 ff; *TFTC* 6.5:229 (June 1909); Li Shih-yueh, p. 45.

In Kiangsi province, two of the five gentry preparatory members, Yü Chao-fan and Ho Tsan-yuan, were elected to the provincial assembly. A third, Wu Ch'ing-t'ao, the Associate Director of the preparatory office, was elected to the provincial assembly in his native Hupeh. In Chihli province, it is not known who represented the gentry on the preparatory office, but Chin Pang-p'ing, one of the two senior active officials in the province, was appointed later as the General Secretary of the National Assembly. Similarly, not all members of the Chekiang preparatory office are known, but of two known to us, Ch'en Ching-ti (its Associate Director) was elected. In Hupeh, four of the six preparatory members were elected, among them T'ang Hua-lung, who was reelected Chairman of the Assembly and Hsia Shou-k'ang and Chang Kuo-jung, who were elected Vice-Chairmen.

In Kwangsi, of the three members of the preparatory office elected to the assembly, Ch'en Shu-hsün became Chairman and T'ang Shang-kuang Vice-Chairman. For Kwangtung and Kirin, we do not have any information on the preparatory members. In Honan, all three preparatory members were elected to the provincial assembly, and, as in Hupeh and Hunan, one of them was elected Chairman and the other two Vice-Chairmen. In Hunan, out of eight preparatory members, except for the senior provincial officials who served as preparatory members, five were elected and they dominated the chairmanship and vice-chairmanship.

117. For example, we need only look at a book advertisement in the constitutionalists' magazine, *Kuo-feng pao* 1:13 (28 June 1910). Meng Sen, a member of the Kiangsu Provincial Assembly, is listed as the author of four separate works: *Fa-hsueh t'ung-lun, Tzu-i-chü chang-ch'eng chien-shih, Ti-fang tzu-chih ts'ai-cheng lun-kang,* and *Ti-fang tzu-chih ch'ien-shuo.* Yang T'ing-tung, an expectant member for the Kiangsu Provincial Assembly, is given as the author of *Ch'in-ting hsien-fa ta-kang chiang-i* and *Tzu-i-chü chih-wu hsu-chih;* T'ao Pao-

lin, a member of the Chekiang Provincial Assembly, appears as the author of *Hsin-pien hsien-hsing fa-chih ta-i* and *Tiao-ch'a hu-k'ou chang-ch'eng shih*. In addition, Liu Ch'ung-yu, Vice-Chairman of the Fukien Provincial Assembly, translated Oda Man's *Hōgaku tsūron*.

Meng Sen was the editor and a leading writer of *Tung-fang tsa-chih*. He was first named as editor in 5.7, in which his first column on constitutionalism was published. After 6.3 (April 1909), a new editor named Ch'en Chung-yi replaced him, though Meng's articles on constitutionalism continued to appear. Ti Pao-hsien, a member of the Kiangsu Provincial Assembly, wielded a great deal of influence as the editor of the important daily newspaper *Shih-pao*. Cf. Ko Kung-ch'en, *Chung-kuo pao-hsueh shih*, p. 187.

118. Chang P'eng-yuan, *Li-hsien-p'ai*, pp. 63–77. Li Shou-k'ung, "Ko-sheng tzu-i-chü lien-ho-hui yü hsin-hai ko-ming," and "Ch'ing-mo chih tzu-i-chü."
119. Mo Pei, pp. 39–42; see also Chapter 6 in this volume.
120. Mo Pei, p. 274.
121. Hu Ssu-ching, "Mi-ch'en li-hsien yin-huan ping ch'ou-hsien san-ts'e ch'ing chi-hsiu nei-chih i tu hsieh-mou che," in *Huang-ch'ao hsu wen-hsien t'ung-k'ao* 399:11497.
122. *Hsuan-t'ung cheng-chi*, pp. 758–759.
123. *Chung Po-i hsien-sheng fang-wen chi-lu*, pp. 21–22, quoted in Chang P'eng-yuan, *Li-hsien-p'ai*, p. 31. The original is preserved in manuscript in the Institute of Modern History, Academia Sinica.
124. *Hai-fang tang*, Railway Section, pp. 953–954.
125. Bland, p. 125.
126. USDS, 893.00/492, quoted in Chang P'eng-yuan, *Li-hsien-p'ai*, p. 30; Cameron, p. 122.
127. Chang P'eng-yuan, *Li-hsien-p'ai*, p. 26.
128. Ibid., pp. 284–287, 298–302. In "The Constitutionalists," in Mary Wright, ed., *China in Revolution: The First Phase, 1900–1913*, p. 152, Chang presented his view on the basis of only the 98 members of provincial assemblies who were elected to the National Assembly, and memberships of the provincial assemblies in five provinces (Fengtien, Shantung, Shensi, Hupeh, and Szechwan) for which relatively detailed information on the social background of provincial-assembly members is available. However, the information for Fengtien, Shansi, and Hupeh is far less adequate than that for Shantung and Szechwan. For Hupeh, for which there is better information than for Fengtien or Shensi, the social background of only 20 members (20.4%) out of 98 is known, as opposed to 93% for Shantung and 87% for Szechwan. The statistics for Shantung and Szechwan shown in this book differ from my own calculations, and his definition of *sheng-yuan* is not clear to me.
129. See Chapter 2.
130. Chang P'eng-yuan, "Ch'ing-chi tzu-i-chü i-yuan ti hsuan-chü chi ch'i ch'u-shen chih fen-hsi," pp. 18–20. The backgrounds of chairmen and vice-chairmen are known: 30 out of 60 were *chin-shih* degree-holders, 18 were *chü-jen* degree-holders, 5 were *kung-sheng* degree-holders, and 3 were *sheng-yuan* degree-holders.

131. For example, among the 113 Chekiang gentry who petitioned the Governor for the protection of railway rights, no one as low as a *chü-jen* was found among the gentry from Hangchow and Chia-hsing prefectures, which had produced many more scholars and gentry for a long time, whereas, in Wenchou and Ch'ü-chou prefectures, no one even as high as a *chü-jen* was found. Mo Pei 1:39–42.
132. Contrary to Chang P'eng-yuan, who recognized the importance of higher-level gentry, some scholars have stressed the fact that holders of lower degrees were numerically dominant in the provincial assembly; see John Fincher "Political Provincialism and the National Revolution," p. 212, and Mary Wright, "Introduction" to *China in Revolution*, p. 19. Wright has argued that holders of lower degrees were more varied in background and occupation and, because of this variety, functioned differently than the holders of higher degrees, who clung to the status quo. As a result, the lower gentry were more interested in national than in local matters. Though the distinction between higher and lower is not clearly stated, it seems that higher degree means *chin-shih* and lower degree all the rest. These opinions are different from my own and neglect the fact that most of the active leaders of the national constitutional movement, the chairmen and vice-chairmen of provincial assemblies, held higher degrees.
133. *Cheng-chih kuan-pao*, no. 762, 27:475.
134. Liu Chin-tsao's comment on self-government, in *Huang-ch'ao hsu wen-hsien t'ung-k'ao* 395:11; also Ou-chia Lien's memorial, ibid. 400:11,516.
135. Bland, pp. 125, 127. The prohibition against gambling in Kwangtung was widely reported in the newspapers during 1910–1911.
136. *Cheng-chih kuan-pao*, no. 1155, 40:198 (13 January 1911); *TFTC* 7.11:87 (December 1910).
137. "Ti-fang yao-wen," *Shih-pao*, 12 October 1910.
138. Ibid.
139. Hu Ssu-ching, "Ch'ing pa hsin-cheng che" (Memorial requesting the discontinuance of the new policies), dated 16 June 1910, *T'ui-lu shu-kao* (1913), included in *T'ui-lu ch'üan-shu*. Chang P'eng-yuan, *Li-hsien-p'ai*, p. 24, n. 13, introduced a story from a satirical novel, *Yü-pei li-hsien*, in which an opium addict acquired the eligibility by buying land, mistaking membership in the provincial assembly for officeholding.
140. Chang P'eng-yuan, *Li-hsien-p'ai*, pp. 30–31.
141. Ibid., pp. 248–250.
142. Ibid., pp. 277–280.
143. Ibid., pp. 248–250.
144. "Lun li-hsien tang i ti-fang tzu-chih wei chi-ch'u," *TFTC* 2.12:216–218 (January 1906).
145. Concerning opportunities for the gentry of *chü-jen* rank and below, see "Cheng-wu-ch'u i-tsou chü-kung sheng-yuan liang-yü ch'u-lu pien-fa," *Kuang-hsu cheng-yao* 32:4b–5a; "Hui-i cheng-wu-ch'u i-tsou fu pien-hsiu Yuan Li-chün tsou yü-pei li-hsien che," *TFTC* 5.1: 13–15 (February 1908). Ch'en Kung-lu described this problem briefly in *Chung-kuo chin-tai shih*, pp. 584–585.

146. "Hunan tzu-i-chü chih-shih," *Shih-pao,* 3 January 1910.
147. Chang I-lin 8:466.
148. Chung-li Chang, *The Chinese Gentry,* p. 138.
149. Their ratios for Kweichow and Shantung, however, are remarkably different. It seems that definitive conclusions cannot be drawn from these statistics. Fincher's statement (p. 212) that "the 1909 electorate was a somewhat larger proportion of the population than the post-Taiping gentry" assumes, for instance, that Chang's figures are actual rather than estimated.
150. *Cheng-chih kuan-pao,* no. 1149, 26:279–280.
151. See, for example, "Shih-ping," no. 2, *Shih-pao,* 28 December 1919, and "Ching-shih chin-hsin," *Shih-pao,* 17 January 1912.
152. Mou Shu-tzu, "Lun ko-sheng ch'ing-yuan kuo-hui tai-piao chi-ying ch'ou-pei ti-fang tzu-chih," pt. 3, *Shun-t'ien shih-pao,* 17 November 1908.
153. T'an Ssu-t'ung, "Fu-tzu ta-jen han-chang," no. 10, in *T'an Ssu-t'ung ch'üan-chi,* p. 307.
154. *TFTC* 1.1:46 (March 1904).
155. The report of the *Times* reprinted in the *North China Herald,* 18 February 1910, p. 359.
156. Bland, p. 125.
157. Ibid., p. 127.
158. A report on the provincial assembly from T'ai-yuan, Shansi, in the *North China Herald,* 30 October 1909, p. 250.
159. *TFTC* 6.11 (December 1909).
160. Though Fincher (pp. 197–198, 202) emphasized the cooperative relationship between the governor and the provincial assemblies, different perspectives on this matter should be considered. Further analyses of the concrete activities of the provincial assemblies are needed to clarify the relationship.
161. *Cheng-chih kuan-pao,* no. 266, 10:394–395.
162. "Hsuan-t'ung yuan-nien ta-shih chi," *Kuo-feng pao* 1.1:3–4 (1910) stated that, "ever since Chang Chih-tung and Yuan Shih-k'ai were appointed to the Grand Council (in 1907), the central government has become more powerful. For the past year or two there has been heated controversy about the centralization of power in political circles." Immediately after the outbreak of the rebellion in Wu-ch'ang, the revolutionary proclamation stated that "the Ch'ing Court made every effort to centralize power forcefully under the guise of constitutional reform." *Chung-kuo ko-ming chi,* pp. 5–8. This statement shows how seriously the people regarded the centralization of power by the Ch'ing Court.
163. The description of the character of governors is based on Liang Ch'i-ch'ao, "Tzu-i-chü ch'üan-hsien chih-wu shih-lun," in *Yin-ping-shih wen-chi,* pp. 36–38.
164. Cf. Chapter 6 in this book.
165. "Lun cheng-fu chung-yang chih-ch'üan chih wu," *TFTC* 4.2:21–26 (April 1907).
166. Yü Shih-mei's memorial is found in *Hsuan-t'ung cheng-chi* 13:248–250, entry for *jen-tzu* day, 5th month, 1st year. See also Liang Ch'i-ch'ao, "Tzu-i-chü ch'üan-hsien chih-wu shih-lun," *Yin-ping-shih wen-chi,* pp. 35–39.

167. According to Ting Wen-chiang, p. 307, many of the writings of the Office to Draw Up Regulations for Constitutional Government were pre-drafted by Liang. Probably because of this, Liang refuted Yü Shih-mei's argument and supported the regulations of the provincial assembly.

6. The Soochow-Hangchow-Ningpo Railway Dispute
"Ch'ŏngmal kangch'ŏl ch'ŏllo pun'gyu (1905–1911) wa sinhae hyŏngyŏng chŏnya ŭi sinsach'ŭng hyangbang"

1. Sino-British relations over the Soochow-Hangchow-Ningpo railway are discussed in Fujii Masao, "Shinmatsu Kō Setsu ni okeru tetsuro mondai to burujoa seiryoku no ichi sokumen"; Chao Chin-yü, "Su-Hang-Yung t'ieh-lu chieh-k'uan ho Chiang-Che jen-min ti chü-k'uan yun-tung"; Yamashita Yoneko, "Shingai kakumei no jiki no minshū undō"; I-tu Sun (Jen), *Chinese Railways and British Interests, 1898–1911*. Another important article is Lee En-han, "The Chekiang Gentry-Merchants versus the Peking Court Officials: China's Struggle for Recovery of the British Soochow-Hangchow-Ningpo Railway Concession." Because this chapter was completed before the publication of Lee's article, I have not referred to Lee here. Lee's article is a useful supplement to mine, although our approaches to the topic differ. Lee has made use of British Foreign Office documents which I could not consult. These documents reveal that Sheng Hsuan-huai secretly informed the British government that his real intention was to benefit the British government and that his problematic leak about tacit nullification of the preliminary contract was merely an excuse given to the anti-loan activists in order to save face (p. 236).
2. In the Sino-British railway dispute, the people of Chekiang had more at stake than the people of Kiangsu, since about three-fourths of the projected railway would cross Chekiang province. Therefore, this present study centers on the activities of Chekiang activists.
3. Chang Chien, "Cheng-wen lu," chüan 1, p. 45, in *Chang Chi-tzu chiu lu*.
4. For Japanese interest, see Sheng Hsuan-huai's letter of the 7th day, 5th month, 24th year of Kuang-hsu to Li Fu-hsiang, in his *Sheng Hsuan-huai wei-k'an hsin-kao*, p. 78; for German interest, see I-tu Sun (Jen), pp. 69 ff.
5. *Ch'ing-chi wai-chiao shih-liao* 126:404.
6. Wang I-nien, *Wang Jang-ch'ing hsien-sheng chüan-chi*, p. 135.
7. The British and Chinese Corporation was established by the Hui-feng Bank and Jardine, Matheson & Co. in 1898 at the initiation of the British government in order to undertake the construction and management of railways in China. See Hsieh Pin, *Chung-kuo t'ieh-tao shih*, p. 41.
8. The full text of the preliminary contract is contained in Mo Pei, ed., *Chiang-Che t'ieh-lu feng-ch'ao*, p. 7. This publication (to be cited as *Feng-ch'ao* in this chapter) is a collection of various materials on the railway dispute, including official documents and newspaper articles. It was originally published in Shanghai in two volumes in 1909 and was reprinted in Taipei in 1968. Unfor-

tunately, the original dates of publication of these documents are rarely given.
9. See *Shina keizai zensho* 5:297. Neither did the British hurry in developing many Chinese mines whose concessions they had already secured, a situation of which Chinese movements calling for the nullification of such concessions made good use. For this problem, see Lee En-han, *Wan-Ch'ing ti shou-hui k'uang-ch'üan yun-tung*, pp. 162–163, 178.
10. *Ch'ing-chi wai-chiao shih-liao*, 207:392–395. The petition was referred to in a memorial of the Foreign Board in December 1907.
11. Ibid. 171:454.
12. According to *Feng-ch'ao*, pp. 76, 85, Li was General Director of the Shanghai Merchants Association.
13. *Shina keizai zensho* 5:297; *TFTC* 2.11 (December 1905).
14. Sheng En-i et al., *Yü-chai ts'un-kao* 14:2a–2b.
15. Ibid. 14:2b.
16. Ibid. 12:3b. Article 13 of "Ch'ung-ting t'ieh-lu chien-ming chang-ch'eng" (The revised regulations on railway construction), announced on 19 November 1907 (*Shina keizai zensho* 5:98–104), stipulated clearly that the survey should be completed within six months after the conclusion of the railway contract, and that construction should start within a second six-month period. In the case of mining, also, the Chinese often resorted to the same stipulations in regard to the completion of surveys and the beginning of work in order to offset concessions that had been given to foreign powers.
17. Lee En-han, "Chung-Mei shou-hui Yueh-Han lu-ch'üan chiao-she."
18. Ibid., pp. 131–138. These movements continued until September of the next year.
19. Fujii Masao, p. 23.
20. Liu Chin-tsao, *Ch'ing-ch'ao hsu wen-hsien t'ung-k'ao* 364:11109 (commentary).
21. Details involving the establishment of the Chekiang Railway Company can be found in *TFTC* 2:8 (September 1905) and 2:11 (December 1905).
22. *Ta-Ch'ing Te-tsung shih-lu* 547:5031, entry for *ting-yu* day, 7th month (26 August 1905); *Kuang-hsu cheng-yao* 31:54b–55b entry for 7th month (August 1905).
23. Liu Chin-tsao, 365:11098.
24. Ibid.
25. *Ta-Ch'ing Te-tsung shih-lu* 548:5040 entry for *i-ch'ou* day, 7th month (23 September 1905).
26. *Feng-ch'ao*, pp. 14–15. Prior to this, on 26 October, Sheng had asked the boards of Foreign Affairs and Commerce to negotiate with the British Minister to China (*Feng-ch'ao*, pp. 31–35).
27. Ibid., p. 16.
28. Ibid., p. 17; and Sheng En-i et al., *Yü-chai ts'un-kao* 14:4b.
29. *Feng-ch'ao*, p. 18; and Sheng En-i et al., *Yü-chai ts'un-kao* 12:30a.
30. Ibid. 14:5a.
31. See *Feng-ch'ao*, pp. 19–26, for documents exchanged between the Chekiang Governor and the British Consul.

32. Liu Chin-tsao, p. 11108, a memorial of the 14th day, 9th month, 33rd year (20 October 1907); and *Feng-ch'ao*, pp. 35–38.
33. Ibid.
34. *Shina keizai zensho*, pp. 313–314.
35. See note 32 above.
36. *Ta-Ch'ing Te-tsung shih-lu* 579:5306 entry for *jen-yin* day, 9th month (20 October 1907); and Liu Chin-tsao, p. 11108.
37. Hsieh Pin, pp. 357–359.
38. "Ko-sheng t'ieh-lu hui-chih" in *TFTC* 4:9–11 (October–December 1907).
39. *Ch'ing-chi wai-chiao shih-liao* 206:381–382; and *Feng-ch'ao*, pp. 269–271.
40. *Ta-Ch'ing Te-tsung shih-lu* 581:5324 entry for *jen-wu* day, 10th month, 33rd year (29 November 1907); *Feng-ch'ao*, p. 49.
41. *Feng-ch'ao*, pp. 261, 272.
42. Liu Chin-tsao, "Che-lu kai-lueh", in *Ch'ing-ch'ao hsu wen-hsien t'ung-k'ao*, pp. 11130–11131; and Fujii Masao, p. 24. The others included Hsu Ting-lin, Yang T'ing-tung, and Wang T'ung-yü of Kiangsu and Chang Yuan-chi, Sun T'ing-han, and Sun I-jang of Chekiang.
43. This was originally proposed by Liang Shih-i, Director of the General Railway Bureau. Sheng En-i et al., *Yü-chai ts'un-kao* 73:4b–5a.
44. The text of the Sino-British loan agreement can be found in *Hai-fang tang* (Archives on maritime defense), V, 583–592. The full text of the compromise pact between the Board and the local railway companies is recorded in *Hai-fang tang*, pp. 621–625; and in Liu Chin-tsao, *Ch'ing-ch'ao hsu wen-hsien t'ung-k'ao*, p. 11116.
45. Yuan Shih-k'ai, stressing that the loan agreement was very advantageous to the Chinese side, said that, although the preliminary contract stipulated that the terms of the railway's final contract would be identical to those of the Shanghai-Nanking railway contract, the loan agreement did not include two undesirable features of the former pact: mortgaging the whole property and the revenues of the railway, and the lenders' (British) financial supervision of the line. See *Ta-Ch'ing Te-tsung shih-lu* 587:5367, entry for *keng-shen* day, 2nd month, 34th year (6 March 1908); and Shen Tsu-hsien, pp. 203–204.
46. By that time, the construction of the railway linking Shanghai and Chia-hsing was almost completed. In such a situation, the government authorities thought that the line from Shanghai to Chia-hsing might be of no use if the railway between Soochow and Chia-hsing were to be constructed as originally projected. Therefore, they changed the terminus and the name of the railway.
47. *Hai-fang tang*, pp. 717–718 entry for 10th day, 11th month, 34th year (3 December 1908). Fujii Masao (p. 24) seems to have been mistaken when he identified the director as Shih Chao-chi.
48. *Feng-ch'ao*, p. 10. Although the letter itself does not carry a date, it must have been September because it said that the memorial from the Board of Commerce to the Throne on the establishment of the Chekiang Railway Company in August was made "the previous month."
49. Ibid., pp. 11–12.

50. Ibid., pp. 14–15.
51. How the Chekiang gentry supposed wrongly is given in the recollection of Liu Chin-tsao, the Vice-Director of the Chekiang Railway Company and the author of *Ch'ing-ch'ao hsu wen-hsien t'ung-kao.* See p. 11109.
52. "Chung-kuo ta-shih chi," *TFTC* 7.8 (September 1910).
53. *Kuang-hsu cheng-yao,* chüan 33; and *Ta-Ch'ing te-tsung shih-lu* 581:5324, entry for 24th day, 10th month, 33rd year (29 November 1907).
54. See note 52 above.
55. *Ta-Ch'ing Te-tsung shih-lu* 582:5329, entry for *chia-wu* day, 11th month, 33rd year (11 December 1907); *Yü-chai ts'un-kao* 14:7a.
56. According to Chang I-lin, a private secretary of Yuan Shih-k'ai, Yuan said, "Sheng Hsuan-huai is to blame for the current railway dispute. Why do people put the blame on me just as I have taken charge of the Board of Foreign Affairs?" Chang recommended Yuan to invite representatives of the Kiangsu and Chekiang railway companies and give them access to all relevant documents. Chang I-lin, *Hsin-t'ai-p'ing-shih chi,* p. 476. The memorial of the Board of Foreign Affairs mentioned above (26 November 1907) spoke of opening those documents to the public, convinced that the British had never agreed tacitly to the nullification of the preliminary contract. At this point, noted Chang, the argument of the native-financed railway construction subsided at last. According to a report in *Chung-wai jih-pao* (quoted in *Feng-ch'ao,* p. 495), Yuan complained that Sheng "had glossed over the facts, thereby causing the dispute."
57. See the biographical sketch of Sheng Hsuan-huai appended to the opening chüan of *Yü-chai ts'un-kao,* p. 48b; Albert Feuerwerker, *China's Early Industrialization: Sheng Hsuan-huai and Mandarin Enterprise,* p. 78; *Feng-ch'ao,* p. 495.
58. *Feng-ch'ao,* pp. 95–97, 113–118, 135.
59. Ibid., pp. 269–271; *Ch'ing-chi wai-chiao shih-liao* 206:381–382.
60. *Feng-ch'ao,* pp. 219–220, 236. Wang K'ang-nien, who was one of the promoters of the Chekiang Railway Company and a noted Shanghai journalist, stated in his "Su-Hang-Yung-lu shih-mo lueh-chi," p. 7, that Wu Kang died of accidental medication by a doctor and T'ang Hsu of a disease. Wang reproached T'ang Shou-ch'ien for fabricating the two deaths by hunger strike. Wang's description of the railway dispute is full of additional personal abuse against T'ang Hsiu-ch'ien beyond the disagreement over the two deaths. I do not know what made Wang attack T'ang in such a way.
61. *Feng-ch'ao,* pp. 39–42. The names of the signatories are found here, 113 in all. See *Ta-Ch'ing Te-tsung shih-lu,* 581:5323, entry for the 19th day, 10th month, 33rd year (24 November 1907).
62. *Feng-ch'ao,* pp. 69–70.
63. Ibid., pp. 249–252.
64. *Ta-Ch'ing Te-tsung shih-lu* 580:5313; 581:5319,5329; *Feng-ch'ao,* p. 241.
65. A detailed description of the Chekiang Citizens' Anti-Loan Association can be found in *Feng-ch'ao,* pp. 95–98, 113–118, 135, 241.
66. Chang P'eng-yuan, *Li-hsien-p'ai yü hsin-hai ko-ming,* p. 274. Wang participated

in the joint memorial of the 113 Chekiang people as a representative of Chinhua prefecture. He was later elected to the prefectural assembly in his home area. In some sources, Wang T'ing-yang is referred to as Wang Fu-ch'uan.
67. *Feng-ch'ao*, pp. 95–97.
68. Ibid., pp. 130, 134, 332–333, 342, 355–368, 388–392, 414, 428.
69. A report on 10 January 1908, in *Huai-pao*, quoted in Chao Chin-yü, p. 56.
70. See Ku Nai-pin, "Che-chiang ko-ming chi," quoted in Chao Chin-yü, p. 55; "Che-chün Hang-chou kuang-fu chi," in *Chung-hua min-kuo k'ai-kuo wu-shih-nien wen-hsien*, pt. 2, 4:134; *Feng-ch'ao*, p. 339. For the Chekiang students' meeting in Japan on 28 September, see *Feng-ch'ao*, pp. 361–362.
71. Ibid., pp. 90–94, 331, 337, 344, 354, 368–370, 373, 402, 406.
72. Ibid., pp. 239, 259–260, 375. According to *Feng-ch'ao*, the movement for a memorial through the Censorate and for a pan-national students' association centered around the Metropolitan University in early October.
73. *Ta-Ch'ing Te-tsung shih-lu* 581:5321 entry for *kuei-yu* day, 10th month (20 November 1907); *Feng-ch'ao*, pp. 239–240.
74. *Feng-ch'ao*, p. 139.
75. Ibid., pp. 124, 378–382, 400.
76. The name of Ma Liang appears 16 times in the two volumes of *Feng-ch'ao*. No other leader's name appears as often.
77. *Feng-ch'ao*, pp. 119–121, 135.
78. *Ta-Ch'ing Te-tsung shih-lu* 579:5306 entry for *jen-yin* day, 9th month (20 October 1907); *Feng-ch'ao*, p. 45.
79. *Feng-ch'ao*, p. 44.
80. Ibid., pp. 45, 47, 60–61.
81. Ibid., p. 103.
82. Ibid., p. 274. According to *Feng-ch'ao*, p. 412, the subscription of 13.4 million yuan was reported to the shareholders' meeting of the Kiangsu Railway Company on 13 November, while a memorial of Wang Wen-shao in November (*Kuang-hsu cheng-yao*, chüan 33) reported that it totaled 15.4 million yuan.
83. *Feng-ch'ao*, p. 385. The above memorial of Wang Wen-shao showed that the subscription in Chekiang surpassed 27.8 million yuan.
84. *Feng-ch'ao*, pp. 145, 345, 419.
85. Ibid., pp. 39–42, 145, 349, 419.
86. Ibid., pp. 409–413, 419. How much was paid for one share is not known. However, this figure seems to reflect how far short of the subscription the actual sales were.
87. Ibid., pp. 76, 350–351.
88. Ibid., pp. 319–320, 403–405. The Southern City (Nan-shih) was the Chinese district of Shanghai south of the foreign concessions.
89. These included Soochow, Chia-ting, Chia-hsing, Sung-chiang, Ningpo, and Hangchow. Ibid., pp. 81–83, 91–92, 95, 319, 327, 338, 343, 348, 351, 394, 401.
90. These are recorded in more than 15 prefectures including Ningpo, Hu-chou, Chia-hsing, Shao-hsing, Nanchang, Ch'ang-chou, and Soochow. Ibid., pp. 78, 83, 87, 90, 94, 305, 332, 338, 345, 346, 349, 394, 405.

91. Ibid., pp. 121, 124, 345, 372, 402, 403, 406, 407, 408, 483.
92. As an administrative unit, Shanghai belonged to Kiangsu province, but socially and economically it was closer to Chekiang than Kiangsu, forming a community with Hangchow. Cf. the preface of Mary B. Rankin's *Early Chinese Revolutionaries: Radical Intellectuals in Shanghai and Chekiang, 1902–1911*.
93. *Feng-ch'ao*, pp. 95–97.
94. Ibid., pp. 416–417, 489–490.
95. Ibid., pp. 489–490.
96. Ibid., p. 489.
97. Ibid., p. 276.
98. Jean Rodes, *La Chine Nouvelle*, quoted in Mary C. Wright's introduction to *China in Revolution: The First Phase, 1900–1913*, p. 17.
99. *Feng-ch'ao*, p. 490.
100. Ibid., p. 349.
101. Ibid., pp. 130, 133, 377.
102. Ibid., pp. 127, 130, 133, 327, 377.
103. Ibid., pp. 137–138, 374.
104. Ibid., pp. 131, 295, 342, 374, 407, 409.
105. Ibid., p. 388.
106. Ibid., p. 126.
107. Ibid., p. 388.
108. Ibid., p. 273. In Shanghai, there was a move to boycott the circulation of British banknotes issued by the Hui-feng Bank. *Yü-chai ts'un-kao*, 273:4a–b.
109. Ibid.
110. Ibid., p. 79, 466, 471.
111. *Feng-ch'ao*, p. 339. See note 67 above.
112. *Feng-ch'ao*, p. 45. The editor of *Feng-ch'ao* did not indicate clearly where this comment came from, but, to judge from the editorial style of *Feng-ch'ao*, it was presumably published originally in *Chung-wai jih-pao* in Shanghai.
113. *Feng-ch'ao*, p. 116.
114. Ibid., pp. 41, 116.
115. Ibid., pp. 55, 137.
116. Ibid., p. 56.
117. *Ta-Ch'ing Te-tsung shih-lu* 581:5320, entry for *i-ch'en* day, 11th month, 33rd year (12 November 1907). Also on 30 December the same year, it ordered again the Governors of Chekiang and Kiangsu to hold such outlaws in check (ibid. 583:5338). See also *Feng-ch'ao*, p. 239.
118. *Ta-Ch'ing Te-tsung shih-lu* 584:5344 entry for 10th day, 12th month, 33rd year (13 January 1908); and *Feng-ch'ao*, pp. 248, 249, in which is recorded a response to the Grand Council's telegram of 12 November 1907, p. 239; *Hai-fang tang*, p. 549.
119. Chao Chin-yü, pp. 57–58. For popular movements around this time, see Yamashita Yoneko, pp. 127–138.
120. *Feng-ch'ao*, pp. 196–197.
121. Ibid., p. 495.

122. *Hai-fang tang* no. 595 (text dated 22 March 1911).
123. Ibid., p. 656 (text dated 6 July 1908).
124. Ibid., pp. 583–592.
125. Ibid., p. 707 (text dated 22 October 1908).
126. Ibid., pp. 715–716 (text dated 20 November 1908).
127. Ibid., pp. 717–718 (text dated 3 December 1908).
128. Ibid., pp. 712–713.
129. *TFTC* 7.10:78.
130. Bland, p. 239. Editors' note: Among the private papers of J. O. P. Bland, now held at the University of Toronto, there are extensive materials pertaining to the railway issue. Volumes 23 and 24 of the Bland Papers contain his private correspondence with the directors of the British and Chinese Corporation, for which he served as agent in the railway negotiations; Volume 41 includes his "Memorandum on Railway Construction in China," which he drafted in 1906 and presented to the Chinese government on behalf of the Corporation. We are grateful to Stuart Waugh for this information.
131. This is a report of a Peking correspondent of the London *Times* (quoted here from Bland, p. 243). "Su-lu kung-ssu chih you-pu wen" (a communication from the Kiangsu Railway Company to the Board of Posts and Communications), 18 February 1911, which is included in *Hai-fang tang*, p. 943, points out the lack of invested capital for the construction of the northern section of the railway. Editors' note: The English reporter quoted by Bland is none other than Bland himself.
132. *Hai-fang tang*, p. 822 (text dated 10 November 1910).
133. Liu Chin-tsao 366:11109; *Hai-fang tang*, p. 899 (text dated 3 November 1910) points out that Liang Shih-i asked the British and Chinese Corporation to use 2 million yuan for the appropriation of the Kiangsu Railway Company.
134. *Hai-fang tang*, p. 943.
135. According to *Ch'ing-ch'ao hsu wen-hsien t'ung-k'ao*, p. 11116, this is Liu Chin-tsao's own view.
136. *Hai-fang tang*, p. 825 (text of 15 June 1910).
137. Ibid., pp. 947–949 (text of 4 March 1911).
138. Ibid., pp. 899 ff. (text of 3 November 1910).
139. *TFTC* 7.10:78–79.
140. *Hai-fang tang*, p. 946 (text of 3 March 1911).
141. *Ta-Ch'ing hsuan-t'ung cheng-chi shih-lu* 52:914, entry for the 11th day, 4th month, 3rd year (9 May 1911).
142. Chang Chien, *Se-weng tzu-ting nien-p'u*, included as an appendix to Chang I-tsu's *Chang Chien chuan-chi*, p. 66.
143. *Ta-Ch'ing Te-tsung shih-lu* 524:4829 entry for 1st day, 12th month, 29th year (17 January 1904).
144. *Ta-Ch'ing hsuan-t'ung cheng-chi shih-lu* 16:311 entry for 29th day, 6th month, 1st year (14 August 1909).
145. *Tung-fang tsa-chih*, 6.9 (October 1909) and 6.10 (November 1909).
146. Sung Tz'u-kun, *T'ang Shou-ch'ien chuan* 1-2:80–81. T'ang's new appointment was also understood as "the tactic of giving someone formal respect while

indirectly banishing him," devised by Hsu Shih-ch'ang. See Liu Chin-tsao 366:11109.
147. *Ta-Ch'ing hsuan-t'ung cheng-chi shih-lu* 24:435 entry for 16th day, 10th month, 1st year (28 November 1910). According to Sung Tz'u-kun, T'ang went to Peking after he expressed his desire to resign from the provincial judgeship of Yunnan province. There, he met the Prince Regent and delivered his "Wan-yen shu" to him, with a plea for the removal of Yuan Shih-k'ai. On the day he delivered "Wan-yen shu," he was appointed Commissioner of Education in Kiangsu. *TFTC* 7.2:32 (April 1910).
148. *Ta-Ch'ing hsuan-t'ung cheng-chi shih-lu* 38:672, entry for *chia-yin* day, 7th month, 2nd year (17 August 1910).
149. Sheng Hsuan-huai said in a letter to Wu Chung-hsi, Senior Vice-President of the Board of Posts and Communications (25 June 1908): "Having won a victory over the Court, [the gentry of] Soochow, Hangchow, and Ningpo become more and more arrogant and frequently hold meetings. Matters within the purview of our office become more troublesome because of outside interference. Newspapers have recently been criticizing me for accepting the loan." See Sheng Hsuan-huai, *Sheng Hsuan-huai wei-k'an hsin-kao*, p. 117.
150. "Chung-kuo ta-shih-chi," *TFTC* 7.8 (October 1910); *Kuo-feng pao* 1.20 (September 1910); Liu Chin-tsao, p. 11151.
151. *Ta-Ch'ing hsuan-t'ung cheng-chi shih-lu* 38:682 entry for *keng-shen* day, 7th month, 2nd year (23 August 1910).
152. This characterization is taken from "Chung-kuo ta-shih-chi pu-i," *TFTC* 7.9:69.
153. Ibid., 7.9:110–111 (October 1910).
154. Ibid., 7.9:68–69. One petition was that of the company signed by two vice-directors, and the other a petition of the shareholders who were represented by Provincial Censor Hsu Ting-ch'ao and others.
155. *Ta-Ch'ing hsuan-t'ung cheng-chi shih-lu* 40:711 entry for 13th day, 8th month, 2nd year (16 September 1910).
156. Ibid., 41:711 entry for 21st day, 8th month, 2nd year (24 September 1910); "Chung-kuo ta-shih-chi pu-i," *TFTC* 7.10:69–70.
157. Ibid., 7.10:77–79.
158. Ibid., 7.11:96–98.
159. Ibid., 7.12:107–108.
160. According to the source cited in the preceding note, Sheng told the delegates that the Board of Posts and Communications did not have the money to take over the Chekiang and Kiangsu railway companies and suggested that the contract as well as the Loan Deposit Agreement would be nullified by itself. Although this observation appears to be sympathetic to the Chekiang Railway Company, it seems to have been a tactic to extract the money to buy out the companies by abrogating the Loan Deposit Agreement. I presume this is so because the Board of Posts and Communciations asked Britain at this time if the Board could use the loan money, which it had received for railway construction, to buy out the Kiangsu Railway Company. See *Hai-fang tang*, pp. 899 ff.

161. See note 158 above.
162. See Chapter 5 in this book.
163. "Chung-kuo ta-shih-chi pu-i," *TFTC* 7–9:67; *Cheng-chih kuan-pao* 1051:471.
164. *Shih-pao*, 19 March 1910; "Chung-kuo ta-shih-chi pu-i," *TFTC* 7.10:75–77.
165. *Feng-ch'ao*, p. 361.
166. *Shih-pao*, 16 October 1910.
167. See Chapter 5 in this book.
168. For instance, one member of the National Assembly, Shao Hsi, who was from the Chekiang Provincial Assembly, protested that the Office for Drawing Up Regulations for Constitutional Government had infringed on the authority of the National Assembly by sending its own directors to the Chekiang Governor, who followed them blindly. The above description of the debate on T'ang's dismissal in the Chekiang Provincial Assembly is from *Kuo-feng pao* 1.27:2 (November 1910); and *Cheng-chih kuan-pao*, nos. 1067, 1070, 1083, 1086, and 1093 (17 October–5 November 1910).
169. *Kuo-feng pao* 1.25:3,23 (November 1910); see also the passages of *Cheng-chih kuan-pao* cited in note 158 above.
170. *Feng-ch'ao*, p. 133.
171. Ibid., p. 368.
172. Ibid., p. 135.
173. The 11 are: T'ao Pao-lin, Ts'ai Huan-wen, Yü Tsung-lien, Wang Hsu-pin, Ting Chung-li, Wang Yü-kun, Ch'en Chi-liang, Wang Tso, Ts'ai Ju-lin, Wang T'ing-yang, and Yeh Kao-shu. Ch'en Chi-liang seems to be Ch'en I-liang, who is included in the list of 113 persons in the *Feng-ch'ao* list.
174. *Feng-ch'ao*, pp. 39–42; Chang P'eng-yuan, *Li-hsien-p'ai*, pp. 270–274.
175. For Shao Hsi's argument against the loan, see *Feng-ch'ao*, pp. 183 ff. Later, as we have seen, he became a member of the National Assembly and took an active part in the incident of T'ang Shou-ch'ien's dismissal.
176. *Feng-ch'ao*, p. 274; Chang P'eng-yuan, pp. 258–263.
177. All were key members of the Constitutional Preparatory Association (see Chapter 5). Among the members of the Association who were active in the anti-loan movement were Lei Fen, Li Hou-yu, Chang Yuan-chi, Meng Chao-ch'ang, and Wang Ch'ing-mu. See Chang Yü-fa, *Ch'ing-chi ti li-hsien t'uan-t'i*, p. 368; Fujii Masao, p. 28; *Feng-ch'ao*, pp. 471 ff.
178. For the relation between the members of the provincial assembly and the enlightened intellectuals, see Chapter 5 in this book.
179. I-tu Sun (Jen), p. 72.
180. *Feng-ch'ao*, p. 179.
181. Ibid., p. 120.
182. An editorial from *Shih-pao*, reprinted in *Feng-ch'ao*, p. 158, stated: "At a time when the constitution is being prepared, the rights of the people should not be suppressed."
183. Chang Chien, "Cheng-wen lu," in his *Chang Chi-tzu chiu lu* 3:180, 181. The same phrase is found in a speech by Ma Feng-po to the merchants of Shanghai's Southern City, who said that the Court was "turning its back on constitutionalism by suppressing the spirit of the people." See *Feng-ch'ao*, p. 404.

184. *Feng-ch'ao*, p. 380. This is a part of his speech to the Kiangsu Railway Association on 9 November 1907.
185. Bland, p. 241.
186. Ibid., pp. 237–238.
187. Sheng Hsuan-huai, *Sheng Hsuan-huai wei-k'an hsin-kao*, p. 117; Bland, pp. 33, 240.
188. *Feng-ch'ao*, p. 60.
189. Ibid., p. 120.
190. Ibid., p. 113.
191. See "Hui-chih Su-Che jen-min jen-ku chü-k'uan ch'ing-hsing" in *Chung-hsing jih-pao* (Singapore), 31 December 1907. This article is also included in *Chung-hua min-kuo k'ai-kuo wu-shih-nien wen-hsien*, 1st ser., 16:668. *Feng-ch'ao*, pp. 384–385, noted his speech but did not report its content.
192. For example: "There is no way to defend ourselves against the Westerners but to achieve independence through revolution. If the Ch'ing Court is determined to fight against them [the foreigners], I shall certainly assist the dynasty." Ch'en T'ien-hua, "Ching-shih chung," in *Chung-hua min-kuo k'ai-kuo wu-shih-nien wen-hsien*, 1st ser., 16:155. See also Ch'en's "Meng hui-t'ou," in ibid., 1st ser., 16:178.
193. *Feng-ch'ao*, p. 61.
194. *TFTC* 7.10:76.
195. *Feng-ch'ao*, p. 79. A comment appeared in *Chung-wai jih-pao* also stating that people should not be obedient to the Ch'ing Court. See *Feng-ch'ao*, p. 45.
196. Chang Chien, *Se-weng tzu-ting nien-p'u*, p. 63. As we have seen, in February 1911, when the Governor General of Chihli province asked about the introduction of the foreign loan, it was T'ang Shou-ch'ien, Chang Chien, and Cheng Hsiao-hsu who received the inquiry (p. 66). After the Wuchang Uprising, Yuan Shih-k'ai said to some of the Manchu nobility: "It is possible to subjugate Li Yuan-hung and Ch'eng Te-ch'üan [recruited from government army officers and officials], but not possible to subjugate those who represent the people, like Chang Chien, T'ang Shou-ch'ien, T'ang Hua-lung [of Hupeh], and T'an Yen-k'ai [of Hunan]." It is clear that T'ang was the Chekiang representative, so it is most probable that he was the person with whom Chang Chien could discuss the politics of the time. Also, we have to remember that, during the Revolution, a telegram sent jointly by Chang Chien and T'ang Shou-ch'ien to the soldiers of northern China in support of the revolutionary cause made a great contribution to the success of the Revolution. See Chang Chien, "Cheng-wen lu," in *Chang Chi-tzu chiu-lu* 3:189.
197. *Feng-ch'ao*, p. 273.
198. Chang Chien, "Cheng-wen lu," in *Chang Chi-tzu chiu-lu*, pp. 2355–2358.
199. Chang Chien, *Se-weng tzu-ting nien-p'u*, p. 66.
200. Liu Hou-sheng, p. 184.
201. From Ma Feng-po's speech to the Southern Shanghai Merchants and Students Association, in *Feng-ch'ao*, p. 404.
202. Ibid., p. 326.

203. *Chung-kuo ko-ming chi* 1:5–8. The proclamation seems to be implying not only the Szechwan railway protection movement, but also the constitutional movement, the movement to recover foreign privileges, and the Chekiang-Kiangsu railway disputes.
204. Liu Hou-sheng showed how the Soochow-Hangchow-Ningpo railway dispute became a contributing factor in enhancing T'ang Shou-ch'ien's esteem among the gentry of southeastern China. Liu in his *Chang Chien ch'üan-chi* (p. 189) said that T'ang could not be compared with Chang Chien during the period of the Boxer Rebellion (1900), but he was as popular as Chang at the time of the Republican Revolution because of his conspicuous activities in the railway disputes. T'ang's appointment as Governor of Chekiang in the Revolution owed much to the support of Ch'u Fu-ch'eng, who was a representative of the provincial assembly as well as a member of the T'ung-meng-hui. Ch'u supported T'ang because he realized that only T'ang held the people's respect and could save Chekiang from the kind of disaster that Hunan had suffered. In Hunan, where the gentry's power was strongly felt, Chiao Ta-feng, a member of the T'ung-meng-hui of lower social standing, became military governor (*tu-tu*) but was assassinated eight days later. The rival commanders of the New Army in Chekiang, T'ing Pao-hsuan and Chou Cheng-t'an, were thus unable to claim the position over T'ang. On this account, see Ch'u Fu-ch'eng's "Chekiang hsin-hai ko-ming chi-shih."
205. Ma Hsu-lun, "Wo tsai hsin-hai che-i-nien," p. 173.
206. Chang Chien, *Se-weng tzu-ting nien-p'u*, p. 72. Because the same group that was active in the anti-loan movement took the lead in Chekiang and Kiangsu after the Wuchang Uprising, the two provinces remained calm during that turbulent period. (Liu Hou-sheng, p. 183.) Hangchow, where the Manchu garrison was stationed, avoided a bloody showdown between the Manchus and the Chinese because of T'ang's influence. (Chang Chien, "Cheng-wen lu," in *Chang Chi-tzu chiu-lu*, chüan 3; Ma Hsu-lun.) There is other evidence of T'ang's leadership around the year 1911. A report of the Japanese Consulate in Hangchow stated: "T'ang did not take the post of secretary of communication in the Nanking provincial government, although he was chosen for that post. His decision seems to have been influenced by the people of Chekiang, who complained to the Nanking provisional government that T'ang's absence might result in a popular disturbance and could adversely affect the Chekiang Railway question." (Japanese Foreign Ministry microfilm MT, 1,6,1,50,108; 7 January 1912.) When the Nanking government sought to secure the American loan with the Shanghai-Hangchow-Ningpo Railway in order to finance the Nanking provisional government, T'ang strongly opposed the idea, and so it was never realized. (Hsu Lun, "Chang Chien tsai hsin-hai ko-ming chung ti cheng-chih huo-tung, in *Hsin-hai ko-ming wu-shih-chou-nien chi-nien lun-wen-chi* 2:417.) This episode also shows that T'ang was firmly adhering to nationalistic principles and was greatly concerned with the interests of the people of Chekiang.
207. Liu Hou-sheng, p. 183. Prior to the independence of Shanghai and Soochow there were only 4 independent provinces, but just five days after the independence of the two cities 14 provinces followed suit.

208. Hsu Lun 2:412–413; Chang Chien, *Se-weng tzu-ting nien-p'u*, p. 72, and his *Chang Chi-tzu chiu-lu* 3:189.
209. Kondō Hideki, "Shindai no ennō to kanryō shakai no shūmatsu," Table 6. See also my comments on his article, in *Chungguk kŭndaesa yŏn'gu*, pp. 437–448; Ping-ti Ho, pp. 246–247.
210. *Feng-ch'ao*, pp. 293–295.
211. Fujii Masao, p. 28.
212. *Feng-ch'ao*, p. 403.
213. Ibid., pp. 404–405.
214. Ibid., pp. 385–388.
215. *Min-li pao*, 26 February 1911, quoted from Kojima Yoshio, "Shingai kakumei ni okeru Shanhai dokuritsu to shōshinsō," in *Chūgoku kindaika no shakai kōzō: Shingai kakumei no shiteki ichi*, p. 117.
216. *Feng-ch'ao*, p. 378. Li P'ing-shu was elected President of the Kiangsu Railway Association at the 9 November 1907 meeting. He was also an executive member of the Kiangsu Railway Company. Before that, he had been a county magistrate and a private secretary of Chang Chih-tung. On his career, see Fujii Masao, p. 28, and Kojima Yoshio, p. 119. Shen Man-yun was one of the originators of the Kiangsu Railway Association. (*Feng-ch'ao*, p. 2747.) He sent an anti-loan petition to the Chekiang Governor as a representative of Southern City merchants. (*Feng-ch'ao*, p. 319.) Yeh was one of the originators of the Kiangsu Railway Company and expressed some radical opinions at its meeting (*Feng-ch'ao*, pp. 378, 381).
217. Kojima Yoshio, p. 119.
218. Fujii Masao, pp. 28–29.
219. *Feng-ch'ao*, p. 65.
220. "Chiang-li yeh-shang chang-ch'eng" in Liu Chin-tsao 391:11405–11406, promulgated in 1903, encouraged the gentry to invest in manufacturing and commercial business. An editorial entitled "Lun shih-jen pu-ch'ing-ch'iu shih-yeh chih fei" appeared in *Chung-wai jih-pao* of 21 June 1904. See Lee En-han, *Wan-Ch'ing ti shou-hui k'uang-ch'üan yun-tung*, p. 159. With this encouragement, businessmen of gentry origin increased; but they do not seem to have had good relations with those merchants who were running small traditional businesses.
221. In a meeting discussing the Chekiang Railway question in Tokyo, Chang Ping-lin, who was in exile around this time, severely criticized the "deceiving and arrogant" nature of the gentry leadership. He pointed out that, if they were entrusted with the strike, they would pretend at first to lead the strike but would soon be reconciled with the government, so they should not be trusted as leaders in such a matter (*Chung-hsing jih-pao*, 1 March 1908). The article in this newspaper is included in *Chung-hua min-kuo k'ai-kuo*, 1st ser., 16:672. He correctly pinpointed an aspect of gentry leadership at the time; in fact, the gentry opposed the strike.
222. Sheng Hsuan-huai, *Sheng Hsuan-huai wei-k'an hsin-kao*, p. 117.
223. T. W. Overlach, *Foreign Financial Control in China*, pp. 61–62, quoted in Lee En-han, *Wan-Ch'ing ti shou-hui*, p. 272.

224. *Feng-ch'ao*, p. 429. The edict of 14 October 1908 on the Chekiang Railway dispute included the phrase "to accomplish diplomacy by manifesting great faithfulness." See *Ta-Ch'ing Te-tsung shih-lu* 579:5306, entry for *jen-yin* day, 10th month, 34th year.
225. Included in *Feng-ch'ao*, p. 455.
226. Horikawa Tetsuo, "Shingai kakumeizen no riken kaishū undō," pp. 9–12.
227. *Feng-ch'ao*, p. 495.
228. Sheng Hsuan-huai, "Lu-Hang-Yung wen-t'i."
229. Sheng Hsuan-hui, *Sheng Hsuan-huai wei-k'an hsin-kao*, p. 117.
230. *Shina tetsudō gairon*, p. 215.

BIBLIOGRAPHY

Ajia jimmei jiten アジア人名辞典. Sōgensha, 1940.

Araki Toshikazu 荒木敏一. "Yōsei ninen no hikō jiken to Ten Bun-kyō" 雍正二年の罷考事件と田文鏡. In *Tōyōshi kenkyū* 15.4:100–119 (March 1957).

Bland, John Otway Percy. *Recent Events and Present Policies in China*. London, Heinemann, 1912.

Cameron, Meribeth Elliott. *The Reform Movement in China, 1898–1912*. Stanford, Stanford University Press, 1931.

Chang Chien 張謇. *Chang Chien jih-chi* 張謇日記. 15 ts'e. Nanking, 1962.

——. *Chang Chi-tzu chiu-lu: chuan-lu* 張季子九錄：專錄. 3rd. ed. Taipei, Wen-hai ch'u-pan-she, 1965 reprint.

——. *Se-weng tzu-ting nien-p'u* 嗇翁自訂年譜. In Chang Hsiao-jo, *Nan-t'ung Chang Chi-chih hsien-sheng chuan-chi*. 1904. Taipei, Wen-hai ch'u-pan-she reprint, 1965.

Chang Chih-tung 張之洞. *Ch'üan-hsueh-p'ien* 勸學篇. In *Chang Wen-hsiang-kung ch'üan-chi*, chüan 201–203, 1937. Taipei, Wen-hai ch'u-pan-she reprint, 1963.

——. "Chang Hsiao-ta shang-shu tien chih Hsu hsueh-shih shu" 張孝達

尚書電致徐學使書. In Su Yü, ed., *I-chiao ts'ung-pien* 翼教叢編 6:1a. 1898. Taipei, Wen-hai ch'u-pan-she reprint, 1970.

Chang Chung-li. *The Chinese Gentry: Studies of Their Role in Nineteenth-Century Chinese Society*. Seattle, University of Washington Press, 1955.

———. *The Income of the Chinese Gentry*. Seattle, University of Washington Press, 1962.

Chang Hsiao-jo 張孝若. *Nan-t'ung Chang Chi-chih hsien-sheng chuan-chi* 南通張季直先生傳記 Shanghai, 1930. Taipei, Wen-hai ch'u-pan-she reprint, 1965.

Chang I-lin 張一麐. "Ni-fu chün-chi chang-ching nei-ko chung-shu Yin K'o-ch'ang" 擬復軍機章京內閣中書尹克昌. In *Hsin-t'ai-p'ing-shih chi*. Taipei reprint, 1966.

———. *Hsin-t'ai-p'ing-shih chi* 新太平室集. Taipei, Wen-hai ch'u-pan-she reprint, 1966.

Chang I-tsu 張怡祖. *Chang Chien chuan-chi fu-lu* 張謇傳記附錄. Taipei reprint, 1965.

Chang P'eng-yuan 張朋園. *Liang Ch'i-ch'ao yü Ch'ing-chi ko-ming* 梁啟超與清季革命. Nankang, 1964.

———. "Ch'ing-chi tzu-i-chü i-yuan ti hsuan-chü chi ch'i ch'u-shen chih fen-hsi" 清季諮議局議員的選舉及其出身之分析. In *Ssu yü yen* 5.6:13–23 (Taipei, March 1968).

———. *Li-hsien-p'ai yü hsin-hai ko-ming* 立憲派與辛亥革命. Academia Sinica, Institute of Modern History Monograph Series no. 24. Taipei, 1969.

Chang Ping-lin 章炳麟. "Yü Ma Liang shu" 與馬良書. In *T'ai-yen wen-lu ch'u-pien* 太炎文錄初編. 6 chuan. 1917–1919. Included in *Chang-shih ts'ung-shu*. 1924.

Chang Te-chün 張德鈞. "T'an Ssu-t'ung ssu-hsiang shu-p'ing" 譚嗣同思想述評. In *Li-shih yen-chiu*, 1962.3:27–60.

Chang Yü-fa 張玉法. *Ch'ing-chi ti li-hsien t'uan-t'i* 清季的立憲團體. Taipei, 1971.

Chao Chin-yü 趙金鈺. "Su-Hang-Yung t'ieh-lu chieh-k'uan ho Chiang-Che jen-min ti chü-k'uan yun-tung" 蘇杭甬鐵路借款和江浙人民的拒款運動. In *Li-shih yen-chiu*, 1959, no. 5.

Chao-lien 昭槤. *Hsiao-t'ing tsa-lu* 嘯亭雜錄. 8 chüan. Shanghai, 1909.

Chao Ping-lin 趙炳麟. *Kuang-hsu ta-shih hui-chien* 光緒大事彙鑑. In *Chao Po-yen chi* 趙柏巖集. 1922.

Ch'en Ch'ih 陳熾. *Yung-shu* 庸書. Shanghai edition, 1898.

Ch'en Ch'iu 陳虬. "Tung-yu t'iao-i" 東遊條議. In *Chih-p'ing t'ung-i* 治平通義. 1893. Excerpts printed in *Wu-hsu pien-fa* 1:217–229.

Ch'en Hsu-lu 陳旭麓. "Kuan-yü *Chiao-pin-lu k'ang-i* i-shu chien lun Feng Kuei-fen ti ssu-hsiang" 關於校邠廬抗議一書兼論馮桂芬的思想. In *Hsin chien-she*, 1964, no. 2.
Ch'en Hung-mou 陳宏謨. "Tzu-hsun ti-fang li-pi yü" 諮詢地方利弊諭. In Hsu Tung, ed., *Mu-ling shu* 2.30a (1848).
Ch'en Kung-lu 陳恭祿. *Chung-kuo chin-tai shih* 中國近代史. 2nd ed. Taipei, 1976.
Ch'en T'ien-hua 陳天華. "Ching-shih chung" 警世鐘. In *Chung-hua min-kuo k'ai-kuo wu-shih-nien wen-hsien* 中華民國開國五十年文獻. 1st ser., 16:155. Taipei, Cheng-chung shu-chü, 1961–1969.
——. "Meng hui-t'ou" 猛回頭. In *Chung-hua min-kuo k'ai-kuo wu-shih-nien wen-hsien*, 1st ser., 16:172–196.
Cheng-chih kuan-pao 政治官報. Taipei, Wen-hai ch'u-pan-she reprint, 1965.
Cheng Kuan-ying 鄭觀應. *Sheng-shih wei-yen* 盛世危言. Canton, 1900.
Ch'ien I-chi 錢儀吉, ed. *Pei-chuan chi* 碑傳集. 1893. Taipei, Wen-hai ch'u-pan-she reprint, 1973.
Ch'ien Mu 錢穆. *Chung-kuo chin-san-pai-nien hsueh-shu-shih* 中國近三百年學術史. Chungking, Shang-wu yin-shu-kuan, 1937.
Ch'ien Yung 錢泳. *Lü-yuan ts'ung-hua* 履園叢話. Taipei, Kuang-wen shu-chü, 1969.
Ch'ing-chi hsin-she chih-kuan nien-piao 清季新設職官年表. Ed. Ch'ien Shih-fu 錢實甫. Peking, Chung-hua shu-chü, 1961.
Ch'ing-chi wai-chiao shih-liao 清季外交史料. Taipei, Wen-hai ch'u-pan-she reprint, 1965.
Ch'ing-i pao ch'üan-pien 清議報全編. Yokohama, Hsin-min she, 1901.
Ch'ing-shih kao 清史稿. Peking, 1928.
Chou Chen-fu 周振甫. *Yen Fu ssu-hsiang shu-p'ing* 嚴復思想述評. Shanghai, Chung-hua shu-chü, 1940.
Chou Hao 周鎬. "Yü Wang Ch'un-hsi shu" 與王春溪書. In Ho Ch'ang-ling 賀長齡, ed., *Huang-ch'ao ching-shih wen-pien* 皇朝經世文編 22.43–44. Taipei, Kuo-feng ch'u-pan-she reprint of 1886 ed.
Chu Shou-p'eng 朱壽朋. *Kuang-hsu ch'ao tung-hua hsu-lu hsuan-chi* 光緒朝東華續錄選集. In *T'ai-wan wen-hsien ts'ung-k'an*, no. 277. Taipei, T'ai-pei yin-hang, 1969.
Ch'u Fu-ch'eng 褚輔成. "Chekiang hsin-hai ko-ming chi-shih" 浙江辛亥革命紀實. In *Chung-hua min-kuo k'ai-kuo wu-shih-nien wen-hsien*, 2nd ser., 4:120.
Ch'ü T'ung-tsu. *Local Government in China under the Ch'ing*. Cambridge, Harvard University Press, 1962.
Ch'üan Han-sheng 全漢昇. "Ch'ing-mo ti hsi-hsueh yuan ch'u Chung-kuo shuo" 清末的西學原出中國說. In Wu Hsiang-hsiang et al. 吳相湘, eds., *Tzu-ch'iang yun-tung* 自強運動. In *Chung-kuo chin-*

tai-shih lun-ts'ung 中國近代史論叢. Taipei, Cheng-chung shu-chü, 1956.

Chung-hua min-kuo k'ai-kuo wu-shih-nien wen-hsien 中華民國開國五十年文獻. Taipei, Cheng-chung shu-chü, 1966.

Chung-kuo chin-tai jen-wu lun-ts'ung 中國近代人物論叢. Peking, San-lien shu-chü, 1965.

Chung-kuo chin-tai ssu-hsiang lun-wen-chi 中國近代思想論文集. Shanghai, Jen-min ch'u-pan-she, 1958.

Chung-kuo hsien-tai-shih ts'ung-k'an 中國現代史叢刊. Ed. Wu Hsiang-hsiang. Taipei, Cheng-chung shu-chü, 1960.

Chung-kuo ko-ming chi 中國革命記. Shanghai, Shang-hai tzu-yu-she, 1912.

Chung-kuo ta-shih chi pu-i 中國大事記補遺.

Chung-wai jih-pao 中外日報. Shanghai.

Cohen, Paul A. *Between Tradition and Modernity: Wang T'ao and Reform in Late Ch'ing China*. Cambridge, Harvard University Press, 1974.

de Bary, Wm. Theodore et al., eds. *Sources of Chinese Tradition*. New York, Columbia University Press, 1960.

Fairbank, John K., ed. *The Chinese World Order: Traditional China's Foreign Relations*. Cambridge, Harvard University Press, 1968.

Fang Tsung-ch'eng 方宗誠. "O-li yueh" 鄂吏約. In Sheng K'ang, ed., *Huang-ch'ao ching-shih wen hsu-pien*, chüan 25, li-cheng 8, shou-ling 2.

Feng Kuei-fen 馮桂芬. *Hsien-chih-t'ang kao* 顯志堂稿. 1876 ed.

——. *Chiao-pin-lu k'ang-i* 校邠廬抗議. Shanghai, 1897. Taipei, Wen-hai ch'u-pan-she, 1971. Reprint of 1897 edition.

——. "Chih yang-ch'i i" 製洋器議. In *Chiao-pin-lu k'ang-i* 2.

——. "Fu hsiang-chih i" 復鄉職議. In *Chiao-pin-lu k'ang-i* 1.

——. "Kung ch'u-chih i" 公黜陟議. In *Chiao-pin-lu k'ang-i* 1.

——. "Sheng tse li-li" 省則例議. In *Chiao-pin-lu k'ang-i* 1.

——. "Shou p'in-min i" 收貧民議. In *Chiao-pin-lu k'ang-i* 1.

——. "Ts'ai hsi-hsueh i" 采西學議. In *Chiao-pin-lu k'ang-i* 2.

Feng Yu-lan 馮友蘭. "Liang Ch'i-ch'ao ti ssu-hsiang" 梁啟超底思想. In *Chung-kuo chin-tai ssu-hsiang-shih lun-wen-chi*. Ed. Shang-hai jen-min ch'u-pan-she. Shanghai, Shang-hai jen-min ch'u-pan-she, 1958.

Feuerwerker, Albert. *China's Early Industrialization: Sheng Hsuan-huai, 1844–1916, and Mandarin Enterprise*. Cambridge, Harvard University Press, 1958.

Fincher, John Howard. "Political Provincialism and the National Revolution." In *China in Revolution: The First Phase, 1900–1913*. Ed. Mary Wright. New Haven, Yale University Pres, 1968.

Fujii, Masao 藤井正夫. "Shinmatsu Kō Setsu ni okeru tetsuro mondai to burujoa seiryoku no ichi sokumen" 清末江浙における鉄路

問題とブルジョア勢力の一側面. In *Rekishigaku kenkyū* 183:22-30 (May 1955).

Fujitsuka Chikashi 藤塚鄰. "Richō no gakujin to Kenryū bunka" 李朝の學人と乾隆文化. In Keijō Teikoku Daigaku Hōbun Gakkai, ed., *Chōsen Shina bunka no kenkyū* 朝鮮支那文化の研究 Tokyo, 1929.

Fujiwara Sadamu 藤原定. "Shindai no hōken shisō to hōkensei no zanzon" 清代の封建思想と封建制の殘存. In *Mantetsu chōsa geppō* 20.4:1-61 (April 1940).

Gernet, J. *Le Monde Chinois*. Paris, Libraire Armand Colin, 1972.

Goodrich, L. Carrington and Chaoying Fang, eds. *Dictionary of Ming Biography: 1368-1644*. New York: Columbia University Press, 1976.

Hai-fang tang 海防檔. Ed. Institute of Modern History, Academica Sinica. Taipei, 1957.

Hashimoto Takakatsu. "Gen Fuku no chūsei hikaku bunka ron" 嚴復の中西比較文化論. In *Tōhōgaku* 41:76-90 (1971).

Hatano Yoshihiro 波多野善大. "Ahen sensō ni okeru tai-Ei kyōkō ron no imi suru mono" アヘン戰爭における對英硬強論の意味するもの. In *Kōza kindai Ajia shisō shi* 講座近代アジア思想史. Tokyo, Kōbundō, 1960.

Hazama Naoki 狭間直樹. "Santō Raiyō bōdō shoron: Shingai kakumei ni okeru jimmin tōsō no yakuwari" 山東萊陽暴動小論=辛亥革命における人民闘爭の役割. In *Tōyōshi kenkyū* 22.2:1-27 (October 1963).

Ho Ch'ang-ling 賀長齡, ed. *Huang-ch'ao ching-shih wen-pien* 皇朝經世文編. Taipei, Kuo-feng ch'u-pan-she, reprint 1963.

Ho Ch'i 何啟 and Hu Li-yuan 胡禮垣. *Hsin-cheng chen-ch'üan* 新政真詮. 1900.

Ho Ping-ti. *The Ladder of Success in Imperial China: Aspects of Social Mobility, 1368-1911*. New York, Columbia University Press, 1962.

Hong Tae-yong 洪大容. "Kŏnjŏng p'ildam" 乾淨筆譚. In *Tamhŏn yŏn'gi* 甚軒燕記, Yŏnhaeng-nok sŏnjip 燕行路選集 ed., 1960.

———. "Kyebang ilgi" 桂坊日記. In *Tamhŏn yŏn'gi*.

Horikawa Tetsuo 堀川哲男. "Shingai kakumeizen no riken kaishū undō" 辛亥革命前の利權回收運動. In *Tōyōshi kenkyū* 21.2:1-37 (September 1962).

Hsi Huang 秘璜, Liu Yung 劉墉 et al. *Huang-ch'ao wen-hsien t'ung-kao* 皇朝文獻通考. 300 chüan. Che-chiang shu-chü ed., 1882.

Hsia Tung-yuan 夏東元. "Lun yang-wu p'ai" 論洋務派. In *Hsin chien-she* 新建設, 1964, no. 5.

Hsiang-hsueh hsin-pao 湘學新報. Taipei, Ta-tung reprint, 1966.

Hsiang-pao lei-tsuan 湘報類纂. Taiwan, Ta-tung shu-chü reprint, 1969.

Hsiao I-shan 蕭一山. *Ch'ing-tai t'ung-shih* 清代通史. Taipei, Commercial Press, 1962.

Hsiao Kung-ch'üan 蕭公權. *Chung-kuo cheng-chih ssu-hsiang shih* 中國政治思想史. Taipei, Chung-hua wen-hua ch'u-pan shih-yeh wei-yuan-hui, 1954.

———. *Rural China: Imperial Control in the Nineteenth Century*. Seattle, University of Washington Press, 1960.

Hsieh Chin-luan 謝金鑾. "Chü-kuan chih-yung" 居官致用. In Hsu Tung, ed., *Mu-ling shu* 1:51–53.

Hsieh Pin 謝彬. *Chung-kuo t'ieh-tao shih* 中國鐵道史. Shanghai, Chung-hua shu-chü, 1934.

Hsin-hai ko-ming 辛亥革命. Ed. Chung-kuo shih-hsueh-hui. Peking, 1957.

Hsin-min ts'ung-pao 新民叢報. Tokyo, 1902–1930.

Hsu Lun 徐崙. "Chang Chien tsai hsin-hai ko-ming chung ti cheng-chih huo-tung" 張謇在辛亥革命中的政治活動. In *Hsin-hai ko-ming wu-shih-chou-nien chi-nien lun-wen-chi* 辛亥革命五十周年紀念論文集. Vol. II. Peking, Chung-hua shu-chü, 1962. II, 417.

Hsu Shih-ch'ang 徐世昌, ed. *Yen-Li i-shu* 顏李遺書. In Wang Han 王灝, ed., *Chi-fu ts'ung-shu* 畿輔叢書. 1879.

Hsu Tung 徐棟, ed. *Mu-ling shu* 牧令書. 1848.

———. *Pao-chia shu* 保甲書. 1848.

Hsu Tzu-ling 徐子苓. "Ying-shang chiao-yü Ts'ao chün mu-chih-ming" 潁上教諭曹君墓志銘. In Miao Ch'üan-sun, ed., *Hsu pei-chuan chi* 46.7a–7b.

Hsuan-t'ung cheng-chi 宣統政紀. Ta-lien, Liao-hai shu-she, 1934.

Hsueh Fu-ch'eng 薛福成. "Pien-fa" 變法. In *Ch'ou-yang ch'u-i Yung-an ch'üan-chi* (1895), 20b–22a.

———. "Hsi-fa wei kung-kung chih li shuo" 西法為公共之理說. *Hai-wai wen-pien* 海外文編. In *Yung-an ch'üan chi*: 3:1b–2a.

———. *Ch'u shih Ying Fa I Pi ssu-kuo jih-chi*, 出使英法意比四國日記. *Hai-wei wen-pien*. In *Yung-an ch'üan-chi*, chüan 3.

———. "Tsai-lun O-lo-ssu li-kuo chih shih" 再論俄羅斯立國之勢. *Hai-wei wen-pien*. In *Yung-an ch'üan-chi*, chüan 3.

Hu Pin 胡濱. *Chung-kuo chin-tai kai-liang-chu-i ssu-hsiang* 中國近代改良主義思想. Peking, Chung-hua shu-chü, 1964.

Hu Sheng-wu 胡繩武 and Chin Ch'ung-chi 金冲及. *Lun Ch'ing-mo ti li-hsien yun-tung* 論清末的立憲運動. Shanghai, Jen-min ch'u-pan-she, 1959.

Hu Shih 胡適 et al. *Hu Shih yü Chung-hsi wen-hua* 胡適與中西文化. Taipei, Shui-niu ch'u-pan-she, 1967.

Liu Hou-sheng 劉厚生. *Chang Chien chuan-chi* 張謇傳記. Hong Kong, Sung-men shu-tien, 1965.

Liu Hung-ao 劉鴻翱. "Feng-chien lun" 封建論. In Sheng K'ang, ed. *Huang-ch'ao ching-shih wen hsu-pien*, chüan 11.

Liu Ping-chang 劉秉章. "Tsun-ch'a Chiang-hsi cheng-shou ting-ts'ao shu" 遵查江西徵收丁漕疏. In Sheng K'ang, ed., *Huang-ch'ao ching-shih wen hsu-pien*, chüan 32.

Lo Erh-kang 羅爾綱. *T'ai-p'ing t'ien-kuo shih-kao* 太平天國史稿. Shanghai, Shang-wu yin-shu-kuan, 1937.

Lojewski, F. O. "Reform within Tradition: Feng Kuei-fen's Proposal for Local Administration." In *Ch'ing-hua hsueh-pao*, n. s. 11:1.2:147–159 (1975).

Lu Chi 陸機. "Wu-teng lun" 五等論. In Hsiao T'ung 蕭統, ed., *Wen-hsuan* 文選, chüan 54.

Lu Shih-chi 魯仕驥. "Ts'ang-chou chih-hsien Hsu-kung Shih-tso hsing-chuang" 滄州知州徐公時作行狀. In Ch'ien I-chi, ed., *Pei-chuan chi*, chüan 102.

Ma Hsu-lun 馬敍倫. "Wo tsai hsin-hai che-i-nien" 我在辛亥這一年. In *Hsin-hai ko-ming hui-i lu* 辛亥革命回憶錄, Vol. I. Peking, Chung-hua shu-chü, 1961.

Marsh, Robert M. *The Mandarins: The Circulation of Elites in China, 1600–1900*. Glencoe, Free Press of Glencoe, 1961.

Meng Sen 孟森. "Tsou-hsiao an" 奏銷案. In Meng Sen, *Ming-Ch'ing-shih lun-chu chi-k'an* 明清史論著集刊. Taipei, Shih-chieh shu-chü, 1961.

Miao Chia-yü 繆嘉譽. "Ch'ung-yang k'o-wen" 崇陽客問. In Sheng K'ang, ed., *Huang-ch'ao ching-shih wen hsu-pien*, chüan 26.

Miao Ch'üan-sun 繆荃孫, ed. *Hsu pei-chuan chi* 續碑傳集. 86 chüan. Chiang-ch'u pien-i shu-chü, 1910.

Mihashi Fujio 三橋富治男. *Osuman Toruko shiron* オスマントルコ史論. Tokyo, Yoshikawa kōbunkan, 1966.

Min-hu pao 民呼報.

Min-li pao 民立報.

Min Tu-ki 閔斗基. "Musul pyŏnbŏp saryŏ yŏngsŭp" 戊戌變法史料零拾. In *Paiksan hakpo* 白山學報 Vol. 8 (1970).

——. "Musul pyŏnbŏp undong ŭi paegyŏng e taehayŏ: t'ŭkhi ch'ŏngnyup'a wa yangmup'a rŭl chungsim ŭro" 戊戌變法運動의 背景에對하여—特히 清流派와 洋務派를 中心으로. In *Tongyang sahak yŏn'gu* 東洋史學研究 5:101–147 (1971).

——. "Ch'ŏngdae 'saenggamch'ŭng ŭi sŏngkyŏk; t'ŭkhi kŭ kyech'ŭngjŏk kaebyŏlsŏng ul chungsim ŭro" 清代生監層의 性格—특히 그 階層的個別性을 中心으로. In *Chungguk kŭndaesa yŏn'gu*.

———. "Ch'ŏngmal sinsa ŭi ŭigi ŭisik kwa kaehyŏk" 清末紳士의危機意識과改革. In *Chungguk kŭndaesa yŏn'gu*.

———. "Ch'ŏng-mal chaŭiguk ŭi Kaesŏ kwa kŭ Sŏngkyŏk" 清末諮議局의開設과 그 性格. In *Chungguk kŭndaesa yŏn'gu*.

———. *Chungguk kŭndaesa yŏn'gu: Sinsach'ŭng ŭi sasang kwa haengdong* 中國近代史研究—紳士層의思想과行動—潮閣. Seoul, Ilchogak, 1973.

———. "Ch'ŏngjŏ ŭi hwangje t'ongch'i wa sasang t'ongje ŭi silje: Chŭngjŏng moyŏk sakkŏn kwa *Taeŭi kangmi-rok* ŭl chungsim ŭro" 清朝의皇帝統治와思想統制의實際—曾靜謀逆事件과 '大義覺迷錄'을中心으로. In *Chungguk kŭndaesa yŏn'gu*.

———. "Chungguk ŭi chŏnt'ongjŏk chŏngch'isang: ponggŏn kunhyŏn nonŭi rŭl chungsim ŭro" 中國의傳統的政治像—封建郡縣論議를中心으로. In *Chungguk kŭndaesa yŏn'gu*, 1973.

———. "Ch'ŏngdae maguje wa haengjŏng chilsŏ ŭi t'ŭksŏng" 清代幕友制 와行政秩序의特性. In *Chungguk kŭndaesa yŏn'gu*.

———. "Sipku segimal chungguk ŭi Kehyŏk undong kwa sanghae ŭi sangin gurup" 十九世紀末中國의改革運動과上海의商人그룹. In *Tongyang sahak yŏn'gu* 東洋史學研究 11:99-126 (1977).

———. *Chungguk kŭndae kaehyŏk undong ŭi yŏn'gu—Kang Yu-wi chungsim ŭi 1898 nyŏn kaehyŏk undong* 中國近代改革運動의研究—康有爲中心의 1898 年改革運動. Seoul, Ilchogak, 1985.

———. "Kankoku ni okeru Chūgoku gendaishi kenkyū ni tsuite" 韓國に於ける中國現代史研究について. Tr. Ho Pei-ch'ung. In *Chikaki-hi Arite*, no. 10 (November 1986).

———. "Kankoku ni okeru Chūgokushi kenkyū no tenkai" 韓國に於ける中國史研究の展開. In T'eng Wei-tsao 滕維藻, Wang Chung-jung 王仲榮, and Okuzaki Yūji 奥崎裕司, eds., *Higashi-ajia sekaishi tankyū* 東アジア世界史探求. Tokyo, December 1986.

Minamoto Ryōen 源了圓. "Bakumatsu ishin no seishin jōkyō" 幕末維新の精神狀況. In Ishida Ichirō, ed. *Nihon bunkashi gairon*.

Miyazaki Ichisada 宮崎市定. *Kakyo: Chūgoku no shiken jigoku* 科擧: 中国の試驗地獄. Tokyo, Chūō Kōronsha, 1963, revised edition, Chūkō shinsho, Vol. XV. Original edition, Osaka, Akitaya, 1946.

———. "Yōsei jidai chihō seiji no jitsujō—shushi yushi to Rokushu kōan" 雍正時代地方政治の実況. In *Tōyōshi kenkyū* 18.3:1-26 (December 1959).

Mo Pei 墨悲, ed. *Chiang-Che t'ieh-lu feng-ch'ao* 江浙鐵路風潮, Vol.

I. Shanghai, 1907. Reprinted 1909. Taipei, Committee on Kuomintang Party History, 1968 photocopy.

Mo Yu-chih 莫友芝. "Wai-chiu Hsia Fu-t'ang hsien-sheng mu-chih-ming" 外舅夏輔堂先生墓志銘. In Miao Ch'üan-sun, ed., *Hsu pei-chuan chi* 43.17a.

Mou Shu-tzu 牟樹滋. "Lun ko-sheng ch'ing-yuan kuo-hui tai-piao chi-ying ch'ou-pei ti-fang tzu-chih" 論各省請願國會代表必應籌備地方自治, part 3. In *Sh'un-tien shih-pao*, 29 September 1908.

Muramatsu Yūji 村松祐次. "Shindai no shinshi jinushi ni okeru tochi to kanshoku: Sekkō-shō Eikō-ken Ko shi shihi giden o megutte" 清代の紳士地主における土地と官職：浙江省永康縣胡氏試費義田をめぐって. In *Hitotsubashi ronsō* 44.6: 24–52 (December 1960).

Nagahama Masatoshi 長濱政壽. *Chihō jichi* 地方自治. Tokyo, 1952.

Nakamura Eiko 中村榮孝, ed. "Jidai kikō mokuroku" 事大紀行目錄. In *Seikyū gakusō* 1:177–184 (1930).

Nakamura Keichoku 中村敬直. "Shōzan sensei shisō hyōgen" 象山先生詩鈔評原. Quoted in Ishida Ichirō, *Nihon bunkashi gairon*.

Nan-yang jih-jih kuan-pao 南洋日日官報.

Nivison, David S. and Arthur F. Wright, eds. *Confucianism in Action*. Stanford, Stanford University Press, 1959.

Nomura Kōichi 野村浩一. "Shinmatsu kōyō gakuha no keisei to Kō Yū i gaku no rekishiteki igi: Jizoku no teikoku no botsuroku" 清末公羊学派の形成と康有為学の歴史的意義：持続の帝国の没落. In *Kokka gakkai zasshi* 71.7:1–61 (July 1957); 72.1:32–64 (January 1958); 72.3:48–112 (March 1958).

——. *Kindai Chūgoku no seiji to shisō* 近代中国の政治と思想. Tokyo, Chikuma shobō, 1964.

Oda Man 織田萬. *Hōgaku tsūron* 法學通論. Tokyo, 1902.

Ŏm Yŏng-sik 嚴永植. "Munsang ŭi yangmu sasang" 文祥의洋務思想. In *Yangmu sasang kwa kŭndae pyŏng-gongŏp ŭi hŭnggi* 洋務思想과近代兵工業의興起. Seoul, 1975.

Ono Kazuko 小野和子. "Shinsho no shisō tōsei o megutte" 清初の思想統制をめぐって. In *Tōyōshi kenkyū* 18.3:99–123 (December 1959).

Onogawa Hidemi 小野川秀美. *Shinmatsu seiji shisō kenkyū* 清末政治思想研究. Kyoto, Kyōtō Daigaku, Tōyōshi Kenkyūkai, 1960.

Pao Yun 寶鋆 et al. *Ta-Ch'ing Mu-tsung i-huang-ti shih-lu* 大清穆宗毅皇帝實錄. 374 chüan. Taipei, Hua-wen shu-chü, 1964.

Pei-yang kuan-pao 北洋官報.

P'i Hsi-jui 皮錫瑞. "Shih-fu-t'ang jih-chi" 師伏堂日記. Reprinted in *Hu-nan li-shih tzu-liao* 湖南歷史資料 2:124 (1959).

Po Ching-wei 柏景偉. *Li-hsi ts'ao-t'ang chi* 澧西草堂集. 8 chüan, Nanking, 1923.

Rankin, Mary B. *Early Chinese Revolutionaries: Radical Intellectuals in Shanghai and Chekiang, 1902–1911.* Cambridge, Harvard University Press, 1971.

Reinsch, Paul S. *Intellectual and Political Currents in the Far East.* Boston and New York, Houghton Mifflin, 1911.

Rodes, Jean. *La Chine Nouvelle.* Paris, 1910.

Saka Chiaki 坂千秋. "Chihō jichi no kaiko to tembō" 地方自治の回顧と展望. In *Jichisei happu gojisshūnen kinen rombunshū* 自治制發布五十周年記念論文集. Tokyo, Tōkyō Shisei Chōsakai, 1938.

Sakai Tadao 酒井忠夫. *Chūgoku zensho no kenkyū* 中国善書の研究. Tokyo, Kōbundō, 1960.

Schiffrin, Harold Z. *Sun Yat-sen and the Origins of the Chinese Revolution.* Berkeley, University of California Press, 1968.

Schwartz, Benjamin I. *In Search of Wealth and Power: Yen Fu and the West.* Cambridge, Harvard University Press, 1964.

———. "The Limits of 'Tradition versus Modernity' as Categories of Explanation: The Case of the Chinese Intellectuals." In *Daedalus* 101.2:71–88 (spring 1972).

Shen Tsu-hsien 沈祖憲 et al. *Jung-an ti-tzu chi* 容庵弟子集. Taipei, Wen-hsing shu-tien reprint, 1962.

Shen T'ung-sheng 沈桐生, ed. *Kuang-hsu cheng-yao* 光緒政要. Shanghai, 1909.

Sheng En-i 盛恩頤 et al. *Yü-chai ts'un-kao* 愚齋存稿. Taipei, Wen-hai ch'u-pan-she, 1963.

———. "Hsing-shu" 行書. In *Yü-chai ts'un-kao.*

Sheng Hsuan-huai 盛宣懷. *Sheng Hsuan-huai wei-k'an hsin-kao* 盛宣懷未刊信稿. Peking, Hsin-hua shu-tien, 1960.

———. "Hu-Hang-Yung wen-t'i" 滬杭甬問題. In *Hai-fang tang, t'ieh-lu* 595: 953–955.

Sheng K'ang 盛康, ed. *Huang-ch'ao ching-shih wen hsu-pien* 皇朝經世文續編. 120 chüan. 1897. Taipei reprint, 1972.

Shih Chin 石錦. "Ch'ing-mo tzu-ch'iang kuan ti nei-jung fen-yeh chi ch'i yen-pien" 清末自強觀的內容分野及其演變. In Li En-han 李恩涵 and Chang P'eng-yuan 張朋園, eds., *Chin-tai Chung-kuo chih-shih fen-tzu yü tzu-ch'iang yun-tung* 近代中國知識份子與自強運動. Taipei, Shih-huo ch'u-pan-she, 1977.

Shih-pao 時報. Shanghai, 1904–1937.

Shimada Kenji 島田虔次. *Shushigaku to Yōmeigaku* 朱子学と陽明学. Tokyo, Iwanami Shoten, 1967.

Shina keizai zensho 支那經濟全書. Tōa Dōbunkai, ed. Shanghai, 1908.

Shina tetsudō gairon 支那鐵道概論. Dairen, 1927.

Shinkoku gyōseihō 清国行政法. Rinji Taiwan Kyūkan Chōsakai dai ichi bu, ed. 8 vols. Tokyo. Kaneko insatsujo reprint, 1936.

Su-erh-na 素爾訥, ed. (*Ch'in-ting*) *Hsueh-cheng ch'üan-shu* 欽定學政全書. Taipei, Wen-hai ch'u-pan-she reprint, 1968.

Suematsu Kaiichiro 末松偕一郎. *Chihō jichi seido yōgi* 地方自治制度要義. Tokyo, 1923.

Sun Chia-nai 孫家鼐. "I-fu k'ai-pan ching-shih ta-hsueh-t'ang che" 議禮開辦京師大學堂摺. In *Wu-hsu pien-fa*, II, 425–429.

——. "Tsou-ch'en ch'ou-pan ta-hsueh-t'ang ta-kai ch'ing-hsing che" 奏陳籌辦大學堂大概情形摺. In *Chung-hua min-kuo k'ai-kuo wu-shih-nien wen-hsien*, Ser. 1, 8:311–313.

Sun I-tu (Jen). *Chinese Railways and British Interests, 1898–1911*. New York, Kings Crown Press, Columbia University, 1954.

Sun I-yen 孫衣言. "Liang hsien-sheng mu-piao" 梁先生墓表. In Miao Ch'üan-sun, ed., *Hsu pei-chuan chi*, chüan 43.

Sun Yat-sen 孫逸仙 "Po pao-huang-pao shu" 駁保皇報書. In *Ko-ming wen-hsien*, III, 222–297. Taipei, 1953.

Sung Chiao-jen 宋教仁. *Wo chih li-shih* 我之歷史 1919. Taipei, Wen-hsing shu-tien reprint, 1962.

Sung Tz'u-kun 宋慈裒. *T'ang Shou-ch'ien chuan* 湯壽潛傳. Nanking, Kuo-shih-kuan, 1948.

Ta-Ch'ing hsuan-t'ung cheng-chi shih-lu 大清宣統政紀實錄. 170 chüan, Taipei, Hua-wen shu-chü, 1964 reprint.

Ta-Ch'ing Shih-tsung hsien huang-ti shih-lu 大清世宗憲皇帝寶錄 159 chüan.

Ta-Ch'ing Te-tsung huang-ti shih-lu 大清德宗皇帝寶錄. 1921. Taipei, Hua-wen shu-chü, reprint 1965.

Ta-i chüeh-mi lu 大義覺迷錄. Original ed. 1730.

Ta-kung-pao 大公報.

Ta-lu tsa-chih 大陸雜誌. 3 chüan. Taipei, 1956.

Tai Wang 戴望. "Ku chih-fang chün-hsien lun po-i" 顧職方郡縣論駁議. In Sheng K'ang, ed., *Huang-ch'ao ching-shih wen hsu-pien*, chüan 24, li-cheng 7, shou-ling, pp. 7a–9b.

Takahashi Tōru 高橋享. "Kosaiwo no buntai hansei" 弘齋王の文體反正. In *Seikyū gakusō* 7:1–14 (1932).

T'an, Chester. *Chinese Political Thought in the Twentieth Century*. Garden City, Anchor Books, 1971.

T'an Ssu-t'ung 譚嗣同. *T'an Ssu-t'ung ch'üan-chi* 譚嗣同全集. Peking, San-lien shu-chü, 1954.

——. "Chih Wang K'ang-nien shu" 致汪康年書. In *T'an Ssu-t'ung ch'üan-chi*, pp. 339–368.

——. "Ssu-wei i-hu t'ai tuan-shu: Pei pao Yuan-chang" 思緯壹壺臺短書—貝報元徵. In *T'an Ssu-t'ung ch'üan-chi*, pp. 389–430.

———. "Shang Ch'en Yu-ming fu-pu shu" 上陳右銘撫部書. In *Hunan li-shih tzu-liao* 湖南歷史資料. Changsha, 1959.

T'ang Chen 湯震. "Tsun-hsiang lun" 尊相論. In *Wei-yen* 危言. Shanghai reprint, 1959.

———. *T'ang Chih-hsien hsien-sheng wei-yen* 湯蟄仙先生危言. Shanghai, 1890.

T'ao Shu 陶澍. "Yen-chin chin-kun pao-ts'ao so-lou-kuei p'ien" 嚴禁衿棍包攬陋規篇. In Sheng K'ang, ed., *Huang-ch'ao ching-shih wen hsu-pien*.

"T'ien-chin fu tzu-chih-chü shih-pan tiao-ch'a chien-ch'ang" 天津府自治局試辦調查簡章. In *Tung-fang tsa-chih* 4.4:172–176 (1907).

Tikhvinskii, S. L. *Chung-kuo pien-fa wei-hsin yun-tung ho K'ang Yu-wei* 中國變法維新和康有為 (The Reform Movement in China and K'ang Yu-wei). Chinese translation of *Dvizhenie za reformy v. Kitae v. kontse XIX v. i Kan Iu-vei*. Peking, San-lien shu-chü, 1962.

Ting Wen-chiang 丁文江, ed. *Liang Jen-kung hsien-sheng nien-p'u ch'ang-pien ch'u-kao* 梁任公先生年譜長編初稿. Taipei, Shih-chieh shu-chü, 1959.

Toriumi Yasushi. "Recent Trends in the Studies on Modernization in Japan." In *Acta Asiatica* 13:106 (Tokyo, 1967).

Tōyama Shigeki. "Reforms of the Meiji Restoration and the Birth of Modern Intellectuals." In *Acta Asiatica* 13:55–99 (1967).

Tsai-tse 載澤 et al. *K'ao-ch'a cheng-chih jih-chi* 考察政治日記. Peking, June 1908.

Tso Tsung-t'ang 左宗棠. *Tso Wen-hsiang kung ch'üan-chi* 左文襄公全集. 13 chüan. Changsha, 1891–1892.

"Tsou-ch'ing li-hsien chih feng shuo" 奏請立憲之風說. In *Tung-fang tsa-chih* 1.5 (8 July 1904).

Tuan-fang 端方. *Tuan Chung-min kung tsou-kao* 端忠敏公奏稿. Preface by Yang Chung-hsi, 1918.

Tung-hua hsu-lu 東華續錄. Ed. Wang Hsien-chien. 430 chüan. Peking 1942.

Tung-hua lu. See *Kuang-hsu ch'ao tung-hua lu*.

Uete Michairi 植手通有. "Meiji keimō shisō no keisei" 明治啟蒙思想の形成. 3 pts. In *Shisō*, nos. 1, 2, 6 (1967).

Vinacke, H. M. *Modern Constitutional Development in China*. Princeton, Princeton University Press, 1920.

Waley Arthur, tr. *The Analects of Confucius*. London, Allen & Unwin, 1938.

Wang Chia-chien 王家儉. "Wen-hsiang tui-yü shih-chü ti jen-shih chi ch'i tzu-ch'iang ssu-hsiang" 文祥對於時局的認識及其自強思想. In *Kuo-li Tai-wan shih-fan ta-hsueh li-shih hsueh-pao*, no. 1 (1973).

Wang Chih 王植. "Shen-shih" 紳士. In Hsu Tung, ed., *Mu-ling shu* 10.24b–25b.

Wang Erh-min 王爾敏. "Ch'ing-chi chih-shih fen-tzu ti Chung-t'i Hsi-yung lun" 清季知識分子的中體西用論. In *Wan-Ch'ing cheng-chih ssu-hsiang shih-lun* 晚清政治思想史論. Taipei, 1969.

Wang Feng-sheng 王鳳生. "Shen-shih" 紳士. In Hsu Tung, ed., *Mu-ling shu* 16.26b–27a.

Wang Fu-chih 王夫之. *Tu T'ung-chien lun* 讀通鑑論. Taipei, Shih-chieh shu-chü, 1962.

Wang Hui-tsu 王輝祖. *Hsueh-chih i-shuo* 學治臆說. In *Wang Lung-chuang hsien-sheng i-shu* 王龍莊先生遺書. 1873.

——. *Ping-t'a meng-hen lu* 病榻夢痕錄. In *Wang Lung-chuang hsien-sheng i-shu*.

Wang I-nien 汪詒年. *Wang Jang-ch'ing hsien-sheng chuan-chi* 汪穰卿先生傳記. Taipei, Wen-hai ch'u-pan-she reprint, 1966.

Wang K'ang-nien 汪康年. "Su-Hang-Yung-lu shih-mo lueh-chi" 蘇杭甬路始末略記. In *Wang Jang-ch'ing hsien-sheng pi-chi* 汪穰卿先生筆記. Taipei, Wen-hai ch'u-pan-she reprint, 1969.

Wang Shih-to 汪士鐸. *Wang Hui-weng I-ping jih-chi* 汪悔翁乙丙日記. Peiping, 1936.

Wang T'ao 王韜. *T'ao-yuan wen-lu wai-pien* 弢園文錄外編. Hong Kong, 1883. Taipei reprint, 1963.

——. "I-yen yuan-pa" 易言原跋. In Cheng Kuan-ying, *Tseng-ting sheng-shih wei-yen*, 2nd ed.

Wang Wei-ch'eng 王維誠. "Wang T'ao ti ssu-hsiang" 王韜的思想. In *Chung-kuo chin-tai ssu-hsiang-shih lun-wen-chi*.

Weng T'ung-ho 翁同龢. *Weng T'ung-ho jih-chi* 翁同龢日記. Taipei, Cheng-wen, 1970.

Wright, Mary C., ed. *China in Revolution: The First Phase, 1900–1913*. New Haven, Yale University Press, 1968.

Wu Hsiang-hsiang 吳相湘. *Sung Chiao-jen – Chung-kuo min-chu hsien-cheng ti hsien-ch'ü* 宋教仁－中國民主憲政的先驅. Taipei, 1965.

Wu-hsu pien-fa 戊戌變法. Chung-kuo shih-hsueh-hui, ed. Shanghai, Shen-chou kuo-kuang-she, 1953. 2nd ed., 1958.

Wu-hsu pien-fa tang-an shih-liao 戊戌變法檔案史料. Kuo-chia tang-an-chü, ed. Peking, Chung-hua shu-chü, 1958.

Wu Jung-kuang 吳榮光. "Yang-min" 養民. In Hsu Tung, ed., *Mu-ling shu* 15.14b–15a.

Yamanoi Yū 山井湧. "Minmatsu Shinsho ni okeru keisei chiyō no gaku" 明末清初における経世致用の学. In *Tōhōgaku ronshū* 1:136–150 (February 1954).

Yamashita Yoneko 山下米子. "Shingai kakumei no jiki no minshū undō: Kō Setsu chiiki no nōmin undō o chūshin to shite" 辛亥革命の時期の民衆運動：江浙地区の農民運動を中心として. In *Tōyō bunka kenkyūjo kiyō*, no. 37 (1965).

Yang Hsiang-chi 楊象濟. "I hsing-ming ch'ien-ku pu shu-hsien" 以刑名錢穀補屬縣. In Sheng K'ang, ed., *Huang-ch'ao ching-shih wen hsu-pien*, chüan 27, *li-cheng* 10, *mu-yu*, pp. 42–62.

Yang-wu yun-tung wen-hsien hui-pien 洋務運動文獻彙編. Ed. Shih-chieh shu-chü. 8 vols. Taipei, 1963.

Yano Jin'ichi 矢野仁一. *Kindai Shina shi* 近代支那史. Kyoto, Kōbundō, 1926.

Yao Ch'un 姚椿, ed. *Kuo-ch'ao wen-lu* 國朝文錄. 82 chüan. 1805.

Yen Fu 嚴復. "Lun chiao-yü shu" 論教育書. In *Yen Chi-tao shih-wen ch'ao* 嚴幾道詩文鈔. Taipei, Wen-hai ch'u-pan-she, 1969.

———. "Shang chin shang huang-ti wan-yen shu" 上今上皇帝萬言書. In *Wu-shu p'ien-fa* 2:311–329.

Yi Tŏk-mu 李德懋. "On *Ssu-k'u ch'üan-shu*" 四庫全書. In Ch'ŏngjang-kuan chŏnsŏ, ed., *Angyŏp-gi* 青莊館全書 盎葉記. Seoul University Press, 1956.

Yŏlha ilgi 熱河日記. *Yŏnamjip* 燕巖記. Pak Yŏng-ch'ŏl 朴榮喆, ed. 5 ts'e. Kyŏnghŭi Press 慶熙, 1932.

Yŏnhaeng-nok sŏngjip 燕行錄選集. Seoul, Sungkyunkwan 成均館 University, 1962.

Yŏndae chaeryu-nok 煙臺在留錄. Liao-hai ts'ung-shu ed. 101 ts'e. Dairen, 1937.

Yu-hsueh i-pien 遊學譯編. Taipei, Tang-shih-hui, reprint 1968.

Yü Shih-mei 于式枚. "K'ao-ch'a Ying Te Jih san-kuo hsien-fa ch'ing-hsing che" 考察英德日三國憲法情形摺. In *Kuang-hsu ch'ao tung-hua lu*. 211 chüan. 1909. Taipei, Ta-tung shu-chü, 1924.

Yü Yueh 俞樾. "Feng-chien chün-hsien shuo" 封建郡縣說. In Sheng K'ang, ed., *Huang-ch'ao ching-shih wen hsu-pien*, chüan 12.

———. "Hsien Jen-fu hsiung chia-chuan" 先任甫兄家傳. In Miao Ch'üan-sun, ed., *Hsu pei-chuan chi* 44: 16a–21b.

Yuan Ch'ang 袁昶. *Fang-kuo-tun-sou* 芳郭鈍叟, pseud. "I-fu chi-yü shih-chien t'iao-ch'en" 議覆寄諭事件條陳. In *Yü-hu wen-lu* 于湖文錄 (n.p.,n.d.).

Yuan Mei 袁枚. "Tsai shu feng-chien-lun hou" 再書封建論後. In Yao Ch'un, ed., *Kuo-ch'ao wen-lu*, chüan 21. 1851.

———. "Ta men-sheng Wang Li-ch'i wen tso-ling shu" 答門生王禮圻問作令書. In Ho Ch'ang-ling, ed., *Huang-ch'ao ching-shih wen-pien* 21: 23–27.

Yuan Shou-ting 袁守定. "Chü-kuan t'ung-i" 居官通義. In Hsu Tung, ed., *Mu-ling shu* 1:31b–42a.

———. *Tu-min-lu* 圖民錄. 1839.

Yueh Yuan-sheng 岳元聲. *Ch'ien-ch'u-tzu wen-chi* 潛初子文集. Cited in Sakai Tadao, *Chūgoku zensho no kenkyū*.

Yung-cheng chu-p'i yü-chih 雍正硃批諭旨. 360 chüan. 1732.

INDEX

Abahai. *See* T'ai-tsung
an-fen ying-sheng 安分營生 (carry on with one's livelihood), 196
an-min 安民 ("let the people live in peace"), 90
an-yü 案語 (commentary), 247n122
Analects, 80
Anhwei, 123, 153, 158, 162, 168, 198, 252n44
Anti-imperialism, 208, 210–211
Anti-loan movement, 181–182, 191–218, 271n206. *See also* Railways; Sino-British loan agreement
Assembled Pearls (*chü-chen* 聚珍) Bureau, 225n44. *See also* Ssu-k'u ch'üan-shu

bakufu-han 幕府藩 system, 61, 232 n14
Bannermen, Manchu, 157, 162, 195, 198
Belgium, political system in, 146–147, 172
Bland, J. O. P., 165, 170, 190, 209–210, 256n111, 267n130
Bluntschli, Johann, 160
Board of Agriculture, Industry, and Commerce, 187, 194, 204, 262n26, 263n48
Board of Civil Office, 94
Board of Foreign Affairs, 186, 187, 188, 190, 193, 194, 197, 201, 210, 211, 217, 262 n26, 264n56
Board of the Interior, 252n44, 253n53
Board of Posts and Communications, 188, 189, 190, 199, 200, 201, 202, 203, 204, 206, 267n131, 268nn149, 160
Board of Punishment, 184
Board of Revenue, 123, 184
Board of Rites, 133, 223n9, 248n130
Board of War, 148
Board of Works, 127
Book of Changes. See I-ching
Book of History, 11
Book of Music, 11
Book of Poetry, 11
Book of Rites, 11
Boxer Rebellion, 112, 138, 217, 271n204
Brenan, Byron, 183
British and Chinese Corporation, 182, 183, 185, 186, 209, 261n7, 267nn130, 133
Bureaucracy. *See chün-hsien*

Canton-Hankow railway, 184
Canton-Kowloon railway, 186
Capital, Chinese, 181, 183, 186–187, 188
Censorate, 117, 124, 164, 185, 191, 193, 265n72
Cha-p'u 乍浦, 183
chaejo chiŭn 再造之恩, 2
Chang Chien 張謇, 74–75, 138, 139; and constitutionalism, 140, 142, 147, 154, 160, 182, 252n40; and railway dispute, 182, 202, 208; and Kiangsu Railway Company, 187; and Ch'ing Court, 209, 211, 212; and 1911 Revolution, 213–214
Chang Chih-tung 張之洞, 54, 74–76, 77, 83, 172, 232n1, 238n83, 260n162, 272n216; and principle/utility concept, 53, 54, 79, 80, 231n1, 233n17; and constitutionalism, 140, 141; and railway dispute, 184, 199, 217–218
Chang Ch'uan-pao 張傳保, 205
Chang Chung-li 張仲禮: on class division in gentry, 23, 26, 29–30, 31, 33, 34, 43, 44, 49, 165, 168, 226n15, 227n28; on gentry and central government, 230n79; on school vs. examination systems, 231n114
Chang Hsi-i 張錫懌 (Chang Hsiang-shen 張鄉紳), 226n13
Chang Hsueh-ch'eng 章學誠, 82
Chang I-lin 張一麐, 149, 159, 168, 252n44, 253nn52,58, 264n56
Chang Kuo-jung 張國溶, 257n116
Chang Pai-hsi 張百熙, 244n73
Chang P'eng-yuan 張朋園, 162, 163, 165, 167, 256nn110,112, 258n128, 259n132
Chang Ping-lin 章炳麟, 91, 248n127, 272n221
Chang Tsai 張載, 236n36
Chang Tzu-mu 張自牧, 113
Chang Yuan-chi 張元濟, 184, 188, 263n42
Ch'ang-ch'ing 長慶, 80–81
Ch'ang-chou, 196, 214, 265n90
Chao Feng-ch'ang 趙鳳昌, 140
Chao-lien 昭槤, 16
Chao Ping-lin 趙炳麟, 191
Che 折 family, 109
Chekiang: *sheng-chien* in, 37, 38; gentry in, 156–157, 163, 164, 214, 259n131, 261n2, 272n221; provincial assemblies in, 159, 257n116. *See also* Soochow-Hangchow-Ningpo railway dispute
Chekiang Academic Circles Anti-Loan Association, 192
Chekiang Citizens' Anti-Loan Association, 191–192, 193, 195, 196, 197, 205, 207, 264n65
Chekiang High School, 192
Chekiang-Kiangsu railway dispute. *See* Soochow-Hangchow-Ningpo railway dispute
Chekiang Provincial Assembly, 205–206, 207, 213, 258n117, 269n168
Chekiang Railway Company, 200, 201; formation of, 184–185, 262n21, 263n48; and anti-loan movement, 187, 191, 194, 202–206, 207, 210, 211, 217, 264nn51,56,60, 268n160, 271n206, 272n221, 273n224
Chekiang Railway School, 191
chen 鎮 (towns), 249n2
Ch'en Chi-liang 陳冀亮 (Ch'en I-liang 陳儀亮), 269n173
Ch'en Ch'ih 陳熾, 54, 82–83, 84, 118, 122, 123
Ch'en Ch'iu 陳虬, 114–116, 238n77
Ch'en Ching-ti 陳敬第, 257n116
Ch'en Chung-yi 陳仲逸, 258n117
Ch'en Hsu-lu 陳旭麓, 234n27
Ch'en Hung-mou 陳宏謀, 42
Ch'en Kuei-lung 陳夔龍, 254n76
Ch'en Pang-jui 陳邦瑞, 184
Ch'en Pao-chen 陳寶箴, 111, 123
ch'en shih chih fa 陳詩之法 (submission of poems to inform rulers of local conditions), 107
Ch'en Shih-hsia 陳時夏, 205, 208
Ch'en Shu-hsun 陳樹勳, 257n116
Ch'en T'ien-hua 陳天華, 134
cheng 政 (political systems), 53
cheng-chiao 政教 (political principles), 239
Cheng-chih pien-ts'uan-kuan 政治編纂館 (Office for Revising Government Institutions), 149, 150, 151, 159, 175, 253nn52,53,58, 254n63, 255n103
Cheng Hsiao-hsu 鄭孝胥, 202, 270n196
cheng-hsueh 正學 (orthodox learning), 59
Cheng Kuan-ying 鄭觀應, 72–74; and institutional reform, 52, 123, 238n77, 245n79; and the West, 54, 55, 117–118, 239n107; on principle/utility concept, 83, 84, 86, 233n17
cheng-tung 正董 (directors-in-chief), 106
Cheng-wu-ch'u 政務處 (Bureau of Government Affairs), 250n10
Cheng Yun-han 鄭雲漢, 110
ch'eng 城 (cities), 249n2
Ch'eng 程 brothers (Ch'eng I 程頤, Ch'eng Hao 程顥), 17, 80, 234n25

Ch'eng-ch'a pi-chi 乘查筆記 (Notes from a mission of inquiry; Pin-ch'un), 113, 242n43
Ch'eng-ch'in 誠勤, 244n79
Ch'eng Chu 程朱 school, 59, 60, 222n4
Ch'eng Chün-sun 程均孫, 193
Ch'eng Han-cheng 程含章, 42
Ch'eng Hao 程顥, 236n36
Ch'eng I 程頤, 236n36
ch'eng-i cheng-hsin 誠意正心 (sincere and purified mind), 62
Ch'eng, King 成, 120, 121
ch'eng-shen 城紳 (absentee landlords), 39
Ch'eng Te-ch'üan 程德全, 151–152, 175, 213, 270n196
chi-i 集議 (listening to public opinion), 129, 130
chi-i 技藝 (technology), 51, 53, 55, 57, 69, 70, 71
ch'i 氣 (material force), 12, 235n30
ch'i 器 (tools), 69, 70
ch'i 器 (vessels), 81, 82, 83, 84–85, 88
Ch'i Feng-o 奇豐額, 3
ch'i-min chih-shou 四民之首 (leaders of the people), 48
ch'i-t'i tao-yung-lun 器體道用論 (*ch'i* is principle, *tao* is utility), 85
ch'i-yung chih-wu 器用之物 (physical mechanisms), 237n69
Chia-ch'ing period, 43, 104, 225n48
Chia-hsing, 38, 192, 207, 214, 259n131, 263n46, 265n90
Chia-ting, 265n89
Chiang-Che t'ieh-lu feng-chao 江浙鐵路風潮 (documentary collection on anti-loan movement), 197, 199, 215, 261n8
Chiang Ch'un-lin 江春霖, 191
Chiang Feng 姜鋒, 52
Chiang Kai-shek 蔣介石, 55
Chiang Kuei-t'i 姜桂題, 198
Chiang Ping-chang 蔣炳章, 155, 257n116
Chiao-pin-lu k'ang-i 校邠廬抗議 (Straightforward words from Chiao-pin Studio; Feng Kuei-fen), 65, 67, 83, 105–107, 116, 122–123, 127, 234n27, 235nn32,34, 243n54
Chiao Ta-feng 焦達峯, 271n204
chieh-tu-shih 節度使 (provincial commissioners), 109
chien-sheng. See sheng-chien
Ch'ien Chin-sun 錢錦孫, 183
Ch'ien-lung 乾隆 era, 2, 3, 4, 7, 13, 19, 24, 35, 46, 103, 223n6, 224n30
chih 制 (institutions), 240n126

"Chih-p'ing san-i" 治平三議 (Three proposals for orderly administration; Ch'en Ch'iu), 115–116
Chih-p'ing t'ung-i 治平通議 (General discussion for orderly administration), 115–116
"Chih yang-ch'i i" 製洋器議 (Feng Kuei-fen), 234n26
ch'ih-li ch'ang tuan 持吏長短 (manipulating officials), 34
ch'ih-tzu 赤子 (children), 24
Chihli: 1898 reform movement in, 122; constitutionalism in, 140, 148; and provincial assemblies, 153, 154, 168, 257n116; leadership in, 156, 172; elections in, 157, 158, 255n89; and railway dispute, 202, 270n196
chihō jichi 地方自治 (local self-government), 160
Chihō jichi ron 地方自治論 (Local self-government; Matsunaga Michikazu), 126
Chihō jichi ronshu 地方自治論集 (Collection on local self-government; German Association of Japan), 126
chin-chien. See sheng-chien
Chin 晉 dynasty, 13
Chin-hua, 265n66
Chin Pang-p'ing 金邦平, 149, 161, 252n44, 253n58, 257n116
chin-shih 進士 (metropolitan graduates): status of, 23, 25, 26, 27, 28, 29, 30, 227n33, 231n114; social aspects of, 44–45, 49; and examination strikes, 46; and debates over feudalism, 100; and provincial assemblies, 121–122, 161, 165, 243n62, 252n44, 256n130, 259n132; number of, 214, 226n15
Ch'in 秦 dynasty, 83, 84, 89, 91, 93, 129; history of, 11, 12, 14; *chün-hsien* system in, 96, 98, 99, 106, 109, 119, 131
Ch'in Kuei 秦檜, 15
Ch'in-lien Revolt, 39
Ch'in Shih Huang-ti 秦始皇帝, 11, 12, 18
Chinese learning. See Chung-hsueh
Ching-shih po-i 經世博議 (Wide-reaching statecraft proposals; Ch'en Ch'iu), 115, 116
Ching-shih wen-pien 經世文編, 27
ching-t'ien 井田 (well-field) system, 108–109
ch'ing 清 (clear), 5, 223n12
Ch'ing, Prince, 149, 197
ch'ing-i 清議 (disinterested opinion), 97

Chi Yun 紀昀, 16, 225n48
Chiu-shih yao-i 救世要議 (Important proposals to save the nation; Ch'en Ch'iu), 115, 116
Ch'iu Chi-heng 仇繼恒, 257n116
Ch'iu Chin 秋瑾, 198
Choch'ŏn-nok 朝天錄 (Records of tributary visits to the imperial capital), 2
Chŏngjo 正祖, King, 3, 222n4
Chosŏn (Yi) dynasty, 2, 9
chou 州 (department), 102, 114
Chou Cheng-t'an 周承燊, 271n204
Chou Chin-chen 周金箴, 189
Chou dynasty, 90, 91, 93, 103, 120
Chou Fu 周馥, 141
Chou-li 周禮 (Rites of Chou), 83, 84, 145
chu 主 (the base), 73
Chu Fu-shen 朱福詵, 191
Chu Hsi 朱熹, 80, 91, 236n36; and Ch'ing rulers, 4, 9, 11, 14, 15–19; Korean attitude to, 9, 11, 12, 15–16, 18, 222n4, 225n50; and Japanese scholars, 58, 59, 64, 234n25
Chu Hsi-en 朱錫恩, 185
chu-shih 主事 (second class secretaries), 252n44
Chu Shih-yen 朱士彥, 38
Chu Shu 朱書, 100–101, 111
chü-jen 舉人 (provincial graduates), 3, 5, 13, 39, 46, 107, 117, 252n44; as officials, 22, 23, 27, 28, 30; status of, 25–26, 29, 34, 37, 49, 231n114; and parliaments, 121, 132, 161, 162, 164, 165, 167, 243 n62, 258n130, 259nn131,145; and reform societies, 127; privileges of, 226nn14,15, 21; use of term, 227n33
Chü-yeh lu 居業錄 (Hu Chü-jen), 16
Ch'u Fu-ch'eng 褚輔成, 271n204
"Ch'u-pi" 除弊 (Eliminating abuses; Wang T'ao), 82
ch'u wei min 黜為民 (reducing [*sheng-chien*] to commoners), 48
ch'ü 區 (parish), 145
Ch'ü-chou, 259n131
Ch'ü T'ung-tsu 瞿同祖: on character of *sheng-chien*, 23, 31, 34, 37, 47, 49; on gentry distinctions, 28, 29, 30, 34, 38, 45; on "ruling class," 31, 227nn28,33, 231n114
chuan-chin-t'ien 卷金田 (charitable land), 44
Ch'üan-hsüeh p'ien 勸學篇 (Exhortation to study; Chang Chih-tung), 54, 56, 74–76, 77, 83, 232n1, 238n83
Ch'üan-kuo shang-t'uan lien-ho-hui 全國商團聯合會 (National Confederation of Merchant Associations), 214, 216
chün chu yü shang, min chu yü hsia 君主於上，民主於下 ("The sovereign is the lord above, and the subject is the lord below"), 69–70
"Chün-fu i" 均賦議 (Discussion of equalization of taxes; Feng Kuei-fen), 37
"Chün-fu shuo-ch'üan chin" 均賦說勸衿 (Persuading the *chin* to equalize taxes; Feng Kuei-fen), 27–28
"Chün-fu shou ch'üan-shen" 均賦說勸紳 (Persuading the *shen* to equalize taxes; Feng Kuei-fen), 27
chün-hsien 郡縣 (bureaucratic) system, 89–136; vs. *feng-chien* system, 89–136, 139, 145, 171, 242n39, 247n122; supporters of, 91, 98, 111; criticism of, 128, 129, 241n4; corruption in, 223n6
"Chün-hsien lun" 郡縣論 (Ku Yen-wu), 92–93, 101, 108, 134, 241n4
chün-kuo 郡國 system, 91
chün-min kung-chu 君民共主 (joint rule by the monarch and the people), 118
Ch'un, Prince (Tsai-feng 載灃), 148
Chung-hang Yüeh 中行說, 7
chung 中 (standard or mean of unchangeable behavior), 73
Chung-hsüeh 中學 (Chinese learning), 73, 74, 75, 76, 78–79, 81–85, 87–88. See also *t'i yung*
Chung-hsüeh wei chu, hsi-hsüeh wei fu 中學為主，西學為輔 (Chinese learning as foundation, Western learning as supplement), 80
Chung-hsüeh wei pen, hsi-hsüeh wei yung 中學為本，西學為用 (Chinese learning as principle, Western learning as utility), 80
Chung-hsüeh wei t'i, hsi-hsüeh wei yung 中學為體，西學為用 (Chinese learning for basic principle and Western learning for practical utility), 51–57, 64–88, 231n1, 232n7, 233nn14, 17, 234n25, 238nn76,85, 240nn126,127
"Chung-kuo chi she i-yüan lun" 中國亟設議院論 (Let China immediately establish parliaments; Han Wen-chü and Liang Ch'i-chao), 132
"Chung-kuo tzu-ch'iang ts'e" 中國自強策 (A plan for China's self-strengthening; Wang K'ang-nien), 132, 138, 139
Chung-t'i hsi-yung. See *Chung-hsüeh wei t'i, hsi-hsüeh wei yung*

Chung Ts'ai-hung 鍾才宏, 164
Chung-wai jih-pao 中外日報 (Universal gazette), 197, 199, 211, 249n4, 264n56, 266n112, 270n195
"Ch'ung-ting t'ieh-lu chien-ming chang ch'eng" 重訂鐵路簡明章程 (The revised regulations on railway construction), 262n16
Committee for the Investigation of the Principles of Modern Politics and Government, 144
Committee of Ministers. See Hui-i cheng-wu-ch'u
Confucianism, 3, 4, 11, 122, 231n102; and gentry, 22, 24, 32, 38, 41, 45, 48, 256n111; and principle/utility concept, 53, 55, 56, 58–64, 68, 69, 82, 235n28, 236n36; and reform, 78, 79, 83, 84, 85, 87, 133; and feng-chien system, 101, 104
Constitutional movement: and principle/utility concept, 54; and local self-government, 112, 113, 133, 134, 137, 140–147, 172, 175, 213, 221n3, 250n18; and Ch'ing Court, 133, 213, 248nn129,130; proponents of, 140–144, 163, 250n10, 252n40, 258n117; leaders of, 164–165, 259n132; and railway dispute, 181, 182, 184, 188, 269n183, 271n203; and antiloan movement, 198, 205–206, 208, 209, 211. See also Emperor: memorials to; tzu-i-chü

Darwin, Charles, 131
Degree-holders, 25–28, 36, 45, 49; and provincial assemblies, 117, 125, 126, 132, 165, 248n135, 259n132; privileges of, 226n14. See also shen-shih; specific degrees
Democracy, 86, 119, 129, 234n27. See also Elections
Dorgon, 13
Duke Ch'i, 103
Duke Sung, 103
Dutch Learning. See Rangaku
Dzungars. See Mongols

Eikoku chihō jichi ron 英國地方自治論 (Local self-government in England; Yonekane Mizawa), 126
Elections, 156, 157–158, 159, 160–162, 168, 176, 178, 255n88; Western parliamentary, 117, 118; in America, 234n27. See also Voting, qualifications for
Elites. See shen-shih
Emperor, 24, 31, 99, 120; and provincial assemblies, 77, 78, 123, 153, 155, 159, 163, 172, 173; and principle/utility concept, 80; memorials to, 122, 131, 158, 245nn88,89,90, 250n10, 251n39, 252n40, 263n48; and reform, 129, 132, 163; and railway dispute, 210, 186, 190. See also ku-wen; individual emperors
Empresses Dowager, 66, 77
England: political system of, 139, 144–145; and Chinese railways, 181–182, 261n1. See also Sino-British loan agreement
Erh ya 爾雅, 16
Examination strikes, 45–46, 231n102
Examination system, 21, 26, 40, 43, 44, 49, 81, 167; and school system, 25, 27, 32, 226n2, 231n114; reform of, 67, 76, 77, 80, 114; and chün-hsien system, 104, 110

fa 法 (methods), 240n126
fa-ku 法古 (taking the past as model), 90
fan-chen 藩鎮 system, 248n127
Fan Kung-hsu 樊恭煦, 187
Fan Tsung-yin 范宗尹, 100
fang-chen 方鎮 (autonomous military command zones), 91, 96, 97, 100–101, 109, 112
Fang Hsuan-ling 房玄齡, 11
Fang Ta-shih 方大湜, 35
Fei Chin-wu 費舍吾, 241n24
fen 分 (division), 105
fen-chih 分治 (divided administration), 106
feng-chien 封建 (feudal) system, 89–136; late-Ch'ing debates over, 89, 105–112, 113, 116, 126–136, 138, 139, 145, 172, 242n39, 249n1; and institutional reform, 52, 92–100, 248n127; and provincial assemblies, 137, 172, 175
Feng Hsu 馮煦, 153
Feng Kuei-fen 馮桂芬, 27–28, 37; on principle/utility concept, 83, 87, 236n50; and reform, 102, 105–107, 111–112, 116, 117, 122–123, 125, 126, 127, 234n26, 235nn32,34, 236nn40,49. See also individual works
Feng Mao-lung 馮夢龍, 110
Feng Ssu-luan 馮斯欒, 110
feng-su 風俗 (public morale), 239n102
Feng Te-i 封德彝, 98
Feng Yu-lan 馮友蘭, 53
Fengtien, 154, 167
Feudalism, 52, 57, 72, 89–136. See also feng-chien
Filial piety, 4, 56, 58, 70
Fincher, John, 259n132, 260nn149,160

France, 140, 146, 172
fu 府 (prefecture), 145
"Fu hsiang-chih i" 復鄉職議 (On the reinstitution of local posts; Feng Kuei-fen), 105–107
Fu-hui ch'üan-shu 福惠全書 (A complete book concerning happiness and benevolence; Huang Liu-hung), 25, 27
fu-ku 復古 (returning to the ancient), 67, 71
fu-sheng 附生 (supplementary licentiate), 26, 165
fu-tung 副董 (assistant directors), 106
fu-yung 附庸 (subordinate areas), 248n127
Fuchow, 158
Fujii Masao 藤井正夫, 263n47
fuken gikai 府縣議會 (local assemblies), 143
fukenkai 府縣會 (prefectural meetings), 256n105
Fukenkai kisoku 府縣會規則 (law allowing local parliaments), 256n105
fukensei 府縣制 (prefectural system), 256n105
Fukien, 156, 157, 158, 258n117
fukoku kyōhei 富國強兵 (enriching the state and strengthening the armed forces), 63

Gentry. See *shen-shih*
Germany, 142, 160, 183
Gneist, Rudolf von, 160
Governors, provincial, 94, 97, 102, 111, 124, 173
Grand Council, 117, 148, 184, 191, 194, 198, 203, 260n162, 266n118
Great Learning. See *Ta-hsueh*

Hai-fang tang 海防檔 (Archives on maritime defense), 263n44, 267n131
Hai-kuo t'u-chih 海國圖志 (Illustrated gazetteer of the maritime nations; Wei Yuan), 63
Hai-ning, 198
Hai-yen, 198
Han dynasty, 5, 7, 34, 90, 91, 94, 98, 118, 124, 128, 130
Han Kao-tsu 漢高祖, 11
Han Learning, 15, 17, 225n48
Han-Sung che-chung 漢宋折衷 (compromise between the Han and Sung schools), 17

Han Wen-chü 韓文舉, 132
Hangchow: voting in, 158; and railway dispute, 182, 183, 195, 197, 204, 207, 211, 259n131, 265n89; mass rallies in, 191, 192, 196; gentry in, 213, 214, 268n149. See also Anti-loan movement; Soochow-Hangchow-Ningpo railway dispute
Hanlin Academy, 43, 155, 156, 164, 184, 187, 191, 207, 244n77
Hao-ch'eng 郝成, 3
hao-i shen-chin 好義紳衿 (public-spirited gentry), 33
Hashimoto Sanai, 58
ho 合 (measure of grain), 37
ho (unity), 105
Ho Chao-hsun 何肇勳, 127
Ho Ch'i 何啓 (Ho Kai), 120–121, 122, 131, 138, 243n59, 249n3
ho-chih 合治 (integrated administration), 106
Ho-chung-kuo shuo 合眾國說 (On the United States; Liang T'ing-nan), 113
Ho Lang-hsien 何閬仙, 192
Ho Ping-ti 何炳棣, 23, 30–31, 44, 48, 49, 227nn28,31,32,33
Ho-shen 和珅, 16
Ho Tsan-yuan 賀贊元, 257n116
hojok 胡族 (barbarian tribe), 2
Hong Tae-yong 洪大容, 6, 9
hsi 西 (Western), 85
hsi-hsueh 西學 (Western learning), 73, 74, 75, 76, 79–80, 83, 84, 87–88, 111, 123, 240n126
hsi-jen ch'i-shu chih hsueh 西人器數之學 (Western technological learning), 57
Hsia-shih, 192, 198
Hsia Shou-k'ang 夏壽康, 257n116
Hsia Tung-yuan 夏東元, 52–53
Hsia Yin-kuan 夏寅官, 257n116
hsiang 鄉 (administrative unit), 106, 109, 145
hsiang-chü li-hsuan chih 鄉舉里選制, 94
Hsiang-chün chih 湘軍志 (Treatise on the Hunan Army), 80
Hsiang-hsueh hsin-pao 湘學新報, 80
hsiang-huan 鄉宦 (upper local gentry), 32. See also *hsiang-shen*
hsiang-kuan 鄉官 (local officials), 102, 119, 129, 131, 134, 144
Hsiang-pao 湘報 (The Hunan journal), 80
hsiang-she 鄉社 (rural convenant) system, 142, 143
hsiang-shen 鄉紳, 25, 32

hsiang-yueh 鄉約, 44
Hsiao Ho, 蕭何, 11
Hsiao Kung-ch'üan 蕭公權, 31, 37, 39, 44, 46, 99, 229n66, 243n59
Hsiao-t'ing tsa-lu 嘯亭雜錄 (Chao-lien), 16
Hsiao-wen Emperor, 4
Hsieh Chin-luan 謝金鑾, 24
hsien 縣 (county), 102, 114, 249n2
hsien-che 賢哲 (worthy), 91
Hsien-cheng ch'u-kang 憲政初綱 (preliminary outline of constitutional government), 252nn40,43
Hsien-cheng pien-ch'a-kuan 憲政編查館 (Office to Draw up Regulations for Constitutional Government), 153–154
hsin 心 (mind), 64
Hsin-cheng chen-ch'üan 新政真詮 (True explanations of the new policies; Ho Ch'i and Hu Li-yuan), 120
hsin-cheng chü 新政局 (institutional reform bureaus), 125, 246n98
hsin-i 信義 (faith), 217
hsin-shu 心術 (mental discipline), 62
Hsin-wen-pao 新聞報 (Daily news), 199
Hsiung-nu 匈奴, 7
Hsu Ch'i 徐琪, 183
Hsu Chih-ching 徐致靖, 244n78
Hsu Hsi-lin 徐錫麟, 198
Hsu K'uan-ch'ing 徐冠卿, 223n12
Hsu pei-chuan chi 續碑傳集, 35, 43
Hsu Shih-ch'ang 徐世昌, 141, 148, 175, 268n146
Hsu Ting-ch'ao 徐定超, 191, 268n154
Hsu Ting-lin 許鼎霖, 187, 188, 257n116, 263n42
Hsu T'ung 徐桐, 74
Hsuan-t'ung 宣統, 170, 251n35
Hsueh Fu-ch'eng 薛福成, 54, 57, 69, 70–72
"Hsueh-hsiao p'ien" 學校篇 (Huang Tsung-hsi), 132
Hsueh Hsuan 薛瑄, 16
Hsueh-shih lu 學仕錄 (Tai Chao-ch'en), 37
hsun-i chih kuan 訓議之官 (advisory officials), 245n88
Hu-chou, 192, 195, 214, 265n90
Hu Chü-jen 胡居仁, 16
Hu-kwang, 172, 254n76
Hu Li-yuan 胡禮垣, 120–121, 122, 131, 243n59
Hu Pin 胡濱, 65
Hu Shih 胡適, 55

Hu-shu, 183, 186
Hu Ssu-ching 胡思敬, 134, 167, 168, 252n43, 253n51
Hu Yü-fen 胡燏棻, 184
Hu Yuan 胡瑗, 64, 236n36
Huan-yu chi-lueh 宦遊紀略 (Kao T'ing-yao), 46
Huang Chang-chien 黃彰健, 245nn89,90
Huang I-feng 黃逸峯, 52
Huang Kuei-chun 黃桂鋆, 127
Huang Liu-hung 黃六鴻, 25, 27
Huang Shao-ch'i 黃紹箕, 184
Huang Tsun-hsien 黃遵憲, 129–131, 139, 237nn67,69, 247n117
Huang Tsung-hsi 黃宗羲: views of *feng-chien* system, 92, 95–96, 97, 100, 102, 109, 111–112, 132; on rule of law, 103; and reform of *chün-hsien* system, 125, 128, 129, 135; influence of, 133–134, 248n129
Huang Yen-p'ei 黃炎培, 208
Hui-feng Bank, 261n7, 266n108
Hui-i cheng-wu-ch'u 會議政務處 (Committee of Ministers), 144, 148, 151
hui-i-t'ing 會議廳 (council), 149, 252n47
Hui-tien shih-li 會典事例 (Regulations of government), 33, 42. See also *Ta-Ch'ing hui-tien shih-li*
Hunan, 130, 132, 139, 249n7, 271n204; radical reform movement in, 74, 75, 76, 111, 128; provincial assembly in, 156, 168, 170, 257n116
Hung-hsien Emperor, 218
Hundred Schools, 79
Hung Hsiu-ch'üan 洪秀全, 43
Hupeh, 154, 156, 166, 167, 168, 213, 257n116
Hwang Chae 黃梓, 3–4

i 義 (righteousness), 12, 13, 15
i 藝 (techniques), 81–82
I-ching 易經 (Book of Changes), 62, 81, 234n25
i-hsueh 異學 (heretical teachings), 59
i-k'o 藝科 (technical categories), 81
i-lang 議郎 (imperial councillors), 117, 124, 245nn88,89
i-li 義理 (teaching of the sages), 80
i-shih-hui 議事會 (deliberative council), 150
i shou wei t'i, i chan wei yung 以守為體, 以戰為用 (Take defense as the *t'i* [basic principle] and combat as the *yung* [utility]), 65

i tzu-li wei t'i, i t'ui-ch'eng wei yung 以自立為體，以推誠為用 ("Take the establishment of one's own character as *t'i* [basic principle] and the extension of one's sincerity to the outer world as *yung* [utility]"), 65

i-yuan 議院 (parliament), 124, 132, 238n77

Imperial Academy, 26, 102

Imperial Chinese Railway Administration, 182, 183, 189

i-ya min-ch'i 抑壓民氣 (suppressing the spirit of the people), 209

Japan, 134, 140, 141, 197, 256n108; ethics/technology in, 52, 56, 57, 58–64, 232n14; elections in, 138–139, 176, 256n111; political system of, 139, 141, 147, 159–160; Chinese students in, 139, 149, 155, 159, 163, 164, 175, 205, 242n39, 252n44, 265n70

Jardine, Matheson & Co., 182–183, 261n7

Jehol, 2, 3, 7, 8, 14, 223n15

Jehol Diary. See *Yŏlha ilgi*

jen-hsin 人心 (human will), 239n102

jen-lun 人倫 (universal humanity), 69

Jih-chih lu 日知錄 (A record of daily knowledge; Ku Yen-wu), 134, 241n4

Jih-pen hsien-fa i-chieh 日本憲法義解 (Exposition of the Japanese Constitution; Chang Chien), 140

Jih-pen i-hui-shih 日本議會史 (History of the Japanese Diet; Chang Chien), 140, 142

Jih-pen kuo-chih 日本國志 (The governmental system of Japan), 237nn67,69

Jih-pen pien-cheng k'ao 日本變政考 (A study of the political reform in Japan; K'ang Yu-wei), 125

Jih-pen shu-mu chih 日本書目志 (Index to Japanese publications; K'ang Yu-wei), 126

jitsugaku 實學 (practical learning), 235n31

Jordan, Sir John, 186, 208

jōri 條理 (reason), 56

Ju-lin wai-shih 儒林外史 (The scholars; Wu Ching-tzu), 38

Juan Yuan 阮元, 225n48

Jung-lu 榮祿, 122

kaikoku ron 開國論, 87

kang-ch'ang ming-chiao 綱常名教 (traditional social doctrine), 54

K'ang-hsi Emperor, 4, 6, 7, 9, 100–105, 224n28

K'ang, King 康, 120, 121

K'ang Yu-wei 康有為: and principle/utility concept, 54, 55, 76, 78–79, 80, 82, 238n83, 239n90; and Chang Chih-tung, 74, 75, 77; and Reform Movement, 113–114, 123, 124–126, 160, 232n12, 237n67, 238n77, 239n98, 242n46, 245nn88,89,90; on local self-government, 139–140, 246n98, 249n9

Kansu, 8, 155, 198

K'ao-ch'a cheng-chih-kuan 考察政治館 (Office for the Investigation of the Principles of Modern Politics and Government), 153

Kao Feng-ch'i 高鳳岐, 151

Kao T'ing-yao 高廷瑤, 35, 46

Kao-tsung (Emperor), 15

Katō Hiroyuki 加藤弘之, 58, 236n35

keisei saimin 經世濟民 (statecraft), 59

Kiangnan, 4, 39

Kiangsi, 154, 156, 166, 202, 257n116

Kiangsu: gentry in, 37, 138, 203, 214; provincial assemblies in, 154, 155, 156, 208, 255n103, 257nn116,117; voting in, 157, 158, 203, 255n89; railway dispute in, 163–164, 181, 182, 187, 188, 190, 212–213, 217, 261n2; and 1911 Revolution, 182, 210; and anti-loan movement, 191–192, 193, 197, 198, 200, 210, 216, 266n92

Kiangsu-Chekiang railway, 188, 190. See also Soochow-Hangchow-Ningpo railway dispute

Kiangsu Railroad Association, 163–164, 193, 207, 270n184, 272n216

Kiangsu Railway Company, 187, 193, 194, 195, 200, 201, 207, 264n56, 265n82, 267nn131,133, 268n160, 272n216

Kim Ch'ang-ŏp 金昌業, 4, 6, 7, 223nn14,15

ko-chih 格致 (the investigation of things), 83

ko-chih chih hsueh 格致之學 (empirical study), 237n69

ko-ming lun 革命論 (theory of Mandate of Heaven), 12, 13, 100, 103

Ko Pao-hua 葛寶華, 184

ko-wu chih-chih 格物致知 (study of the principles of nature), 59, 62

ko-wu ch'iung-li 格物窮理 (to get to the heart of principles through examination of things), 61, 234n25

k'o-shih 科試 (preliminary examination), 26
Kondo Kuniyasu 近藤邦康, 54
Korea, 1–3, 9. *See also* Yŏlha ilgi
Ku-chin t'u-shu chi-ch'eng 古今圖書集成 (Synthesis of books and illustrations of ancient and modern times), 14
Ku Hung-ming 辜鴻銘, 238n83
"Ku T'ing-lin *Jih-chih lu* chih ti-fang tzu-chih shuo" 顧亭林日知錄之地方自治說 (Local self-government theory as seen in *Jih-chih lu* of Ku Yen-wu), 134
ku-wen 古文 (pure style), 222n4
Ku Yen-wu 顧炎武, 34, 44, 247n115; and institutional reform, 92–95, 96, 97, 99, 100, 107, 108, 109, 116, 120, 125; on selection of local officials, 102, 105, 106, 111–112, 119, 121, 126, 127, 128, 130–131, 133, 134, 135
kuan 官 (officials), 106, 167
kuan-ch'üan 官權, 86, 209
Kuang-hsu Emperor, 65, 109, 207, 26n21, 244n73, 252n41
kuang yen-lu 廣言路 (the expansion of communication), 116
kung 公 (public good), 63, 89, 91, 99, 120, 121, 125, 129–130, 131
Kung, Prince, 65–66, 77, 148
Kung Chien-yang 龔健飇, 102, 107, 111, 241n24
kung-chih 公治 (public government), 110
kung-fa 公法 (public law), 247n122
kung-fei 公費 (expense allowance), 168
kung-fu 工夫 (study), 64
kung-ho 共和 (ancient republican) period, 130
Kung-i t'ang 公議堂 (Hall of Public Discussion), 141
kung-kung chih li 公共之理 (public principles), 57
kung-min 公民 (citizens), 139, 249n9
kung-min tzu-chih 公民之治 (civil self-government), 246n98
kung-sheng 貢生 (senior licentiates), 26, 28, 30, 34, 36–37, 41, 42, 117, 227n32; as officials, 22, 23, 25, 27, 31, 107, 167, 227n33. *See also sheng-chien*
"Kung-ch'e shang shu" 公車上書 (K'ang Yu-wei), 124
kung t'ien-hsia 公天下 (treating the empire as a public domain), 93, 101
kung-t'ui 公推 (public recommendation system), 234n26

K'ung chiao 孔教 (Confucianism), 55
Kuo-ch'ao ch'i-hsien lei-cheng 國朝耆獻類徵, 35
Kuo-feng pao 國風報, 257n116
Kuo-hui 國會 (National Assembly), 54, 114, 124, 138; and provincial assemblies, 143, 147, 152, 156, 163, 166, 168, 174, 252n44, 257n116, 258n128; and railway dispute, 205, 206, 269nn168,175. *See also* Tzu-cheng-yuan; *tzu-i-chü*
kuo-min 國民 (citizens), 193, 195, 207, 209, 210, 211, 214
Kuo Sung-t'ao 郭崇燾, 78, 239n102
Kwangchow, student strike at, 231n10
Kwangsi, 138, 150, 154, 155, 156, 168, 249n3, 257n116
Kwangtung, 46, 138, 259n135; and provincial assemblies, 150, 154, 156, 166, 249n3, 257n116; elections in, 157, 158, 255n91
Kweichow, 3, 102, 162, 260n149
kyōgi yōron 公議輿論 (valuing public opinion), 63
kyōshin 鄉紳 (local elite), 22, 226n2

Lamaism, 8, 9. *See also* Tibet
Lang-jun-yuan conference, 148–149, 152, 162, 175
Lao Nai-hsuan 勞乃宣, 253n61
Lawsuits, 24, 37, 41–42, 43, 228n4
Lee En-han 李恩涵, 261n1
Lei Fen 雷奮, 188, 208, 257n116, 269n177
Levenson, Joseph, 85
li 理 (principle), 58, 60, 61, 64, 101, 234n25
li-cheng 里長, *li-chia* captain, 35
li-chia 里甲 system, 35
li-chien-sheng 例監生 (student of imperial academy by purchase), 26, 30, 32, 34, 36
Li 李 family, 109
Li Hou-yu 李厚佑, 183, 194, 269n177
Li Hsing-yuan 李星沅, 37
Li Hung-chang 李鴻章, 55, 65–66, 76–78, 172, 230n79, 239n90
Li Kang 李綱, 100
li-kung-sheng 例貢生, 23, 26, 28, 30, 31, 36
Li Pai-yao 李百藥, 91
Li P'ing-shu 李平書, 215, 272n216
Li shih erh ch'iu chu yeh 禮失而求諸野 ("Having lost the rituals, seek them among the uncivilized peoples"), 235n34

Li Ssu 李斯, 11, 14, 91
li t'ien-hsia 理天下 (establishing good government), 90
Li-tse hu-yen 蠡測卮言 (Unrestrained observations from one of limited experience; Chang Tzu-mu), 113
Li Tse-hou 李澤厚, 54, 55, 65, 232n10
Li Tuan-fen 李端棻, 127
Li Yuan-hung, 黎元洪, 270n196
Liang Chang-chü 梁章鉅, 44
Liang Ch'i-ch'ao 梁啟超, 53, 54, 55, 74, 75, 79, 80, 109–110, 111, 112, 231n1, 238n83, 239nn90,107, 244n73; and Reform Movement, 123, 127, 128, 129, 132, 134, 232n12, 237n67, 238n83; and constitutional movement, 143, 159, 174, 252n40, 261n167; view of parliament, 244n74; on popular rights, 244n77; on local government, 246n98
Liang-feng 兩峰, 5
Liang-Kiang 兩江, 140, 141, 191, 198
Liang Shih-i 梁士詒, 200, 263n43, 267n133
Liang T'ing-nan 梁廷枏, 113
Liang Tun-yen 梁敦彥, 186, 190
Liaotung, 8
lin-sheng 廩生, 26, 34, 165
Lin Wei-chen 林維臻, 182
Literati: Chinese, 5, 9–10, 11, 14, 15, 16, 17, 18, 69, 77; Korean, 11, 15, 16; treatment of, 34; and settlement of disputes, 42; and public opinion, 63, 129; and local government, 102. *See also shen shih*
Liu Chin-tsao 劉錦藻, 184, 200, 211, 264n51
Liu Ch'ung-yu 劉崇佑, 258n117
Liu Hou-sheng 劉厚生, 212, 271n204
Liu Hung-ao 劉鴻翱, 104–105
Liu Pang-chih 劉邦驥, 166, 167
Liu Tsung-yuan 柳宗元, 91, 98, 100, 101, 103, 104, 105, 110
Liu Yung-ch'ang 劉永昌, 257n116
Lo Ch'eng-jang 駱成讓, 245n80
Loan Deposit Agreement, 199–206, 210, 268n160. *See also* Sino-British loan agreement
Local self-government, 92, 95, 97, 105, 110, 112, 137, 138, 139, 253n62; Western, 107; late Ch'ing debates on, 112–136, 139, 249n2; and centralized power, 146, 147, 171–172, 173, 176, 260n162; and rule of avoidance, 150. *See also tzu-i-chü*
Lord Huan 桓 of Ch'i 齊, 103
Lord Wen 文 of Chin 晉, 103
lou-kuei 陋規 (customary fees), 24
Lu, state of, 11

Lu Chi 陸機, 90
Lu Hsiang-shan 陸象山, 15, 16
Lu Jun-hsiang 陸潤庠, 187
Lu Sheng-nan 陸生楠, 101, 111
Lu Tsung-yü 陸宗輿, 142, 169, 252n44
Lü Liu-liang 呂留良, 101, 111
Luan-chou 灤州, 154
lun-ch'ang ming-chiao 倫常名教 (traditional ethics), 66
lun-chi 倫紀 (ethics and moral discipline), 75
"Lun chiao-yü shu" 論教育書 (A letter on education; Yen Fu), 240n126

Ma Chien-chung 馬建忠, 69, 72
Ma Feng-po 馬逢伯, 211, 269n183, 270n201
Ma Liang 馬良, 193, 208, 209
Magistrates, county, 24, 26; duties of, 24; and gentry, 28, 42; and *sheng-yuan*, 34, 35–37, 45–47; and feudal system, 94, 95, 102, 106, 107–108, 112, 114, 115, 117; and local officials, 119, 125, 126, 128, 135
Manchus, 1, 2–3, 5, 12, 13, 14, 80, 271n206; compared with Chinese, 6–7; Sinicization of, 6–7; and Mongols, 7; and Chinese literati, 15, 18
Mandate of Heaven. *See ko-ming lun*
Maruyama Masao 丸山茂樹, 235n28
Matsunaga Michikazu 松永道一, 126
May Fourth Movement, 87
Meiji Restoration, 52, 56, 57, 58, 64, 87, 232n14, 246n94
Mencius, 11, 13, 62, 80, 83, 104
Meng Chao-ch'ang 孟昭常, 208, 257n116, 269n177
Meng Sen 孟森, 133, 164, 248n129, 257nn116,117
Merchants, 161, 162, 215–216, 256n110, 269n183, 272n220
min-cheng-chü 民政局 (civil government bureaus), 125, 126, 246n98
min-ch'üan 民權 (popular political rights): and principle/utility concept, 54, 55, 74, 75, 76; and debates on self-government, 120–121, 123, 126, 128, 134, 136, 140, 248n127; and constitutional system, 209, 269n182; and gentry, 216, 244n77
min tang 民黨 (people's party), 209
Minamoto Ryōen 源了圓, 58

Mines, 181, 184, 236n50, 262n9,16
ming 明 (bright), 5, 223n12
Ming dynasty, 5, 9, 13, 17, 79, 92, 107, 224 n28; and Korea, 1–2, 10; and local self-government, 134; gentry in, 22, 28, 32, 41, 171
Ming-i tai-fang lu 明夷待訪錄 (A plan for the prince; Huang Tsung-hsi), 95–96, 97, 129, 134
Ming T'ai-tsu 明太祖, 224n35
ming-t'i ta-yung 明體達用 (understand the principles and perceive their practical utility), 236n36
Mission to Investigate the Practice of Constitutional Government in Foreign Countries, 144, 175
Mito school 水戶學, 59
mo 末 (branch), 54, 69, 70, 72, 78, 79, 81, 83, 234n25
Modernization, 52–55, 56, 137, 232n14
Monarchism, 129, 131, 133, 139, 235n27, 246n98, 247n108
Mongols, 7, 8
Mou Shu-tzu 牟樹滋, 256n107
mu-ch'ien ho-chü wei-ch'ih 目前和局維持 (seek immediate stability), 77
Mu-ling shu 牧令書 (The magistrate's handbook), 27, 33, 35
mu-yu 幕友 (private secretaries), 24, 106, 107–108, 114, 115, 223n6, 252n44
munch'e panjŏng 文體反正 (restore the orthodoxy of literary style), 3

Nakamura Keichoku 中村敬直, 236n35
Nan-hai kuan-chih i 南海官制議 (Discussions of political systems; K'ang Yu-wei), 125–126, 139–140, 249n9
Nan-hsueh-hui 南學會 (Southern Study Society), 75
Nanchang, 265n90
Nanking, 214, 271n206
National Assembly. See Kuo-hui
Nationalism, 70, 71, 72, 182, 192, 207, 208, 210, 218
nei-ko chung-shu 內閣中書 (a secretary of the Grand Secretariat), 252n44
Neo-Confucianism, 16, 56, 59, 61, 62, 64, 234n25; Chu Hsi School of, 9, 58, 60; and Western science, 60
New Army, 195, 213, 216, 271n204
New Policy (1901), 175
"Ni shang huang-ti wan-yen shu" 擬上皇帝萬言書 (Ten-thousand-word memorial intended for the Emperor; Yen Fu), 131
Ninghsia, 寧夏, 8
Ningpo, 192, 195, 196, 204, 265nn89,90, 268n149
Nishimura Shigeki 西村茂樹, 58
Nomura Kōichi 野村浩一, 56, 57, 233nn16,17
Nü-chieh pao-lu-hui 女界保路會, (Women's Association for the Preservation of Railway Rights), 196
Nü-kuo-min chü-k'uan-hui 女國民拒款會 (Women's Citizens' Anti-Loan Association), 196

Office to Draw Up Regulations for Constitutional Government, 159, 160, 169, 171, 173, 174, 253n61, 254n63, 261n167
Office for Revising Government Institutions. See Cheng-chih pien-ts'an-kuan
Onogawa Hidemi 小野川秀美, 55, 236n40, 238n77
Opium War, 39, 59, 113
Ortai 鄂爾泰, 102, 241n24
Otsuka Taiya 大塚退野, 235n31
Ou Chia-lien 歐家廉, 158

Pak Chae-ga 朴齊家, 5–6, 222n4, 225n48
Pak Chi-wŏn 朴趾源, 2–19, 34, 49, 222n4, 223nn5,9, 224nn22,35,38, 225 nn41,48. See also Yŏlha ilgi
Pan Ku 班固, 90
P'an T'ing-yun 潘庭筠, 10
Pao-Che hui 保浙會 (Chekiang Preservation Society), 127
pao-chia 保甲 system, 33, 36
Pao Ch'uan hui 保川會 (Szechwan Preservation Society), 127
Pao-kuo hui 保國會 (Society for Preserving the Nation), 127
pao-lan tz'u-sung 包攬詞訟 (proxy lawsuits), 41–42, 43
Pao Shih-ch'en 包世臣, 135, 248n134
Pao-Tien hui 保滇會 (Yunnan Preservation Society), 127
Pao-wang hui 保亡會 (Society to Prevent the Destruction of the Nation), 195
Parliamentary system: Western, 55, 67, 68, 69–70, 72, 78, 234n26; and principle/utility concept, 73, 83; and debates on local self-government, 92, 113, 114–116, 117–118, 119, 120, 121, 138, 135, 249n2; and Reform Movement, 123–136,

Parliamentary system *(continued)*
  234n26, 238n77, 247n117; and local assemblies, 142, 160, 164, 171, 175, 177, 251n36
Pei-chuan chi 碑傳集, 35, 43, 46
Peking (Yen; Yŏn), 2, 3, 4, 5, 203, 205, 210
pen 本 (root), 64, 69, 70, 72, 78, 79, 81, 83, 234n25, 240n126
People's Public Association for Railways and Mines (Kiangsu), 193
pi-t'an 筆談 (written conversation), 5
"P'i Han" 闢韓 (In refutation of Han Yü; Yen Fu), 131
P'i Hsi-jui 皮錫瑞, 75
pieh-hao 別號 (courtesy name), 35
pien ch'eng-fa 變成法 (changing established institutions), 113
pien-fa 變法 (institutional reform) group, 74, 77, 78–81, 84, 85–86, 92, 232 n2, 242n46; vs. *yang-wu* movement, 52, 53, 70, 86; and popular rights, 54, 248 n127; and national sovereignty, 66, 70; and imperial power, 68
"Pien-fa" 變法 (Reform; Hsueh Fu-ch'eng), 71
"Pien-fa" 變法 (Reform; Wang T'ao), 82
"Pien-fa p'ing-i" 變法平議 (Ordinary proposals on reform; Chang Chien), 138, 139
"Pien-fa tzu-ch'iang" 變法自強 (Reform and self-strengthening; Wang t'ao), 82
Pin-ch'un 斌椿, 113, 242n43
pin-kuan 賓館 (guest houses), 114
p'in-kuan 品官 (ranked officials), 30
p'in-shih 貧士 (poor gentry), 43
P'ing-p'ing yen 平平言 (Fang Ta-shih), 35
Political bureaus, see *min-cheng chü*
Political systems, 72, 77, 78, 81, 82, 84, 89, 97. See also Parliamentary system
Principle/utility. See *t'i-yung*
Provincial assemblies. See *tzu-i-chü*
pu 輔 (complementing), 66
pu-jen 不仁 (brutal), 100
Public opinion, 151–152, 155
Pukhak 北學 ("Learn from Ch'ing") school, 3

Railway-rights preservation movement (Szechwan), 182
Railways, 66, 73, 77, 157, 163, 181–218
Rangaku 蘭學 (Dutch Learning), 59
Reform Movement of 1898, 122–136, 138, 170, 231n4, 236n44, 238n77, 246n98, 247n117, 248n127, 249n1; and principle/utility concept, 78–81, 82, 83, 84, 87, 232n12, 240n126; and debates over political feudalism, 105, 111, 112, 113, 114–116. See also *pien-fa*
Regionalism, 182, 209, 210
Regulations of the Provincial Assembly, 160, 168, 173, 174, 206
Republican era, 55, 91
Revolution of 1911, 92, 163, 182, 202, 207, 210, 213, 218, 270n196, 271n204
Rights Recovery Movement, 172, 184. See also Soochow-Hangchow-Ningpo railway dispute
Rule of avoidance, 128; abolition of, 94, 107, 114, 119, 144, 150, 175; opposition to, 95, 97, 102, 105, 126, 127, 130, 131, 133, 134, 145; and private secretaries, 108, 125
Russia, 140, 142
Russo-Japanese War of 1904–1905, 112, 140

sakoku jōi 鎖國攘夷 (closing the country and expelling the barbarians), 59, 62, 66
Sakuma Shōzan 佐久間象山, 56, 57, 59–62, 63, 64, 233n35, 235nn27,28
san-kang wu-lun 三綱五倫, ("the three duties and five moral obligations"), 69
San-yuan-li 三元里 incident, 231n102
School system, 21, 25, 26, 27, 32, 49, 73, 130; and examination system, 226n2, 231n114
Schwartz, Benjamin, 240nn126,127
Secret societies, 198, 216
Self-strengthening, 67, 70, 82, 232n2
Shang Ch'i-heng 尚其亨, 147
shang hsia hsiang-ch'üan 上下相權, 245n79
shang ku 尚古 (valuing the institutions of antiquity), 94
Shang Yang 商鞅, 11, 14, 18
Shanghai, 107, 154, 213, 271n207; merchants in, 162, 194, 195, 215, 265n88, 269n183; and railways, 183, 190, 191, 192, 193, 196, 198–199, 204, 211, 214, 266nn92,108
Shanghai-Hangchow-Ningpo Railway, 188, 199, 200, 201, 209, 271n206
Shanghai Merchants Association, 194, 262 n12
Shanghai-Ningpo Railway Corporation, 185
Shansi, 43, 45, 142, 143, 154, 156, 162, 168

Shantung, 3, 102, 142, 156, 162, 165, 168, 260n149
Shao Hsi 邵羲, 208, 269nn168,175
Shao-hsing, 195, 196, 198, 214, 265n90
Shao Yung 邵雍, 236n36
she-kuan (probationary appointment), 97
shen 紳 (official gentry), 22, 23, 25, 28–29, 30, 34, 37, 40, 226n21, 230n79; and tax engrossment, 33; and wealth, 44; and sheng-chien, 47–48
Shen Chia-pen 沈家本, 143, 184
shen-chin 紳衿 (ruling class), 227n28
Shen-chou jih-pao 神州日報 (North China daily news), 217
Shen Mao-chao 沈懋昭 (Shen Man-yun 沈縵雲), 194, 215, 272n216
Shen-pao 申報 (Shanghai daily news), 199
shen-shih 紳士 (gentry): relationship to central government, 21, 95, 152; definition of, 21–23, 27–28, 226n2, 227n33; basic characteristics of, 25–28, 137; three divisions of, 27–28; debates on structure of, 28–32; and land, 44; and reform, 76, 93, 135–136; and politics, 96–97, 161; in local administration, 102, 106, 107, 112, 115, 117, 122, 126–127, 128, 130, 131, 133; and provincial assemblies, 139, 141, 150–151, 162–163, 165, 177, 205; and railway disputes, 181–191, 272n221; changing attitudes of, 207–218. See also sheng-chien
shen tso-yu 慎左右 (taking care in selecting assistants), 113
Shen Tun-ho 沈敦和, 184
Shen-tung chü 紳董局 (gentry association; Shantung), 142
Shen Yun-p'ei 沈雲沛, 205
sheng 升 (grain measure), 37
sheng 省 (province), 249n2
sheng-chien 生監 (sheng-yuan–chien-sheng stratum), 21–49; definition of, 21–23, 227nn31,35; and state power, 23, 32–37; relationship to local government, 23–24, 107, 230n79; behavioral patterns of, 24; problem of, 28–32; political aspects of, 32–42; beating the, 35–37; and tax-engrossment, 37–38, 43; anti-official character of, 37–41, 230n79; and tax resistance, 38–39, 230n79; and proxy lawsuits, 41–42; poverty of, 43–44, 47; social aspects of, 43–49; social mobility of, 44–45, 47; relation to commoners of, 48, 227n22; and parliaments, 132, 161, 165, 167. See also sheng-yuan

Sheng Hsuan-huai 盛宣懷: and railway dispute, 164, 182, 183, 199, 210, 216, 218, 264nn56,57, 268n149; and abrogation of Sino-British contract, 184, 185–186, 187, 189, 205, 261n1, 268n160; removal and return of, 190–191, 203
sheng-jen chih tao 聖人之道 (the Way of the Sages), 55
Sheng-shih wei-yen 盛世危言 (Warnings to a seemingly prosperous age; Cheng Kuan-ying), 78, 83, 117, 118, 123, 243n55, 245n79
Sheng-wu chi 聖武記 (Military history of the Ch'ing dynasty), 80
sheng-yuan 生員 (students), 3, 22, 23, 227nn21,22,32; status of, 25, 26, 27, 28, 29, 32, 34, 36–37; privileges of, 30, 226nn14,15; and public works, 33; and engrossment, 37; and lawsuits, 42; immobility of, 44–45, 47; collective actions of, 45–49; and reform, 106, 107, 136; as advisers to magistrates, 117; and parliaments, 121, 132, 160, 161, 243n62; and provincial assemblies, 157, 160, 161, 165; and chien-sheng, 228n35; uprisings of, 231n107; definitions of, 258n128. See also sheng-chien
"Sheng-yuan lun" 生員論 (Ku Yen-wu), 32
Sheng Yun 升允, 155
Shensi, 8, 45, 155, 162, 256n110
shih 士 (or shih-chin 士衿; scholar gentry), 22, 23, 25, 27, 28–29, 30, 226n21, 327n31; treatment of, 34, 35, 36, 37, 228n50; and tax resistance, 38–39; and sheng-yuan, 45, 49
shih 勢 (contemporary conditions), 64, 73, 101, 104
Shih Chao-chi 施肇基, 263n47
Shih Chao-tseng 施肇曾, 189, 199
shih-chia 世家 (hereditary feudal families), 130
shih-chin 是今 (affirming the present), 90
shih-chung 時中 (a standard or mean within fluctuation), 73
Shih K'o-fa 史可法, 13, 225n41
Shih-pao 時報, 164, 198, 199, 211, 258n117, 269n182
shih-ta chih-li 事大之禮 (a smaller country serving a larger one), 1
shih-ta-fu 士大夫 (upper gentry elite), 22, 27, 44, 226n2
shih-ta shih-hsing 事大使行 (dispatch of envoys of submission), 1

Shih-wu Hsueh-t'ang 時務學堂 (Shih-wu Academy, Hunan), 111, 132, 244n73

Shih-wu-pao 時務報, 132, 244n73

shih-yeh 實業 (modern style Chinese industry), 215

Shinmatsu seiji shisō kenkyū 清末政治思想史研究 (Onogawa Hidemi), 238n77

shu 數 (fate), 12

shu-shih 庶士 (lower literati), 30

shuang-hsuan jih-yueh 雙懸日月 ("the sun and the moon together are suspended in the sky"), 5

Shun 舜, 11, 58, 62, 64, 95, 98, 120, 121, 233n16

Shuo-wen 說文, 16

Sino-British contract of 1890, 181, 182, 184, 185, 187, 190, 264n56

Sino-British loan agreement, 186–191, 263n45; movement to abrogate, 191–206, 207, 216, 217

Sino-Japanese War, 113, 181

Sinocentrism, 9–14, 63

Six Boards, 76, 77, 97, 115

Six Classics, 79

Six Ministries, 238n77

Sonnō jōi ron 尊王攘夷 (Honor the Emperor, Expel the barbarians), 59

Soochow, 193, 213, 214, 252n44, 263n46, 265nn89,90, 268n149, 271n207

Soochow Anti-Loan Association, 209, 210

Soochow-Hangchow-Ningpo railway dispute, 163, 181–218, 271n204; background of, 182–191

Southern Academy, 127–128, 129, 130, 244n77

Southern Shanghai Merchants and Students Association, 215, 270n201

Southern Study Association (Hunan), 170

Spring and Autumn Annals, 9, 13, 15

Spring and Autumn period, 109, 110

ssu 私 (private advantage), 63, 89, 99, 120, 121, 129–130, 131

ssu-Han 思漢 (longing for a Chinese ruler), 9, 10, 11, 12, 13, 224n30

Ssu-k'u ch'üan-shu 四庫全書 (Complete Library of the Four Treasuries), 14–15, 16, 18, 225nn44,48

Su Shih 蘇軾, 104

Su-Sung area, 27

Suematsu Kaiichirō 末松偕一郎, 253n62

sui 遂 (administrative unit), 109

Sui dynasty, 120

Sun Chia-nai 孫家鼐, 65, 80, 122, 123

Sun Hsing-yen 孫星衍, 225n48

Sun I-jang 孫詒讓, 188, 263n42

Sun Pao-ch'i 孫寶琦, 140, 141, 142, 145, 149, 187, 250n10

Sun T'ing-han 孫廷翰, 188, 263n42

Sun Yat-sen 孫中山, 138, 139, 246n98, 249n3

Sung-chiang, 196, 265n89

Sung Chiao-jen 宋教仁, 255n104

Sung dynasty, 15, 16, 64, 79, 91, 100, 104, 107, 109, 112, 128, 236n36

sung-hu 訟戶 (lawsuit households), 38–39, 42

sung-kun 訟棍 (pettifoggers), 42

Sung Po-lu 宋伯魯, 80

Sung Tz'u-kun 宋慈袌, 268n147

Sung Yü-jen 宋育仁, 132

Sungkyuankwan University (Seoul), 222n2

Szechwan, 155, 156, 165, 182, 216, 218, 271n203

Ta-Ch'ing hui-tien shih-li 大清會典事例 (The regulations of government of the great Ch'ing dynasty), 27, 48

Ta-hsueh 大學 (Great learning), 60

Ta-i chüeh-mi lu 大義覺迷錄, 9, 16

ta-i ming-fen 大義名分 (correct human relationships), 59

ta-t'ung 大同 (great unity), 82

Ta-kung-pao 大公報, 140, 250n10

Tai Chao-ch'en 戴肇辰, 37

tai-chien 臺諫 (imperial censor), 118

Tai Hung-tz'u 戴鴻慈, 141, 147, 252n40

Tai Wang 戴望, 108–109, 111

Taiping Rebellion, 37, 43, 44, 66, 230n79

T'ai-tsung 太宗 (Abahai), 1, 11

Tamhŏn yŏn'gi 湛軒燕記 (Description of a journey to Peking; Hong Taiyong), 9

tan 石, 37

T'an Hsien 譚獻, 123

T'an Ssu-t'ung 譚嗣同, 84, 85, 128–129, 170, 240n124, 244n73

T'an Yen-k'ai 譚延闓, 270n196

T'ang 湯, 103

T'ang Chen. *See* T'ang Shou-ch'ien

T'ang dynasty, 11, 90, 91, 96, 100, 101, 104, 109, 112, 118, 128

T'ang Hsu 湯緒, 191, 264n60

T'ang Hua-lung 湯化龍, 257n116, 270n196

T'ang Shang-kuang 唐尚光, 257n116

T'ang Shao-i 唐紹怡, 200
T'ang Shou-ch'ien (T'ang chen) 湯壽潛, 83–84, 116–117, 123, 190, 199, 212, 267n146, 270n196; dismissal of, 199–207, 210, 211, 213, 214, 216, 264n60, 267n146, 269nn168,175; popularity of, 271n204; leadership of, 182, 197, 214, 216, 271n206; and Chekiang Railway Company, 184; as editor of *Shih-wu-pao*, 244n73
T'ang Ts'ai-ch'ang 唐才常, 238n83
tao 道 (circuits), 125, 246n98
tao 道 (the Way): and principle/utility concept, 57, 58, 61, 63, 67, 69, 70, 71, 73, 80, 81, 84, 234n25, 235n30, 237n67, 240n126; universality of, 69, 82, 84, 88; and political feudalism, 100, 104, 246n93
tao-ch'i 道器, 81–85, 87–88, 235n30
Tao-kuang reign, 37, 248n130
T'ao Ch'i-piao 陶七彪, 192
T'ao Hui-fu 陶慧斧, 207
T'ao Pao-lin 陶葆霖, 257n117, 269n173
T'ao Shu 陶澍, 37
Tax engrossment, 37, 38, 43
Taxes: collection of, 24, 37, 39, 42, 229n66; grain-tribute, 27, 28, 29, 36, 37, 38, 42, 157; resistance to, 37, 38, 39, 40, 43, 48, 145–146; land, 38, 154; and voting rights, 164; and representation, 208–209; and government, 228n44
Te-ch'ing, 192
Technology, Western, 51, 66, 67, 70, 74, 76, 78, 81, 83, 84; origins of, 113. *See also* *chi-i* (technology); *t'i-yung*; Japan: ethics/technology in
Tempō 天保 period, 59
tenchi kōri 天地公理 (self-evident truth of heaven and earth), 56, 57
teng-k'o lu 登科錄 (examination class lists), 3
Tenney, Charles, 165
tenri 天理 (heavenly principle), 56
Three Dukes, system of, 238n77
Three Dynasties (San-tai), 63, 64, 67, 68, 69, 73, 96, 101, 104, 119, 128, 235nn32,34, 237n69
ti-fang tzu-chih 地方自治 (local self-government), 160. *See also* Local self-government
ti-pao 地保 (local constables), 39
Ti Pao-hsien 狄葆賢, 164, 258n117
Tibet, 7, 8, 14. *See also* Lamaism
t'i 體 (principle), 53, 70–71, 73, 80, 83, 84, 85
t'i-yung 體用 (principle/utility), 53–88, 232n7

T'ieh-liang 鐵良, 140, 148, 149, 151, 152, 162, 166, 175, 252n53
t'ien 天 (Heaven), 64
t'ien-hsia wei-kung 天下為公 ("the world should be for the public"), 63
T'ien Wen-ching 田文鏡, 46
Tientsin, 165
Tikhvinskii, S. L., 242n46
Ting Chung-li 丁中立, 269n173
Ting Wen-chiang 丁文江, 261n167
T'ing Pao-hsuan 童保暄, 271n204
tōdō seigei ron 東道西藝論, 233nn14,25, 236n35
tōyō dōtoku seiyō geijutsu ron 東洋道德西洋藝術論 (East Asian ethics and Western technology), 56, 57, 58–64, 86, 87, 233n25, 236n35
Toyotomi Hideyoshi, 2
Tsai-tse 戴澤, 144, 146–147, 148, 151, 152, 169, 251n39, 252n43, 255n104
Ts'ai Huan-wen 蔡煥文, 269n173
Ts'ai Ju-lin 蔡汝霖, 269n173
tsao-hua chih ling 造化之靈 (spirit of nature), 57
Ts'ao Ju-lin 曹汝霖, 149, 161, 252n44, 253n58
Ts'ao Shen 曹參, 11
Ts'en Ch'un-hsuan 岑春煊, 150, 151, 152, 159, 175, 253n53
Tseng Ching 曾靜, 43, 101
Tseng Kuo-fan 曾國藩, 17, 55, 64–65, 76, 230n79, 236n36
tseng-sheng 增生 (supplementary licentiate), 26, 165
Tso Tsung-t'ang 左宗棠, 81
Tsuda Masamichi 津田真道, 58
"Tsun-hsiang lun" 尊相論, (On enhancing the prestige of the ministers; T'ang Chen), 117
Tsungli Yamen 總理衙門 (Office of Foreign Affairs), 124
tu 都 (township), 229n66
Tu Ju-hui 杜汝晦, 11
Tu-shu chi 讀書記 (Hsueh Hsuan), 16
tu-tu 都督 (military governor), 271n204
Tu t'ung-chien lun 讀通鑑論 (On reading the *Comprehensive Mirror*; Wang Fu-chih), 97–99
Tu Yu 杜佑, 91
t'u 圖 (ward), 229n66
T'u-min lu 圖民錄 (Yuan Shou-ting), 45
T'u-shu chi-ch'eng 圖書集成, 15
Tuan-fang 端方, 141, 147, 148, 159, 160, 250nn11,39, 252nn40,43

Tung-fang tsa-chih 東方雜誌 (Eastern miscellany), 134, 140, 142, 143, 156, 160, 164, 170, 173, 175, 248n129, 250n10, 258n117

tung-kuan 冬官 (public works management), 83

t'ung-shih 童試 examination for *t'ung-sheng*, 45

Tung-yu t'iao-i 東遊條議 (Itemized proposals from an eastern tour; Ch'en Ch'iu), 114–115, 116

T'ung-chih Emperor, 66, 108, 109

t'ung hsia-ch'ing 通下情 (knowing the feelings of those below), 113

T'ung-hsiang 桐鄉, 198

T'ung-meng hui 同盟會 (revolutionary alliance), 39, 192, 271n204

t'ung-sheng 童生 (degree aspirants), 28, 31, 45

tzu-chih yen-chiu-so 自治研究所 (research centers for self-government), 163

Tzu-cheng-yuan 資政院 (National Assembly), 147, 150

tzu-i-chü 諮議局 (provincial assemblies), 92, 112–113, 122, 124, 133, 136, 137–177, 252n47, 253n53, 269n178; debates on establishment of, 138–147, 249n2; establishment of, 147–158, 175, 254n76; regulations of, 154–155, 156, 159, 160, 166, 168, 254n63, 256n111; characteristics of, 159–168; authority of, 168–177; and anti-loan movement, 205–208; membership of, 258n128

Tzu-i-chü ch'ou-pan-ch'u 諮議局籌辦處 (Provincial Assembly Preparatory Office), 154, 156

Tzu-i-chü ch'uang-pan-chü 諮議局創辦局 (Provincial Assembly Inaugural Bureau; Hupeh), 154, 156

Tz'u-hsi 慈禧 (Empress Dowager), 112, 140, 147, 148, 252n41

Uete Michiari 植手通有, 58, 61–62, 233n25, 235n28

United Anti-Loan Meeting of Chekiang Schools, 207

Voting, qualifications for, 117, 122, 138–139, 160–163, 164, 256n111. *See also* Elections

Wang An-shih 王安石, 13
Wang Ching-wei 汪精衛, 55
Wang Ch'ing-mu 王清穆, 187, 269n177
Wang Erh-min 王爾敏, 231n1
Wang Fu-chih 王夫之, 82, 84, 92, 97–99, 106, 109, 111, 133
Wang Hsu-pin 王序賓, 269n173
Wang Hu-ting 王鵠汀, 5, 10–11, 12, 13–14, 224nn35,38
Wang Jung-pao 汪榮寶, 149, 252n44, 253n58
Wang K'ang-nien 汪康年, 132, 138, 139, 184, 249n4, 264n60
wang-kuo 亡國 (ruin of the nation), 202
Wang Mang 王莽, 13, 98, 224n38
Wang Min-hao 王民皞, 3
Wang Sun 王遜, 46
Wang Ta-hsieh 汪大燮, 186
Wang T'ao 王韜, 52, 69–70, 72, 82, 237n60
Wang T'ing-yang 王廷揚 (Wang Fu-ch'uan 王孚川), 192, 207, 264n66, 269n173
Wang Tso 王佐, 269n173
Wang T'ung-yü 王同愈, 187, 188, 257n116, 263n42
Wang Wen-hsao 王文韶, 65, 184, 188, 191, 192, 194, 216, 236n36, 265nn82,83
Wang Yang-ming 王陽明, 17
Wang Yü-kun 王予袞, 269n173
Warring States period, 110
Wei Cheng 魏徵, 98
Wei-chin period, 90
wei-hsin-p'ai 維新派 (reform faction), 242n46
Wei Kuang-t'ao 魏光燾, 140
Wei Lü 衛律, 7
wei-ta pu-tiao 尾大不掉 (lit., "the tail is too big to wag"), 103
Wei-yen 危言 (Words of warning; T'ang Shou-ch'ien), 83–84, 116–117, 123, 243n54
Wei Yuan 魏源, 53, 63, 65
Wen-chou, 259n131
Wen-hsiang 文祥, 77, 78
Wen Su 溫肅, 164
Weng Fang-kang 翁方綱, 6
Weng T'ung-ho 翁同龢, 65, 82, 123
Western affairs. *See yang-wu*
Western learning. *See hsi-hsüeh*
wo-pei 臥碑 (stele of restraint), 41
Women's Association for the Preservation of Railway Rights. *See* Nü-chieh pao-lu-hui
Wright, Mary, 258n128, 259n132
wu 物 (things), 56
Wu 武, 103

Wu Chao 吳炤, 5, 6
Wu Ch'ing-t'ao 吳慶燾, 257n116
Wu Chung-hsi 吳樂光, 268n149
Wu-hsu pien-fa 戊戌變法, 135
Wu-hsu pien-fa tang-an shih-liao 戊戌變法檔案史料, 135
Wu Kang 鄔鋼, 191, 264n60
Wu Le-kuang 吳樂光, 32-33
Wu Lei-ch'uang 吳雷川, 207
wu-li 物理 (principle of things), 59
Wu-li t'ung-k'ao 五禮通考 (Comprehensive study of the five rites), 80
wu-lun 五倫 (five relations), 59
Wuchang Uprising, 209, 212, 213, 260n162, 270n196, 271n206
"Wu-teng lun" 五等論 (Lu Chi), 90

Yang Hsiang-chi 楊象濟, 102, 107-108, 111
Yang Hsiang-lan 楊相蘭, 123
Yang Jui 楊銳, 123, 244n73
yang-min 養民 (nourishing the people), 33
Yang Shen-hsiu 楊深秀, 80
Yang Shih-ch'i 楊士琦, 149
Yang T'ing-tung 楊廷棟, 188, 257nn116,117, 263n42
Yang Tu 楊度, 253n61
Yang Tu-sheng 楊篤生, 255n104
yang-wu 洋務 (Western affairs) group, 51-52, 65, 71, 74, 76-78, 81, 232nn2,14, 239n107, 242n46; and principle/utility, 53, 55, 56, 85, 86-87; and political rights, 54; and *pien-fa* group, 70, 86, 232 n2. See also *pien-fa* group
Yano Jin'ichi 矢野仁一, 15
Yao 堯, 11, 58, 62, 64, 95, 98, 120, 121, 233 n16
Yao Shao-shu 姚紹書, 151
Yao Tzu-liang 姚子良, 209, 210
Yeh Ch'ang-ch'ih 葉昌熾, 123
Yeh Hui-chün 葉惠鈞, 215
Yeh Kao-shu 葉誥書, 269n173
Yen-ch'eng 嚴誠, 9, 10
Yen Fu 嚴復, 85, 131, 240n126, 247n122
Yen Hsin-hou 嚴信厚, 184
yen-lu 言路 (communication with the ruler), 61
Yen Mao-yu 顏茂猷, 28
Yen Shih-ku 顏師古, 105
Yen Yuan 顏元 (pseud: Ssu-ku-tzu 思古子 ["Man who yearns for ancient times"]), 99-100, 104, 111
Yi dynasty. See Chosŏn dynasty
Yi T'oegye 李退溪, 235n31
Yi Tŏk-mu 李德懋, 222n4, 225n48

Yin Chia-ch'üan 尹嘉銓, 3, 223n5
Yin-ping shih wen-chi 飲冰室文集 (Liang Ch'i-ch'ao), 238n83, 239nn90,107
Yŏlha ilgi 熱河日記 (Jehol diary), 1-19, 34, 49, 222n3
Yoko Shōnan 橫井小楠, 56, 58, 62-64, 235n31
Yonekane Mizawa 米金彌澤, 126
Yŏngjo 英祖 reign, 2
Yŏnhaeng-nok 燕行錄 (Records of visits to Yen [Peking]), 1-3, 222n4
Yoshida Shōin 吉田松陰, 58
Yu Tŏk-kong 柳得恭, 5, 8, 16, 225 n48
Yü 虞, 13
Yü Chao-fan 喻兆蕃, 257n116
Yü Min-chung 于敏中, 16
Yü-pei li-hsien kung-hui 預備立憲公會 (Constitutional Preparatory Association), 154, 269n177
Yü p'i li-tai t'ung-chien chi-lan 御批歷代通鑑輯覽 (Comprehensive mirror of successive dynasties imperially annotated), 13
yü-shih 御史 (counselor), 118
Yü Shih-mei 于式枚, 173, 250n10, 256n107, 261n167
Yü Tsung-lien 俞宗廉, 269n173
Yü-yao 余姚, 192
Yü Yueh 俞樾, 109, 111
Yuan Ch'ang 袁昶, 126-127, 244n73
"Yuan ch'iang" 原強 (On power; Yen Fu), 131
"Yuan-chün" 原君 (Huang Tsung-hsi), 95, 248n129
Yuan dynasty, 7
Yuan Mei 袁枚, 28, 103-104, 111
yuan-pen 原本 (basis), 66
Yuan Shih-k'ai 袁世凱, 140, 191, 218, 252n44, 268n147, 270n196; and constitutionalism, 141, 148, 152, 252n43, 253 n58; and provincial assemblies, 153, 169, 175; and British loan, 188, 190, 199, 217
Yuan Shou-ting 袁守定, 45
"Yuan-tao" 原道 (On the Way; Wang T'ao), 82
Yueh Yuan-sheng 岳元聲, 28
Yun 禹, 95
yung 用, 53-56, 70-71, 73, 76, 80, 83, 84, 85
Yung-cheng Emperor, 9, 16, 43, 45, 101, 102, 111, 223n12, 241n24
Yung-lo Emperor, 14
Yung-lo ta-tien 永樂大典, 14
Yung-shu 庸書 (Mediocre writings; Ch'en Ch'ih), 118, 123
Yunnan, 102, 202, 268n147

HARVARD-YENCHING INSTITUTE MONOGRAPH SERIES
(titles now in print)

8 and 9. *The Ancient Na-Khi Kingdom of Southwest China,* 2 volumes, by Joseph F. Rock
11. *Han Shi Wai Chuan: Han Ying's Illustrations of the Didactic Application of the* Classic of Songs, translated and annotated by James Robert Hightower
12. *Money and Credit in China: A Short History,* by Liensheng Yang
13. *Civil Service in Early Sung China, 960–1067: With Particular Emphasis on the Development of Controlled Sponsorship to Foster Administrative Responsibility,* by E. A. Kracke, Jr.
16. *Sonq Dynasty Musical Sources and Their Interpretation,* by Rulan Chao Pian
17. *An Introduction to Sung Poetry,* by Kojiro Yoshikawa, translated by Burton Watson
18. *A History of Japanese Astronomy: Chinese Background and Western Impact,* by Shigeru Nakayama
19. *The Izumi Shikibu Diary: A Romance of the Heian Court,* translated and with an introduction by Edwin A. Cranston
20. *Miraculous Stories from the Japanese Buddhist Tradition: The Nihon Ryōiki of the Monk Kyōkai,* translated, edited, and with an introduction by Kyoko Motomochi Nakamura
21. *The Chinese Short Story: Studies in Dating, Authorship, and Composition,* by Patrick Hanan
22. *Songs of Flying Dragons: A Critical Reading,* by Peter H. Lee
23. *Early Chinese Civilization: Anthropological Perspectives,* by K. C. Chang
24. *Population, Disease, and Land in Early Japan, 645–900,* by William Wayne Farris
25. *Shikitei Sanba and the Comic Tradition in Edo Fiction,* by Robert W. Leutner
26. *Washing Silk: The Life and Selected Poetry of Wei Chuang (834?–910),* by Robin D. S. Yates
27. *National Polity and Local Power: The Transformation of Late Imperial China,* by Min Tu-ki
28. *T'ang Transformation Texts: A Study of the Buddhist Contribution to the Rise of Vernacular Fiction and Drama in China,* by Victor H. Mair
29. *Mongolian Rule in China: Local Administration in the Yuan Dynasty,* by Elizabeth Endicott-West